PETROLEUM PROGRESS AND PROFITS

A History of Process Innovation

M.I.T. PRESS RESEARCH MONOGRAPHS

PETROLEUM PROGRESS AND PROFITS:
A History of Process Innovation
by John L. Enos

STRATEGY AND STRUCTURE:
Chapters in the History of the Industrial Enterprise
by Alfred D. Chandler, Jr.

SOCIAL FACTORS IN ECONOMIC DEVELOPMENT:
The Argentine Case
by Tomás Roberto Fillol

JOHN LAWRENCE ENOS

PETROLEUM
PROGRESS AND PROFITS

A History of Process Innovation

THE M.I.T. PRESS

MASSACHUSETTS INSTITUTE OF TECHNOLOGY

Cambridge, Massachusetts

1962

To My Family

PREFACE

IN its crude state, petroleum is relatively useless; to transform it into gasoline, kerosene, diesel fuel, lubricating oil, and other products is the function of the petroleum refiner. Today he carries out this job with great skill and economy. But this has not always been true. Fifty years ago, the petroleum-refining industry would not have deserved such praise. Although petroleum had already been a major item of commerce for half a century, refining processes were still primitive. The typical refinery contained small pieces of equipment with which a few simple operations were carried out under hazardous conditions. In the last fifty years, accompanying and stimulated by the revolution in transportation through the introduction of the automobile and the airplane, important advances in refining technology have been made.

The purpose of this study is to reveal more about the nature of technological progress. Why did it come about? Who contributed to it? What barriers did inventors and innovators face, and what resources were they able to draw upon? What were the effects of technological progress upon all those who deliberately or unwittingly played a role in its achievement? These are some of the questions to which the investigation is addressed.

The petroleum-refining industry was selected for this study because it is an industry in which advances in technology have been both substantial and rapid. It affords several observations of new techniques, brought about by men most of whom are still living. Its expenditures for research and development have been substantial, probably larger than any other nonmilitary industry; for example, the concentration of scientific talent which yielded one of the process innovations described in this study was probably greater than any other prior to the development of the atomic bomb.

In the refining of petroleum, the most important process is cracking, by which gasoline is produced from fuel oil. Approximately half of the total volume of gasoline is manufactured by this technique. Chemically, cracking consists of splitting large hydrocarbon molecules into smaller ones. The cracking reaction is carried out under conditions of high temperature and pressure, and is promoted by catalysts.

As a subject for study, the cracking of petroleum has the advantage that there have been not one but four waves of innovations. Each new technique has tended to supplant its predecessor. The first of the four waves of cracking innovations reached its crest in 1913, when the first cracking process to produce gasoline was introduced. The second wave swelled in 1921-22, when a series of more efficient cracking processes were developed. The pattern was repeated in the third wave in 1936 and the last subsequent to 1942. Both the increasing importance of cracking in petroleum-refinery operations and the successive introduction and demise of new cracking processes revealed by the graph on page 261.

In order to yield a better understanding of this highly technical subject, engineering principles as well as economic and historical analyses were used in the study. An attempt was made to provide a quantitative as well as a qualitative measure of technological progress. This involved calculations of the amounts of each of the resources — capital, labor, raw material, and energy — which are applied to the manufacture of petroleum products. When these calculations had been made for each of the cracking processes, it was possible to determine the changes that have occurred in the productivity of each of the inputs.

Technological progress also has economic and social effects. The social effects are manifested in the nature of the environment in which individuals' work. These effects have been most vivid in the activities through which technological progress is accomplished, namely research and development. During the past half century, the character of the organizations which have carried out research and development, the quality of the products they have manufactured, and the resources they have had at their command have changed significantly. From being the burden of a few lonely and dedicated men, research has become so institutionalized that its offspring — technological progress — is as much a product of the petroleum-refining industry as gasoline.

The economic effects of technological progress are equally important, for new methods of manufacture can change the payments to individuals, the behavior of firms, and the structure of industry. In this study each of these three changes has been examined. It was possible, for example, to estimate to what extent the gains from technological progress have been distributed to the owners of resources and to the consumers of petroleum products. It was also possible to measure the contribution that successful developments made to the over-all profit of the innovating companies.

This book is divided into seven chapters — six devoted to individual cracking-process innovations, and a seventh which generalizes from the specific events. The procedure within each descriptive chapter is as follows: the need for a technological advance is demonstrated; the various individuals able to make the advance are identified; the research and development carried out by the successful, and by a few of the less successful, are reported; the barriers to progress are noted; the advantages of the new technique are calculated; the distribution of the benefits is estimated; the original installation and subsequent adoptions are described; and the effect upon the behavior and structure of the industry is determined.

Each new cracking process, as originally installed, did not represent the perfection of the art. Rather, throughout the economic life of each process, there were a series of improvements. These improvements are described in the same manner as the original developments, although in less detail. In an industry where startling innovations are relatively infrequent, accumulated improvements tend to contribute just as much to technological progress.

One not very surprising conclusion that can be drawn from the study is that technological progress is profitable. The inventors, the innovators, the companies that made the initial installation, and those which later acquired access to the art were all rewarded, although in considerably different amounts. In general, technological progress has been most profitable to those who initiated it, although the rate of profit accruing to the developers of new cracking processes appears to have declined as the industry matured. Profits have arisen primarily from increases in productivity; each innovation has enabled the refiner to economize on all process inputs. In other words, for a given amount of product, new processes have required smaller amounts of all resources. To be sure, there have been certain shifts in the proportions in which resources are combined, but these are less significant than the reductions in total quantities necessary.

Another conclusion is that there are economies of large-scale operation, that is, that larger plants have lower unit costs. As successive processing innovations have occurred, the range throughout which these economies of scale exist has been extended. In earlier years, difficulties in constructing processing equipment limited the range of scale economies; in recent years the upper limit has been set by the extent of the market.

It is apparent that a study such as this could not have been made without the assistance of the individuals and companies responsible for the technological advances. Not only did the majority of the companies approached make available all of their facilities, but in several cases they contributed even more time and energy than I did. I do wish to single out a few of these individuals, for my debt to them is considerable. Dr. Robert E. Wilson, former Chairman of the Standard Oil Company (Indiana), admitted me to his company and also assisted me in my approach to, others. Mr. David A. Shepard, Executive Vice-President, and Dr. Daniel C. Hamilton, formerly of the Economics Department at the Standard Oil Company (New Jersey) and now of the School of Business at the University of Chicago, permitted me to draw upon the resources of the company and of its subsidiary, Esso Research and Engineering Company. At Esso Research and Engineering Company, Dr. C. E. Starr, Jr., and Mr. B. L. Bragg were particularly helpful. Mr. John G. Woods of the Universal Oil Products Company, Mr. C. G. Kirkbride, formerly President of Houdry Process Corporation, and Mr. Clarence H. Thayer, Vice-President, Manufacturing, of the Sun Oil Company, gave me access to their companies' experience and to their colleagues. Mr. George H. Watkins of the Standard Oil Company (Ohio) has contributed to this study as he has to all of my knowledge of the industry.

In these companies and in others there have been many more people who have helped me throughout this study. By all rights they should be mentioned individually. My excuse for not doing so is that they were so numerous and their help so great that the acknowledgment would add another chapter. The footnotes in which they are identified are expressions of my gratitude.

In addition to direct assistance from the companies, I also received indirect, but to me very important, assistance in the form of a grant from the Sloan Research Fund of the School of Industrial Management at M.I.T. These funds enabled me to travel to the various companies and also to be for one year a research assistant in the Department of Economics.

Our society is sufficiently hospitable to research so that studies such as mine need not be justified. They do, however, need to be encouraged and guided. For encouragement and guidance, I am indebted to Professor M. A. Adelman. Without his help, so generously and warmly given, the project might not have been completed. Without his enthusiasm and example, it certainly would not have been as enjoyable to me as it was. To him go my greatest thanks.

JOHN L. ENOS

Cambridge, Massachusetts
June, 1961

CONTENTS

PETROLEUM PROGRESS AND PROFITS

A History of Process Innovation

1

THE BURTON PROCESS

A_T the beginning of the twentieth century the introduction of two new products, the electric light and the automobile, exerted a profound effect on the petroleum industry. By replacing the kerosene lamp as the main source of artificial illumination, the electric light reduced the demand for kerosene, until then the industry's most profitable product. By replacing the horse as the main mode of transportation, the automobile greatly increased the demand for gasoline, previously of little value. The petroleum industry responded by shifting its attention from kerosene to gasoline, developing in the process new refining techniques and new methods of distribution. The most significant refining technique was to be petroleum cracking, which eventually doubled the amount of gasoline obtainable from crude oil.

The raw material for cracking was the heavy portion of the crude oil, long recognized as a potential source of light hydrocarbons[1] and already utilized in the manufacture of illuminating oil. Competing with coal as a fuel and consequently fetching a low price, the heavy fractions of crude petroleum were readily available for other uses.

The first commercial process for cracking heavy petroleum fractions to yield gasoline was introduced in 1913 by Dr. William Meriam Burton of the Standard Oil Company (Indiana). The development of the Burton process had begun four years earlier, in 1909; the four years were consumed with repeated laboratory and pilot-plant experiments, reports to the board of directors, pleas for permission to build commercial units, and, once permission had been obtained, actual construction of the units themselves. Improvements in the process and in equipment continued after the first units had been installed, to the point where the final units constructed by Indiana Standard in 1922 differed materially from the first Burton stills. Until it was rendered obsolete about 1920, the Burton

---

[1] In 1855, Benjamin Silliman, Jr., a chemistry professor at Yale University, while investigating a sample of crude petroleum, discovered that the application of intense heat to heavy fractions would decompose or "crack" them, yielding volatile products (Charles Singer *et al.*, *A History of Technology*, Vol. V, London: Oxford University Press, 1958, p. 109).

process was the only commercial process for manufacturing gasoline from heavy petroleum oils.

The story of the Burton process is the story of the man whose name it bears. The prime mover was Burton himself; he was responsible not only for the initial invention in the laboratory but also for the fruition of the process in commercial operation. In between came the contributions of several other scientists and technicians, who made complementary inventions without which the process could not have been a commercial success. But these contributions were mainly technical. The development of a successful cracking process needed not only the technical competence of a chemist, but also the imagination and enterprise of a Schumpeterian innovator. Burton had both.

To Indiana Standard, the Burton process soon yielded profits of $150,000,000. The long-run effects were mixed, however; the profits enabled the company to produce its own crude oil, but the success of the process made the company complacent. During the twenties the high standards — technical, economic, and moral — were relaxed, and the company's strength declined. At the same time, the Burton process had demonstrated to the petroleum industry the rewards attainable from innovation and had stimulated the development of improved processes.

Need for a Cracking Process

Around the turn of the century the petroleum industry began to fear a shortage of crude oil. The demand for petroleum products had been increasing very rapidly, more rapidly than new crude-oil production was being developed.

There were two ways in which a shortage of crude oil could be averted; first, more could be discovered, and secondly, the existing supply could be better utilized so as to yield a larger fraction of the products which were in greater demand. In different areas of the country, depending upon the local conditions, emphasis was placed upon one or the other. In California and Texas, which had access to excellent sources of crude oil, and the East Coast, where there was a good market for heavy residual fuels, the emphasis lay upon finding more crude oil.

In the Midwest, because of diminishing local supplies and the high cost of transportation from distant fields, the emphasis lay upon altering the yield structure of the petroleum products. By 1900, production of crude oil in Ohio, West Virginia, and Pennsylvania was past its peak, and by 1904 Indiana also had started to decline. The absolute reduction in the amount of crude oil that could be obtained from the midwestern fields amounted to only a few per cent each year, but when contrasted with the rapidly growing demand for the products, the gap between production and demand grew alarmingly greater each year. Intensified research for new crude-oil supplies led to the discovery of the Illinois field in 1905, but even this proved a disappointment when the production peak was passed in 1908, a mere three years later. The midwestern refiners became dependent on crude oil from Oklahoma, which was more expensive because of the transportation costs. It was natural, therefore, for the refiners to try to reduce their crude-oil requirements. The only way to do this without cutting into their sales of the profitable light products, such as kerosene, gasoline, and solvents, was to increase the yield of those products from each barrel of crude oil.

The potential source of light products was the heavy material that remained after the light products had been distilled. This heavy material, which was called residual fuel oil, or residuum, consisted of all the hydrocarbons that were heavier than kerosene. As heavy fuel oil, the residuum competed with coal, which was readily available in the Middle West and which sold for a low price compared with the price of crude petroleum (see Appendix Table 4).

The members of the industry were well aware of the potential value of this heavy material. For several years there had been a process in operation called coking, which subjected the heaviest of the petroleum fractions to heat in an open still at atmospheric pressure and thereby caused its decomposition into lighter products. The products were mainly kerosene, gas oil (the next heavier distillate), and coke. A little fuel gas and gasoline were also produced. The coking process was not very efficient, because of the low yield of light distillates and also because of the high yield of coke, which settled upon the bottom of the still to a depth of 10 to 15 inches and had to be laboriously dug out by hand.[2]

The existence of the coking process proves that there was some knowledge of the practice of cracking in the petroleum-refining industry. Most refiners knew that heat would cause the heavy fractions to decompose, or crack, into lighter fractions, and that the higher the temperature, the more rapid would be the rate at which cracking took place.

Besides temperature, another variable affects the rate of the reaction — the pressure at which the equipment is operated. In the cracking of heavy petroleum stocks, changes in the pressure at which cracking takes place have a direct and an indirect effect upon the rate of reaction and the product yield. The direct effect of increasing pressure upon the rate of reaction and upon the yield of products has not been fully determined.[3]

---

[2] Robert E. Wilson, "Fifteen Years of the Burton Process," *Industrial and Engineering Chemistry,* October, 1928, pp. 1099–1100.

[3] W. L. Nelson, *Petroleum Refinery Engineering,* 3rd ed., New York: McGraw-Hill Book Co., 1949, p. 595.

This lack of knowledge is of little consequence, however, because it is the indirect effect of pressure that is far more important. In brief, pressure determines which hydrocarbons are subjected to cracking. Cracking begins when the raw material is heated to between 680° and 700° F.[4] If the pressure is that of the atmosphere, as it was in the coking process, over half of the residuum is vaporized and is distilled out of the vessel before the cracking temperature is reached. If the heavy ends are restrained by a pressure greater than atmospheric, all the heavier material will be kept in the vessel. At high pressure, therefore, more than twice the amount of heavy ends will be cracked. With more than twice the amount of reagents entering into the reaction, the yields from cracking under pressure will be proportionately larger.

As significant as the increase in the yield is the change in its structure. It has already been noted that coking, that is, cracking at atmospheric conditions, produces mainly kerosene and gas oil. Under pressure, when the gas-oil portion of the residuum as well as the heavier portions are cracked, the amount of gasoline produced is much greater, and the amount of kerosene and coke correspondingly less. This effect was discovered in 1889 by two English scientists, James Dewar and Boverton Redwood.[5] Their work, together with that of several others,[6] showed later inventors which paths might be fruitful and, perhaps more important, which paths would not. Although Burton was not aware of the Dewar and Redwood patents when he first began his research, he did know the general effects of both temperature and pressure upon the rate of cracking and the yield.[7] Little was known, however, about the temperature and pressure that would be suitable, the equipment that would be necessary to carry out the reaction, and the way that the ideal conditions for carrying out the reaction could be maintained. These were the problems that faced the scientists in the petroleum-refining industry in general, and Burton at Indiana in particular.

Burton's Resources and Experiments

William Meriam Burton was born on November 17, 1865, and grew

---

[4] *Ibid.*, p. 592.

[5] In British patent No. 10,277, and subsequently in U. S. patent No. 419,931, Dewar and Redwood revealed their results and explained their process for distilling and condensing mineral oils and like material under pressure. For a description of Dewar and Redwood's process, see Carleton Ellis, *Gasoline and Other Motor Fuels*, New York: D. Van Nostrand Co., 1921, pp. 221–224.

[6] For a description of early U. S. patents in cracking see Kendall Beaton, *Enterprise in Oil: A History of Shell in the United States*, New York: Appleton-Century-Crofts, Inc., 1957, pp. 234, 235.

[7] Interview with Robert E. Humphreys, November 23, 1954.

up in the town of East Cleveland, Ohio.[8] His father, Erasmus Burton, was a doctor. Early in his life, Burton became interested in chemistry and set up a laboratory in his father's barn. Only a few miles from the Burton home in East Cleveland lived Charles F. Brush, the inventor of the Brush magneto. The young Burton frequently visited Brush, who

[Standard Oil Company (Indiana)]

Office employees at Standard Oil's Whiting, Indiana, refinery in the 1890's. Dr. Burton is in the top row, seventh from the right, at the center of the doorway.

enjoyed showing the youth the mechanical and electrical devices he had built. A sympathetic high school chemistry teacher, William Stinaff, helped him plan his schooling. He attended Western Reserve University

[8] The biographical data on Burton are derived from the following publications: Standard Oil Company (Indiana), *Background Information on W. M. Burton*, November 13, 1944; Standard Oil (Indiana), Public Relations Department, Press Release, December 29, 1954; *William Meriam Burton, A Pioneer in Modern Petroleum Technology*, Chicago: University Press (privately printed), 1952; and from the recollections of his friends Dr. R. E. Humphreys and Dr. R. E. Wilson. A description of the Burton development can be found in P. H. Giddens, *The Standard Oil Company (Indiana): Oil Pioneer of the Middle West*, New York: Appleton-Century-Crofts Inc., 1955, Chapter VI.

and then went to Johns Hopkins, where he received a Ph.D. degree in chemistry in 1889.

He then went to work for the parent Standard Oil Company and after a year with the Standard Oil Company (Ohio) was assigned to another of its subsidiaries, the Standard Oil Company (Indiana). At that time the contribution that a college graduate with an advanced degree in chemistry might make to the industry was only dimly understood. In fact, William P. Cowan, who was then vice president in charge of refining for Indiana Standard, had no idea of what functions a chemist might perform. When Dr. Burton reported to him, Cowan asked him "if he brought his tools along with him."[9]

The parent company had decided that Dr. Burton should run a laboratory at Indiana Standard's Whiting refinery, which was just then being built. For this purpose, Dr. Burton was given the second floor of an old farmhouse close to the shore of Lake Michigan. His first experiments took place in an upstairs bedroom. Many of his instruments he made for himself or had manufactured in the refinery's machine shop. At first the work consisted of the testing of materials, mainly such products as kerosenes, greases, waxes, and lubricating oils. These tests were by no means routine, for standardized methods had not yet been developed, and originality was needed to devise satisfactory tests. But once adequate testing methods were devised, the work, although time consuming, could hardly be considered challenging. It was at this point that Burton first adopted a broader view of the scope of his activity. The technically trained man could do more than determine the physical and chemical characteristics of refinery products; he could also put his knowledge of chemical reactions to work in developing new processes — new ways of manufacturing existing products so as to improve their yields and qualities.

Dr. Burton's first successful development concerned the elimination of undesirable sulfur compounds from certain of the refinery's products. For this work he was promoted to assistant general superintendent of the Whiting refinery in 1892, and in 1896 he became superintendent, at the age of thirty-one.

Dr. Burton's place in the refinery laboratory was filled by Dr. George Gray, also a Johns Hopkins Ph.D. in chemistry. In June of 1900, Indiana hired still another Hopkins man, Dr. Robert E. Humphreys, who was to play a vital role in the development of the Burton method.[10]

---

[9] Personal recollection of Dr. Robert E. Humphreys in interview, November 23, 1954.

[10] Dr. Humphreys remained with Indiana Standard, becoming ultimately vice president in charge of manufacturing and a director. Dr. Gray left the Standard

Dr. Burton recognized that there was a great need for more light petroleum products, and that profits could be made from supplying them. "About 1909 Dr. Burton decided that within a few years demand for gasoline would exceed the quantity available from crude.... There would then be a real incentive to try to make more gasoline, preferably from petroleum."[11] These were the deductions not of a chemist but of

[Standard Oil Company (Indiana)]

Dr. Humphreys in the laboratory of the Whiting refinery (1901).

an entrepreneur, of a man able to see beyond the confines of his own company. He predicted correctly the general acceptance of the automobile, and the consequent growth in demand for gasoline. To him the implications for the oil industry were clear; it would have to adapt its techniques and activities to satisfy the changing needs. Burton was a visionary.

Oil Company (Indiana), shortly after Dr. Humphreys came, to go with the Sunflower Oil Company and subsequently with the Texas Company.

[11] Robert E. Wilson, *op. cit.*, p. 8.

In an age when few of the refinery supervisory personnel had any technical training, Burton was outstanding in his educational background and laboratory experience. Fortunately, his position allowed him to put his training to use in the conception and development of the cracking process. As general superintendent of the Whiting refinery, he had all the facilities and authority needed for his research work.[12] The most obvious was the laboratory, staffed by Humphreys and a new assistant, Dr. F. M. Rogers. Other departments contributed: first, the machine shop, where the novel equipment could be fabricated; secondly, the sales division, whose views on the potential markets for the new products obtained in the cracking process could be obtained; and, thirdly, the accounting staff, whose knowledge of costs and revenues was useful. In 1910, control of the refinery organization was necessary to carry out research and development.

Burton's status as refinery manager was also useful to him in pleading his cause. The position of refinery manager in an oil company is high on the organizational ladder; the manager usually reports to the manufacturing vice-president. The opinions of a refinery manager naturally carry far more weight than those of a man less close to the president of the company. Burton's ability and position, as acknowledged by the board of directors, was perhaps the single most important factor leading to the adoption of his process.

Finally, in Humphreys, Burton had an extremely capable assistant. The successful cracking technique was the invention of a small group of men. The problems of controlling the temperature and pressure during the reaction, building the equipment, separating the products, training the refinery operating personnel, and minimizing coke formation would probably have been insuperable for any one man, no matter how able. Simply manning the laboratory and the pilot plant required two highly trained persons. During the development of the cracking process, the roles of the two men, Dr. Burton and Dr. Humphreys, alternated, each was now the leader, now the follower. When the energies of one man flagged, those of the other were restored. When the faith of one man was diminished, that of the other was renewed. These two men, one working in the refinery headquarters and the other in the laboratory, were equally responsible for the technical development of the process.

---

[12] "Responsibility for dealing with refining problems rested with the Manufacturing Committee.... Among those who participated occasionally were...W. P. Cowan and W M. Burton of Indiana Standard" (R. W. Hidy and M. E. Hidy, *Pioneering in Big Business*, History of the Standard Oil Company [New Jersey], New York: Harper & Brothers, 1955, p. 40). Since the normal complement of the Manufacturing Committee consisted of refinery managers, the individual members tended to have a large degree of autonomy.

These advantages then — vision, talent, training, position, resources, and assistance — were responsible for Burton's ultimate success. Yet success was neither automatic nor immediate. Work on the cracking process continued for approximately eleven years; at least twice all work on the project was halted. The first stage, from 1909 until the first Burton unit was installed in 1913, lasted four years. The second stage, starting in 1913 and consisting of the improvements made on the original Burton process, lasted seven years. About 1920, the process became obsolete, and consequently little additional effort was expended on it. The analysis carried out later in the chapter determines how profitable each stage was, and gives us some insight into the benefits gained during the course of development of a new manufacturing technique.

In the first decade of the twentieth century, research was not considered an integral part of a chemist's work, but because they were enterprising men and had the time available, Burton and Humphreys devoted their creative talents to the solution of current problems. At first the research was on a small scale. They worked on different forms of greases, white medicinal oil, and hydroxysteric acid from oleic acid, which could be used to stiffen candles. When the time came to consider the cracking process, however, the scientists were both willing and able to turn their full talents to the project.

They began their experiments[13] with the knowledge that when a heavy petroleum fraction was heated to a fairly high temperature, it would decompose into a lighter product that would boil in the gasoline range and a more dense product in the form of either a sluggish liquid or petroleum coke. For the raw material to be submitted to high temperatures, Burton chose the most obvious stock, namely the entire heavy fuel fraction. This fraction consisted of all the components of crude oil that boil above the kerosene range: the gas-oil fraction, the lubricating-oil fraction, and the asphaltic residue; in all, about 66% of the total volume of the crude petroleum charged to the refinery. Since this total fraction

---

[13] The published sources on Burton and Humphreys' experiments are Robert E. Wilson, "Fifteen Years of the Burton Process," *Industrial and Engineering Chemistry*, Vol. 20, No. 10, October 1928, p. 1099; Robert E. Wilson, "Pioneers in Oil Cracking," address to the Newcomen Society, Chicago, October 29, 1946; Robert E. Wilson, "Research on a Single Reaction and Its Social Effects," third annual Arthur Dehon Little Memorial Lecture at the Massachusetts Institute of Technology, November 23, 1948; Robert E. Wilson, "Maintaining the Pace of Scientific and Technological Development," address before the Chicago Chemists Club, Chicago, Illinois, September 8, 1954; and United States vs. Standard Oil Company (Indiana), Standard Oil Company (New Jersey), Standard Development Company, *et al.*, District Court of the United States, Northern District of Illinois, Eastern Division, No. 4131, testimony of Robert E. Wilson, commencing October 11, 1926, pp. 1972 ff. The author also interviewed Dr. Humphreys on November 23, 1954, and had access to the Standard Oil Company (Indiana) files on the Burton process.

was of much less value than gasoline and kerosene, and since it represented such a large percentage of the total volume of crude petroleum, the goal was to crack the entire volume successfully. Not only Burton and Humphreys at Indiana Standard, but the other workers in the field also hoped this would be the case.

To their misfortune, the overriding desire to crack the entire heavy fuel fraction led these workers to consider it as a single stock. Burton realized that narrower "cuts," boiling over a shorter range, might behave entirely differently when subjected to cracking. So he and Humphreys divided it into several portions. By this segregation of raw material he obtained from the lighter fractions simultaneously a high yield of cracked gasoline and a low formation of coke. From his willingness to sacrifice the broader goal of cracking the entire group of heavy ends to the narrower one of cracking a limited fraction came success.

The procedure Burton and Humphreys used was to pass the raw material through a heated tube, where it was first vaporized and then decomposed. In order to gain a better understanding of the cracking process, the investigators tried varying the conditions of their experiment: they varied the temperature at which the cracking took place, the amount of time that the cracking stock was submitted to the high temperatures, and the type of stock that was charged. They found, much to their satisfaction, that under certain conditions yields of 20 to 30% of material boiling in the gasoline range could be obtained. Unfortunately, they also discovered that the high yield of gasoline was accompanied by an equally high yield of very light, gaseous hydrocarbons and of coke, which lined the inside walls of the heated tube and greatly reduced the amount of heat that could be transferred to the vapors trapped in the tube. As a final blow, the quality of the cracked gasoline was found to be poor, and the impurities were very difficult to remove with existing methods of treatment.

In the course of the experiments, it became evident that the rate of cracking increased as the temperature rose. This result suggested to Burton and Humphreys that they try to crack the gas-oil fraction at much higher temperatures than could be obtained in the heated tube. In order to study cracking at very high temperatures, they decided to bubble the gas-oil vapors, unadulterated by oxygen, through a bath of molten lead. As they had suspected, the cracking reaction took place very quickly, and a high yield of gasoline was obtained. But when placed in the fuel tank of an automobile, the gasoline obtained from cracking at high temperatures was found to be completely useless. Unstable hydrocarbons in the gasoline polymerized, and a gummy substance was deposited on the walls of the tank, the gasoline lines, and the combustion chamber. Worst of all, the carburetor of the automobile would become plugged after the car had run only a few miles.

During the next sixteen months Humphreys and Rogers worked with the heated tube and the lead bath, while Burton took what time he could from his job as refinery manager to supervise the work and to submit his own ideas. These were productive months, for at the end of them Humphreys knew that moderate cracking temperatures give the best yield of motor gasoline. He also knew that of the various narrow petroleum stocks the best suited for cracking was probably the gas-oil fraction.

In the experiments in the laboratory, there were no serious obstacles to isolating the gas-oil fraction from the remainder of the heavy ends and subsequently cracking it. The gas oil had been heated, had vaporized at a temperature slightly below that at which cracking began to take place, and had been subjected to cracking conditions while in a gaseous state. This was quite possible in the laboratory, where the amounts dealt with were very small and where cracking temperatures were reached very rapidly. In the refinery, however, large volumes of the cracking stock would be processed at one time. Since the amount of heat that could be transferred into the mass of liquid would be considerably less, relative to the volume of the liquid, than that which could be transferred in the laboratory — i.e., since the rate of temperature increase was less — the problem of preventing the gas oil from escaping from the still before it could be cracked was much more difficult to solve. In the coking process — cracking at atmospheric pressure — when a large volume of heavy ends was heated, the gas oil was distilled before cracking temperatures were reached. The most valuable material, the gas oil, thereby left the heating zone before any cracking took place.

Two courses of action were open to Humphreys and Rogers. The first was to promote the cracking reaction by the use of catalysts. Little was known then of catalysts except for the fact that some materials will accelerate the rate of reaction without themselves being materially affected. Humphreys therefore chose the cheapest and most readily available materials, such as coke, stone, and rubble, and inserted them into the heated tube used in previous experiments. Although slight improvements were obtained by using this method, the results were not sufficiently promising to justify carrying the experiments any further.

Use of Pressure

The second course of action was to use higher pressures. Humphreys and Rogers conceived the idea that if oil could be kept in the still until the cracking temperature was reached, a high yield of gasoline could be obtained. Although this idea may seem obvious now, in 1910 it was a bold innovation.

It took courage to implement their idea. First of all, very little work had been done on the behavior of hydrocarbons at elevated pressures. Humphreys and Rogers were not familiar with any experiments on

[Standard Oil Company (Indiana)]

First experimental laboratory still used by Dr. Humphreys. It is now at the Smithsonian.

heavy hydrocarbons, although they did know that when acetylene, a light hydrocarbon, was subjected to pressure, it was likely to explode spontaneously. Working in a small laboratory with home-made equipment, high temperatures, and a combustible material, it is little wonder that they were wary of adding yet another element of danger to their experiments.

Secondly, they knew that the coke formed in the cracking process sank to the bottom of the vessel, or still, and insulated the contents from the source of heat. In order to maintain the rate of cracking, the temperature of the fire had to be raised, but this increased the possibility of burning a hole in the bottom of the still, which could lead to a disastrous fire.

Thirdly, the chemists were faced with the possibility that even if their laboratory experiments did prove successful, it might be impossible to construct the large-scale equipment necessary for commercial operation of the process. For these three reasons, the first two affecting their own security and the third affecting the value of what they were doing, Humphreys and Rogers proceeded with great caution, mixed with a little fear. As Humphreys himself said, they started out with their hair standing on end.

Before they subjected the laboratory still to greater than atmospheric pressures, they experimented with much smaller apparatus. Out of a solid block of steel a hollow cylinder was machined. Into the cavity one pint of gas oil could be poured, and when the cap was screwed on tightly, it could be heated under pressure. The results of the operation in the miniature still led the chemists to believe that cracking under pressure in a larger still would be more successful than atmospheric cracking. Burton, realizing that his superiors were not sympathetic, purposely refrained from discussing his experiments. This silence may have reduced his chances for immediate success, for more men were needed in the laboratory as the work progressed, but it was better to work shorthanded than not to work at all.

The first run on the laboratory still was made with a pressure of 10 pounds per square inch greater than atmospheric. A little cracking of the gas-oil fraction was obtained. Slowly and cautiously, in 5-pound steps, the pressure was increased until a total of 25 pounds greater than atmospheric was attained. As the pressure increased, more of the gas oil remained in the still, there to be cracked into gasoline and a liquid residue which was heavier in weight and darker in color than the original gas oil. During this process, little coke was formed.

As the pressure increased, so did the danger to the chemists in the laboratory and to the office workers in the refinery office just a few feet away. Lacking in technical training and standing to gain little from the success of the experiments while they had much to lose from possible failure, the clerks were probably not the most sympathetic of observers. Perhaps it was from one of them that W. P. Cowan, by now president of Indiana Standard, learned of the research being carried out at the Whiting refinery. He ordered the chemists to stop any dangerous work and to restrict their research to less hazardous pursuits.

While proceeding with work on other methods of cracking, not involving pressure, the two chemists investigated earlier discoveries. They found that other scientists had successfully and safely subjected heavy oils to high temperatures and pressures in small vessels with thick walls. At a meeting of a chemical society at Warsaw, Indiana, about this time, Humphreys fortuitously became engaged in conversation with a certain Dr. Penniman, who was employed by another oil company. Penniman mentioned that he too had heated heavy oils under pressure and had reached a total pressure of 50 pounds before he discontinued his experiments.[14] Although Penniman had not pursued his research, his results were sufficient to arouse Humphreys' enthusiasm again and to prompt him to report the results of the conversation to Burton. Armed with the knowledge that heavy hydrocarbons could be heated under pressure safely, encouraged by the favorable results of his earlier work at low pressures, and ever aware of the great advantages to be gained if he were successful, Burton obtained permission to continue, and the work resumed.

With somewhat greater confidence, Burton and Humphreys increased the pressure, 5 pounds at a time, until they had reached a limit of 75 pounds per square inch above atmosphere. At this pressure they found that little gas oil was distilled; the major portion remained in the still, where it could be cracked. The cracking process produced a reasonably good yield of a fuel suitable for use in internal-combustion engines.

By now Burton and Humphreys understood the over-all relation between the boiling range of the charge stock, the yield of gasoline, and the formation of coke. Cracking residuum under a pressure of 75 pounds yielded more coke than gasoline, but cracking gas oil at the same pressure yielded 20 to 25% gasoline and very little coke. Only when cracking was continued and the percentage yield of gasoline approached 40% did the deposit of coke become substantial.

Next, their main efforts were devoted to determining the operating conditions for producing the best yields. They learned that if the amount

[14] Penniman also said that upon reaching a pressure of 50 pounds, he had distilled the light product off by using steam to reduce the partial pressure. This would indicate that Dr. Penniman's experiments were carried on at a lower temperature than those of Humphreys and therefore at a temperature below which a significant amount of cracking can take place. The materials that he distilled may have been little more than the lighter hydrocarbons in the raw material.

of heat supplied to the still per unit time was increased, the rate of distillation would be increased too, but the resulting distillate would have less desirable characteristics. On the other hand, if the rate of heat transfer was greatly reduced, the improvement in the distillate would be more than offset by the extremely low rate of gasoline production. A balance had therefore to be struck between utilization of the process equipment and quality of the cracked gasoline.

It was one thing to determine the proper operating conditions; to control the conditions was another. The optimum rate of firing coal to the furnace had to be found, and this rate had to be adhered to. The optimum pressure in the still had to be obtained and kept constant throughout the run. It was possible to control the pressure by regulating the outward flow of gas formed during the cracking process. This pressure-control valve could have been installed at any point in the equipment beyond the outlet to the still itself. Humphreys placed it in a pipe located beyond the condensing equipment. The pressure valve was thus in the dry gas line, that is, in the line which carried off to the refinery fuel system the hydrocarbon vapors which were not condensed into the motor gasoline. In this way the gasoline was condensed under pressure, which increased the amount of light ends recovered in the gasoline and improved the gasoline yield.

One further variable in the process, the composition of the vapor from the still, had to be dealt with. What materials were to be permitted to enter the condensing section? In answering this question, Dr. Humphreys made a contribution that was vital to the success of the cracking process. In essence his solution was to prevent the distilled material heavier than gasoline from being condensed along with the gasoline, that is, to return the heavy material to the still, where it could again be subjected to the high temperatures. At the temperature and pressure utilized for cracking in the Burton process, the vapors given off consisted of approximately one quarter of material boiling in the gasoline range and three quarters above the gasoline range. If these vapors had been collected and condensed at this point, the resulting distillate would have been one quarter gasoline and three quarters kerosene and gas oil. It would have needed to be redistilled several times before the gasoline was completely separated. After the distillate had been separated and treated in this way, the gasoline would have been perfectly suitable for use as a motor fuel; but the kerosene would have had very little market value, for partially cracked kerosene is a poor illuminant.

It was, therefore, necessary to reduce the quantity of kerosene and gas oil that condensed with the gasoline. Humphreys achieved this by the invention of what he called a "run-back." The run-back was a crude but fairly effective distillation column in which the kerosene and gas oil condensed and ran back into the still but from which the gasoline vapors escaped unaffected.[15] Actually the run-back was a long inclined pipe of large diameter connected at its lower end to the top of the still and at its upper end to the condensing apparatus (No. 7 in patent illustration). As the gasoline and kerosene vapors rose in the pipe, they were subjected to cooling from the air in the atmosphere on the other side of the pipe wall. Kerosene, because of its lower boiling temperature, would

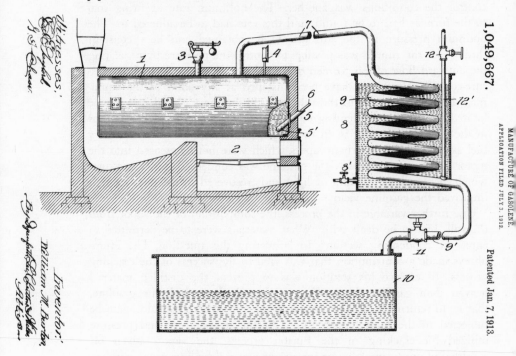

Illustration from Burton's cracking patent.

condense on the walls of the pipe and would drip down into the inside of the still. Back in the still once again, it would crack a little more, increasing the over-all yield of gasoline. Thus Humphreys' run-back managed simultaneously to give some control over the composition of the cracked distillate and to improve the quantity of gasoline obtained.

[15] Humphreys did not know of the more advanced types of distillation columns — for example, the bubble tower — then in use in the synthetic alcohol industry. With this knowledge, he might have been able to adapt the bubble tower for use in the cracking process. As it was, the bubble tower was not applied to the petroleum-refining industry until the fall of 1916.

UNITED STATES PATENT OFFICE.

WILLIAM M. BURTON, OF CHICAGO, ILLINOIS, ASSIGNOR TO STANDARD OIL COMPANY, OF WHITING, INDIANA, A CORPORATION OF INDIANA.

MANUFACTURE OF GASOLENE.

1,049,667. Specification of Letters Patent. **Patented Jan. 7, 1913.**

Application filed July 3, 1912. Serial No. 707,424.

To all whom it may concern:

Be it known that I, WILLIAM M. BURTON, a citizen of the United States, residing at Chicago, in the county of Cook and State of
5 Illinois, have invented a new and useful Improvement in the Manufacture of Gasolene, of which the following is a specification.

My invention relates to an improvement in the treatment of the high boiling-point re-
10 sidual portions, and particularly the residue of the distillation of the paraffin group or series of petroleum after the lower boiling point distillates have been removed to obtain a low boiling-point product of the same
15 group or series.

The great and growing demand during the past ten years for gasolene has induced a large increase in the supply by improvements in the method of distilling from crude
20 petroleum the naphthas, the boiling points of which range from about 75° F. to 350° F. This leaves the illuminating oils, the boiling points of which range from about 350° F. to about 600° F., and the lubricating oils and
25 waxes and, as residue, fuel-oil and gas-oil, with boiling-points ranging from about 600° F. to 700° F. The increasing demand for gasolene has induced attempts to obtain it from this residue; but these attempts, while
30 successful in producing gasolene, have invariably, so far as I am aware, as the result of lowering the boiling point, changed the general formula of the paraffin group $(C_nH_{2n}+2)$ to that of the ethylene group
35 (C_nH_{2n}), rendering the product unmarketable because undesirable by reason of its offensive odor, for the removal of which no suitable treatment has been found.

A known method of treating the fuel and
40 gas oils, forming the aforesaid residue of distillation of the paraffin series of petroleum, for obtaining therefrom a low boiling-point product involves subjecting the liquid to be treated to a temperature sufficiently
45 high to secure so-called destructive distillation, and conducting the resultant vapors through a condenser by way of a pipe or conduit connecting it with the still, but having a loaded valve interposed in the conduit
50 between the condenser and still to maintain pressure in the latter of the vapors of distillation on the liquid. While this practice produces the desired effect of lowering the boiling point of the liquid, the condensed
55 product, for reasons which I do not attempt

to explain, is found to have been converted into distillates belonging to the objectionable ethylene group, referred to.

The object of my invention is to provide a method of treating the aforesaid residue of the paraffin group of petroleum by distillation and condensation of the vapors thereof, whereby the resultant product of low boiling-points shall be of the same paraffin series and thus free from the objection mentioned or, in other words, whereby conversion of the petroleum of that series into products belonging to the ethylene series shall be avoided. This object I accomplish by raising the boiling point of the liquid residue and increasing the heat-influence thereon while undergoing distillation by maintaining backpressure on said liquid of the vapors arising therefrom by distillation, as has hitherto been done as aforesaid, and also maintaining the vapors themselves under pressure throughout their course from the still through the condenser and while undergoing condensation.

Suitable apparatus devised for the practise of my improvement is illustrated in the accompanying drawing by a broken view in vertical longitudinal section, diagrammatic in character, showing parts in elevation.

A boiler-like holder 1 for the liquid residue to be treated surmounts a fire-chamber 2 and is shown to be equipped with a safety-valve 3 to relieve excessive pressure in the holder, a pressure-gage 4, and a temperature-gage 5, the preferable construction of which is that illustrated of a tube 5¹ extending inclinedly into the holder through its head and closed at its inner end, for containing mercury, or by preference oil, and adapted to have withdrawably inserted into it through its outer, open end a suitable thermometer 6 for immersion into the contents of the tube under subjection to the heat in the holder. A conduit 7 leads from the top of the holder and inclines upwardly therefrom, to induce the return-flow into it of unvaporized portions of the liquid, to a condenser 8, the tank of which is shown to be provided with a lower draw-off cock 8¹. The condenser-coil 9 discharges at its lower end through a pipe-extension 9¹ thereof, of any desired length, into a receiver 10 for the products of condensation. In this pipe, and thus beyond the discharge-end of the coil, is contained a shut-off valve 11, and it is desir-

Specification from Burton's cracking patent.

Together with Burton's concept of heating, distilling, and condensing under pressure, Humphreys' method of separation constituted the main technical achievements of the Burton process.

It might be asked at this point why an even higher pressure was not utilized during the process. Chemists had found that the higher the pressure, the greater the amount of gas oil that was subjected to the cracking process, and therefore the higher the gasoline yield. If an operating pressure of 75 pounds provided a higher yield than 50 pounds, 100 pounds' operating pressure should provide a still higher yield. Why then was this higher pressure not utilized?

It was neither a lack of interest in higher pressures nor a lack of knowledge of what they might provide, but rather a lack of suitable high-pressure equipment. This is not the only instance in which an improvement in the manufacturing technique was frustrated by a physical inability to carry out the improvement. At this point, and throughout the development of the various cracking processes, advances in cracking frequently had to wait for advances in mechanical and structural engineering.

In this case Burton and Humphreys were their own mechanical and structural engineers, designing and having built in the refinery machine shop the vessels, piping, and cooling equipment necessary to process the gas oil. In 1911, the technique of welding had not been developed, and high-pressure vessels were constructed of riveted plates. The rivets were driven through the plates and pounded home by air hammers. On the surface of the still, the riveted seams were the weakest area. In constructing the stills the limit on the thickness of the shell was therefore set by the air pressure in the refinery. A higher air pressure in the refinery would have permitted the use of thicker steel plates and sounder seams. Seventy-five pounds was the highest pressure that Humphreys felt his equipment could stand. In his calculations, he used an arbitrary safety factor of 400%, based on the strength of steel at ordinary temperatures. In 1911, however, very little was known about the characteristics of steel at elevated temperatures; by taking the strength of steel at ordinary temperatures as his basis, Humphreys had substantially overestimated its strength at higher temperatures. Later research disclosed the safety factor in the original Burton stills was only about 50%.

In addition to determining the upper limit of operating pressure, the equipment that was available also limited the capacity of each unit. Had it been possible to build a larger still, many advantages would have been gained. Humphreys believed that larger-scale operations would be more profitable. A larger still required no more labor for its operation. The increase in the internal volume of the vessels and the piping was

greater than the increase in surface area of the equipment. Since the
capacity increased in proportion to the volume, and the cost of construction increased in proportion to the surface area, benefits of lower capital
cost per unit of capacity could thus be achieved from larger-scale equipment. The limit was set therefore by the largest steel plates that were
then available. The biggest standard size was 30 feet by 10 feet. Two steel
plates could not be riveted together end to end to provide a still 60
feet long, because the seam would not hold when directly subjected to
the heat from the furnace. Because the bottom of the still had to be
seamless, the length of the longest plate determined the length of the

[Standard Oil Company (Indiana)]

An early Burton still.

still. For the same reason, diameters could not be greater than the maximum plate width of 10 feet, for the side seams had to be above the liquid
level of the cracking stock in the still. Consequently, the original Burton
stills were 8 feet in diameter, and 30 feet in length.[16]

Adopting the Burton Process

Once the experimental work at high pressures was resumed toward the
end of 1910, the main problems were solved quite speedily. By the middle

[16] Standard Oil Company (Indiana), "Historical Summaries of Products and
Manufacturing Processes," report by J. K. Roberts to Dr. O. E. Bransky, October 7,
1938, pp. 4–5.

of 1911, Burton, Humphreys, and Rogers had a very good idea of how the process was to be carried out. They knew what characteristics the charge stock should have; they had been able to specify the ideal operating conditions; they had designed the actual refinery equipment; and they had constructed and were operating a pilot plant.[17] From the beginning of 1911 until the middle of 1912, the development of the Burton process was delayed not by technical considerations but by the inability to secure funds to construct the equipment. It required a change in the organization of Indiana Standard to bring the Burton process to commercial operation.

In order to install the cracking equipment, Burton had to gain permission from the board of directors of the parent company, the Standard Oil Company (New Jersey). Filled with enthusiasm for the cracking process, Burton went to New York. He presented his material: an explanation of the nature of the cracking process, drawings of the process equipment, an estimate of $1,000,000 as the capital cost of building the first six batteries of pressure stills and attendant facilities, and a calculation of the profits to be expected from the installation.[18] According to statements Burton himself made some years later, the estimated rate of return on the investment was quite attractive, high enough to recover the investment in somewhat less than a year.[19]

In spite of this favorable estimate and the persuasiveness of Dr. Burton, who himself was completely convinced of the merit of his process, the request was turned down. One reason for the decision is known; the graphic answer has come down through the decades. "No, you'd blow the whole State of Indiana into Lake Michigan."[20]

This reason was in itself an adequate explanation for the refusal. The board of directors was composed of men with little training or experience in the chemistry of petroleum. Having lived through an age of boiler explosions in trains, ocean ships, and river steamers, they were well aware of the hazards of processing hydrocarbons under pressure. Little wonder that, removed geographically and temperamentally from the

[17] Drawings of the settings for the first and second batteries of 8-foot by 30-foot pressure stills were completed by October 30, 1911; see the Standard Oil Company (Indiana) memorandum dated October 20, 1936, on the "Construction Details, Burton and Burton-Clark Pressure Stills," signed by William B. Plummer.

[18] W. M. Burton, "Address of Acceptance," Perkin Medal Award, *Industrial Engineering Chemistry*, Vol. 14, 1922, pp. 162–163. This payout calculation was probably made by Burton himself, for Humphreys has no recollection of its being done at the Whiting refinery laboratory.

[19] For the assumptions and calculations underlying the payout calculation, see the deposition of William M. Burton, filed with the Income Tax Unit, Treasury Department, County of Cook, State of Illinois, in November 1922.

[20] Robert E. Wilson, "Pioneers in Oil Cracking," *op. cit.*, p. 12.

successful experiments in the laboratory and pilot plant, they were reluctant to agree to the project. Profits could be made in investments requiring less physical risk. Burton was asking for $1,000,000 to be invested in a process which at this point had not been proved in commercial operation. Burton, himself, was certain that his process would be successful, but the directors probably found it difficult to divorce his emotional commitment from his scientific evaluation. The directors had not conceived of the idea of cracking a narrow-range boiling stock under pressure; they had not carried out the long and dangerous experiments in the laboratory and in the pilot plant; they had not known the obstacles to success and therefore could not have been as impressed by the apparent solution of the problems. They had to consider the investment in terms of its alternative, in terms of the other projects to which several hundred thousand dollars could be appropriated. It is little wonder that they withheld their approval.

Furthermore, at this time, the Standard Oil Company (New Jersey) was particularly unwilling to assume such a risk, for it was vulnerable enough without taking on additional commitments. Jersey Standard had just lost the antitrust case in the United States Circuit Court of the Eastern District of Missouri, which had held it to be "a combination or a conspiracy in restraint of trade."[21] The court had ordered the dissolution of the trust. The very life of the company was in jeopardy, and it could not concern itself with improving its conditions of life should it survive.

After the adverse decision, Burton returned to Chicago. His disappointment did not last long, however. Within a few weeks the Supreme Court upheld the dissolution decree, and in the middle of May the breakup of the Standard Oil Company (New Jersey) was confirmed. On September 1, 1911, Jersey Standard distributed to its stockholders the equities which it held in its thirty-three subsidiaries.[22]

The scene was set for a reversal. Now in order to have the Burton process installed, permission would have to be obtained not from the directors of the Standard Oil Company (New Jersey) but from those of the new, independent Standard Oil Company (Indiana). One of the directors of the new company was Burton himself. To his colleagues, Burton renewed his plea. For the purpose of constructing the same

[21] United States vs. Standard Oil Company of New Jersey et al., 173 Fed. Rep., 197–200. On May 15, 1911, the Supreme Court upheld the lower court's decision (Standard Oil Company of New Jersey et al. vs. The United States, 221 U. S. 1).

[22] Moody's Analyses of Investments, 1916, New York: Moody's Investors Service, 1916, p. 1121. Stockholders of the Standard Oil company (New Jersey) received 9,990 shares of Indiana common stock for each 983,383 shares of Jersey common stock held prior to the dissolution.

six batteries that he had requested earlier, Burton now asked for $800,000.[23]

Whereas in New York the risk had seemed to outweigh the possible gain, in Chicago the balance was in the opposite direction. After the divorcement, Indiana Standard was left with adequate refining and marketing facilities but was dependent upon outside suppliers for its crude oil.[24] Without a sure source of its chief raw material, the company was eager to reduce the amount of crude oil that it had to purchase in order to meet its rising sales commitments. By requiring less crude oil per gallon of gasoline, the Burton process would make this reduction possible.[25]

As significant as the tangible advantages to be gained by reducing the company's dependence upon outside suppliers of crude oil was the intangible effect of Dr. Burton's personality. He was well known by his fellow board members; his technical background and his success in running the Whiting refinery were respected. When it came to making the final decision, the directors felt that they could rely upon his recommendation.

Following the authorization of the expenditure, construction was started on the first six batteries of sixty stills. Each of these stills consisted of a drum, 8 feet by 30 feet, built to withstand a pressure of 75 pounds. From the top of each still two long inclined pipes 12 inches in diameter (Humphreys' run-backs) took off. At the top end of the run-backs were condensing coils, and connected to the coils were the vessels in which the liquid was separated from the gas. Above each battery towered a smokestack, which exhausted the flue gas from the furnace of each still. The stills were placed side by side and from above looked like a set of gigantic Fourth-of-July rockets. Construction was completed in November 1912, and the first battery of stills began operation in January 1913.[26] From that day on, the manufacture of petroleum products was revolutionized.

[23] Standard Oil Company (Indiana), Press Release on W. M. Burton, November 13, 1944, p. 5. Total assets of the Indiana company in 1913, the first year for which statistics are available, were $49,190,085. Earnings in the same year were $14,687,696. (Moody's *Analyses of Investments, 1916*, New York: Moody's Investors Service, 1916, p. 1118.)

[24] J. G. McLean and R. W. Haigh, *The Growth of Integrated Oil Companies*, Boston: Harvard Graduate School of Business Administration, 1954, p. 210.

[25] *Ibid.*, "For a number of years after the dissolution decree in 1911, the Standard Oil Company (Indiana) remained a refining and marketing company and made no significant attempt to acquire crude oil production" (p. 254). The authors attribute this policy to the close ties that were retained between Indiana Standard and its former suppliers of crude oil under the pre-1911 arrangements (p. 255); equally important was the crude-oil saving accomplished through cracking.

[26] R. E. Wilson, "Pioneers in Oil Cracking," *op. cit.*, pp. 13–17.

Success was apparent from the beginning. The Burton units performed as had been expected, doubling the yield of gasoline from crude oil. At a manufacturing cost of 44¢, 9.8 gallons of gasoline worth 11.5¢ per gallon were obtained from a barrel (42 gallons) of gas oil worth 2.27¢ per gallon. The profit was 25¢ for each barrel of gas oil processed.[27] It seemed that within two years Indiana Standard would recover the money spent on the first sixty units. And the price of gasoline, rather than falling with increased production, was rising with the increased popularity of the automobile.

Persuaded by these arguments that additional installations would be profitable, Indiana Standard rapidly increased the number of Burton units. Another sixty units were authorized for the Whiting refinery and were put into operation between May and November of 1913.[28] Construction of sixty units more was begun in December of 1912 at the refinery in Wood River, Illinois, across the Mississippi River from St. Louis. Another sixty units were constructed at the Sugar Creek, Missouri, refinery. In Casper, Wyoming, Indiana Standard installed in 1914 as its sole processing equipment twenty Burton units, which operated on gas oil purchased from other refiners in the Wyoming crude-oil field.[29] As Burton observed, the "company was increasing its Burton Process just as fast as the equipment could be built with the funds at hand."[30]

Fortunately profits accrued so quickly that the funds on hand increased at a very rapid rate. According to one estimate, during the rest of the decade one half of the company's profits were derived from the use of the Burton process.[31] Moreover, during 1913 and 1914, there were within the company few competing uses for funds. The company had an excellent marketing organization, which was easily able to dispose of the increased volume of products. The supplies of crude oil were adequate,

[27] See Appendix Tables 9, 12, and 13.

[28] Standard Oil Company (Indiana), "Historical Summaries of Products and Manufacturing Processes," *op. cit.*, pp. 2–5; also "Construction Details, Burton and Burton-Clark Pressure Stills," memorandum by W. B. Plummer, November 20, 1936.

[29] *Ibid.*

[30] Letter from William M. Burton to Mr. Seubert dated Chicago, September 12, 1922, sworn before W. F. Roberts, Notary of the Public, May 16, 1924, and entered as Exhibit 9 in Indiana Standard's presentation in its claim for a refund from the Burton Process Patent: U.S. Treasury Department, Income Tax Unit, State of Illinois, County of Cook.

[31] Standard Oil Company (Indiana), "Claim for Refund on Burton Process Patent," brief presented to the Income Tax Unit, U.S. Treasury Department, State of Illinois, County of Cook.

and it was even possible to purchase from other refiners the immediate charge stock for the Burton stills, gas oil, at a moderate cost.[32]

By using Burton stills to process gas oil purchased from outside sources, Indiana Standard was obtaining the profits of innovation. In this case, these profits arose from the difference between the productivity of the input, gas oil, in its old use (as an industrial fuel only slightly superior to heavy fuel oil) and the productivity in its new use (as a raw material for gasoline). Moreover, since Indiana Standard had patented the Burton process, and since the Burton process was the only commercial cracking process, these profits were not quickly eliminated by competition. The most profitable innovation is the one that cannot be imitated.

Operating and Marketing Problems

One potential problem, the rebellion of the refinery workers who would be faced with the task of operating pressure stills, was avoided because of the foresight of the refinery management. Knowing that Dr. Humphreys had worked day after day without injury to himself during the development of the process, the workers saw that it was possible to operate safely. In addition, each process crew was given careful training by Humphreys on a commercial-sized unit located near the Whiting refinery laboratory. There, the men who were to operate the stills in the refinery familiarized themselves with the cracking operations, and at the same time aided Humphreys in his continuing investigation of the factors controlling the cracking operation. After this training, the stillmen were content to assume their operating duties in the refinery. Fortunately for the company there were no serious accidents during the first few years, although numerous fires did break out.

By the existing standards of the time, the stillmen's lives were not unduly hazardous; less fortunate, however, were the laborers who cleaned out the stills. In the Burton process, the length of the run was determined by the thickness of the coke deposited on the walls of the still. When it had become dangerously thick, the fire under the still was extinguished and the residual oil was pumped out. Steam was blown through the empty still in order to remove any hydrocarbon vapors and thus prevent explosion. The still then sat empty and unattended until it had cooled off sufficiently for the man who scraped the coke off the inside walls to enter. The sooner the man entered, the more quickly the still could be cleaned out and put back into operation; however, the sooner he entered, the hotter he found it inside the still. A compromise

[32] In the last six months of 1914, the fraction of total gas-oil charge that was purchased from outside refiners was 16%, assuming 40% gas-oil recovery from distilling crude oil (Standard Oil Company [Indiana], *Whiting Refinery Cost and Yield Records*).

was worked out: the cleaners, clad in asbestos suits, entered the stills when they cooled to 250°F. and began immediately the laborious job of chipping away the carbon until the still wall was completely revealed.

Perhaps of more immediate concern to the company was the resistance that it met in marketing the new product, cracked gasoline. Burton was content to obtain a product with the same *chemical* characteristics as straight-run gasoline.[33] He reported that the cracked gasoline from the pressure still was suitable as a fuel for internal-combustion engines, for it vaporized in the carburetor and burned in the cylinder just like straight-run gasoline.

But when the marketing department took over this new fuel, they found that its *physical* properties were anything but ideal. Cracked gasoline had a yellow hue, and to the consuming public, which was accustomed to finding impurities in the gasoline it bought, the yellow color seemed yet another adulterant. Even more serious was the offensive odor of the cracked gasoline. During the cracking process, some of the sulfur compounds present in the charge stock were broken down into hydrogen sulfide, which gave the gasoline a bad smell. The customer quickly became aware of this odor, for in many of the automobiles at that time, including the Ford, the gasoline tanks were under the front seat. Any gasoline spilled on the floor board while the tank was being filled remained there under the nose of the operator as a potent reminder of the presence of the cracked gasoline.[34]

The marketing department's first action was to sell this new product, cracked gasoline, to the outlets to which it sold regular gasoline. A new brand name, "Motor Spirit," was imported. Because of its color and odor, it was offered at 10.5¢ a gallon, a discount of 3¢ a gallon from the price of regular gasoline.[35] The 3¢ discount was set by the structure of the gasoline market in 1913; at the time of the introduction of Motor Spirit, a regular gasoline and a low-grade gasoline, selling for 3¢ less, were both offered. Motor Spirit was thought to be competitive with the latter product.[36] But the public's reaction to Motor Spirit was unfavorable.

[33] William M. Burton, letter to Mr. Seubert, *op. cit.*, "This product . . . was thoroughly satisfactory from the standpoint of operations in an engine. . . ."

[34] The one advantage which cracked gasoline in its raw state had over straight-run gasoline was its high octane; in 1913 this advantage was not recognized. Even if it had been, the engines of the day were not designed to utilize a fuel of higher octane than that available in straight-run gasoline. It was only in the mid-twenties that this characteristic of cracked gasoline came to be appreciated.

[35] William M. Burton, letter to Mr. Seubert, *op. cit.*

[36] *Ibid.*: The low-grade gasoline did not volatilize in the carburetor as readily as the regular grade because it included heavier fractions. In refining terminology, the low-grade gasoline was described as having a high end-point, i.e., as requiring a higher temperature for complete vaporization.

The bad color and odor more than offset the lower price; in fact, the public gave little evidence of being willing to buy Motor Spirit at any price.[37]

Indiana Standard now found it necessary to treat the gasoline chemically to improve odor and color. Fortunately this required no new technique, for, like other refining products, the cracked gasoline could be treated with sulfuric acid. Some new treating equipment was necessary, but the sums involved were minor and the step was taken rapidly. When treated, the cracked gasoline was nearly indistinguishable from the normal, straight-run product. There was no reason to continue marketing cracked gasoline at the lower price, so refiners "sneaked in say 25% of cracked gasoline in their gasoline blend with 75% of straight run."[38]

In addition to the problems created in manufacturing and marketing a new product, the Burton cracking process made severe demands upon the equipment itself. From the beginning of research on cracking under pressure, Burton and Humphreys had been preoccupied with improving the safety and the performance of the equipment. This preoccupation did not cease when the first commercial units were installed at Whiting. Refinery personnel knew that heating oil under pressure was dangerous, but they were not reminded of it as long as the hot oil was kept in confinement. Unfortunately, fires frequently broke out, usually in the places where sections of pipes were joined together or where the still plates were riveted.[39] The repeated cycles of expansion and contraction, caused by the heating and cooling phases of the cracking process, permitted oil to seep through. Upon contact with the air, the hot oil would catch on fire and start a frightening although not necessarily serious conflagration. In order to prevent these fires in the existing equipment, it was necessary to wedge calking material between the joints, often while the unit was under pressure. In the beginning, to instill confidence in the operators, Humphreys himself would work on the burning stills with a calking hammer. The net result of this playing with fire was to encourage Indiana Standard, and through it the manufacturers of

[37] Standard Oil Company (Indiana) vs. Globe Oil and Refining Company, United States Circuit Court of Appeals, 7th Circuit, No. 5511, October 1935 (appeal following suit in U.S. District Court, Northern District of Illinois, Eastern Division, Nos. 10,770 and 12,503); testimony of Russell Wiles (attorney for the plaintiff), pp. 457–458.
[38] Universal Oil Products Company vs. Winkler-Koch Engineering Company and Root Refining Company, District Court of the United States, District of Delaware, Nos. 716 and 895; testimony of Hiram J. Halle, p. 808.
[39] Interview with Robert E. Humphreys, November 23, 1954; also R. E. Wilson, "Pioneers in Oil Cracking," op. cit., p. 18, and his "Fifteen Years of the Burton Process," op. cit., p. 1101.

petroleum-refinery equipment, to develop vessels and piping better able to withstand the severity of operation at high temperature and pressure.[40]

Process and Equipment Improvement

But the desire for greater safety in operations was not the only stimulus to the improvement of cracking equipment. This incentive was combined with that of cost reduction. Even before the cracking process was installed in the refinery, Burton and Humphreys recognized that the ways in which the cost of manufacturing could be reduced were limited. One possibility was to reduce the fuel costs; but within the limits set by the design of the Burton process, the possibility of improving the efficiency of combustion was slight, and the savings that might be achieved were small compared with those that could be gained elsewhere.

Two other possibilities were reductions in capital and labor costs. Any modification of the process or the equipment which could increase the capacities of the stills and thereby reduce the fixed costs[41] would be advantageous.

There were two ways of increasing the capacity of the units: first, by operating them at a constant rate of cracking for a longer time before shutting them down, and second, by increasing the rate of cracking so that within a certain time interval a larger amount of cracked material would be produced. Thus the first affected the amount of raw material that was cracked, and the second affected the rate at which the cracking took place.

The variable which determined how much raw material could be cracked in any run was the amount of coke that was deposited upon the walls of the still. For a given quantity of gas oil that was charged to the Burton stills, the amount of coke formed was determined by the severity with which the material was cracked; the greater the fraction of gas oil cracked, the more coke formed. Therefore, if the length of the run were to be increased, under a constant rate of cracking, it would be necessary somehow to prevent the coke from adhering to the walls of the still. In 1911, Humphreys conceived the idea of placing perforated plates inside the still, following the contour of the bottom and raised a few inches above it. By investigating the cracking of a body of oil, he discovered that the coke was formed within the mass of the oil itself rather than upon the metal surfaces of the vessel. Coke was deposited upon the still bottom by the precipitation of the coke particles. Humphreys reasoned that by placing grids just above the bottom of the still,

---

[40] Robert E. Wilson, "Fifteen Years of the Burton Process," *op. cit.*, pp. 1101, 1104.

[41] In the petroleum-refining industry, where labor is highly skilled and output fluctuations are not severe, labor tends to be thought of as a fixed cost.

he would trap many of the coke particles before they reached the bottom. The stills could therefore be operated for a longer time before the deposit of coke on the still wall itself reduced the rate of heat transfer and forced the unit to be shut down. He designed the "false-bottom plates," to be hinged at either side so that they could be raised from the bottom of the still to facilitate cleaning.[42]

In 1914, the first 120 Burton stills, which had been constructed at the Whiting refinery between January 1913 and February 1914, were equipped with the plates.[43] Some laboratory data that were obtained later when the original Burton patent itself was being valued for tax purposes[44] indicate that the false-bottom plates raised the yield of a Burton still charged with gas oil from 23.87% to 26.42% of gasoline. If we assume that slightly higher temperatures could be used when the false-bottom plates were installed, so that the entire cycle of operations (charge, heat, crack, pump-out, cool, and clean) took no longer, the effect of the false-bottom plates would be to increase the still's capacity to produce gasoline by approximately 2.5%.[45] In terms of manufacturing an equal amount of gasoline by means of the two different pieces of equipment, a saving of approximately 10% of the raw material cost could be achieved. With gas oil worth 2.5¢ per gallon in 1913, this amounts to a cost reduction of 1.07¢ per gallon of gasoline, or 8.0% of the total cracking cost.

It also seemed possible to effect savings by improving the composition of the cracked distillate. If it contained fewer of the components heavier than gasoline, the distillate would require less subsequent processing, and consequently less fuel would be consumed.

The original Burton units relied on the long, inclined vapor lines of Humphreys' run-backs to separate the hydrocarbons in the vapor that would boil at high temperature from those that would boil at low temperature. Even though it would have reduced the strain on the subsequent processing steps, perfect separation using the run-backs would have required a rate of cracking so slow as to entail extremely

[42] U.S. Patent 1,122,003. "Method of Distilling Hydrocarbons," patented December 22, 1914, by R. E. Humphreys.

[43] Standard Oil Company (Indiana), "Historical Summaries of Products and Manufacturing Processes," *op. cit.*, p. 2.

[44] Standard Oil Company (Indiana), Oil and Gas Evaluation Section, "Memorandum Showing Valuation of Burton Patent," Whiting, Indiana, February 21, 1922.

[45] These experimental data can be compared with those derived from Whiting refinery operations for the period February-June 1913. In 1913, the yield of gasoline, based upon the actual material charged to the Burton pressure stills was 23.3%. In the last six months of 1914, by which time most of the stills were equipped with false-bottom plates, the yield of gasoline was 25.4%. The improvement in gasoline yield over the year and a half was 2.1%.

high capital, labor, and fuel costs. Capital and labor costs would have been high because the capacity of the unit to produce gasoline would have been extremely low, and the fuel cost would have been high because of the constant vaporizing and condensing of the heavier materials. A balance had to be kept between a high rate of cracking on the one hand, and an adequate fractionation of the cracked vapors on the other. Improvement could result, therefore, only from a new fractionating technique.

Two new fractionating techniques were developed in the first few years after the installation of the original Burton stills: the air-cooled radiator and the bubble tower. The air-cooled radiator looked like a harp whose strings were replaced by pipes; it was placed at the upper end of Humphreys' run-back lines, where it subjected the uncondensed vapors to further cooling. It was the development of John B. Moore, one of the refinery employees at the Whiting plant.[46] These radiators were added to the third battery of sixty stills installed at Whiting between February 1915 and August 1916.[47]

Although no analysis is available of the specific merits of the Moore radiator, a comparison of the operation of a Burton still with one run-back line and the same still with two run-back lines indicates the benefits to be gained from better fractionation. In this experiment, the second run-back line would increase the degree of fractionation approximately as much as the Moore radiator. The Burton still equipped with one run-back line produced 52.37% distillate on charge, of which 50.45% was gasoline, giving a yield of gasoline on gas-oil charge of 26.4%.[48] In the Burton still equipped with two run-back lines, 49.80% distillate was produced from the gas-oil charge, and of this distillate 59.4% was gasoline, giving an over-all gasoline yield of 29.6%, an increase of 3.2% over the still with one run-back line. With better fractionization, the final yield of pressure distillate is smaller but has a higher proportion of gasoline in it. This means that more of the material heavier than gasoline was returned to the stills to be cracked once again, and that the burden on the subsequent distillation facilities was reduced.

The increased volume of cracked gasoline was not obtained without extra cost, however. Additional fuel was required to vaporize the greater volumes of cracked gasoline and heavier reflux material, but the cost of the extra fuel consumed did not detract enough from the profits

[46] U.S. Patent 1,130,318. "Apparatus for Distilling Petroleum Oils," John B. Moore, filed October 19, 1914, and patented March 2, 1915.
[47] Standard Oil Company (Indiana), "Historical Summaries of Products and Manufacturing Processes," *op. cit.*, p. 2.
[48] Standard Oil Company (Indiana), "Memorandum Showing Valuation of Burton Patent," *op. cit.*

to be gained from the Moore radiator to prevent its being well worth while to install. In fact, a rough estimate of the value of the invention, based on a capital cost of $1,067 per still[49] for the marginal investment in the Moore radiator shows an increase in gasoline output of 111 gallons per day. Taking into account the saving in gas oil that the higher yield of gasoline permitted, total cost was reduced by 1.02¢ per gallon of gasoline produced, or 8.2%.[50] At this rate, the investment in the radiators was returned four times during the first year.

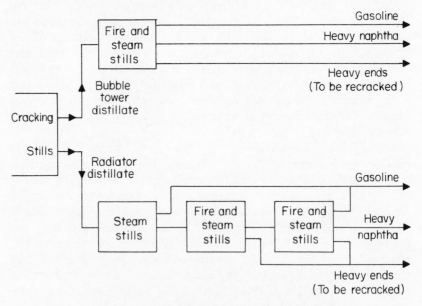

Flow chart for the rerunning of cracked distillate.

Source: Standard Oil Company (Indiana), "Report of Flow of Materials at Whiting Plant," by W. H. Holland, November 10, 1920. The treating stages have been omitted from the chart.

Although the radiator substantially improved the Burton apparatus, the processing scheme for fractionating the distillate into its various products was by no means perfect. The flow chart above illustrates the advantages which could have been gained by better fractionation. Even

[49] Walter F. Rittman, a consulting engineer, estimated that the cost of the radiator was roughly 8% of the total cost of a Burton unit. See Standard Oil Company (Indiana) vs. Globe Oil and Refining Company, U.S. Circuit Court of Appeals, 7th Circuit, October 1935, No. 5511, p. 299. The capital cost of a single Burton unit, without the Moore radiator, was approximately $13,300.

[50] This return is derived solely from the increase of 3.2% in gasoline production and the equal reduction in pressure distillate bottoms, the gasoline being valued at 13.5¢ per gallon, the pressure distillate bottoms at 2.5¢ per gallon, and the capacity of the Burton unit being taken as 88.5 barrels per day of gas-oil charge.

with Moore radiators as integral parts of the Burton units, it was necessary to submit the distillate to three rerunning steps before the final product was obtained. First the pressure still distillate was rerun, yielding gasoline and tar. Then the tar itself was rerun so that an additional heavy naphtha could be recovered. Finally the additional heavy naphtha was rerun, yielding gasoline, kerosene, and tar. In each instance, the material charged to the rerunning stills had to be heated, and the distilled products had to be cooled. A much better development, of course, would have been a method of fractionation which would yield the final products after only one fractionating stage.

The next innovation in fractionation, the "bubble tower," indicated the path along which this development was to take place. In the bubble tower, as in all other distillation columns, a material composed of two or more components boiling at different temperatures is separated into two or more fractions, at least one of which will boil above and at least one of which will boil below the average of the feed. Within the tower, the components are in both vapor and liquid states, the vapor rising and the liquid falling. The closer the contact between vapor and liquid, the better the fractionation. The temperature at the bottom of the tower is considerably higher than that at the top. As vapors enter the tower, they rise to successively colder zones. In each zone, the component which condenses at that temperature becomes a liquid, leaving the materials that boil at a lower temperature in a vapor state. When the top of the tower is reached, only the lightest materials are left, and they are still in a vaporous form when they leave the tower. Likewise only the heaviest materials remain at the bottom of the tower, and these are withdrawn as a liquid.

Fractional distillation had been recognized and applied in industries other than petroleum refining before 1915, first in the manufacture of alcohol.[51] At approximately the same time that the principle of distillation was applied to products from the Burton stills, it was applied to the fractionation of crude petroleum in California.[52]

The bubble tower adopted by the Standard Oil Company (Indiana) at its Whiting refinery was the invention of two of its employees, Frank R. Lewis and Thomas S. Cooke.[53] Their research was carried out at

[51] W. L. Nelson, *Petroleum Refinery Engineering*, 3rd ed., *op. cit.*, p. 5.

[52] E. H. Leslie, *Motor Fuels*, New York: The Chemical Catalogue Co., 1923, pp. 178 ff.

[53] Lewis and Cooke filed a patent application on the bubble tower on May 7, 1917. The application was granted on October 4, 1921, and assigned the patent number 1,392,584. In a subsequent suit, the patent was held invalid, as having been anticipated in the prior art (Standard Oil Company [Indiana] vs. Globe Oil and Refining Company, *op. cit.*, pp. 6–8).

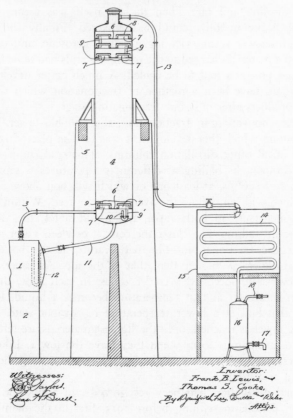

F. B. LEWIS AND T. S. COOKE.
ART OF DISTILLING PETROLEUM OILS.
APPLICATION FILED MAY 7, 1917.

1,392,584.   Patented Oct. 4, 1921.

Illustration from Lewis and Cooke's bubble-tower patent.

Whiting prior to the autumn of 1916. Tests on a commercial-scale unit
in November and December of that year were successful, and the bubble
towers were put into operation on fifty Burton stills constructed between
February 1917 and August 1918.[54] The towers were designed to operate
at the pressure of the stills, which was then 90 to 95 lb./sq. in., compared
with 75 lb./sq. in. in 1915.[55] The temperature at the bottom of the tower
was kept at 595° F., equal to the end point of kerosene. This tempera-

[54] Standard Oil Company vs. Globe Oil and Refining Company, *op. cit.*, testimony of Walter F. Rittman, pp. 291, 292; and Standard Oil Company (Indiana),
"Historical Summaries of Products and Manufacturing Processes," *op. cit.*, pp. 4, 5.
[55] Standard Oil Company (Indiana), "Historical Summaries of Products and
Manufacturing Processes," *op. cit.*, p. 2.

[Standard Oil Company (Indiana)]

Row of bubble towers used to fractionate products from the improved
Burton-Clark cracking equipment.

ture was chosen deliberately so that all kerosene and lighter products
would be in the overhead fraction.[56]

The addition of the bubble tower in the cracking process had two
major benefits. First of all, it increased the yield of gasoline in the
pressure distillate. The boiling range of the bubble-tower distillate was
narrower than the distillate from the radiators, and subsequent rerunning
steps were reduced from three to one, with a concomitant reduction in
cost.

The second effect of the installation of the bubble tower was to permit
an increase in the cracking capacity of the Burton units. Before the
bubble tower was introduced, the capacity of the Burton stills had been
limited by the distillation operation. Cracking could have been carried
on at a higher rate in the still itself, but the increased volume of vapor

[56] Testimony of Walter G. Whitman, Standard Oil Company (Indiana) vs. Globe
Oil and Refining Company, *op. cit.*, p. 113.

could not have been fractionated without returning a larger fraction of the gasoline to the still and permitting much more of the heavier material to escape into the pressure distillate. Following the adoption of the bubble tower, the two operations were in balance, with the result that the full capabilities of the equipment could be utilized.

An estimate of the value of adding the bubble tower to the cracking unit requires two assumptions. First, a value must be assumed for the improvement in product yields that occurred through better fractionation. Because no comparison between distillation with radiators and with bubble towers was to be found in refinery records, the value was inferred from a statement that the bubble tower permitted a 4.5% higher yield of gasoline on charge than did the Moore radiator.[57]

The second assumption concerns cracking capacity. Accompanying the improvement in fractionation was an increase in the daily capacity of the Burton units of 53%, achieved primarily by increasing the temperature at which the cracking took place.[58] The combined effect of these increases in capacity and gasoline yield would be a reduction of 1.34¢ per gallon of gasoline, or 11.8% of the total cost.

Only new Burton units were equipped with bubble towers, for it was more profitable to keep the old units in continuous service. It was fortunate that bubble towers were not universally adopted, for in January 1922 two of the towers ruptured simultaneously, killing twenty men and causing the rest of the installations to be condemned.[59]

The setback was not permanent, however, for the evil lay, not in distillation under pressure, but in the prolonged subjection of the metals to corrosion. One of the advantages of the bubble tower had been the reduction in corrosive compounds found in the finished gasoline, the gaseous product.[60] Since the concentration of corrosive materials in the vapors from the bubble tower was less than that in the distillate feed,

[57] Standard Oil Company (Indiana) vs. Globe Oil and Refining Company, U.S. Circuit Court of Appeals, No. 5511, testimony of Walter F. Rittman, p. 309. Rittman also recalled that the cost of the bubble tower was higher than that of the Moore radiator, representing 25% rather than 8% of the capital cost of the respective cracking units (*ibid.*, p. 299). This gives $4,450 as the approximate capital cost of the bubble tower.

[58] In the relevant temperature ranges the rate of cracking doubles for each increase of 22°F. (Robert E. Wilson, "Pioneers in Oil Cracking," *op. cit.*, p. 22.) In 1920 those Burton units equipped with bubble towers were processing 157 barrels per stream day whereas those with radiators were processing only 103 barrels per day (Standard Oil Company [Indiana], W. W. Holland, "Report of Flow of Materials at Whiting Plant," November 10, 1920).

[59] Standard Oil Company (Indiana) vs. Globe Oil and Refining Company, *op. cit.*, testimony of Walter G. Whitman, p. 113.

[60] District Court of the United States, Northern District of Illinois, Eastern District, Decision in Equity 10,770 and 12,503, p. 2.

the concentration in the liquid residue was necessarily greater. The metal of which the towers were constructed was not able to withstand these concentrations. The development of alloy steels, with their characteristic resistance to the debilitating effects of corrosive substances at high temperatures, followed in part therefore from the accidents at the Whiting refinery.[61]

With one addition, which was more in the nature of an improvement in the operation of the process than it was a new piece of equipment, Indiana Standard's contributions to the art of distillation (but not to cracking) ended with the bubble tower. This final improvement actually took place before the introduction of the radiator and consisted of tying together the gas lines from all the stills.[62] Before these were joined, the pressure in each still was built up by the gas generated at the beginning of the cracking reaction. When the stills were tied together, this preparatory operation was eliminated, because the excess gas generated during the cracking reaction in the other stills could be utilized to bring the freshly charged still to operating pressure quickly.

The Tube Still

As significant in the progress of cracking as the improvements in distillation were the nearly simultaneous improvements in gas-oil decomposition. Here the most important innovation was the tube still. Unlike Moore, Lewis, and Cooke, who made one major contribution each, the inventor of the tube still was for many years to play a significant role in the development of the cracking art. The man responsible for this innovation was Edgar M. Clark, in 1913 the manager of Indiana Standard's refinery at Wood River, Illinois. Unlike Burton and Humphreys, Clark had had no formal academic training beyond elementary school. He began work as a railroad station agent. In 1890, he went to the Standard Oil Company, for which his father was also working, as an hourly paid laborer. His mechanical aptitude, inventive genius, and energy manifested themselves early and resulted in his promotion within the refinery organization.[63] Clark became assistant superintendent of the Whiting refinery, working directly for Burton, and, in 1907, was made manager of the new refinery that Standard was building at Wood River.

Through his friendship with Burton, Clark was well aware of the development of the Burton process. He had also had an opportunity to practice it when Indiana installed forty Burton stills at Wood River, soon

---

[61] R. E. Wilson, "Pioneers in Oil Cracking," *op. cit.*
[62] U.S. Patent No. 1,132,163, granted on March 16, 1915, to E. M. Clark.
[63] Standard Oil Company (Indiana) vs. Globe Oil and Refining Company, *op. cit.*, testimony of Walter F. Rittman, p. 1461.

after work was begun on the first sixty stills at Whiting. The work was well under way by December of 1912, and by the following July the refinery was turning out cracked gasoline.

[Standard Oil Company (Indiana)]

E. M. Clark.

Clark's position in the company organization was different from that of Burton's other colleagues: he was not a chemist by training; he alone was not stationed at the Whiting refinery; and his rank, unlike that of the others, was not subordinate to Burton's (at least until Burton was promoted to vice president in 1916). He was well aware of the developments in cracking that were made after 1909, but was far enough from the scene to be able to gain the perspective that was lacking to those immersed in the actual work. Having a great mechanical aptitude, he was perhaps able to see that Burton was unconsciously limiting his choice of alternatives to those that lay within the possibilities of immediate fulfillment, with the equipment that could be constructed at the time. This combination of distance without isolation, and of knowledge without commitment, was crucial.

Clark was working within the same frame of reference as Burton—trying to crack a light virgin gas oil into gasoline by utilizing high temperatures and pressures. His solution to the problem was so different, however, that as first adopted it changed the operation of the Burton

process substantially, and, as subsequently improved, it supplied the
basic principles for an entirely new cracking process which was to
render Burton's obsolete. But we are concerned in this chapter with the
Burton process and its improvements; the second application of his
concept will be taken up in the story of the Tube and Tank process.

Clark's idea was to confine the cracking to a bank of tubes through
which the oil flowed rapidly. In the tubes, the ratio of surface area to
volume was much greater than it was in the large-diameter Burton still.
The rate of heat transfer and consequently the rate of cracking was
much higher. As the gas oil heated in the tubes, the liquid became
turbulent. The turbulence kept in suspension the coke that was formed
during the cracking reaction and so limited deposits on the tube walls.
Since much of the coke formed in the cracking zone was removed from
the tubes, the operation could be carried on for a longer time before
the unit had to be shut down and cleaned out. In addition, the tubes
presented less of a cleaning problem than did the Burton stills. They
were small enough to be cleaned with a mechanical reaming tool, much
as a tobacco pipe is cleaned by a pipe cleaner. Also it was no longer
necessary before beginning the cleaning to wait for the still to cool.

Clark began his own research while the first Burton stills were being
constructed at Whiting.[64] In operating the experimental cracking still,
Burton had experienced difficulty with "hot spots." When the still was
shut down, the bulges caused by the expansion of the shell wall had to
be hammered out. Repairs took time and weakened the steel.

Clark learned of this operating problem during his summer vacation
in 1912, which he spent at Whiting. While trying to find a cure for hot
spots, Clark became aware of the similarity between cracking units and
steam boilers. In both types of equipment, liquids were heated under
confinement to high temperatures and pressures; vapors were generated
and subsequently condensed. In the construction of the Wood River
boiler house, he had departed from custom and installed Vogt tubular
boilers, which represented an advance over the familiar horizontal-return
boilers. It was natural therefore that he should have thought of applying
the principle of a tubular still to the cracking process.

Clark's first experiments were made with a cracking coil of 1-inch steel
tubing, 30 feet long, which was wrapped around a length of 12-inch pipe
set upright. Mornings, he would light a gas fire under the coil, extinguish
it on the way to lunch, start it again upon his return an hour later, and
cease operations at the end of the working day. This regimen was

[64] The story of Clark's experiments is drawn primarily from interviews in
December 1955 and March 1956 with his former associates, J. R. Carringer and
Dr. N. E. Loomis.

somewhat severe for a refinery manager, so after a week he asked the chief inspector at the refinery control laboratory, J. R. Carringer, to assist him. Working part time, they operated the coil on light and heavy gas oils, and determined the yields of gasoline.

Two events — an explosion in the experimental still at Whiting and the authorization to install sixty Burton units at Wood River — led Clark to accelerate his research. He quickly constructed a horizontal tube still, composed of thirty-six tubes, $1\frac{1}{4}$ inches in diameter and 3 feet long, rolled into a cast-iron header. The cracked oil circulated from the tubes into a reservoir holding about 25 gallons, which was elevated above the still. By 1913, Clark had impressed a crew to'run the still twenty-four hours a day, and was achieving gasoline yields equal to those Burton obtained, but on a wider range of gas-oil stocks.

This tube still, the genesis of the commercial Burton-Clark cracking unit, was followed shortly by a larger experimental unit. In the larger unit the tube bed was composed of thirty tubes $1\frac{1}{2}$ inches in diameter and 5 feet long, and the reservoir was a vertical drum 4 feet in diameter and 6 feet high. The reservoir was, for the first time, also kept under pressure. Clark realized that the gas oil, entering the drum from the tubes without being reduced in pressure, would continue to crack, even though no heat was being supplied. He also learned that the apparatus could be charged, and a complete cracking cycle carried out, several times before the drum had to be cleaned out. Having cracked gas oil successfully on his apparatus, Clark then applied for a patent on the invention.[65]

In continuing the development of the idea of cracking in a tube, Clark was faced with two alternatives. On the one hand, he could apply the tube principle to the Burton process, adapting it so as to take advantage of cracking in tubes rather than in the still itself, and yet retaining the other features of the Burton process. On the other hand, he could focus his attention on the cracking in the tubes themselves, using this as the nucleus of a new process which might have inherent advantages over the Burton process. In 1914, he chose the former course, partly because Indiana Standard wanted to build cracking units incorporating the tube principle and partly because no pumps were available which could circulate hot oil at high pressures.

By September 11, 1914, Clark had designed the new tube-still units, and in April 1915, the first twenty Burton-Clark units began operation at the Wood River refinery. In August of the same year, twenty units were installed at the Whiting refinery. Before December 1920, an additional

[65] U.S. Patent No. 1,119,496, "Method of Distilling Petroleum," to E. M. Clark; application filed April 20, 1914, and patent granted December 1, 1914.

210 units were built at Wood River, Whiting, and the company's refineries at Sugar-Creek, Missouri, and Casper, Wyoming,[66]

The Burton-Clark unit differed from its predecessor mainly in the construction of the cracking section. The still, in which the cracking took place in the Burton process, was elevated to a point approximately 4 feet above the ceiling of the furnace. Underneath, inside the furnace itself, were inserted forty-five 4-inch cracking tubes, each 29 feet in length. These tubes lay along an inclined plane, lowest in the convection section of the furnace and rising steadily through the convection and radiation sections.[67]

[Standard Oil Company (Indiana)]

First Burton-Clark tube cracking still (at the Wood River, Illinois, refinery), about 1914.

Circulation of the cracking stock, which was effected in Clark's laboratory apparatus by means of a pump, was facilitated in the commercial unit by the natural flow of the oil in the inclined tubes. By the time the gas oil reached the radiation section of the furnace, it had begun to crack. The

[66] Standard Oil Company (Indiana), "Construction Detail Burton and Burton-Clark Pressure Stills," memorandum by William B. Plummer including drawing of tube stills A. 4375, September 11, 1914. Also Standard Oil Company (Indiana), "Historical Summaries of Products and Manufacturing Processes," *op. cit.*, pp. 4, 5.

[67] U.S. Patent 1,388,514. "Distillation of Petroleum Hydrocarbons," E. M. Clark, application filed December 14, 1915, and patent granted August 23, 1921. See also Standard Oil Company (Indiana) vs. Globe Oil and Refining Company, *op. cit.*, testimony of L. C. Moore, p. 739.

cracked vapors were propelled through the tubes by the hydrostatic pressure of the heavier liquids above them at a rate sufficient to carry much of the coke created during the cracking reaction out of the cracking tubes.

The still, now removed from the source of heat, acted as a reservoir from which the cracking stock could be removed and into which the cracked vapors and uncracked liquid could be forced. As in the Burton process, the vapors rose to the top of the still and flowed through the runback line. Thereafter the processing scheme was the same as in the earlier installation.

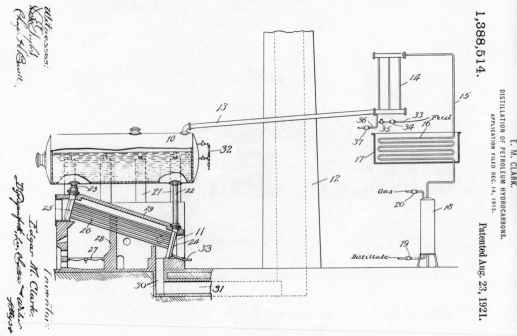

Illustration of E. M. Clark's tube-still patent.

Just as Burton and Humphreys had been faced with problems in obtaining suitable equipment three years earlier, so Clark found that some of the apparatus needed for the installation of the cracking tubes was not available. His main problem was in obtaining tube headers — long hollow cylinders of metal divided into compartments, each of which received the effluent from one of the cracking tubes. The construction of the headers was a more formidable job than was that of the tubes themselves. Ultimately the process equipment manufacturer that equipped the Wood River refinery with steam boilers, the Henry Vogt Machinery Company in Louisville, Kentucky, was able to construct them. In order to build headers which could withstand the high temperatures and pressures incident to the cracking operation, the Vogt Company had to borrow a 1,200-ton hydraulic press from the Louisville and Nashville Railroad,[68] where it had presumably been used in the manufacture of steam engine boilers.

The capacity of these Burton-Clark units, however, was greater than the volume of oils which could be charged to the reservoirs, for capacity was not set by the volume of contents in the still but by the amount of coke that was deposited in the tubes. Since the tubes were not filled with coke after the original 9,150 gallons were cracked, Clark found that he could now add 7,500 gallons more of fresh gas oil during the cracking phase of the cycle.[69] Under this mode of operation, the tube stills could be operated for 48 hours before the accumulation of coke forced a shut-down, as compared with only 24 hours in the case of the original Burton units. Since the other phases of the operating cycle took the same amount of time (pumping, cooling, cleaning, and so on), the cycle efficiency of the Burton-Clark was one-third greater than that of the original Burton units. In his correspondence with Burton, Clark emphasized the importance of the higher capacity of the tube-stills by means of a cost comparison.[70] Assuming process labor to be a fixed cost, dependent solely upon the number of stills in the refinery, he calculated that the forty 8-foot by 30-foot Burton shell stills at Wood River, charging 165,000 gallons of gas oil a calendar day, incurred a process labor cost of $163.26. The same forty stills revamped to permit cracking in the tubes would process 220,000 gallons of gas oil daily at a process labor cost of $131.26. On the basis of 100 gallons of gas-oil charge, the reduction in direct labor cost would be from 9.9¢ to 6.0¢, or 39.4%. Clark estimated the capital cost of changing the forty Burton shell stills to tube stills to be $133,000, and the recovery of the investment to require a little less than four years. Clark also claimed additional economies in fuel, maintenance, and a higher gasoline yield per unit of charge.

The basis for the claim of higher gasoline yield is not clear. It seems unlikely that under similar temperatures and pressures and with similar distillation facilities a Burton-Clark unit would yield a higher percentage of gasoline than did an original Burton unit. What is more likely is that the higher yield resulted from Clark's running the units at a higher pres-

[68] Standard Oil Company (Indiana), letter from E. M. Clark to W. M. Burton, February 23, 1916.

[69] Standard Oil Company (Indiana), letter from E. M. Clark to W. M. Burton, March 10, 1916. The original 9,150 gallons had been made up of 8,250 gallons in the still plus 900 gallons that filled the tubes.

[70] Standard Oil Company (Indiana), letter from E. M. Clark to W. M. Burton, February 23, 1916.

sure, for shortly after he installed his first tube units, Clark experimented with pressures in the range of 110 lb./sq. in.[71] At this pressure, materials boiling in the kerosene range, which would have vaporized in the Burton process, would be retained in the cracking section, there to be broken down when subjected to the high temperatures.

The claims for lower maintenance cost and lower fuel cost seem valid. The maintenance cost would have been reduced by the substitution of mechanical cleaning for the laborious hand scraping. The fuel saving would have resulted from the higher mean-temperature difference between the source of heat and the gas oil. Since the Burton-Clark still could be entirely insulated, the heat loss to the atmosphere that took place from the upper half of the direct-fired Burton still was eliminated.

TABLE I

Cost Reductions Achieved by the Introduction and Improvement of the Burton Cracking Process

Process Equipment	Year Introduced	Cracking Cost (cents per gallon of gasoline, 1913 prices)	Cost Reduction, as % of the Previous Cost
Crude Distillation	before 1913	18.7	—
Burton Process			
Shell still	1913	13.5	28
with false-bottom plates	1914	12.4	8
with radiator	1915	11.4	8
Tube still	1915	11.1	2
with bubble tower	1916	9.8	12

Sources: Appendix Table 12 and references cited in text. Costs exclude royalties.

Because there is so little information on the merits of the last three claims, we can take account only of the increase in capacity and of the decrease in direct labor in calculating the cost reduction gained by installing the Burton-Clark stills. Assuming the capital cost of a Burton-Clark unit to be the same as the Burton unit itself,[72] the reduction in the total cost of manufacturing gasoline was 0.27¢ per gallon, or 2.4%.

[71] In a letter to Burton dated November 23, 1916, Clark reported distillate production at pressures of 98 and 107 lb./sq. in. In a second letter four days later Clark expressed his belief that higher pressures were both possible and also beneficial, saying, "I hope that you will conclude very quickly that we have the right to run at any pressure up to 400 lbs., and advise us that we may again increase pressure."

[72] This assumes that the cost of building tubes into the Burton-Clark unit was equal to the cost of building false-bottom plates in the Burton.

When the new tube stills were being built, an additional advantage was discovered. In the Burton units no seams were permitted on any part of the surface that was subjected to the heat from the furnace. When the Burton-Clark still was elevated above the fire, to serve the function of a reservoir, this limitation on the location of seams was eliminated. It then became possible to have seams located closer to the bottom of the still, which meant that for a given size of steel plate the diameter could be increased. So the 8-foot by 30-foot stills of the Burton process were replaced with 10-foot by 30-foot stills, which raised the capacity of each still from 8,250 to 13,300 gallons. Twenty of these new tube still units were installed at Wood River in April 1915, and forty more were operating by October 1916.

[Standard Oil Company (Indiana)]

Burton-Clark cracking units arranged in a battery.

In all, four improvements were made on the Burton process: in chronological order, false-bottom plates, the radiator, the tube still, and the bubble tower. In terms of novelty and future promise the tube still was outstanding; as Table 1 illustrates, however, the other improvements were probably more profitable. In combination, the improvements matched Burton's original contribution, a phenomenon we shall also observe in subsequent process innovations.

Licensing the Burton Process

From the beginning, the originators of the Burton process were faced with the problem of whether to restrict its operation to their own company or to permit others to practice it. The advantages and disadvantages of allowing others to use it were numerous; the main advantage was thought to be the income that would be received from royalties, the main disadvantage the over-all increase in gasoline production that would result from the widespread introduction of the process. Burton and Colonel Stewart, then the chief attorney for the firm, recognized that if Indiana Standard were the only company to practice cracking, the amount of cracked gasoline added to the nation's supply of automotive fuel would be relatively small. With the demand for gasoline expected to increase extremely rapidly as the automobile became widely accepted, the price of gasoline would rise substantially.[73] As sole operators of a process for manufacturing gasoline from a cheap raw material, gas oil, Indiana Standard would profit a great deal.[74] But it was difficult not to license the process, particularly when the former members of the Standard Oil "trust," with whom Indiana's executives were still on good terms, conjured up feelings of loyalty for the "Standard Oil" family.[75]

There seems to have been no fear that the company would be threatened by the development of a competitive process. Two reasons for this self-assurance may be advanced, the first of which was a conviction within Indiana Standard that the Burton process was the best possible way to crack those components of crude oil heavier than kerosene. The second reason was its strong patent position. Starting with Burton's own concept of cracking under pressure, all the inventors made application for and received within a very short time the patents covering their claims. The

[73] William M. Burton, Exhibit No. 8, "Claim for Refund on Burton Process Patent," affidavit submitted to the Income Tax Unit, Treasury Department, in November 1922, p. 5.

[74] An outside engineering firm, called in by Indiana Standard to give its estimate of the value of the Burton invention for tax purposes, calculated the expected returns over the life of the patent both on the assumptions of licensing and of not licensing. The discounted returns (with the yearly discount increasing from 7% to 15% as the payments extended farther into the future) were estimated at $165,000,000 (profits $125,000,000, royalties $40,000,000) with licensing and $252,000,000 without. The difference between the two sums is explained primarily by the higher prices for gasoline and crude oil assumed in the second case. The assumption of a rise in the price of gasoline was justified on the ground that the supply schedule of the industry would not have shifted as far in the direction of greater quantities at any given price had the Burton process been available solely to one firm. (Ford, Bacon, and Davis, Inc., Engineers, "Report on the Fair Market Value of the Burton Process Patent as of March 1, 1913," in the files of the Standard Oil Company [Indiana], p. 2.)

[75] Interview with Walter C. Teagle (formerly president, Standard Oil Company [New Jersey]), October 18, 1955.

original patents (Burton's, which covered cracking, and Humphreys', which covered distillation) had actually been granted within a few weeks and two years, respectively, of the operation of the first Burton stills. In addition, the Burton patent was quite broad, and covered in its claims the basic principles of cracking. With such strong patent protection, and with the memory of a long and harrowing history of research and development which they assumed any competitor would have to experience, it is little wonder that Indiana Standard felt itself invulnerable.

Not to be separated from the question of whether or not to license was the question of the amount of royalty to charge. No precedent had been set in the petroleum-refining industry, but in other industries licenses had been granted, and the fairness of the charge had been adjudicated in legal suits, in which the royalties had ranged up to 50% of the profits obtained from using the patented process.[76] The final decision, made by the board of directors, was to license the Burton process for a fee of 25% of the profits from the cracking operation. Indiana was to specify the accounting procedure to be used in calculating profits.[77]

The average royalty received by the Standard Oil Company (Indiana) during the first seven years of licensing was about 17¢ per barrel (42 gallons) of charge,[78] although profits and consequently payments varied from one licensee to another, depending upon local market conditions and the firm's operating efficiency. The royalty income from the licensing of the Burton process patents was considerable. Starting with $74,000 in 1914, the first year in which the process was licensed, yearly royalties rose to $2,000,000 by 1917.[79]

In addition to paying royalties, the licensing companies were forced to make other concessions in order to be permitted to use the Burton process. The terms of the contract that the licensee signed defined the geographical area within which he could sell his cracked gasoline. No sales outside the

[76] In United States vs. Berdan Fire-Arms Company, 26 Ct. Cls., 48, 156 U.S. 552, 50% of the savings were thought reasonable (cited in "Memo for Mr. J. Howard Marshall," Chief Counsel, Office of the Petroleum Coordinator for War, December 1, 1942).

[77] A copy of the license together with the method for determining profits was submitted by Indiana in the suit Standard Oil Company (Indiana), Standard Oil Company (New Jersey), Standard Development Company et al. vs. The United States of America, Transcript of Record, Supreme Court of the United States, October Term, 1930, No. 378, pp. 162–167.

[78] Standard Oil Company (Indiana), testimony of Mr. Wiles; reported in the minutes of the hearing afforded representatives of the Standard Oil Company (Indiana) in the office of the Chief, Natural Resources Sub-Division, Income Tax Unit, Treasury Department, U.S. Government, on July 14, 1921.

[79] See Table 14 in the Appendix.

specified area were allowed.[80] The purpose of the territorial limitation was to prevent any refiner from dumping excess gasoline into the markets which were supplied by the Standard Oil Company (Indiana).[81]

A limit was set on the scope of the license. The licensees were permitted to contract only for the rights to operate the Burton process; they had to solve the major problems of constructing the equipment and operating it efficiently themselves. As Indiana Standard's attorney admitted,

> we have developed at Whiting certain theoretical aspects of what goes on in these stills which have turned out to be of very great value as a "rule of thumb." They are almost scientifically demonstrated truths which we have not disclosed to anyone. There is no reason why we should, in patents, or elsewhere and our reports have been written for our own confidential information, and as such one could hardly read them without being brought up to date on matters we could "spill out" as technical information but wouldn't for anything in the world.[82]

By being restricted to the patent alone, the licensees were in the position of the hunter who is given a hunting license, but finds he must still buy a gun and learn how to shoot.

Predictably, licenses were first granted to the other Standard Oil companies. The initial license, carrying the right to sell cracked gasoline in all the Canadian provinces, was secured by the Imperial Oil Company in 1914. Negotiations had been initiated by Walter C. Teagle, then president of Imperial and a member of the board of directors of Imperial's major stockholder, the Standard Oil Company (New Jersey). The success of the Burton development had been publicized widely in the trade publications,[83] and Teagle's interest in licensing the process had been aroused. In the discussions Indiana Standard was represented by President Cowan, like Teagle a man with a very strong personality. Their bargaining centered on the size of the royalty; since Teagle was attempting to gain only the international rights and since Indiana did not operate outside the United States, there was no conflict over marketing territories. Both Teagle and Cowan made concessions and finally agreed upon a royalty rate of 25% of the profits from operating the cracking process.[84]

[80] Standard Oil Company (Indiana), "List of Early Burton Process Licensees," letter from Pike H. Sullivan to Congers Reynolds, March 24, 1950.

[81] These territorial limitations were removed in 1920 at the time of the agreement between the Texas Company and Indiana Standard on the cross-licensing of the Burton and the Holmes-Manley processes (ibid.).

[82] Standard Oil Company (Indiana), testimony of Mr. Wiles, op. cit.

[83] See, for example, two articles by H. G. James, "Serious Condition in Oklahoma Field," Oil and Gas Journal, June 4, 1914, p. 34, and "Kansas-Oklahoma Field Conditions," Oil and Gas Journal, June 25, 1914, p. 32.

[84] Interview with Walter C. Teagle, October 18, 1955. Mr. Teagle did not recall the specific nature of the concessions.

In 1914 licenses were also granted to the Standard Oil Company of Kansas, which was permitted to sell cracked gasoline only in that state, and to the Solar Refining Company, which was limited to Ohio. The Standard Oil Company (New Jersey) and Magnolia Petroleum Company received licenses in 1915; Tidewater Oil Company, the first firm not formerly a member of the Standard Oil group, and two others, in 1916; and nine more from 1917 to 1921.

What were the results of this licensing policy? On the one hand, Indiana Standard's very willingness to license its radically new and profitable development within a year of the first installation inevitably set a precedent. That the first significant innovation in cracking should have been made available to a number of firms at terms which were not onerous established a pattern. It was fortunate that such a precedent was set when it was easy to establish a generous policy. Had the first innovation been restricted in its use to the innovating firm, the tendency would have been for the second innovation to receive the same treatment.

The larger the company that carried out a process innovation, the more likely it was to be restricted. A small innovator would probably gain more by having a large portion of the industry adopt his process and pay him royalties than he would by applying it solely to his own operations. A larger innovating firm might find it more profitable to prevent outsiders from using its process, because if it were very large they would be likely to be in competition. If they did adopt it, the whole industry's supply would shift rather than just the cost schedule of the large innovating firm. Actually, in petroleum refining in 1913, the dividing line between promoting and refusing licenses would probably have been drawn close to firms of Indiana Standard's size.

It is not surprising, therefore, that Indiana Standard's licensing policy was discriminatory in certain of its aspects. The license was not available to all refiners: those who marketed in its area could not obtain a license at all, and those who operated outside its market could not sell within it. This enabled Indiana Standard, at least in the short run, to restrain competition within a large part of the Midwest. It also tended, however, to increase competition in the long run within just that area. As we shall see in Chapters 2 and 3, the main innovations achieved after the introduction of the Burton process originated in the Midwest, in fact, right within Indiana Standard's market. The effect of the restrictive licensing policy was to stimulate enterprising competitors, rather than frustrate them. Had they not been deprived of the use of the process, they might have made no such efforts. In summary, the licensing policy enabled Indiana Standard to gain a reward for its endeavors — a reward large enough to make others envious of it, but not so large as to daunt the aspiration of its competitors.

Profits

The general feeling among the executives of Indiana Standard was that one-half of the profits of the company from 1913 through 1922 were attributable to the inventions in cracking. Our own estimate of the profits generated by the development of the cracking process, based upon the rate of return experienced by Burton process licensees as presented in Appendix Table 14, is $123,000,000 for the same period. This figure represents 34% of Indiana Standard's total profits of $366,000,000 for the nine years.[85] Our estimate does not make allowance for certain special advantages Indiana Standard enjoyed. First, it was able to build and operate cracking plants more quickly than licensees.[86] Second, Indiana Standard had acquired during the period from 1909 to 1913 much of the know-how necessary to design and operate the equipment profitably. Its licensees, however, did not have the accumulated knowledge of four years' experiments when they began building and operating cracking units. Nor were they able to benefit appreciably from the experience of the inventors, for Indiana Standard considered its technical skills to be beyond the province of the Burton-process patents, and therefore outside the coverage of its licenses. Consequently, the innovator, at least at first, produced at lower cost than its licensees. Third, through "customs plants," cracking units built adjacent to competitors' refineries, Indiana Standard was able to carry out more cracking than the over-all level of operations in its own refineries would permit. From these refiners Indiana Standard could purchase gas oil, which it would then charge to the cracking units.[87] In this

[85] *Moody's Analyses of Investments, 1916; Moody's Rating Books, 1922,* and *Moody's Manual of Investments, 1926,* New York: Moody's Investors Service.

[86] This is evident from a comparison of the first two columns of Appendix Table 14.

[87] Standard Oil Company (Indiana), "Historical Summaries of Products and Manufacturing Processes," *op. cit.,* pp. 4, 5; the location, numbers, and dates of installation of custom plants are tabulated below:

Refinery	Location	Number of Burton Units	Date of Installation
United Oil Company of Denver	Florence, Colorado	6	February 1917
		2	July 1918
		2	November 1919
Midwest Refining Company of Denver	Greybull, Wyoming	20	June 1917
		20	May 1919
	Laramie, Wyoming,	10	November 1920
		10	December 1921
	#2 Plant	40	January–July 1920
Mutual Oil Company of Denver	Glenrock, Wyoming	8	June 1922

way, Indiana profited from the higher value of gas oil as a cracking stock than as an industrial fuel. Since the demand for fuel oil, the alternate use for gas oil, was relatively low in the mountain areas of the West where the customs plants were located, the differential was quite sizable. Customs plants enabled Indiana Standard, a vertically integrated firm, to expand in one phase of its operations without losing its balance.

Although the average profits from cracking were splendid, they were not uniformly so. By 1919 the peak of approximately $20,000,000 a year had probably been reached. In fact, if the volume of cracked gasoline had not increased steadily, the peak would have arrived three years earlier, for it was in 1916 that the profit per unit of output was at a maximum.[88] That the highest average and total profits were reached four and seven years, respectively, after the cracking process was introduced indicates that the profits resulting from innovation were not dissipated quickly by competition from imitating firms.

Profits, when retained, facilitate the growth of a company. A comparison between the rate of growth of the assets of Indiana Standard and that of several other oil companies shows that from 1912 to 1921 Indiana surpassed the other companies of the Standard Oil group. The average annual rate of increase in the total assets of the Standard Oil Company (Indiana) from 1912 to 1921 was more than one and a half times (24.1% compared with approximately 15%) that of the other five former members of the Standard Oil "trust" (see Table 2). Indiana Standard alone kept pace with the two thriving independents, Gulf Oil and The Texas Company. Assuming half of this growth to have resulted from the success of the cracking process, the inventions of Burton and his associates were responsible for the superior showing of the company.

The growth of Indiana Standard was limited mainly to crude-oil production. With its excellent refining and marketing facilities, the company was sufficiently integrated to see the advantages therein and yet, lacking crude-oil production, not fully enough integrated to be able to achieve the ultimate reward, high and fairly steady profits, through the ability to insulate itself from the effects of changes in the supply and demand of crude petroleum and its products. The dissolution of the Standard Oil "trust" had left Indiana Standard without its own source of crude oil and its own transportation facilities. For the first few years the company was able to rely upon purchase contracts with small crude-oil producers and upon the pipe lines acting as common carriers. But the rapid growth in the number of automobiles and the incidence of World War I

[88] In 1916, the estimated profit per gallon of cracked gasoline was 6.9¢; thereafter it dropped to 5.6¢ in 1917 and 5.2¢ in 1918. For the average profits, and for the assumptions upon which they are based, see Appendix Table 14.

TABLE 2
Total Assets of Eight Major Oil Companies, 1912, 1921, and 1924

Company	Total Assets (millions of dollars)			Average Annual Rate of Increase (%)	
	1912	1921	1924	1912–1921	1921–1924
Standard Oil Company (Indiana)	43.9	305.7	361.5	24.1	5.8
Standard Oil Company (New Jersey)	370.0	1,115.9	1,244.9	13.3	3.7
Standard Oil Company (New York)	92.2	333.2	406.2	15.3	6.9
Standard Oil Company of California	67.3	276.7	352.8	16.5	8.4
Atlantic Refining Company	28.6	111.1	131.0	16.3	5.6
Ohio Oil Company	65.6	90.5	97.7	4.2	2.6
Gulf Oil Corporation	28.2	272.8	379.5	25.5	11.6
The Texas Company	52.0	356.0	375.7	23.8	1.8

Sources: Assets—"Standard Is Strong in Disunion," Business Week, June 22, 1946 (the Standard Oil companies, Atlantic Oil Company, and Ohio Oil Company for 1912); Moody's Manual of Investments, 1912, 1913, 1923, and 1926, New York: Moody's Investors Service, 1912, 1913, 1923, and 1926, respectively (remainder). Total assets for Gulf Oil Corporation as of 1911; 1912 not available. Average annual rate of increase for Gulf, therefore, based on period 1911–1921.

increased greatly the demand for the products of crude oil. As a result of a sizable increase in demand for crude oil, a raw material whose short-run supply curve was relatively inelastic, and of the general price inflation accompanying the war, the price that Indiana Standard paid rose sharply from 2.8¢ per gallon in 1915 to 6.7¢ per gallon in 1918.[89] At the same time, there was the almost universal fear that the supplies of crude oil were being exhausted by the unprecedented withdrawal. In order to insure an adequate source of crude oil at a stable price, therefore, Indiana Standard used a large share of the profits generated in the refining stage of the business for the purchase of crude-oil wells in the midcontinent and Wyoming fields.[90] Resources were allocated to purchasing existing crude-oil production and gathering pipe lines rather than to drilling wells because of the lower risk and the more sudden flow of crude oil to the company's refineries.

Stagnation in Research

In the years after 1913, the company's research potential did not increase as fast as might have been expected on the basis of its initial success.

[89] See Appendix Table 4.
[90] See P. H. Giddens, op. cit., Chapter IX; also J. G. McLean and R. W. Haigh, op. cit.

Burton was no longer in a position to do research as he had in the period
from 1909 through 1913. The Whiting research laboratory, where the company's research facilities were concentrated, had eight technical employees
in 1912; by 1920 it employed only six more, and by 1922 had lost four
of these six employees. New laboratory facilities had been added here,
which partly compensated for the lack of technical personnel, but the

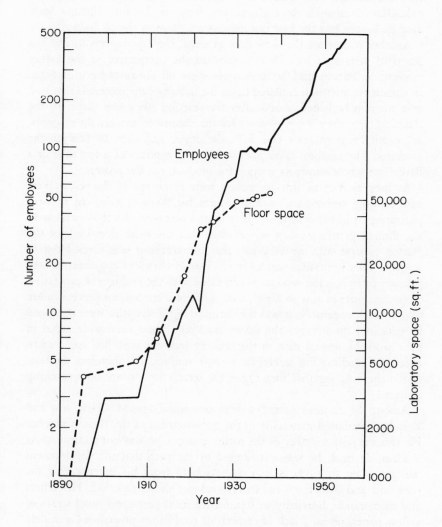

**Growth of Whiting research laboratory, Standard Oil Company (Indiana),
1890-1955.**

meager growth of research staff, after the grand success of the company's earlier research effort, seems strange. In part, the failure to increase the staff of the laboratory can be accounted for in two ways. First, many technically trained men were given operative responsibilities in the refinery; technical skills were no longer restricted to the laboratory staff. Second, the education of chemists was interrupted by the war, and those who did graduate were greatly in demand by the chemical and armament industries. Even with those allowances, however, by 1918 Indiana Standard no longer had the best research organization in the oil industry.

Another reason for the slow pace of technological progress in Indiana Standard after 1916 can be attributed to the perspective of the earlier innovators. Burton and his colleagues were all chemists by profession. In chemistry, attention is placed upon the nature of the materials involved in a reaction both before and after the reaction has taken place. In the chemical laboratory it is customary for the chemist to analyze the reagents, to permit them to react one with the other, and then to analyze the products. The reaction takes place within the confines of a test tube or a flask. The whole emphasis is upon the product, not the process.

As long as men of this persuasion were in charge of the research on new refining techniques, it was natural for them to think of refinery processing as incorporating so many batch operations. To those who were not limited in this way, it was evident that the main drawback of the Burton process was the very fact that the cracking was carried out in batches. This limitation was most obvious to chemical engineers, whose primary interest is the process. When faced with the problem of processing large quantities of raw material, they think of a continuous process rather than a batch system. So it was the chemical engineers who were equipped by education to advance the art of cracking. These men were aided in their work by several men in the refining industry who had had experience with cracking but lacked the formal training, and therefore the bias, of the chemist; together they began the search for a continuous cracking process.

Among the most important of these men was Edgar M. Clark, who had already contributed materially to the improvement of the Burton process. He was the only member of the earlier group who was not a chemist. As a self-made man, he was not limited by the path that the development had taken up to 1913, as was obvious both from his invention of the tube still and also from his correspondence of that period. His letters and memoranda, hurriedly written for the most part upon small scraps of yellow paper, reveal a lack of respect for established procedures, a widely ranging inventiveness, and an impatience with details. He was constantly trying to find new ways of operating the existing equipment and seemed quite irritated at the necessity to obtain clearance before many of the experiments could be tried out. He made his requests in an imperious manner and with great frequency until they were finally granted. Here was a man who had many ideas about cracking and who was eager to achieve a status which would assure him that they would be appreciated.

Burton's side of this correspondence is no longer available, so it is impossible to tell whether he was sympathetic to Clark's ideas. That he then believed the Burton process to be as efficient a process as man could invent we know, for it was not until 1923, three years after the introduction of the first continuous cracking process, that he realized that it had been supplanted. Dr. Robert E. Wilson recalls writing in a report comparing the Burton process with the new Tube-and-Tank and the Holmes-Manley processes that "we might as well recognize the fact that the Burton process is obsolete." Burton observed sadly, but for the first time, that it could not be expected to be the best process indefinitely. Burton's attitude was also expressed in his behavior when first informed of the Cross process, another of the early continuous cracking processes. He was quite skeptical of the claim, and did not bother to answer the letters sent him by its promoter.[91]

It is amazing how brief was Indiana Standard's technological supremacy. Although the Burton process was used by Indiana Standard until 1927, and by others even later than that, no significant improvements were made after 1916. The false-bottom plates, the radiator, the bubble tower, and the cracking tubes were all developed within three years of the original installation. No further improvements were made by other companies, for their energies were directed toward the development of continuous cracking processes. Within Indiana Standard the situation was different. The endeavors of Burton and his associates had paid off handsomely, and in the period from 1915 through 1920 the rewards flowed in. By all measures the Standard Oil Company (Indiana) had prospered as a result of the cracking innovations. It is easy to see that the company might well be satisfied with the results of the Burton process.

[91] See the letters from R. M. MacCormac of Kansas City, Missouri, to the Standard Oil Company (Indiana) on November 6, 1918, November 18, 1918, November 27, 1918, and January 8, 1919. Mr. MacCormac represented the Morgan Oil and Refining Company, of Kansas City, which had acquired the rights to the Cross process and which was attempting to promote it to the industry. MacCormac hoped that Indiana Standard would purchase some of the Morgan stock, for it "will be better for everybody to deal with you, who could recognize the fundamental features in the process and understand and appreciate its scope" (letter of November 18, 1918). Ultimately Indiana Standard joined with Gasoline Products Company (which bought out the Morgan interests), but it was not the desire to take part in another process innovation that prompted this alliance.

There was little incentive to breed a new goose when the one it already had was laying golden eggs.

The Results of the Burton Process

In the development of the Burton process, Indiana Standard showed both the requirements for and the results of a successful innovation. The first requirement was a visionary and energetic man, technically well trained and in close contact with both the manufacturing facilities and the

[Standard Oil Company (Indiana)]

Dr. Burton and Dr. Humphreys in 1946. In the background is a Fluid Catalytic Cracking unit.

management of the corporation. Burton's abilities were known to the refinery personnel and to the board of directors. In a development of this size, it was also necessary that the innovator be backed by a capable research team, experienced in the field under investigation, working in harmony, and with their eyes on the same goal.

In the development of the Burton process, the greatest barriers to success lay within the firm itself. The first barrier was the technical difficulties that had to be surmounted before the determinants of the cracking reaction could be established and a suitable cracking unit designed. In the era of the Burton invention, there was little communication between engineers working for different organizations; most of the technical problems, therefore, had to be solved by the personnel working on a project — that meant by people within a single organization. Had there only been available an accumulated fund of knowledge and outside experts, the necessity to rely solely upon internal resources would have been eliminated. Yet in spite of this limitation, the Burton process was introduced and, in the years following its introduction, was improved. The improvements were significant both in making the Burton process more profitable to operate and in contributing materially to the advance of petroleum technology.

The second barrier lay in the organization of the original Standard Oil Company (New Jersey). Only when he was able to present his project to a local board of directors secure in the tenure of their office was Burton guaranteed consideration. Once the location of responsibility had been changed from New York to Chicago, however, the installation of the Burton process was assured. What legal action by society, as represented in the antitrust prosecution, had started, persuasion by the individual was able to finish.

The barriers to innovation outside the firm were not so substantial, primarily because it was not imagined that the Burton process would alter substantially the structure of the petroleum industry or the market for its main product, gasoline. The opposition to the installation of the Burton process came primarily from the small refiners in the midcontinent area who were unable to acquire the rights to the Burton process and at the same time did not have the necessary technical skill to invent a competitive technique.[92]

To the consumer of motor gasoline, motor gasoline containing both straight-run and cracked gasoline seemed no different from the product he had formerly accepted. After the disastrous Motor Spirit campaign, the cracked gasoline was treated to remove the color and odor. To the person who could judge it only by its physical characteristics, the new blend of virgin and cracked gasoline was indistinguishable from the old. Besides, with the rapid growth in the demand for gasoline, the automobile driver would hardly have been likely to turn down a product which performed just as well as the one to which he was accustomed.[93]

[92] H. G. James, "Serious Condition in Oklahoma Field," *op. cit.*, and his "Kansas-Oklahoma Field Conditions," *op. cit.*
[93] Since the chemical characteristics of the cracked gasoline were different from those of virgin gasoline, certain state regulations governing quality had to be

The final external barrier was the technological one of inadequate capital equipment. The size and strength of the vessels, piping, and auxiliary equipment available to Burton and his colleagues set the limits on their cracking process. The dimensions of the steel plates determined the capacity of the shell stills; the thickness and the technique of joining determined the operating pressure. The lack of steel impervious to corrosion condemned the bubble towers, and the nonexistence of a pump which could transfer oil at high temperatures and pressures prevented Clark's research on the tube-still from being extended. Because of its similarity to equipment already developed for the generation of steam, Clark's tube-still was sturdier and more versatile than Burton's shell still.[94] In summation, it was the state of the art of constructing refinery equipment that set the maximum size of a single cracking plant.

Once the barriers to innovation had been overcome, the firm received substantial royalties from its licensees and made large profits from its own refining operations. Together these royalty payments and profits yielded Indiana Standard approximately $150,000,000 during the first twelve years of the Burton process.[95] With this is contrasted the total cost of the development, about $236,000.[96] The cost of development was returned nearly ten times in 1913, the first year of operations. Considering royalties alone, up to 1924, the undiscounted rate of return on the investment in research and development over the period 1913 to 1924 was over 800% per year. As a result of the innovation, Indiana Standard was able to strengthen its refining and marketing departments and to expand into other phases of the petroleum industry. It improved markedly its competitive position, mainly at the expense of other firms operating in its own market area. The firm thus took full advantage of the monopoly position granted it under the patent laws.

The results were not wholly beneficial; by failing to expand its research

amended. Dr. Humphreys and Colonel Stewart visited the legislatures of those states — North Dakota, South Dakota, Minnesota, Wisconsin, Iowa, Illinois, Indiana, Michigan, Missouri, Kansas, and Oklahoma — in which Indiana Standard marketed gasoline, in order to promote the amendments. (Interview with Robert E. Humphreys, November 23, 1954.)

[94] The operating pressure on the tube stills was later raised from 95 to 300 lb./sq. in., with improved performance. Operations ceased on the shell stills in 1917, but the tube stills were continued until 1931. (Standard Oil Company [Indiana] vs. Globe Oil and Refining Company, *op. cit.*, testimony of Louis C. Moore, pp. 740 ff.)

[95] This estimate compares with Ford, Bacon, and Davis' figure of $165,000,444 for the value of the Burton patent over its entire life of seventeen years, and with Indiana Standard's claim of $150,000,000 for income-tax purposes.

[96] U. S. vs. Standard Oil Company (Indiana) *et al.*, District Court of U. S., Northern District of Illinois, Eastern Division, in equity No. 4131, testimony of Robert W. Stewart (president, Standard Oil Company [Indiana]), p. 3283.

activities, Indiana Standard lost its leadership in the struggle to improve refining technology. Overconfident and holding to a licensing policy that stimulated competitive research, it encouraged others to continue the development of the cracking art. From 1913 to 1919, the Burton process was supreme as a competitive instrument. By 1925, however, its share of the total cracked gasoline output had shrunk to less than half of the industry's, and by 1929 to less than 10%.[97] The Burton process, quickly adopted, was also quickly cast aside. Indiana Standard, its owner, began a bold competitor; it ended a sedate giant.

Because cracking added a major new activity to petroleum refining, the Burton process affected the entire industry as well as the innovating firm. First of all, it stimulated a burst of energy on the part of imitative entrepreneurs. Some of this entrepreneurial energy was directed at developing processes which were as much like the Burton process as was possible without actually infringing upon the Burton patent. The rest was spent developing new processes which would crack fuel oil as well as gas oil, and which would operate continuously. By increasing the pace of its research activity, the industry showed that it had recognized the value of the contributions that technically trained men could make. The chemist, as well as men in other sciences who gained a reputation by association, began to play a greater role in the affairs of the industry.

Contributions were also made by men in other industries. Realizing the interrelation between developments within the petroleum-refining industry and those in the industries that supplied its equipment, refiners began to show an awareness of and concern for outside innovations. It was some time before the liaison between the refining industry and the equipment manufacturers became effective, but at least a start had been made.

Second, the Burton process changed the product mix in the refining industry. Before 1913, the industry had turned out its products in the physical proportions in which they occurred in crude petroleum. Refining consisted mainly of separation and purification. The introduction of the Burton process changed it to a chemical-processing industry. The proportions in which the products were manufactured now could be different from the proportion in which their constituents occurred in the raw material. Before cracking, gasoline was approximately 15% of the product mix. After the introduction of cracking the proportion could be varied anywhere from 15% to 40%. The industry became much more flexible, and the processing scheme more readily adaptable to changes in the relative demands for its products.

Third, the Burton process influenced the structure of the petroleum industry. The main effect was observed in the refining segment. At the

[97] See Appendix Table 1.

time of the Burton invention the refining industry was relatively competitive and easy to enter; it required little technical skill and produced
homogeneous products. Afterwards this was not true. Those immediately
affected by the cracking process were the small refiners. Located primarily
in the oil fields, the small refiners were usually associated with crude-oil
producers but lacked any distributing organization. They sold their products — limited to gasoline, kerosene, and fuel oil — in the spot market.
As such they were subject to the wide fluctuations that occurred in wholesale prices. Moreover, many lacked access to pipe lines and were required
to ship their products by tank car, a more expensive means of transportation.[98] To these competitive disadvantages was added a financial vulnera-
bility resulting from their small size; they were not constituted to survive
severe shocks. The cracking process provided such a shock. In the words
of one reporter:

> The small refiners of the Mid-Continent field are in desperate straits. . . .
> A year ago gasoline was retailing in the market for .162. In December the
> price of crude was reduced from 1.05 to 85¢ for Mid-Continent. But about
> that time the reconstructed refineries with the new patented pressure process
> of making motor gasoline got into working order and there was a flood of
> motor gasoline—100 per cent more motor gasoline being taken now from the
> same amount of crude as a year ago and instead of gasoline retailing in the
> market for .162 as a year ago, it is now retailing at .122 and is going lower.[99]

Not only was the position of the existing small concern made less secure
by the introduction of the Burton process, but also entry into the refining
branch was made more difficult. Greater technical skill was needed to
construct and operate a refinery incorporating the cracking process, and
larger sums were necessary to build the additional cracking and rerunning
facilities.[100] By making the refinery more complex to design, more expen-

---

[98] In 1914 the transportation cost from the midcontinent fields to the Gulf was
3¼¢ per barrel by pipe line and 5¼¢ per barrel for independent refineries shipping
by tank car (H. G. James, "Kansas-Oklahoma Field Conditions," op. cit., p. 33).

[99] H. G. James, "Serious Condition in Oklahoma Field," op. cit., p. 34. The picture
may not have been as bad for the small refiner as it was painted. The year 1914
was less prosperous for the large oil companies as well. Also, in 1914 and 1915,
eighteen new refineries were built in Kansas and Oklahoma, an increase of 50% in
the number of refineries then in existence in these two states (R. F. Bacon and W. A.
Hamer, The American Petroleum Industry, New York: McGraw-Hill, 1916, vol. II,
pp. 52–53).

[100] In 1913 the capital investment necessary to build and operate an efficient small
refinery, without cracking, was approximately $250,000; this was made up of 30
miles of crude-oil gathering lines ($40,000), a 2,000 barrel-per-stream day plant with
storage facilities for 250,000 barrels ($60,000), working capital ($100,000), and tank
cars ($50,000) (H. G. James, "An Oil Refining Tale of Two States," Oil and Gas
Journal, September 11, 1913, pp. 10–12). Assuming a gas-oil yield of 40% on crude,
a refinery this size would have provided the charge for eight Burton units. Eight

sive to build, and more difficult to operate and maintain, the Burton process effectively reduced the chances for success of the small independent operator.

Moreover, Indiana Standard's policy of licensing the Standard Oil companies first discriminated against the independents, although this did not prevent some of the larger independent integrated concerns from growing even more rapidly.

The nation's economy, although unaware of the Burton process, was also affected by its introduction. The rapid increase in the number of new automobiles, together with the improvement in the network of roads, led to a rapid increase in the demand for gasoline. Had the cracking process not been invented, six additional gallons of crude oil would have been required for each gallon of cracked gasoline in order to satisfy the demand at the existing price. This estimate is based upon three assumptions:

1. that one gallon of straight-run gasoline can be obtained from each six gallons of crude oil,
2. that one gallon of cracked gasoline can be obtained from the gas oil in six gallons of crude oil, and
3. that the amount of crude oil produced would depend on the amount of gasoline demanded rather than upon the demand for any of the other refined products.

An increase in crude-oil production of this magnitude could not possibly have been achieved under the existing price structure. The probable results would have been a small increase in crude-oil production, accompanied by a substantial increase in crude-oil and petroleum-product prices. By doubling the yield of gasoline from each barrel of crude oil, the Burton process conserved a vital natural resource and damped what would have been in the last few years of World War I an even greater rise in the prices of petroleum products.

The final effect of the Burton process was to provide the basis for the research and development programs of all the other oil companies. As we shall see in subsequent chapters, these programs have brought forth new products and processes that have benefited consumers of petroleum products, as well as stockholders and employees of oil companies. All sectors of the economy have gained from the advances in the oil industry's technology — advances which were initiated by the inventors of the Burton process.

---

shell stills and their auxiliary equipment would have cost approximately $100,000; to this should be added more working capital to cover the larger volume of cracked products. Assuming the extra working capital to amount to $50,000, the total capital required for the addition of cracking facilities would have been $150,000. This represents an addition of 60% to the original capital investment.

2

THE DUBBS PROCESS

As soon as the results of Burton's work became known, other inventors began to develop competitive cracking processes. Within a few years, several had achieved success, and in 1920 and 1921 alone, ten processes were introduced.[1] One of the chief of these new cracking techniques was the Dubbs process, developed by Jesse A. and Carbon P. Dubbs and promoted by the Universal Oil Products Company (UOP).

Of this second wave of cracking process innovations, the Dubbs process is of interest mainly for three reasons: first, the process was made available to everyone in the petroleum-refining industry; second, the licensee was entitled to all the technical know-how surrounding the process as well as to the claims revealed in the process patents; and third, UOP offered complete protection against any suits brought by the owners of competitive processes. In addition, the story of the development of the Dubbs process depicts the contributions that could be made by individuals whose background lay outside the boundaries of the petroleum-refining industry, and the profits to be made by inspired research and determined behavior. Finally, it shows how the United States patent system can, by granting a monopoly on the practice of the revealed art, encourage productive research; and also how it can, by a very generous interpretation of the validity of patent claims, cause industrial havoc.

The Dubbs process was erected on four pillars: money, research, patents, and promotion. The money came from Jonathan Ogden Armour, whose family fortune had been made during one of the earliest technological revolutions, the one that took place in the meat-packing industry. With the results of the shift from batch to continuous processing readily apparent in the meat-packing industry, Armour was willing to apply the same principles to a less mechanized industry.

[1] The processes which were commercially successful and the approximate dates of their introduction were as follows: Coast (1920), Fleming (1920), Emerson (1920), Dubbs (1920), Jenkins (1921), Greenstreet (1921), Cross (1921), Holmes-Manley (1921), Tube-and-Tank (1921), and Isom (1921).

We shall devote separate chapters to the Dubbs process and to the Tube-and-Tank. The Cross and Holmes-Manley processes will be referred to in that section of Chapter 3 devoted to patent litigation.

60

There is a parallel between the technological developments in the meat-packing and in the petroleum-refining industries. In an abattoir, the processes of slaughtering and rendering the animal were originally carried out by one individual. This is similar to the batch process in cracking, where the operation took place in one vessel. The revolution in each case was to make the process continuous; this required mechanization and a (dis-)assembly line in meat packing, and continuous flow in cracking. The principle of having the material that was being processed moved past stations at which the same event always took place was the same, for in a continuous process the physical and chemical conditions are constant at any one point.

[Armour and Company]

J. Ogden Armour.

J. Ogden Armour

With the death of his father, Philip Danforth Armour, in 1901, J. Ogden Armour inherited the major portion of Armour and Company.[2] It was a large and smoothly functioning organization, and its inheritance made its new owner, already an aristocrat, into a plutocrat. Although only a freshman at Yale, Armour returned to Chicago to take control of the

[2] Armour and Company was a family concern. J. Ogden Armour himself held 72% of the stock of the company. The rest was held by his cousins and nephews. See "The Salvaging of the Armour Fortune," *Fortune*, April 1931, pp. 49–57.

company. Aided by the war, by more efficient utilization of by-products, by vertical integration, and by enterprising management, Armour and Company's yearly sales grew from $100,000,000 in 1901 to a peak of nearly $1,000,000,000 in 1918.

Accompanying the increase in sales was an equivalent increase in profits. In 1917, for example, Armour and Company's net profit was $21,000,000, of which J. Ogden Armour's personal share was $15,000,000.[3] With income far beyond his private expenses, and with a determination to achieve original entrepreneurial success in other fields, Armour began to invest in novel enterprises.

Assisting Armour in deciding where to invest his money were two friends: Robert J. Dunham, his personal advisor, and Julius Reichmann, a member of the Chicago law firm which handled most of Armour and Company's legal work.

One of their first ventures was the purchase of the Standard Asphalt and Rubber Company of Independence, Kansas. This company had been launched in 1906 to manufacture asphalt and a synthetic rubber from the heavy residues from petroleum-refining operations. In order to obtain the residues, the company built a refinery on the edge of an oil field yielding a crude oil unusually rich in asphalt. To improve the natural qualities of the petroleum asphalt, the company developed a process which involved blowing air into the liquid residue; this oxidation process was licensed to a number of the major oil companies. But because of the many problems which arose, chief of which was the inadequacy of storage facilities, the company lost money steadily, incurring in 1914 a deficit of $300,000.[4]

Hiram J. Halle

In order to rescue the company from bankruptcy, Dunham called in Hiram J. Halle, who had made his reputation two years before by resurrecting two dying firms for the Continental and Commercial National Bank, of which J. Ogden Armour was a director and the largest stockholder. A bachelor, Halle was free to devote himself completely to his work, which he performed with great vigor. Small in stature and not handsome, he compensated for physical shortcomings by aggressiveness in business. He was well suited for his ultimate position as president of UOP.

In November 1914, Halle took over the management of Standard Asphalt. Soon afterwards, he enlarged the plant at a cost of $250,000. With greater operating efficiency and the stimulus of war in Europe, the company was able in 1915 to show a profit of $350,000. During this first

---

[3] *Ibid.*, p. 49.
[4] *Ibid.*, p. 52.

[Universal Oil Products Company]

Hiram Halle.

year, Halle held no official position in the company, but in 1916 he was made president.

As a corporate entity, the Standard Asphalt and Rubber Company played no part in the development of the Dubbs process, but from this firm were drawn some of the money which financed the research, the patent upon which the legal strength was based, and two of the main figures in the story. The patent was the first resource to be utilized. As this patent was to occupy a prominent role in the lively legal action on the continuous thermal cracking processes, we shall investigate it in more detail than its scientific value might seem to justify.

Jesse A. Dubbs's Patents

In 1913, the Armour group had purchased for $25,000 several patents issued to Jesse A. Dubbs, the manager of a small independent California oil refinery. The majority of these patents covered the process of manufacturing asphalt and had been acquired as protection for Standard Asphalt, whose own patents were due to expire in four or five years. These patents were purchased from Dubbs by a partner of Reichmann's, Frank L. Belknap, the counsel for Standard Asphalt and Rubber Company. Belknap had systematically been searching the United States for patents covering asphalt manufacture, calling on all manufacturers known to be using novel methods. He had learned of Jesse Dubbs's research from Jesse's son, Carbon Petroleum Dubbs, an employee of Standard Asphalt.[5]

When visiting Dubbs, Belknap found, besides the patents covering asphalt manufacture, one application covering the use of temperatures and pressures greater than atmospheric in refinery operations. Coming from Chicago and knowing of Burton's work in the cracking of heavy petroleum fractions by the use of elevated temperatures and pressures, Belknap observed the resemblance between certain aspects of Dubbs's application and the Burton patent.[6] He and Carbon P. Dubbs persuaded Jesse Dubbs to sell not only the asphalt patents but everything in his patent file.[7]

The date of Jesse Dubbs's patent application, 1909, preceding Burton's by four years, was significant. Equally significant, however, was the purpose to which Dubbs put the high temperatures and pressures, and this was a long way from cracking. Dubbs's stimulus came not from the desire to produce more gasoline from a given amount of crude oil, but from the need for making the local Santa Maria crude oil amenable to refining. Mixed in with the crude oil so that it formed an extremely durable emulsion was a large amount of salt water. The refiners in the area found it almost impossible to break down this emulsion; the water would not settle out to any extent upon storage, nor would it separate during the distillation process. Given the existing techniques, therefore, Santa Maria crude was practically worthless, and sold for only 10¢ a barrel.[8]

The low price gave Dubbs an incentive to eliminate the water to get a cheap raw material for his asphalt manufacture. He devised a way of breaking the emulsion by using high temperatures and high pressures. His apparatus consisted essentially of two chambers, within which the emulsion was heated, followed by a condenser and a receiver. After passing through the heating sections, the distillate-water mixture no longer formed an emulsion, and in the final tank (numbered 11 in the drawing) settled into two layers. The water drained off from the bottom of the collection tank while light hydrocarbons were removed from the top. The heavy fractions were drawn off from the bottom of the large

[5] The intricate and sometimes sordid story of the acquisition and ownership of Jesse A. Dubbs's patents was finally revealed in two court cases: Daily vs. Universal Oil Products Company, District Court, Northern District of Illinois, Eastern Division 43C1162 (*U. S. Patents Quarterly*, Vol. 75, October-December 1947, pp. 341–360), decided November 26, 1947; and the appeal, Daily vs. Universal Oil Products Company *et al.*, 43C1162, decided September 5, 1948 (*ibid.*, Vol. 79, October-December 1948, pp. 258–259).

[6] "Salvaging the Armour Fortune," *op. cit.*, p. 52.

[7] Interview with W. H. Behrens, former secretary of UOP, December 28, 1955.

[8] *Ibid.*

heated tubes, cooled, and finally combined with the distillate from the receiver so as to reconstitute the crude oil.

Since Jesse Dubbs's apparatus fulfilled its function of breaking the emulsion, he and his three sons, Leland A., E. J., and C. P., who was then working for his father, built a commercial unit on the Rice Ranch Oil Company lease on the Santa Maria field. The plant was constructed in the early part of 1909 and went into operation in June.[9] On November 20,

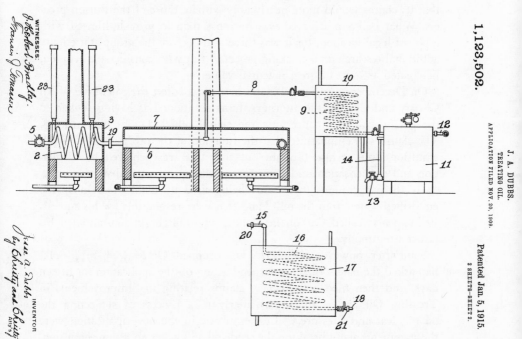

Illustration from Jesse Dubbs's emulsion-breaking patent.

1909, Jesse Dubbs filed a patent application. In the patent application, he described the primary purpose of the apparatus — to break an intractable crude oil and water emulsion by subjecting it to heat and pressure.[10] It was recognized that during this process some distillation occurred. Dubbs's attorneys for this patent application were the Pittsburgh firm of Christy and Christy, for Dubbs had originally come from Pennsylvania and had retained his contacts there.

[9] U. S. Patent No. 1,123,502, "Treating Oil," granted to Jesse A. Dubbs, Patent File.
[10] *Ibid.*

For four years the patent was kept pending. There is no indication of any attempt on the part of Dubbs to delay its consideration. It seems rather that the patent office, then as now, was far behind in its work.

The end of this period of inaction coincided with Frank Belknap's offer to purchase all of Jesse Dubbs's patents and patent applications. With the emulsion-breaking patent application soon to become the property of Standard Asphalt and Rubber Company, Belknap began to amend it so that its claims would more nearly approximate those of the Burton process. What Belknap achieved was no more than to provide himself with a potent legal weapon, for it was three years before the group started any additional research on a cracking process.[11] But with considerable acumen, he created an asset of great potential value.

On December 20, 1913, Belknap's name first enters the patent file. With Christy and Christy, the attorneys, he is mentioned as having spoken to the patent examiner concerning the claims which Dubbs was making. The claims still emphasized that the function of the process was to break emulsions, but it also brought out that this was achieved by distillation and condensation under pressure. Belknap reported that it was precisely these operations that were "being used by Dubbs to remove the emulsified water from the oil"[12] and that were responsible for his success. Belknap also called Carbon P. Dubbs, who obligingly substantiated his father's testimony.

Soon after, however, all subtlety was dropped. On May 28, 1914, Belknap asked the patent office to suspend action on the application for fifteen days, and then filed entirely new claims relating to "Improvements in Treating Oil and . . . more particularly to a process of subjecting the oil to Heat and Pressure."[13] Less emphatic in the new application were the statements about breaking the crude oil and water emulsion: emulsion-breaking is listed only as one of the applications to which heat and pressure can be put. In the words of the patent itself,

among the salient objects of the invention are to provide an improved method of treating oil wherein both the vaporization and condensation take place under the pressure of the generated vapors; to provide a method which is particularly adapted for the removal of the finely divided particles of water from emulsified hydrocarbon oils; to provide a method which will permit the oil being continuously subjected to the required heat and pressure in both the still and condenser without the interruption of its flow; to provide a

[11] "The Salvaging of the Armour Fortune,"*op. cit.*, p. 52.
[12] U. S. Patent No. 1,123,502, Patent File.
[13] *Ibid.*

method by which this may be safely and economically done; and in general to provide an improved method of the character referred to.[14]

Not to be underestimated in the claim was the mention of continuous flow. It is not surprising that a California refiner should be more aware of the advantages of continuous processing than Burton, for it was in California that the first continuous unit relying on a single furnace to provide the necessary heat was conceived and built. Only one year before Belknap began to amend Dubbs's patent application, a successful plant for the continuous distillation of crude oil had been built at Fellows, Kern County, California, for the Santa Fe Railroad Company.[15] Compared with other crude oils in the United States, California crude oil was an extremely heavy material with a relatively small fraction of light distillate products. Once the light materials had been removed, the remaining heavy material could be sold immediately as fuel oil, for which there was a great demand in California because there were no competitive fuels. Thus a process which could separate quickly the light hydrocarbons from the heavy had great merit.

Universal Oil Products Company

By November 24, 1914, Belknap had completed the purchase of Dubbs's patents. The National Hydrocarbons Company was established for the sole purpose of holding the inventions; its name was changed shortly after to Universal Oil Products Company (UOP) when it was discovered that another company of the same name already existed. J. Ogden Armour held 20% of the stock in the new company, and Jesse A. Dubbs 30%. Armour gave the rest to his business associates: Robert Dunham received 20%, Edward J. Leszynsky, then president of Standard Asphalt 20%, F. W. Croll 5%, W. A. Levering 3%, and Frank Belknap 2%.[16] These gifts were to be among the most munificent in history.

Meanwhile, Jesse Dubbs's patent application continued on its way. On October 29, 1914, Walter M. Cross, then a chemistry professor in the Kansas University Medical College, but later to gain fame as the inventor of his own continuous cracking process, appeared before the patent examiners as an expert witness on behalf of Dubbs's claims.[17] Finally on

---

[14] Quoted in E. H. Leslie, *Motor Fuels*, New York: The Chemical Catalogue Co., 1923, p. 379.

[15] *Ibid.*, pp. 177–178; this was the Trumble process for continuous crude distillation, utilizing a pipe-still heater.

[16] Daily vs. Universal Oil Products Company, *op. cit.*, p. 348.

[17] U. S. Patent No. 1,123,502, Patent File; that he was brought in as an expert witness implies that Walter Cross knew quite a bit about petroleum chemistry, but it does not tell us whether he had already conceived the idea of his own cracking process, or whether he was made aware of its potentialities at this meeting.

January 5, 1915, Dubbs's patent was granted, a little over five years after the application was made and in a considerably altered form.

With a patent for pressure distillation in its possession, UOP instituted an entirely different kind of activity. Halle, who "largely created the policies ... and ... conducted the affairs of the company"[18] decided to bring suit against the Standard Oil Company (Indiana). As *Fortune* relates the event,

> . . . Universal proposed to attack the validity of the Burton patent under which the Standard of Indiana was licensing other refiners. President W. P. Cowan of Indiana came to Mr. Armour and a meeting was arranged between Halle and Dunham acting for Universal, and Colonel Robert W. Stewart and Dr. Burton, speaking for Indiana. They exchanged offers but came to no agreement. Thereupon, Universal, with former Senator James A. Reed as counsel, brought suit against Indiana in Kansas City for infringement of the Jesse A. Dubbs patent.[19]

By initiating the suit against the Standard Oil Company (Indiana), UOP became claimant to a large sum of money, for the legality of all the cracking operations carried out by Indiana Standard and by its licensees was at stake. But at the same time, for a few years at least, UOP prejudiced the direction in which their own research activities would be channeled. Since they were attacking Indiana Standard on the basis of the Jesse Dubbs's patent, UOP would necessarily have to show that cracking could be accomplished using Dubbs's apparatus. For this reason, their energies had to be restricted to demonstrating cracking with already defined equipment.

Substantiating the claims in Jesse Dubbs's patent required the construction and operation of a pressure unit which could crack gas-oil stocks, and

---

[18] Universal Oil Products vs. Winkler-Koch Engineering Company and Root Refining Company, District Court of the U. S., District of Delaware, Nos. 716 and 895, p. 760.

[19] "The Salvaging of the Armour Fortune," *op. cit.*, p. 52. W. M. Behrens recalls that Indiana offered $25,000 as a settlement, far short of UOP's demand for 10% of the common stock of Indiana Standard. In 1915, this fraction of the company's stock had a par value of $6,000,000 and a market value approximately three times as great. (Interview with W. M. Behrens, December 28, 1955.) No judgment was ever reached on the suit; it was dropped when UOP was sold to Shell Union Oil Company and the Standard Oil Company of California in 1931. During the fifteen years that the case was in the courts, 22,000 pages of testimony were taken. The suit cost Universal Oil Products Company $1,800,000, and Indiana Standard can be assumed to have spent a similar amount. After settling the suit, UOP signed an agreement with Indiana Standard, Jersey Standard, the Standard Oil Development Company, The Texas Company, and Gasoline Products Company, in which each guaranteed not to sue any of the companies party to the agreement or any of their licensees on the ground of patent infringement. ("Shell and Standard Buy Dubbs Process," *Oil and Gas Journal*, January 15, 1931, p. 65.)

this in turn required capital and engineering know-how. The former was obtained in 1916 when Halle sold Standard Asphalt and Rubber Company to Cities Service Company for $3,000,000.[20] J. Ogden Armour turned over his share of about $2,000,000 to Halle and UOP. A laboratory was built on two acres formerly part of Standard Asphalt's refinery.

Carbon Petroleum Dubbs

In selecting a staff to carry out experiments on the apparatus described in the Dubbs patent, Halle drew once again upon the Dubbs family. Jesse himself had retired, but his son, Carbon P. Dubbs, then in his middle thirties, was active and equally skilled. He had previously managed the refinery of the Pittsburgh Asphalt Company in Pennsylvania, and so was familiar with refining practices. Dubbs was the most enterprising of the group that began to fill UOP's laboratory.

[Universal Oil Products Company]

Carbon P. Dubbs.

One of his first collaborators was Dr. Gustav Egloff, an able and extremely articulate scientist. Like Burton and Humphreys, Egloff was a chemist, having completed his studies at Columbia University in 1915. After graduation, he worked a year for the Bureau of Mines and a year for Aetna Chemical Company before joining UOP in 1917. Egloff's

[20] *Ibid.*

technical contributions to the continuous cracking processes were, next to Carbon P. Dubbs's, to be the most significant, and later he was to show an even wider range of interest than his superior.[21]

Three other scientists were hired to work at Independence: Dr. Jacques C. Morrell, who, like Egloff, had received his advanced degree from Columbia; Colonel George Burrell, who had been active in research in helium during World War I; and Lester Kirschbraun, who carried out research on asphalt-based paints. Walter Cross also contributed his talents.[22]

Halle was not averse to starting a research program based on Jesse Dubbs's process. He felt that in the long run his energies could be better devoted to the manufacture of gasoline, which was in great demand, than to asphalt. In addition, he may well have been drawn to the idea of beginning with a new organization rather than being called in to patch up an old one.

For two years, all research and development activities were carried out in the laboratory located at Standard Asphalt's plant. Then research was shifted to Riverside, Illinois, a suburb of Chicago. Chicago was a more hospitable environment, and much closer to the center of Armour's, Halle's, and Dunham's other activities. Carbon P. Dubbs also made the move and, in addition to working at Riverside, built a laboratory in his home at Wilmette.

Process Development

It was at the laboratory in his home that Dubbs conceived the idea of "clean circulation," which was to be his major contribution to the process.[23] Clean circulation refers to the principle of recirculating that portion

[21] Gustav Egloff worked for UOP the remainder of his life, becoming ultimately its director of research. His research in cracking and other processes resulted in over 300 patents. He died on April 30, 1955 (see his obituary in the *New York Times*, May 1, 1955).

[22] Interview with W. H. Behrens, December 28, 1955.

[23] The fact that the development took place in C. P. Dubbs's private laboratory led to some dissension between UOP and himself. Dubbs had entered into private negotiations with The Texas Company in an attempt to sell them the results of the work he was doing in Wilmette (interview with W. H. Behrens, December 28, 1955). When UOP learned of this, they offered to give Dubbs $25,000 plus 15% of UOP profits in exchange for all of his personal research. A contract legalizing this exchange was signed in 1919 (Daily vs. Universal Oil Products Company, *op. cit.*, p. 355). Subsequently, Dubbs became dissatisfied with the way in which "profits" was being defined and, in 1928, was given instead 150 shares of the common stock of the company (United Gasoline Corporation and the stockholders of Universal Oil Products Company, and Others, "Purchase Agreement," January 2, 1931, Exhibit B, pp. 37, 38).

The idea of "clean circulation" was also conceived by Otto Behimer, working then for The Texas Company. Behimer's patent application preceded Dubbs's, but

of the cracked distillate heavier than gasoline back to the cracking coil, there once again to be subjected to the cracking conditions. In C. P. Dubbs's apparatus (shown on page 72), vapors from the reaction chamber flowed to a fractionating tower, yielding pressure distillate containing a high percentage of gasoline from the top, and a clean hot condensate called reflux from the bottom. According to the technique of clean circulation, it was this reflux that was to be returned to the cracking zone. The reflux diluted the heavy material in the coils and thus reduced substantially the formation of coke. With less coke being formed, the process could be used to crack reduced crude oils as well as gas oil, whereas batch processes such as the Burton could only crack gas oil or other distillates from crude oil. The Dubbs units therefore could act as scavengers for otherwise relatively worthless refinery stocks.

With the combination of continuous flow, derived from the Jesse Dubbs patent, and of clean circulation, the Dubbs process had two improvements over the Burton. The fact that it was a continuous process meant that the oil flowed steadily from one zone to the next, permitting the removal of the cracked material, particularly the coke, from the cracking zone before it could adhere to the sides of the tubes. Thus it increased the length of the operating cycle. Since the conditions at each point in the unit were constant, the process was easier to control than was the Burton, where the cracking materials stayed within the still and changed chemically during the operation. The disadvantage to continuous flow by itself, without the addition of clean circulation, was that the gasoline yield would have been less than that obtained from the Burton process. In order to obtain an equivalent yield, by once-through operation alone, it would have been necessary at this time to crack quite severely, and this would have resulted in a very heavy deposit of coke in the cracking tubes, which would in turn have shortened the length of each run. By recycling some of the cracked materials to be cracked once again,

---

Dubbs's was granted instead and no interference was stated. Indiana Standard was not able to use the Behimer patent in its defense against the suit by UOP, however, because Behimer was hired by UOP in 1927 with a ten-year contract calling for a yearly salary of $25,000 (interview with M. C. Dufincz, Standard Oil Company [Indiana], November 23, 1954). In 1931, Behimer and Dubbs each backed out of one claim, Behimer relinquishing the concept of "clean circulation" and Dubbs that of circulation under positive pressure, this being the concept underlying the hot-oil pump (United States Patent Office, Concession in Behimer vs. Dubbs, Interference No. 52,305, signed May 8, 1931; and Concession in Behimer vs. Dubbs, Interference No. 56,320, signed on the same date. Dubbs's patent was 1,302,620, filed March 19, 1919 and issued October 4, 1921. Behimer's was 1,840,012, filed on January 30, 1923 and issued January 5, 1932. A description of both patents and of their history in the patent office is given in David McKnight, Jr., "A Study of Patents on Petroleum Cracking," *University of Texas Publication No. 3831,* Austin, Texas: University of Texas, August 15, 1938, pp. 19–22, 73–78).

clean circulation permitted an increase in the yield of gasoline, based on the original charge of virgin gas oil or reduced crude. In the Burton process, to be sure, the heavy distillate was frequently recracked, but the stock was not obtained until several rerunning operations had been completed. Dubbs, by subdividing the streams from the cracking coils, was able to separate the cracked materials of medium weight from the heavy, and to return them, still hot, to the coil. And the fact that the cracked material was returned hot rather than cold reduced the amount of fuel necessary to carry out the entire cycle. Just as the Burton still and Humphreys' runback were integral parts of the Burton process, so were Jesse Dubbs's continuous flow and Carbon Dubbs's clean circulation integral parts of its successor.

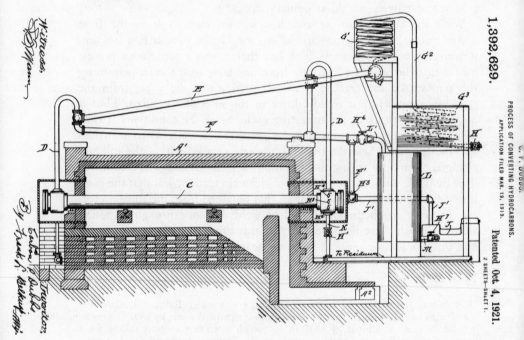

Illustration from Carbon P. Dubbs's "clean-circulation" patent.

While the research was being carried on in Riverside, Illinois, two pilot plants were built in Independence, Kansas.[24] The first was constructed before 1917, and probably bore a great resemblance to Jesse Dubbs's emulsion-breaking plant. The design of the emulsion plant, as given in the

[24] Universal Oil Products Company vs. Winkler-Koch Engineering Company and Root Refining Company, District Court of the United States, District of Delaware, Nos. 716 and 895; testimony of Hiram J. Halle, p. 762.

Jesse A. Dubbs patent, would not appear to lend itself well to cracking, particularly in regard to the heating coil. The figure on page 65 shows a helical coil, with the axis of the helix parallel to the ground. Such a design would place the lower bends considerably closer to the flame than the upper bends. More coke would therefore be formed and would remain at the bottom of each spiral. This would result in shorter runs and an extremely difficult coke removal problem. In actuality, it did not perform effectively.[25]

[Universal Oil Products Company]

Pilot-plant unit at Independence.

The second unit at Independence was constructed in 1917 or 1918 and probably incorporated the clean-circulation concept.[26] The unit, illustrated in the patent sketch, differed from Jesse Dubbs's apparatus in that the heating pipes were laid parallel to one another and in a horizontal plane (C in the figure on page 72), and in that the recycle stock was circulated from the vapor run-back line (F) through a transfer line (F¹) and back

[25] Interview with W. H. Behrens, December 28, 1955.
[26] Universal Oil Products Company vs. Winkler-Koch Engineering Company and Root Refining Company, *op. cit.*; also U. S. Patent No. 1,392,629, granted to C. P. Dubbs, "Process of Converting Hydrocarbons," application filed March 19, 1919, and granted October 4, 1921.

into the charging line (at H⁵), where it mingled with the virgin gas oil. As
in Jesse Dubbs's apparatus, so in his son's the soaking tubes were directly
fired.

This plant was modified shortly afterwards. The number of tubes in
the heating section was increased from five to ten. The ten pipes, each
20 feet long and constructed of 4-inch extra-heavy pipe, were set in two
rows, six in the lower and four in the upper. The hot oil from the heating
furnace discharged into four expansion chambers, each consisting of a
20-foot length of 10-inch extra-heavy pipe, connected in series. By then,
Dubbs had discovered that the cracking would take place in the expansion
chamber without any additional heat, and so the four lengths of 10-inch
pipe were not set in a furnace but were simply insulated to prevent excessive heat loss. The gas oil leaving the heating coils was held at a temperature of approximately 820°F., and a pressure of 135 pounds.[27]

This temperature was considerably higher than that in the Burton process, where the gas oil was kept between 700° and 720°F. By increasing
the temperature at which the reaction took place by approximately 70°,
the Dubbs process was able to obtain a rate of cracking about eight times
as great as that of the Burton. The relatively high pressure prevented
hydrocarbons in the light gas-oil range from being distilled. Dubbs was
able to utilize this pressure economically, as his equipment was the standard type developed for high-pressure use in steam boilers. Having no
reservoir comparable to Burton's still, he was less limited in the pressures
he could use.[28]

For the next year or so, many pilot-plant runs were made on the second
Independence unit. Different types of gas oil were charged to the cracking
coil, yields were obtained, and the gasoline was tested in the engine of
Dr. Egloff's car in order to determine its quality. A high fence had been
built around the two acres at Independence in order to discourage un-
wanted visitors, but by the beginning of 1919, Halle decided that it was
time to open the doors and to display the process to a few prospective
licensees.[29] He first approached the Shell Union Oil Corporation.

Licensing

The Shell group had at Wood River, Illinois, across the Mississippi
from St. Louis, a refinery which was operated by the Roxana Petroleum

[27] Universal Oil Products Company vs. Winkler-Koch Engineering Company and
Root Refining Company, *op. cit.*, pp. 822–828.
[28] This unit is described in E. H. Leslie, *Motor Fuels* (New York: Chemical Catalog
Co., 1923), pp. 379 and 389; in Carlton Ellis, *Gasoline and Other Motor Fuels* (New
York: Van Nostrand Co., 1921), pp. 270–271; and in Universal Oil Products vs.
Winkler-Koch Engineering Company and Root Refining Company, *op. cit.*, pp. 762–
763.
[29] *Ibid.*, p. 763.

Company. We can imagine two reasons why Halle chose Roxana; first, it belonged to a large organization with many refineries. Second, it operated in the same area as Indiana Standard, and thus was at a competitive disadvantage, not being permitted to license the Burton process.

The Dubbs unit was demonstrated to Daniel Pyzel, head of refinery design for the Royal Dutch/Shell group, in February, 1919.[30] Shortly before, Halle and Dubbs had seen W. A. J. M. van W. Van der Gracht, the Roxana president. Halle told Van der Gracht,

> that the process was one that could be operated so-called continuously and that the bane of the cracking art, the formation of carbon on the heating elements, had been solved by us through our clean circulation method . . . that . . . the process would require less plant investment . . . that the labor cost would be substantially less . . . and that the process would not necessarily be limited to the use of the light gas-oil charging stocks which had theretofore been used exclusively.[31]

Van der Gracht seemed impressed but informed Halle that Pyzel would have to recommend the installation. Pyzel was leaving for San Francisco that night, so Halle did not have more than an hour or two to discuss the agreement with him but, with his characteristic persistence, asked to sit through Pyzel's dinner so that he could continue the discussion. One week later, Halle followed Pyzel to San Francisco and persuaded him to return for the demonstration. Pyzel was also impressed and began to negotiate with UOP. On December 12, 1919, the Roxana Petroleum Company took a license to operate the Dubbs process.[32]

During 1919, other private demonstrations of the Dubbs process were carried out at Independence for the benefit of a few firms.[33] As the industry became aware of the Dubbs process, there was some agitation by those not invited to be granted a chance to observe its operation. At the instigation of Judge C. D. Chamberlain of the National Petroleum Association, Halle arranged a public display, beginning on June 22, 1919, and continuing for twelve days. Twenty-one men belonging to the Western Refiners Association attended this demonstration and later submitted a report describing the process.[34]

[30] Pyzel shunned any organizational title and role, acting almost as an independent consultant for Royal Dutch/Shell. C. P. Dubbs gives Pyzel great credit for his contributions to the design of the Dubbs process.

[31] Universal Oil Products Company vs. Winkler-Koch Engineering Company and Root Refining Company, op. cit., p. 780.

[32] Ibid., pp. 780–781; also "Development of Dubbs Process," Oil and Gas Journal, January 15, 1931, p. 65.

[33] Universal Oil Products Company vs. Winkler-Koch Engineering Company and Root Refining Company, op. cit., p. 788.

[34] See National Petroleum News, September 4, 1919, pp. 25–26. Eight of the group of companies represented by the twenty-one men were ultimately to take licenses

It was during the demonstration of the Dubbs process to the Western Refiners Association that Halle enunciated the licensing policies of the Universal Oil Products Company. The Dubbs process, he stated, was to be made available to all refiners without reservation or discrimination. The performance of the units would be estimated from UOP's own pilot-plant data, and the yields would be guaranteed. The royalty rates would be identical for everyone, and would be based not on profits but on the number of barrels of gas-oil charge. The rate was set at 15¢ per barrel of fresh feed, the same figure that was stated by UOP and Shell in their agreement. The licensees could obtain all the technical know-how and could adopt any improvements made by UOP in the future. The license would thus cover not just the use of the patents themselves but rather the cracking process as described in the agreement (called in legal terminology the "definable field"; this includes within its definition the technical skills).[35] Finally, and probably to the small refiner most important, Halle said that he would put a "defend and hold harmless" clause in each license. To the small refiner, this was a great advantage, for he was always afraid of being sued out of existence. With the welter of cracking processes that were beginning to appear, and with the harrowing litigation that ensued, many refiners felt that the risk of taking an unprotected license was greater than they could afford to bear.[36]

In this meeting Halle steadfastly held his ground on his policy of non-discrimination. "Some wanted to know whether they could get exclusive licenses and that was refused. Others wanted to make special arrangements and that was refused."[37]

Both Shell and the small refiners belonging to the Western Refiners Association expressed some concern over the limited capacity of the demonstration unit. Its 72 barrels per day did not compare favorably with the Burton unit, which charged 89 barrels per day, let alone with the Burton-Clark, whose capacity with a bubble tower was 225. Halle and Dubbs had already anticipated this problem — by increasing the size of the furnace and by adding a dephlegmator, an early distillation tower, they figured that they could attain a capacity of at least 250 barrels per day. They told the small refiners these prospects; with Shell they went further and

on the Dubbs process. (Universal Oil Products Company vs. Winkler-Koch Engineering Company and Root Refining Company, *op. cit.*, pp. 847–848.)

[35] W. Meredith Behrens, "Oil Industry," paper delivered before Forum on Patent Licensing, Practicing Law Institute, 20 Vesey Street, New York.

[36] On the other hand, there were some small refiners who imitated the successful processes in their plants, hoping because of the confusion in the courts to escape penalization, or because of their small size to escape notice.

[37] Universal Oil Products vs. Winkler-Koch Engineering Company and Root Refining Company, *op. cit.*, p. 788.

guaranteed that the unit at Roxana would be capable of charging that volume.

Construction of First Units

In order to familiarize themselves with the problems to be expected in building and operating a unit of that size, UOP constructed at Riverside a prototype of the Roxana unit.[38] In spite of the fact that at the time of its completion it was larger than the Burton-Clark units and therefore the largest cracking unit in the world, this unit was used solely for research and development. Halle resisted the temptation to enter the refining industry; he wanted to take no chance of alienating his future customers.

Building the prototype turned out to be a wise step, for the work at Wood River did not progress very favorably.[39] Construction had been started in 1920, shortly after Shell signed the license agreement. Since the Roxana unit had to be bigger than the Independence pilot unit, the number of tubes in the furnace was doubled, the new unit containing four coils of five tubes each. The hot oil flowed from the coil to a series of unheated 10-inch tubes set horizontally. From there the vapors were taken to a dephlegmator set at a considerable elevation, so that the hydrostatic pressure in the recycle line would be equal to the pressure drop in the cracking tubes and the soaking tubes. Had the dephlegmator not been elevated, the virgin gas-oil charge would have flowed into the dephlegmator through the recycle line. The direction of flow for the clean recycle was from the bottom of the dephlegmator to the entrance to the cracking coil and then, with the virgin gas oil, into the coil itself.

The capacity of the Dubbs unit was limited by the height to which the dephlegmator could be raised. If the charging rate to the unit were increased, the pressure drop in the coil and in the soaking tubes would increase and would then be greater than the hydrostatic pressure in the recycle line. By comparing the flow sheets of the modified Roxana unit[40] and the second unit,[41] one sees that increasing the capacity of the units required hoisting the dephlegmator even higher; in the second Roxana unit it was over 60 feet above the ground.

Construction of No. 1 plant at Roxana was completed in March 1921, but Dubbs and his co-workers encountered difficulty in operating the unit.[42] They were unable to obtain the 21% yield of gasoline on the basis

[38] J. G. Alther, "Gasoline, Yesterday, Today, and Tomorrow," address given February 2, 1943, p. 17 (in files of UOP).
[39] Universal Oil Products Company vs. Winkler-Koch Engineering Company and Root Refining Company, op. cit., pp. 833–837.
[40] Ibid., p. 119.
[41] Ibid., p. 135.
[42] Kendall Beaton, Enterprise in Oil: A History of Shell in the United States, New York: Appleton-Century-Crofts, Inc., 1957, p. 244.

of 250 barrels per day charge, mainly because they were unable to clean out the unit within the twenty-four hours guaranteed by UOP in its license. On the tenth run, in December 1921, the unit exploded, killing two men.[43] Dubbs fired the engineer who had designed the No. 1 unit, Robert T. Pollock, and replaced him with two other engineers, Lyman C. Huff and Lewis E. Winkler.

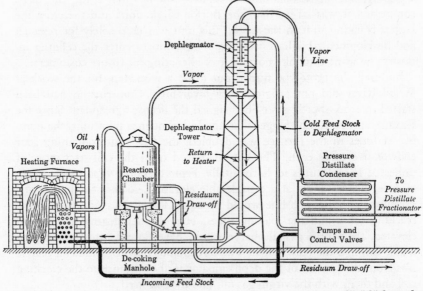

[Shell Oil Company]

Flow sheet of early Dubbs unit.

The explosion of No. 1 unit was a severe blow to the young process company. It seemed that the expansion tubes would have to be completely redesigned and that the cracking coil would have to be modified before a satisfactory unit could be delivered. This meant dismantling Roxana No. 1 unit and, apart from the small percentage of the outlay that was covered by insurance, taking a loss on its construction.

On Carbon P. Dubbs fell the responsibility for creating a new and satisfactory design. It was at this point that he finally broke away from Jesse Dubbs's precedent of using long tubes of fairly large diameter for the soaking chamber. Regulating the level of the liquid in these tubes in order to distribute the vapors equally had been extremely difficult. Moreover, leaks had sprung where the tubes were joined to the headers. The only

[43] Universal Oil Products Company vs. Winkler-Koch Engineering Company and Root Refining Company, op. cit., p. 135.

way to eliminate these faults was to design a radically different soaking system.

Dubbs now saw that a single chamber of greater diameter would fulfill the function much better. It could contain the same volume of oil vapors with less surface area, and it would be less likely to become clogged. The expansion chamber he adopted was approximately 4 feet in diameter and 30 feet long. It was equipped with two vents and a safety valve, the last an added precaution against explosion. The furnace was redesigned so that

[Shell Oil Company]

Four Wood River Dubbs plants in May 1925.

the tubes were laid in nine rows, the number of tubes in each row alternating between three and four. The dephlegmator was raised still higher in order to increase the pressure in the recycle leg. The single receiver house was abandoned in favor of the conventional pump house with the pressure distillate condenser located on the roof. The modified Roxana unit, designated number 1-A, bore little resemblance to its predecessor, either in its physical appearance or its process design. But it had taken a serious accident to bring about a change in the established way of designing the cracking unit.

To Halle, the period following the explosion was also one of strain. On the one hand, he had to pacify Pyzel and the other Shell employees, and accept their modifications in the equipment design and construction. We have a reference to this in Pyzel's testimony during one of the suits, when he said, "After . . . number 1 blew up, there was quite a considerable delay because of . . . questions to be settled, but finally a new plant was built."[44]

On the other hand, Halle had to persuade J. Ogden Armour that the Dubbs process still held great promise and that he should invest more money in UOP. The $2,000,000 with which Armour had originally financed the company had long ago been spent, and over $4,000,000 more was to be necessary before No. 1-A unit at Roxana would begin operation.

Armour's Financial Difficulties

J. Ogden Armour's funds were no longer inexhaustible. Before and during World War I, with the tremendous growth of Armour and Company and with its high profits, he had been able to provide several million dollars without strain upon either his personal fortune or his holdings in the company, but by the end of 1921, things had changed considerably. In that year, Armour and Company showed a deficit of over $31,000,000.[45] Two other ventures, the Armour Leather Company and the Sutter Basin project, the latter a large-scale irrigation scheme in the Sacramento Valley, had accumulated between them deficits of nearly $16,000,000. In order to finance these and other enterprises, Armour was forced to borrow from Armour and Company. By the end of 1922, his personal debt amounted to $56,000,000. To invest more money in the Universal Oil Products Company at a time like this required great courage and considerable confidence in Halle.[46]

Armour's colleagues in the Chicago financial world apparently did not share his confidence. When Armour and Company was finally taken over by the banks which were its main creditors, J. Ogden's securities were appropriated too. To the bankers, Armour's block of stock in UOP, now augmented through purchase of Jesse A. Dubbs's share from Dubbs's widow, seemed to be just another of his worthless holdings.[47] It had had deficits every year since its founding; in fact, it was only in the year of the locusts, 1922, that UOP earned its first revenues, a meager $5,784.60.[48]

[44] *Ibid.*, p. 931.
[45] "The Salvaging of the Armour Fortune," *op. cit.*, pp. 49–50.
[46] Those in Shell close to the venture had the same confidence in Halle as did Armour (comment by Kendall Beaton).
[47] "The Salvaging of the Armour Fortune," *op. cit.*, p. 51.
[48] Universal Oil Products Company vs. Winkler-Koch Engineering Company and Root Refining Company, *op. cit.*, Vol. V, pp. 48a, 49.

Their refusal to assign any value to the stock is therefore understandable.

Had J. Ogden Armour failed a year or more before he did, he might well have carried Universal Oil Products with him. But fortunately for Halle, Dubbs, and the small refiners, J. Ogden Armour's downfall did not come until the end of 1922. By then the Roxana unit 1-A was operating satisfactorily, a second unit was being built, and other licenses were being negotiated. For UOP, the time of harvest had arrived.

The harvest was not abundant enough to fill the needs of both UOP and Armour, however. Just as royalties began to flow in, J. Ogden Armour's assets passed into the hands of his creditors.[49] Had he been able to hold them off, he would have seen the royalties from the Dubbs process increase to over $1,000,000 within two years (see Appendix Table 15). In 1924, Shell alone paid over $237,000, for besides the two units at Roxana, it had also built a unit at Martinez, California. In 1925, the royalties were over $2,000,000. But the costs of designing and testing additional Dubbs units which other refiners now began to install were incurred before royalties began to flow in, and in July, 1926, the company urgently needed $100,000 more to meet current expenses.[50]

Mrs. Armour, who had received the 400 shares in UOP that her husband owned in exchange for providing him with $1,500,000 that he needed for the Sutter Basin project, was unable to supply the money. Halle could have obtained funds through the sale of the foreign rights, but that would have meant accepting $200,000 less than his offering price. With his characteristic boldness, he refused the lower price.

Just at this time, by a great stroke of fortune, J. Ogden Armour received Liberty bonds that were worth $150,000 from a friend of his, Harry Tammen, co-owner of the newspaper *The Post* in Denver, Colorado. Mr. Tammen sent this loan entirely on his own initiative without the knowledge of UOP's plight. Halle, upon their arrival, took the Liberty bonds to a bank as security, borrowed $135,000, and put the funds into UOP.[51] This was the last financing that UOP ever needed.

Improvements

The second unit installed at Roxana cost about $60,000 to build and had twice the capacity — 500 barrels per day — of the first.[52] In doubling the capacity of the unit, however, it was not necessary to double its size. The

[49] "The Salvaging of the Armour Fortune," *op. cit.*, pp. 50–51.
[50] *Ibid.*, p. 55.
[51] In exchange for the loan, and all of Armour's other benefits, Halle took over J. Ogden Armour's personal affairs. It was not until two years later, a year after Armour's death, that his obligations were finally met (*ibid.*).
[52] Universal Oil Products Company vs. Winkler-Koch Engineering Company and Root Refining Company, *op. cit.*, Vol. VI, p. 500.

number of tubes in the furnace only needed to be increased from 32 to 39; the dephlegmator was elevated higher and more plates were added, but the size of the vessel itself did not have to be changed. The 500-barrel-per-day unit was reproduced for other refiners.[53] Many of those who operated in the midcontinent area had a raw material much like Roxana's and therefore could use equipment which was a mere duplication of a Roxana unit. The uniformity of design was reflected in lower capital cost, because the amount of engineering resources necessary to design and build the unit were reduced and because the equipment suppliers became familiar with the type of materials needed.

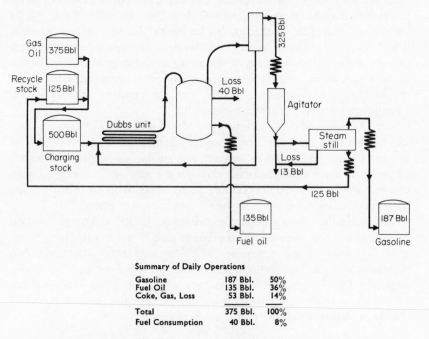

Summary of Daily Operations

Gasoline	187 Bbl.	50%
Fuel Oil	135 Bbl.	36%
Coke, Gas, Loss	53 Bbl.	14%
Total	375 Bbl.	100%
Fuel Consumption	40 Bbl.	8%

Flow chart of 500-barrel-per-day Dubbs unit cracking typical midcontinent gas oil.

Buying a standardized unit from what was now becoming a well-established process-design company aided the small refiner in his competitive struggle against the large company in that it made it easier for him to obtain outside capital. Hoping to adopt an entirely new and unproved process, the small refiner, upon approaching banks or other investors for funds, would find them reluctant to finance him, partly because of his

[53] *Ibid.*, testimony of Hiram J. Halle, pp. 783, 788–789, 847. The second refiner to take a license was the Sinclair Refining Company on March 29, 1923.

lack of resources and partly because of the high risk entailed in process innovation. If he used the Dubbs process, however, the second limitation would tend to disappear, for the outside investor would be certain that the processing claims would be met.[54] He would also be presented with a more accurate estimate of the total capital requirements. Thus, by reducing the risks, UOP, in presenting the standard Dubbs unit to the small refiner, was improving his chances of competing in the future with the large integrated concerns.

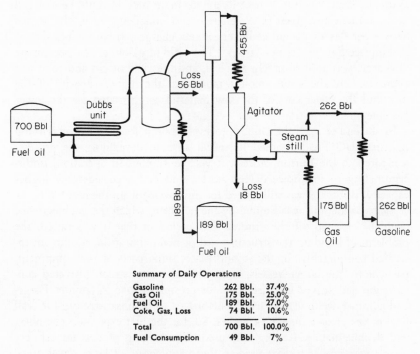

Summary of Daily Operations

Gasoline	262 Bbl.	37.4%
Gas Oil	175 Bbl.	25.0%
Fuel Oil	189 Bbl.	27.0%
Coke, Gas, Loss	74 Bbl.	10.6%
Total	700 Bbl.	100.0%
Fuel Consumption	49 Bbl.	7%

Flow chart of 500-barrel-per-day Dubbs unit cracking fuel oil.

One feature of the Dubbs unit that delighted the small and large refiners alike was its flexibility. Its predecessor, the Burton process, and its most promising competitor, the Cross, were unable to operate on any feed stock heavier than light gas oil. Shell, foreseeing that virgin gas oil, as furnace oil, would rise in price, urged UOP to experiment with charging heavier hydrocarbons.[55] Dubbs and Egloff, trying different feed stocks in

[54] Interview with G. Egloff, November 4, 1954.
[55] Comment of Kendall Beaton.

the Riverside and Independence units, discovered that heavy gas oils and even heavy fuel oil could be cracked in the units without altering the equipment in any way.

Although no change was needed in the equipment, the operating conditions had to be altered if the fuel was to be cracked effectively. They learned that fuel oil could not be cracked as severely in the furnace without depositing a large amount of coke. Since each barrel of fuel oil could not be as severely cracked as the gas oil, it could not absorb as much heat. Yet the furnace was designed to provide a certain rate of heat transfer. With the same amount of heat liberated, more fuel oil could be charged to the unit in any given time. Therefore, a unit designed to charge 500 barrels per day of gas oil could effectively charge 700 barrels per day of fuel oil (see flow charts pp. 82–83).[56] The yield of gasoline, as a percentage of charge, was approximately 3% less, and the yield of gas and coke was approximately the same amount more, but the higher capacity of the unit and the lower cost of the raw material compensated for the lower gasoline yield.

By the end of 1923, the Dubbs process had been accepted by the refining industry. UOP had attained its initial aims in developing the process: compared to the Burton process, it was continuous in operation, undiscriminating in its choice of feedstocks, and had a considerably higher capacity. But there was still a need for improvement. In the first place, the capacity of the unit was limited by the height to which the dephlegmator could be elevated off the ground. For each foot that it was raised, the problems of building the structure and of maintaining the equipment increased considerably. In the second place, some parts of the equipment, particularly the larger vessels, were difficult to construct.[57] Riveted construction had proved unsatisfactory for pressures above 95 pounds. Forge-and-hammer welding was tried, but proved to be unsatisfactory for wall thicknesses greater than 1 5/8 inches. So, for the first expansion chambers and dephlegmators, forging was used. The forging process for refinery vessels was similar to that used in the manufacture of large naval guns. But forging was expensive, and even by this method vessels could not be manufactured larger than 6 feet in inside diameter, 40 feet long, and 5 inches thick. Finally, there was a need for better fractionating facilities. From the top of the dephlegmator of the standard 500-barrels-per-day unit came pressure distillate, which was composed of gas, gasoline, and heavier

[56] For yields when cracking fuel oil, see flow chart on p. 83. For yields when cracking virgin gas oil, see G. Egloff, "Cracking Process Aids Industry," *Oil News*, April 5, 1923. (The yields in the chart on p. 82 are based on a mixed charge of virgin gas oil and clean recycle.)

[57] L. C. Huff, "Importance of Cracking Equipment in the Modern Refinery," *Petroleum Mechanical Engineering*, October, 1930.

material boiling in the kerosene and gas-oil ranges. As in the Burton process, the pressure distillate needed further processing, which in turn required more equipment, fuel, and manpower, and, unless the refining processes were very well integrated, more intermediate storage. Ideally, refiners would have preferred the cracking unit to produce cracked gasoline that would meet the specifications of a finished product. This would have meant making a cut at approximately 400°F., so that the materials vaporizing above that temperature would be separated from those vaporizing below. To do this required better fractionating equipment and a greater understanding of the distillation operation.

By the end of 1926, these three problems had been essentially solved. No single company was responsible for these improvements, for many were working on the problems simultaneously. Shell was primarily responsible for the improvement which had the most significant effect upon increasing the capacity of the unit. In 1922 or 1923, Dubbs learned that Shell engineers in California had designed and built a hot-oil pump.[58] No previous pump could work under the temperatures and pressures existing in the recycle stream, although Behimer had conceived of the idea. With the new pump, equipped with better packing, the capacities of the cracking units were no longer limited by the height to which the dephlegmator could be elevated.[59] The pump alone raised the capacity of the Dubbs unit from 500 to 700 barrels per day.

Through the 1920's, refiners and process-development firms continued to reduce the cost and increase the permissible size of the vessels and other pieces of cracking equipment. Electric welding, which permitted the inside diameter of vessels to be increased from 6 feet to 10 feet, was developed. Other equipment improvement, to quote Lyman C. Huff, the engineer who designed the No. 1-A unit, consisted of

> heavy seamless-steel tubing in iron-pipe sizes, alloy steel tubing, welded-pipe joints, metal-to-metal high-pressure flange joints, alloy steel studs and bolts,

[58] The development, which probably occurred before 1920, was carried out chiefly by W. W. Thompson, who secured the patent. UOP recognized Shell's contribution by reducing its royalty rate by 25% (Kendall Beaton, *op. cit.*, pp. 249 ff.). The first hot-oil pump was installed by H. Dimmig and P. Keith of UOP's engineering department in 1923 or 1924 (interviews with W. H. McAdams and H. C. Weber, February 13, 1956; also, Universal Oil Products Company vs. Winkler-Koch Engineering Company and Root Refining Company, *op. cit.*, letter from A. G. Bogardus, July 12, 1924, pp. 502–505).

[59] Transitional cracking units were designed with both a hot-oil pump and an elevated dephlegmator, because the hot-oil pumps were still not completely reliable. (Gustav Egloff, "The Simultaneous Cracking and Coking of Heavy Oils by the Dubbs Process," paper delivered before the Oil Section of the American Institute of Mining and Metallurgical Engineers in New York on February 15, 1926, p. 14.) Shortly afterwards, however, the dephlegmator was lowered to the same altitude as the reaction chamber.

alloy-steel forgings and castings, high-temperature and high-pressure case and forged-steel valves and fittings, high-temperature and high-pressure pumps (handling oil up to 800°F. and 1500 pounds pressure), fans for re-circulating flue gases at high temperatures (1100 to 1200 degrees Fahrenheit), high-temperature insulating materials, and many others.[60]

Cracking at higher pressures made it possible to use higher temperatures because vaporization was retarded, and the higher temperatures made possible a higher rate of cracking. With these many improvements, the capacity of the Dubbs unit was increased very quickly from 700 to 1000 and, by 1931, to 4000 barrels per day.[61]

The final problem, that of inadequate fractionating, had also been mate-rially reduced by 1926 through the adoption of improvements in distilla-tion. The distilling operation was, like cracking, of major importance in refining. It was utilized in crude distillation, where crude oil was sep-arated into its fractions at atmospheric pressure, and in vacuum distilla-tion, where heavy oils were separated into their fractions at reduced pressures. The stimulus to better fractionation was greater in the crude-oil distilling operation because the volumes of product were larger, and so it was here that the main development took place. Once a suitable theory of distillation had been expounded it was applied to the separation of the products from the cracking process. The desired result, namely, the pro-duction of specification gasoline from the cracking unit, was obtained.

A successful attempt was also made to reduce fuel consumption. As the units increased in size, it became profitable to recover heat from the main streams by means of heat exchanges. Engineering relationships underly-ing that exchange were investigated and, for each cracking unit, calcula-tions were made in order to determine the ideal amount of heat exchange surface to install.[62]

Yet another improvement was made in maintenance, where the cost of cleaning out the soaking drum was lowered by permitting the coke to be removed more quickly. Around the inside of the chamber was coiled a steel chain supported by lugs, which were in turn welded to the inside of the vessel. When the chamber was full of coke, the chain was hoisted out by a winch, breaking the coke up into small lumps. The coke then fell out of the vessel through the open manhole at the bottom.

The final improvement was in the operating technique. By cracking less severely and by removing the heavy cracked material from the soaking

[60] L. C. Huff, op. cit. Electric welding provided benefits in other industries, too. "The Modern High Pressure Boiler, for example, owed its rapid development largely to the pioneer work done in developing cracking equipment." (Ibid.)

[61] "The Salvaging of the Armour Fortune," op. cit., p. 55.

[62] See W. L. Nelson, Petroleum Refinery Engineering, 3rd ed., New York: McGraw-Hill Book Co., 1949, pp. 763-764.

chamber more quickly, refiners were able to reduce coke formation. Less coke meant less cleaning time and consequently higher capacity. Moreover, the residual oil from this so-called low-level operation was a better fuel and commanded a better price.[63]

One effect of the increase in capacity of Dubbs units was to expand the range within which economies of scale operated. By 1930, a refiner needed a 4000-barrel-per-day cracking unit to achieve lowest average costs. Before this stage in their development, cracking units were still small enough to enable the small refiner to receive the benefits of economies of scale. A 500-barrel-per-day Dubbs unit of 1924 would fit into a plant which was processing approximately 1000 barrels per day of crude oil, and this was a modest charging rate. But beyond 500 barrels per day, the technological economies of scale had not been very substantial. At higher plant capacity, identical units were installed. With Burton units, economies did result from the operation of multiple units through a reduction in labor cost per unit of output and, through a common gas line, a reduction in the time necessary to bring the stills up to the operating pressure. The advantages of having two or more cracking units tied into a common fuel-gas line had largely disappeared by now, for it had become accepted refining practice to collect the gas from the several refining operations — crude distillation, cracking, and rerunning — in order to utilize all the potential fuel and maintain a stable gas pressure. The net result was that any refiner with a crude-oil capacity of 1000 barrels per day in the early 1920's could operate cracking units at approximately the same cost as any of its larger competitors. But by 1930, this figure had been raised to 8000 barrels per day of crude oil, a capacity greater than that of most nonintegrated refining firms.[64] This hastened the exit of many of the small refiners from the industry.

Purchase of UOP by Major Oil Companies

In 1924, a second large refiner, the Standard Oil Company of California, became interested in the Dubbs process. This was of immediate interest because California Standard was the first company which had been licensed under the Burton process to adopt the new Dubbs process, and of longer-range significance because California was to be one of the firms which would purchase UOP from its private owners. California's Burton-Clark units had not been very profitable; although operating adequately,

---

[63] Kendall Beaton, *op. cit.*, pp. 250–252.

[64] In 1930, there were 257 plants belonging to companies other than the 30 largest in the industry. The average capacity of these plants was 2837 barrels of crude oil per day. (J. G. McLean and R. W. Haigh, *The Growth of Integrated Oil Companies*, Boston: Harvard University, Graduate School of Business Administration, 1954, Appendix Table 23, p. 701.)

the "costs were high"[65] probably because the heavy California gas-oil stocks would not permit operating cycles as long as those possible with lighter midcontinent stocks.

Following a visit by the foremen of California Standard's pressure stills department to the Shell plant at Martinez, where the Dubbs process was being used, and a decision by its patent attorneys that the Dubbs patents were valid, Richard W. Hanna, the superintendent of the company's refineries and a director, called in Halle. Halle arrived on June 12, 1924, and an agreement was reached. In addition to remodeling one of the Burton units for clean circulation, California ultimately built sixteen Dubbs units, eight at their Richmond refinery, and eight more of 2500 barrels' capacity each at El Segundo.[66]

With the operation of all these units, California Standard found that its royalty payments to the Universal Oil Products Company were becoming quite large. From the initial payment of $32,000 in 1926, royalties increased to over $1,000,000 in 1929.[67] With the biggest units coming on stream in 1930, California Standard expected the yearly payment to more than double. Shell too began to feel that the Dubbs-process royalties were becoming a heavy burden on their operations. Shell had paid slightly over $1,000,000 to UOP in 1926; by 1928 this amount had nearly tripled, and a further increase was anticipated for 1930. In spite of these large royalty payments, neither company had made a serious attempt to develop a competitive cracking process.[68]

It would not have been to their advantage to develop a competitive process for less than the amount of the Dubbs royalties plus the cost of installing new equipment to replace the Dubbs units. It could have been argued in the early 1920's, with some justification, that it would be cheaper to develop a new process. Two other integrated firms did just this. But Shell and California Standard thought it would be cheaper to license because they did not believe that they would have to continue paying UOP royalties. As Daniel Pyzel said, ". . . it was our impression that the result of this [the claim by UOP that Indiana Standard had infringed Jesse A. Dubbs's patent] would nullify both [the Jesse A. Dubbs and the 'clean circulation'] patents."[69] If both patents were nullified, then Shell could operate the Dubbs units without a licence from UOP, since the principles under which they were operated would lie in the public domain.

---

[65] Universal Oil Products Company vs. Winkler-Koch Engineering Company and Root Refining Company, *op. cit.*, testimony of Richard W. Hanna, pp. 870–876.

[66] *Ibid.*, testimony of Hiram J. Halle, pp. 807–808.

[67] *Ibid.*, Vol. V, pp. 48a, 49.

[68] Shell did, of course, contribute to the development of the Dubbs process and receive the reduction in royalties.

[69] Universal Oil Products Company vs. Winkler-Koch Engineering Company and Root Refining Company, *op. cit.*, testimony of Daniel Pyzel, p. 941.

At the beginning of the 1920's, it had seemed as if the suit which UOP had initiated back in 1914 against Indiana Standard would be adjudicated momentarily, to the benefit of, among others, the Shell group. But both of the litigants displayed an amazing tenacity. By 1930 the suit seemed no closer to completion than ten years earlier, and Shell and California Standard were in that year to be paying over $6,000,000 in royalties. To avoid paying royalties now seemed impossible; it might be cheaper to buy UOP. Purchase of UOP would not only eliminate royalty payments but also permit the resolution of the UOP–Indiana Standard suit.[70] The money would be welcome to Mrs. Armour, who still held the shares of UOP which she had acquired from her husband.

The negotiations came to an end on January 6, 1931, when the Shell Union Oil Corporation and the Standard Oil Company of California together bought Universal Oil Products for $25,000,000.[71] The royalties from the licensing of the Dubbs process, accumulated between 1920 and 1930, had been adequate to cover the yearly operating expenses of the company and also to repay J. Ogden Armour's creditors for the money which he lent it during its earlier years. The entire sum was profit to the stockholders. The purchase price was divided among the stockholders: Mrs. Armour received approximately $10,000,000, Halle $3,200,000, Carbon P. Dubbs $3,600,000, Belknap $1,100,000, Reichmann $1,300,000, and others the rest.[72] To Halle, Dubbs, Reichmann, and Belknap the proceeds from the sale of UOP represented a return for sixteen years of research and development, of publicizing and promoting. The price was high, but the rewards were great. To the Armours, who supplied the capital necessary to develop the Dubbs process, the return was adequate but hardly rewarding. Assuming that Armour had lent UOP $7,000,000 ($6,000,000 of it up to 1922 when the first royalties were received and $1,000,000 thereafter), his total return on the $7,000,000 was $17,000,000.[73] Taking the average duration of the investment to be thirteen years, this is an annual return of approximately 7%.

[70] "Texas, Indiana, and Jersey were only too happy to contribute to a fund to bring this about so as to put to an end the myriad of patent fights both in the Patent Office and in the courts which had sprung up between them and Universal and their respective licensees over the years." (W. Meredith Behrens, "Oil Industry," address delivered before the Practicing Law Institute, op. cit.)

[71] Of the total purchase price, Shell paid nearly $10,000,000 and Standard Oil of California nearly $5,500,000. Roughly $3,400,000 apiece was contributed by Indiana Standard and Jersey Standard. The Texas Company was allowed $3,000,000 for adding the Behimer-Adams patents to the pool. (United Gasoline Corporation, I, Acquisition of Properties of Universal Oil Products Company and Agreements Supplementary Thereto, pp. 5, 221.)

[72] Ibid.

[73] The amount that J. Ogden Armour spent on all his enterprises is unknown, but it probably exceeded $56,000,000, the amount of J. Ogden Armour's personal debt

Royalty Rates

Although the ownership of Universal Oil Products Company changed in 1931, the Dubbs process retained its original complexion for several years after that. Some larger-scale units were built, but the design of the equipment was not altered appreciably. Of importance both to UOP and to its licensees, however, were four successive reductions in the royalty rates.

When the Dubbs process was first announced to the Western Refiners Association, the royalty rate was set at 15¢ per barrel of fresh charge, the same fee that UOP and Shell had agreed to. In comparison, the Burton royalty rate fluctuated around 17¢ per barrel of fresh charge, based not upon charged stock but upon the profits from the cracking operation. Since the profits were somewhat less during the post-war recession year of 1921, the year the Dubbs process was introduced, we can assume that the two royalty rates were approximately equal. The royalty rate on the Dubbs process stood at 15¢ until 1924, when, in an effort to entice California Standard to take out a license, UOP adopted a sliding scale whereby the royalty rate on the first million barrels of charge per year (2,740 barrels per day) was still computed at 15¢ per barrel of fresh charge, but on each subsequent million barrels per year it was reduced 1¢ per barrel of fresh charge until it reached a minimum of 12¢.[74] This reduction was passed on to all the refiners, although, of course, it benefited the large refiners most. In order to qualify for the lower royalty rates, a refiner would have to have had at least seven 500-barrel-per-day Dubbs units, well beyond the range of most nonintegrated refiners.[75]

---

to Armour and Company ("The Salvaging of the Armour Fortune," *op. cit.*, p. 50). Of these enterprises — Sutter Basin, which consumed over $15,000,000; the Armour Leather Company, which took $11,000,000 more; and all the rest — only UOP turned in a profit. There was no over-all profit, but rather a loss, of such magnitude as few individuals or even organizations could withstand. The social gain may have compensated for the personal loss, although Mrs. Armour probably derived little comfort from this benefit.

[74] Universal Oil Products Company vs. Winkler-Koch Engineering Company and Root Refining Company, *op. cit.*, testimony of Hiram J. Halle, p. 866.

[75] The numbers of "small refiners," their average refining capacity, and their average cracking capacity are listed below:

Year	Number of plants of "small refiners"	Average crude oil capacity of small refiners' plants (barrels per day)	Average cracking capacity of small refiners' plants (barrels per day of charge)
1920	274	1585	n.a.
1925	430	1953	n.a.
1930	257	2837	891
1935	453	1934	453
1940	393	2397	324

In an effort to appeal to the small refiners hit by the depression, the royalty rate was reduced in 1934 to 10¢ per barrel.[76] Lowering the royalty rate at first reduced UOP's royalties by over $1,000,000 a year, but it also encouraged the building of additional Dubbs units, with the result that within twenty-two months UOP's income was restored to its original level.[77]

In 1938, the royalty rate was reduced to 5¢ per barrel. "As the time approached for the expiration in 1938 of the C. P. Dubbs patent, which was the real base of Universal's cracking patent structure, Universal . . . on that date . . . reduced [it] from 10 to 5 cents."[78] The introduction of the Houdry process (see Chapter 4) undoubtedly had an effect, too.

In 1944, it was once again reduced from 5¢ to 3¢ per barrel of charge. Continuous catalytic cracking processes, far superior to thermal cracking, had been introduced during the war, and many refiners planned to build catalytic cracking units after the war. The royalty rate on catalytic cracking had already been established at 5¢ per barrel. Presumably, it was to improve their competitive position with respect to catalytic cracking that UOP lowered the royalties on the Dubbs thermal cracking process. With the expiration of improvement patents recently, all royalties ceased.[79]

Not the least of UOP's activities was that of publicizing the results of their various experiments. Unlike Indiana Standard, which had always been reluctant to communicate the details of its Burton process, UOP believed that by describing the operation of the Dubbs process it would benefit both itself and the refining industry. We might have expected this difference in attitude from the difference in make-up of the two companies; Indiana Standard was primarily a refiner and therefore had to consider the competitive effects of releasing information on the Burton

---

(*Source:* J. G. McLean and R. W. Haigh, *The Growth of Integrated Oil Companies,* *loc. cit.* Column 4 is calculated from Haigh and McLean's aggregate data on cracking capacity. "Small refiners" are defined as all but the largest thirty companies in the refining industry.) From the table we see that few of the small independent refiners in 1925 had a crude-oil capacity of over 7,000 barrels per day, this being the approximate minimum crude-oil capacity necessary to supply seven Dubbs units with cracking charge.

[76] Gustav Egloff, "The Price of Process Know-How," paper delivered at the Symposium on Cost in Chemical Development before the Division of Chemical Marketing and Economics, American Chemical Society, New York, September 14, 1954, p. 8; and W. Meredith Behrens, "Oil Industry," paper delivered before the Practicing Law Institute, *op. cit.,* p. 4.

[77] *Ibid.* The Dubbs process was the only major cracking process not controlled by the large oil companies, and UOP was the only process design company which sought the business of the small refiners. UOP therefore had little competition in this market. An improvement in refining margin in 1935–36 (J. G. McLean and R. W. Haigh, *op. cit.,* p. 118, Exhibit V-2) also stimulated licensing activity.

[78] *Ibid.*

[79] Universal Oil Products Company, *Prospectus,* February 4, 1959, p. 12.

process. It decided, as we know, that it could best retain its competitive advantage by keeping its know-how to itself and by refusing to license anyone who would sell cracked gasoline in its marketing area. Therefore, Indiana Standard, in order to maximize its profits from the manufacture and sale of petroleum products, restrained the licensing of the Burton process. UOP, however, was a process-development company, deriving its revenues entirely from royalties and the sale of technical service. The more widely the Dubbs process was installed, the greater would be the royalties. So UOP, in order to maximize its royalty income, encouraged in every way it could the widespread adoption of the Dubbs process. All of UOP's policies — the uniform royalty rate, which might have been less than UOP could have obtained from certain refiners but without which many of the smaller refiners would not have taken out a license, the "hold harmless" clause in the license agreement, the offer of technical assistance, and the continued improvement of the cracking process — were directly designed to encourage widespread adoption of the process. Had the Dubbs process been invented by a large company, these corollary features might well have been omitted from the over-all license, for they were of greater benefit to the small refiners with their limited financial reserves, legal and technical staffs, and operating skills than to large integrated concerns. Assuming that the large concerns would not have competed strongly with one another in licensing their own cracking processes, they would not have granted such liberal terms. As it was, beginning in about the middle 1920's, the competitive position of the small refiners rapidly grew worse as a result of the growing economies of large-scale operation,[80] the growth in the transportation of crude oil and products by pipe line,[81] and the increasing capital requirements of the new and complex refining processes.[82] But without UOP and the Dubbs process, the position of the small refiner would have become intolerable. UOP did help the small refiner to invest in the most modern cracking process.[83] When combined with special local situations, such as a readily available crude-oil supply (Texas and the midcontinent area), or a demand for specialized products (heavy fuel oil in California and solvents in Michigan), a few of the small refiners were able to survive.

[80] J. G. McLean and R. W. Haigh, *op. cit.*, pp. 567–575.

[81] *Ibid.*, pp. 186–188, 207–211; R. C. Cook, "Control of the Petroleum Industry by Major Oil Companies," TNEC Monograph No. 39, Washington: United States Government Printing Office, 1941, pp. 20–25, 37–39.

[82] *Ibid.*, pp. 553–556, 627.

[83] *Ibid.*, pp. 533, 611; the units referred to in these cases were most likely designed by UOP.

Later Contributions

Even after the purchase of UOP by the five major oil companies, the company retained its independent, and sometimes even belligerent, attitude. According to the terms of the sale of UOP, Halle was to stay on as president for fifteen years.[84] During this period the company continued to reflect the ideas and personality of its leader. He also kept up the pace of research and development, with the result that UOP's technical contributions since 1931 have probably been as significant to the industry and as valuable to the small refiner as was the Dubbs process.

The broadening of UOP's research activities can be traced back to 1927. In that year Egloff wrote a memorandum to Halle arguing that conventional heat and pressure cracking processes were swiftly reaching their maximum efficiency.[85] If UOP were to retain its competitive advantage in process design, it would have to initiate research in at least one of two new fields, catalysis and oxidation. Egloff listed two groups of scientists, one for each field, that he believed would be able to carry out a successful research program. Unable to afford two programs at once, Halle followed Egloff's recommendation and chose catalysis as the more attractive.

UOP then sought the best scientists, regardless of background. Egloff, in Europe for the World Power Conference in 1929, recruited Vladimir Ipatieff, the famous Russian scientist and expert in catalytic reactions. Ipatieff in turn brought to UOP several German scientists — one of whom was Hans Tropsch, the expert in synthesis.

These recruits were responsible for the development of processes achieving catalytic polymerization (1935) and catalytic reforming (1949). They also played a prominent role in the development of the Fluid Catalytic Cracking process (1942).[86] The company has continued to meet the needs of the small refiners by emphasizing economical design and construction of small processing units.

Changes in Ownership

In 1944, the owners of UOP — Shell, California Standard, Texaco, Jersey Standard, and Indiana Standard — set up the Petroleum Research Fund, which was to hold the UOP stock and whose income was to pass

[84] "Shell and Standard Buy Dubbs Process," *Oil and Gas Journal*, January 15, 1931, p. 65. Carbon P. Dubbs left the company in 1931. Mr. Dubbs is still living, maintaining homes in California and Bermuda.
[85] Interview with W. M. Behrens, December 28, 1955.
[86] See the early descriptive articles: V. Ipatieff and G. Egloff, "Polymer Gasolines from Cracked Gases," *Oil and Gas Journal*, Vol. 16, 1935, p. 31; "Platforming," *Petroleum Processing*, April, 1950, p. 351; E. V. Murphree, *et al.*, *Proceedings of the American Petroleum Institute*, Vol. 24, Part III, 1943, p. 91. UOP's contribution to the Fluid Catalytic Cracking process will be described in Chapter 6.

to the American Chemical Society to be used in sponsoring research in petroleum chemistry and chemical engineering.[87] The royalties which UOP's licensees paid were therefore returned to the refining industry in terms of additional research. Recently, the American Chemical Society, through the Guaranty Trust Company, the trustee, sold the stock of UOP to the public. The company thus reverted to its original status as an independent firm.[88]

UOP and the Dubbs Process

The Universal Oil Products Company is a company whose original aims were changed to the benefit of both itself and the firms in the industry it serviced. At its founding, UOP had the primary purpose of holding a series of patents, some of which were to provide supplemental protection to its parent company's holdings and the rest of which were to be the basis

[87] Several reasons might be advanced for this gift. First of all, in October, 1943, C. P. Dubbs's patent on "clean circulation" had been narrowly interpreted and Egloff's on "selective cracking" had been held invalid by the Supreme Court in a decision reached in the case brought by UOP against Globe Oil and Refining Company (Universal Oil Products Company vs. Globe Oil and Refining Company, 322 US 471–487; see Kendall Beaton, op. cit., footnote to p. 258). Since these patents were the major Dubbs process patents still in force, their being held invalid reduced UOP's prospects for future revenues from thermal cracking.

Second, on December 2, 1943, a civil suit had been brought against UOP by the executor of the estate of Macy Belle Hardison, the widow of a former stockholder in Jesse A. Dubbs's California venture, the Sunset Oil and Refining Company (Daily vs. Universal Oil Products Company, District Court, Northern District of Illinois, Eastern Division, 43C1162; decided November 26, 1947). The defendant appealed, but the suit (Daily vs. Universal Oil Products Company et al., 43C1162, decided September 15, 1948) was finally settled out of court. The plaintiff claimed that Jesse Dubbs had not had the right to sell his emulsion-breaking patent to Belknap and Armour, as Dubbs had previously given Sunset an exclusive license on an asphalt patent (No. 646,638) and any other patents that might be issued in relation to it (ibid., p. 343). The oil companies that now owned UOP assuredly did not relish being held accountable for something that happened long before their acquisition. Yet another suit, being tried before Judge Kaufman in Philadelphia, threatened to embroil the owners, innocent bystanders, in an unpleasantness.

Third, the petroleum research done by the American Chemical Society would be of considerable benefit to the owners of UOP in their role of petroleum processors.

Fourth, the owners of UOP were by now carrying out the bulk of their own research and development. UOP's future tended therefore to become tied to the smaller refiners. There was some fear that the Department of Justice was going to accuse the five majors, through their control of UOP, of monopolizing the cracking art. Certainly they did collect royalties from their competitors, small refiners who licensed the Dubbs process, and were open to the accusation of having their research subsidized by small refiners through the instrument of UOP. It could hardly have seemed wise to Shell, California, Texas, Indiana, and Jersey to own a process-development company so vital to the health of a different portion of the industry.

[88] Universal Oil Products Company, Prospectus, February 4, 1959. The total price to the public was $72,500,000; UOP's net worth therefore nearly trebled in the twenty-eight years of its ownership by the five major oil companies.

of a suit against Indiana Standard. Out of this suit, which looked more like a hold-up than a legitimate dispute between two firms, UOP hoped to obtain a large financial settlement.

The prosecution of its suit against Indiana Standard was considered at first to involve only legal activity, but after a while it was discovered that petroleum research and development would also be required in order to prove the viability of Jesse A. Dubbs's process. With this need for research were joined a timely $2,000,000 from J. Ogden Armour, an enterprising corporate manager in the person of Hiram J. Halle, and a vigorous engineer, Carbon Petroleum Dubbs.

When it was discovered that the company could benefit more by obtaining future royalties from its own process than it could ever hope to obtain by forcing Indiana Standard to relinquish past royalties, it began to promote the Dubbs cracking process. Halle's persistent and aggressive salesmanship provided several prospective licensees, but success was obtained only after original contributions by Carbon P. Dubbs and his colleagues. The failure of the No. 1 unit at Roxana forced Dubbs away from the direction of research followed by his father; he had to abandon his heritage before he was able to design an efficient cracking process. It literally took an explosion to alter his train of thought.

UOP licensed more than just a process; in its agreement with its licensees it provided economic, legal, and technical assistance in order to help the refiner in his actual operations. The company's action in providing these additional services was deliberate; as a process company, it had to rely completely on royalties, and therefore its success was determined by its ability to obtain as many licensees as possible.

In this era, the battle between competitive cracking processes frequently took place in the courts rather than in the market place. The value of a process seemed to be determined not only by its ability to carry out its function adequately but also by the number of underlying patents that the owner held. The mechanism of cracking was little understood, and a great deal of research was being done by engineers either as individuals or for corporations. As is common when natural phenomena are being discovered, numerous patent applications were filed with extremely broad claims. The patent office was generous in granting patents, and as a result there was much overlapping coverage. Since the returns from practicing the cracking art were large, there were distinct advantages in obtaining patent control. The disputants frequently turned to the courts, and the ensuing suits consumed large quantities of each firm's resources.[89] Research was greatly hampered by the arbitrariness of the system.

[89] In the decision in Universal Oil Products Company vs. Globe Oil and Refining Company (322 US 484), the court said, "In a process patent in the refining of oil,

A desire to avoid further legal strife was partially responsible for UOP's change in ownership in 1931. Even after the sale, however, UOP retained its customary independence, first through the steadfastness of its president, and subsequently through its autonomous status. The transfers of ownership made little change in the intensity of its research efforts. The success of the Dubbs process was repeated in subsequent inventions. The combined efforts of three men, one rich, the second enterprising, and the third inventive, brought about a lasting organization whose product was technological progress.

---

preciseness of description is essential. It is a crowded art. Hope for success for new patented processes with slight variations from those in use caused large expenditures in testing their efficiency by important companies with staffs of specialists who were skilled in the art."

3

THE TUBE AND TANK PROCESS

Aᴺᴼᵀʜᴱᴿ of the companies engaged in developing a continuous cracking process during and immediately after World War I was the Standard Oil Company (New Jersey). Jersey Standard's activities led to the successful introduction, in 1921, of the Tube and Tank process. Its research was carried out by the first group specifically organized for permanent research in the American petroleum-refining industry.[1] This separate corporate entity, originally named the Standard Development Company, and later the Standard Oil Development Company,[2] was created deliberately to provide an endless stream of new products and processes; it was the industry's first attempt to institutionalize innovation. In this chapter, we shall give the histories of both the Tube and Tank process and the Development Company and describe why and how they came about and what they accomplished.

The story rightly begins with the development of the Burton process. Although Jersey Standard's management, as constituted in 1911, was unwilling to install Burton units in the Whiting, Indiana, refinery of its subsidiary, the new management had begun by 1913 to comprehend the profitability of the cracking process. By this time, of course, Indiana Standard had made a commercial success of Burton's invention and was, by reason of its former owner's cavalier treatment, the sole owner of the process rights. Jersey Standard had to approach the inventors as a supplicant in order to share in the practice of the cracking art.

A Jersey affiliate, the Imperial Oil Company, Ltd., was the first to apply. Its president, Walter C. Teagle, wrote to President Cowan, Indiana's chief officer, within a month after the latter company had begun its sales campaign for "Motor Spirit."[3]

[1] The Royal Dutch/Shell group had initiated a research center in Amsterdam in 1919 (Kendall Beaton, *Enterprise in Oil: A History of Shell in the United States*, New York: Appleton-Century-Crofts, Inc., 1957, p. 505).

[2] In 1955 the company's name was changed to Esso Research and Engineering Company.

[3] George S. Gibb and Evelyn H. Knowlton, *History of the Standard Oil Company (New Jersey) 1912–1927, The Resurgent Years*. New York: Harper and Brothers,

Of the Jersey affiliates, Imperial was the company most in need of increasing its gasoline output. Its gasoline sales in Canada were greater than the capacity of its Sarnia, Ontario, refinery. Before the dissolution of the Standard Oil "trust," Imperial had supplemented the output of its own refinery with imports from Indiana Standard's refinery at Whiting. With the dissolution and resulting realignment of refineries and market areas, a supplementary source for products sold in Canada was less readily available.

[Standard Oil Company (New Jersey)]

Walter C. Teagle.

Teagle was therefore the likely person to appreciate the potentialities of the Burton process. By reason of his personality, his background, and his present status, he was well suited to the role of entrepreneur. Walter Teagle is a tall man, standing over six feet, with a remarkable memory and great energy.[4] Paramount among his qualities are an ability to grasp the economic implications of scientific advances and a masterful skill at

1956, p. 117. These authors investigated both the early history of the Tube and Tank process and the origins of the Standard Oil Development Company. Their work has been referred to frequently in writing this chapter.

[4] S. J. Woolf, "Character Sketch of Walter C. Teagle," *Oil and Gas Journal*, June 25, 1930, pp. 63, 146 Mr. Teagle is the subject of a biography currently being written by Professor G. S. Gibb of the Harvard Business School.

organization. He grew up in Cleveland, in a family which had long been in the oil industry: his maternal grandfather had been one of John D. Rockefeller's partners, and his father had owned a refinery which was subsequently acquired by Jersey Standard. After graduating from Cornell in 1899, he went to work in the industry. By 1913, at the age of thirty-five, he became the president of Imperial Oil Company, Ltd., and a director of the Standard Oil Company (New Jersey).

In his role as president of Imperial, Teagle was anxious to gain permission to operate the Burton process. In his role as a member of the board of directors of the Standard Oil Company (New Jersey), he was able to secure the technical advice and the support of the entire Jersey organization at the bargaining table. Starting in May 1913, he and Cowan discussed the terms of the license but were unable to reach a mutually acceptable solution until January 30 of the following year.[5] By dint of his persistence, Teagle succeeded in obtaining a reduction in the terms Cowan had originally asked, and Imperial signed the license agreement. For the rights to operate the Burton process, Imperial agreed to pay Indiana $15,000 a year. For all yearly amounts of gasoline in excess of 50,000 barrels, Imperial was to pay an extra 30¢ per barrel.

Imperial's agreement covered only the Canadian and European rights to the Burton process; the rights to operate in New Jersey, Maryland, and West Virginia were obtained the following year by Frederick W. Weller, director of the parent organization. An initial battery of forty Burton stills was built at the Bayway, New Jersey, refinery and was placed in operation by October 1915. In order to give assistance in starting up the units, Indiana Standard sent to Bayway some technicians from its own Wood River refinery. It is significant that these men should have come from Wood River rather than Whiting, where the first Burton stills were installed, for it indicates that by 1915 the men at Wood River were equally skilled in the practice of the cracking art. This was the period when Edgar M. Clark, the refinery manager at Wood River, was developing the tube-still unit.

By the spring of 1917, a total of 160 Burton units had been installed at Bayway, and, at the same time, construction was begun on 60 stills at the Baton Rouge refinery of the Standard Oil Company of Louisiana, another affiliate of Jersey Standard. These units added materially to Jersey's ability to manufacture gasoline. In 1916 about 10% of Jersey's domestic output of gasoline was in the form of cracked distillate; in 1917, with the total output of gasoline doubling, the proportion was 16%.[6]

[5] G. S. Gibb and E. H. Knowlton, op. cit., p. 118; also interview with Walter C. Teagle, October 18, 1955.
[6] G. S. Gibb and E. H. Knowlton, op. cit., Appendix 2, Table IX, p. 680.

In 1917, A. Colton Bedford became chairman of the board of the parent Jersey company, and Walter C. Teagle was made its president. Although they had a substantial investment in the Burton process, Bedford and Teagle watched with interest the research that was under way throughout the country on the development of a continuous cracking process.[7] In 1917, notes began to pass back and forth within the organization on the relative merits of batch versus continuous cracking, even though the latter was still in an experimental stage.

Establishing a Research Organization

Both 1917 and 1918 were difficult years for Jersey Standard's refineries. Because of the increased demand for petroleum products brought about by World War I, Jersey Standard ran its refineries at full capacity. But as it increased its refinery output, it became more dependent upon outside producers of crude oil.[8]

Since gasoline was now the major product, it was necessary to increase the yield of gasoline from a given volume of crude oil if Jersey Standard's own crude-oil supplies were to be economized. One potential source of motor gasoline was heavy gas oil, but this material was unsuitable for cracking by the Burton process. In addition the Burton stills could not handle charging stocks obtained from California and Mexican crude oils because of the high sulfur content and consequent corrosion. Yet these were the very crude oils which were most abundant.[9]

Since the Burton process could not crack the stocks that were most readily available, Jersey Standard decided it would have to discover and install a different cracking process. Discovery might well follow from research in any one of three directions. First of all, Jersey Standard could license some process other than the Burton. Secondly, instead of licensing an outside invention, it could employ scientists who could add their own knowledge and skills to the organization. Thirdly, by concentrating all its own research efforts upon cracking, it could attempt to use existing personnel to develop a process.

In 1917 and 1918, the first course was hardly practical. At that time, the Burton process was still the only commercial method of cracking petroleum; the research on the Dubbs, Holmes-Manley, and Cross processes had not been completed. To license an unproved process would not have been a wise decision.

To have followed the third course would have involved great risk, for

[7] *Ibid.*, p. 122; also interview with Walter C. Teagle, October 18, 1955.

[8] In 1919, Jersey Standard had to purchase from others 137,000 barrels per calendar day (bpcd) of the total 178,000 bpcd refined in its United States and Canadian refineries (G. S. Gibb and E. H. Knowlton, *op. cit.*, p. 410).

[9] *Ibid.*, p. 521; also interview with N. E. Loomis, March 31, 1956.

the inventive talents of Jersey Standard's technical men had never been tested. The few technically trained people Jersey Standard employed were primarily engaged in control work. At the refinery in Bayonne, Dr. Clarence T. Robinson, a chemist, and two assistants carried out servicing activities, mainly in the areas of crude-oil evaluation, investigation of complaints, and studies of chemical treating. The work of evaluating the different types of crude oil was quite demanding because all of the Jersey refineries were expanding and, with the shortage of crude oil after the beginning of the war, were charging more diverse types. Jersey Standard also had an inspection laboratory, directed by Dr. George Saybolt and staffed with twenty employees. The emphasis in this laboratory was on product control: refinery products were tested to make sure that they met quality standards, and testing devices and procedures were improved. Finally, there were ten technically trained men in the Engineering Division. These men had the duties of drawing plans for new installations and assisting in their construction.

The three technical groups had achieved little in process development. None of them felt any responsibility for promoting technological progress, and none was concerned particularly with refining processes; they concentrated rather on the product or the equipment. Their efficiency was judged mainly on their success in holding down the operating costs of existing equipment. They adhered strictly to their regular duties, fearing criticism if they departed, for several of the refinery managers were not oversympathetic to process research.[10] Finally, they had had little experience with patent administration and knew little of the complexities of the cracking art.

With little hope of success from following either the first or the third courses, Jersey Standard was forced to select the second, to hire people from outside its own organization. This course appealed to Teagle personally. Since Jersey Standard was the largest refiner in the country, its Burton process royalty payments to Indiana Standard were substantial, rising in 1916 to over $1,000,000 a year.[11] Teagle did not wish to pay royalties of a similar magnitude to yet another outside company in order to license a continuous cracking process.[12] Moreover, he was eager for Jersey to carry out its own research and development. Motivating him were an "interest in petroleum chemistry and . . . a far-ranging hope of fostering great technical progress in the industry, which he felt had been backward."[13]

[10] G. S. Gibb and E. H. Knowlton, *op. cit.*, pp. 124–5, 528.
[11] *Ibid.*, Table 19, p. 521.
[12] Interview with Walter C. Teagle, October 18, 1955.
[13] G. S. Gibb and E. H. Knowlton, *op. cit.*, p. 522.

The choice now facing Jersey Standard's board of directors was which scientists to hire. Teagle asked himself who was the outstanding man and answered Edgar M. Clark.[14] The refining men at Jersey Standard had observed his Burton operations and knew of his own improvements to the art. They were friendly with several of the Wood River refinery employees, who had informed them of his talent at managing a large organization. These three elements, experience in cracking, inventiveness, and entrepreneurial skill particularly recommended Clark to the Jersey company.

With the intention of hiring Clark, A. C. Bedford asked Dr. Burton to let him transfer his allegiance from Indiana Standard to Jersey Standard. Burton replied that under no circumstances could Clark be spared. Undaunted, Bedford approached Clark himself and found that he was willing to work for Jersey Standard. Thus late in 1918, Clark went to work as manager of Jersey's Bayway refinery at a salary of $18,000 a year. Teagle also hired two members of Clark's staff: Dr. N. E. Loomis, formerly a professor of physics and chemistry at Purdue, and J. R. Carringer, who had had much experience in refinery operation and in the cracking technique.

Clark's decision to move from Wood River to Bayway is fairly easy to explain. In the first place, the salary offered him by Jersey Standard was very attractive. In the second place, he was given free rein in his cracking experiments. While working for Indiana Standard he had written to Burton, his superior, letters whose tone indicated that he felt restricted in his research efforts. At Bayway he was given a much greater degree of independence. The Jersey Standard refineries were rather loosely organized, and each refinery manager enjoyed a large degree of autonomy.[15] Moreover, Teagle and the rest of the board of directors were extremely anxious that a new cracking process be developed and were willing to grant Clark and his assistants all the help that they needed.

For the development of a new cracking process, let alone for an entire program of technological development, Clark realized that Jersey Standard would need two other elements besides his own talents. The first of these would be a group whose members were familiar with patent law as it related to the problems of developing and licensing new processes. From his own experience at Indiana Standard, Clark had seen the complexity of developing a new process. If Jersey Standard were to avoid infringing on the patents of others and if it were to obtain a maximum return from licensing the process, it would have to have competent legal advice. At Indiana Standard the patent law firm of Dryenforth, Lee, Chritton and

---

[14] Interview with Walter C. Teagle, October 18, 1955.
[15] G. S. Gibb and E. H. Knowlton, *op. cit.*, pp. 34, 35.

Wiles had proved to be valuable counsel. Clark had been particularly impressed by a junior partner in the firm, Frank A. Howard. An engineer by training, Howard was well suited for legal work which required a knowledge of engineering. Clark asked him to represent the law firm in their relations with Jersey Standard.

With Howard, Clark discussed the second element that he felt was lacking in the Jersey Standard organization, outside technical assistance. Jersey Standard had consultants of its own, but Clark felt that they were not

[Affiliated Photo-Conway]

Frank A. Howard, 1944.

aware of the latest developments in the cracking field. He remembered two able scientists with whom he had been in contact while with Indiana Standard, Ira Remsen of Johns Hopkins University and Robert A. Millikan of the University of Chicago. In order to enlist their assistance, Clark channeled much of Jersey Standard's patent work to the Dryenforth firm, which was well suited to take care of patent matters and was able to act as liaison with the two consultants.

In one of his letters to the Bayway refinery manager, Howard suggested that Jersey Standard set up a permanent development department.[16] He argued that a large and wealthy organization desiring to carry out a program of research over several years should not trust its research activities

[16] *Ibid.*, p. 524.

to small groups of men in the various refineries — men who had current operating responsibilities which would always tend to have a higher priority than research, who would be divided in their loyalties between the refinery manager and the research head, and who were so scattered geographically as to make communication between groups extremely difficult. Howard believed that the process development group should be independent of the operating level and should have as its primary purpose the furtherance of technological progress. Such an organization could recruit men who wished to do research and, by providing an environment that was sympathetic to their needs, could encourage them to be their most creative. Clark was responsive to these ideas and showed Howard's letters to Walter Teagle.

The directors of Jersey Standard were in complete agreement with Howard's theories. Aware of the research which the federal government had felt it necessary to initiate during the war,[17] learning of the success of the Germans in their research efforts, listening to the promptings of the universities and technical schools, and seeing that several American companies, General Electric for one, had set up their own research organizations, Teagle recognized the advantages of a separate research and development staff.[18] He also feared that R. C. Holmes of The Texas Company, who was then directing a group of engineers engaged in developing a continuous cracking process, held the same beliefs, in which case what might once have been merely advantageous might prove a competitive necessity. He therefore encouraged Clark to enlist Howard's aid in planning a permanent research organization and by June 1919 had agreed in principle to Howard's suggestions. Bedford was informed of the action and added his support.

Howard was then hired to establish and administer the Development Department. Its primary function was to discover, test, and carry forward to the commercial stage ideas arising in the field of petroleum technology.[19] In general, it was expected that most of the original ideas would come from outside Jersey Standard, for Howard felt that their own resources could best be allocated to applying the ideas of others rather than fostering basic research. The department was divided into four groups: one to search for new ideas, a second to carry out process development, a third to supply laboratory facilities, and a fourth to administer patents.

[17] Bedford was chairman of the National Petroleum War Service Committee in World War I (*ibid.*, pp. 238, 239).
[18] Interview with Walter C. Teagle, October 18, 1955. A history of the General Electric Research Laboratory is given in Kendall Birr, *Pioneering in Industrial Research*, Washington: Public Affairs Press, p. 195.
[19] G. S. Gibb and E. H. Knowlton, *op. cit.*, pp. 525–529.

Members of the Development Department of the Standard Oil Company
(New Jersey) in January 1923. Beginning in the left foreground: Joseph
Conway, William Reif, Ross H. Dickson, Henry H. Hewetson, Philip L. Young,
A. A. Wells, Horace M. Weir, A. H. Tomlinson, Harold Sydnor, Charles
Johnson, John McGurk, James Simpson, Herbert Johnson, Robert Lebo,
H. G. M. Fischer, Jackson R. Schonberg, N. E. Loomis, J. A. Britton, Jr., M. D.
Mann, Frank Howard, C. A. Soars, D. L. Ferguson, C. F. Pester, and Joseph
Loefler.

Two consultants were hired, one of whom, Remsen, was already connected indirectly with Jersey Standard, and the other of whom, Warren
K. Lewis, was head of the Chemical Engineering Department at the
Massachusetts Institute of Technology. Remsen was paid $100 a day to
give advice on organic chemicals and Lewis $2,500 a year to advise on
problems in distillation. By February 1920 the Development Department
had fifty-five employees, and by the end of that year a total of $327,000
had been spent.[20] In a little over a year, therefore, Jersey spent half again
as much as the entire estimated cost of the Burton process development.

Evolution of the Tube and Tank Process

The emphasis of the Development Department's work was on continuous cracking; the result was the Tube and Tank process. "Certain features
of this process had already been worked out by Clark before he left the
Indiana Company to come to Jersey Standard."[21] But between the principles and the actuality, between the laboratory and the refinery, many

[20] *Ibid.*, pp. 526, 528.
[21] *Ibid.*, p. 533.

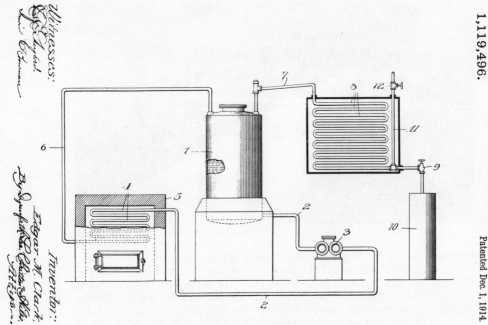

Illustration from E. M. Clark's continuous-flow patent.

barriers arose. Because of Jersey Standard's economic strength and its dedication to a long-range program of research, there was little fear that the development would be stopped because of lack of financing. Likewise because of the enterprise of Teagle, Howard, and Clark, there would be no shortage of inspiration and sustenance. But there were technical problems and legal pitfalls.

The technical problems arose out of the nature and variability of the cracking charge stocks. The first material selected for examination was the heavy, high-viscosity residual fuel derived from Panuco crude oil.[22] Since this Mexican crude oil was cheap and abundant, there was an incentive to process it in existing facilities. It could be distilled in the Jersey Standard's crude-oil stills, but the main product of the distillation was heavy residual fuel oil, which deposited a large amount of coke when it was cracked and therefore was not suitable as charge to the Burton units.

Clark conceived the idea that the Panuco oil might be used as cracking stock if it were permitted to yield fuel gas as well as gasoline.[23] A high yield of fuel gas would compensate for the low yield of gasoline to be expected

[22] Interview with N. E. Loomis, March 31, 1956.
[23] Ibid.; at the time Jersey Standard was selling fuel gas to the utility companies for the purpose of enriching water gas.

from cracking so intractable a charge stock. Clark and Loomis therefore applied their main efforts to cracking the residual fuel oil from Panuco crude oil. At Bayway, Loomis built a small cracking coil consisting of several horizontal banks of 2-inch tubes.[24] A pressure of 75 lb./sq. in. was maintained on the coil. The oil flowed continuously through the tubes and into a separator from which the gas and gasoline were drawn off as vapors. In order to keep the heavy, viscous charge stock from clogging the pipes, Loomis introduced steam into the flowing oil, much as was being done in the Greenstreet cracking process.[25]

To the surprise of the research team, they found that they were not only achieving a little cracking but that they were also reducing the viscosity of the fuel oil. By improving the flow characteristics of the fuel oil, they had made it more valuable as an industrial fuel. This technique of carrying out mild cracking in order to reduce the viscosity of the charge stock was named "vis-breaking."

By 1919, vis-breaking had been developed to the point where Jersey Standard had built one small commercial unit at Bayway, a few larger ones at Bayonne, New Jersey, and several more at the company's refinery at Tampico, Mexico, all to operate with Panuco fuel oil.[26] Their capacity was approximately 250 barrels of charge stock per stream-day, equal to that of a single Greenstreet coil.

At Bayway, J. R. Carringer suggested placing a drum 6 feet by 30 feet on top of the cracking coil, in order to increase the length of the time that the oil was kept at the cracking temperature.[27] Chemical equilibrium

[24] Ibid.

[25] The Greenstreet process was one of the first continuous cracking processes. (E. H. Leslie, Motor Fuels, New York: The Chemical Catalog Co., Inc., 1923 pp. 330–341). The pressure ranged between 75 and 150 lb./sq. in., and the temperature between 900 and 1200°F. The temperature was thus considerably higher in the Greenstreet process than in the Burton process, and as a result the oil was in a vapor phase when the cracking took place. The yield of gasoline was approximately equal to that obtained from the Burton process. Vapor-phase cracking never was very widely adopted because of problems of excessive coke formation in the cracking tubes, high consumption of steam, and poor gasoline quality (W. L. Nelson, Petroleum Refinery Engineering, 3rd ed., New York: McGraw-Hill Book Co., 1949, pp. 597, 603; also E. H. Leslie, op. cit., p. 332).

[26] Interview with N. E. Loomis, March 31, 1956; also G. S. Gibb and E. H. Knowlton, op. cit., pp. 533, 534. Bayonne refinery had been selected as the site for the bigger units because its crude runs were greater and therefore it could provide a larger volume of cracking stock. Unfortunately, a bad fire occurred in one of the Bayonne units, and as the Bayonne refinery manager had never been sympathetic to experimenting with the new process, the emphasis on research was transferred back to Bayway (ibid.).

[27] Interview with N. E. Loomis, March 31, 1956. Previously, the process group had tried adding a second coil in order to increase the residence time (interview with F. A. Howard, October 17, 1955), but a drum was cheaper to construct and easier to maintain.

was not reached during the time that the oil remained in the cracking tubes alone, so that adding the drum had the result of increasing the yield of gasoline.[28] At first, the drum was lightly fired, but soon Loomis discovered that the heat loss from the body of oil was not so great as to interrupt cracking.[29] Four cracking coils, with 4-inch tubes and with drums superimposed, were constructed at Bayway in 1920. These were operated at a pressure of 100 pounds and, like the earlier coils, charged 250 barrels per day.

At about the same time, Clark and Loomis realized that these coil and drum (or Tube and Tank) units, besides being able to process stocks which the Burton units could not handle, were superior to the Burton units in processing light gas oils. The superiority of the Tube and Tank units was discovered when the men in the process section of the Development Department began experimenting with cracking gas oil in the liquid phase.[30] In liquid-phase operation, the problem of coke deposit in the cracking tubes was reduced, although the operating pressure had to be increased so as to prevent the cracking stock from vaporizing. In a pilot plant, pressures up to 900 lb./sq. in. were applied. Most of the work was done at pressures between 200 and 250 pounds, however, for this was the range within which they expected the commercial units to be operated.[31]

With liquid-phase operation, the greatest difficulty encountered was the excessive formation of coke in the soaking drum. The heaviest oil would settle to the bottom of the drum while cracking took place and, in the final minutes of the reaction, deposit much coke. The process group had the idea of drawing off liquid from the bottom of the drum during the reaction, so as to remove the coke-forming material from the chamber. Although the bottom draw-off reduced the percentage yield of gasoline slightly, it increased the time that the equipment could be operated before

[28] For the same reason, E. M. Clark added a second reservoir to each of the Burton units at Bayway, giving them a double-domed appearance (ibid.; for the effect of time upon the yield of gasoline, see W. L. Nelson. op. cit., p. 583–585).

[29] Interview with F. A. Howard, October 17, 1955. In the laboratory apparatus, where the surface-to-volume ratio was higher than that in plant-scale equipment, it had been necessary to add heat to the drum in order to keep the cracking reaction going. To see that this relatively high heat loss did not persist as the size of the equipment was increased was a significant observation.

[30] Interview with Harold Sydnor, March 15, 1955. Working with Dr. Loomis in the process section were H. Sydnor, C. Soars, M. R. Meecham, A. Forman, H. Noel, R. H. Dickson, H. Hewetson, A. Tomlinson, and J. Britton. In the laboratory section under Dr. Robinson were H. Wier, H. D. Mann, J. Schonberg, and D. Ferguson (ibid.; also interview with N. E. Loomis).

[31] Interview with Harold Sydnor, March 15, 1955. Pressures above 500 lb./sq. in. had been opted by the inventors of the Cross process (E. H. Leslie, op. cit., pp. 373–378) and those below 100 fell within the range of Burton operations.

being shut down for cleaning. The increase in capacity more than compensated for the reduction in gasoline yield.

In its operation, the Tube and Tank process was similar to the Dubbs process. Gas oil was cracked in the steel tubes suspended in the furnace; the mass of oil flowed to an unfired drum where the cracking continued; the light cracked materials, leaving the drum in a vapor state, were fractionated, yielding gas, gasoline, and material to be recycled, and the liquid material became fuel oil.

By 1920, therefore, the development group had designed, built, and operated a small-scale unit which would process both light and heavy cracking stocks. From a technical point of view this flexibility was all to be desired, but the applicability of the process to cracking light gas oil made it susceptible to legal challenge. In fact, Howard's former law partner, Russell Wiles, who still represented Indiana Standard, had warned him that Jersey Standard's research and development would be likely to result in an infringement on the Burton patents. Heightened was "the danger — the inevitability, almost — that the work at Bayway would infringe upon one or more of the scores of patents that had already been issued." [32]

Observing the course of the patent litigation between the Universal Oil Products Company and the Standard Oil Company (Indiana), and knowing of the great amount of work that was being done to develop other continuous cracking processes, Howard thought it unlikely that he would be sued for infringement and so continued the experiments. But he took the precaution of strengthening Jersey Standard's legal position to make it at least as strong as any other single company's by purchasing the cracking patents of independent inventors. The most valuable acquisitions were the patents and applications of Carleton Ellis. [33]

Ellis was already well known to members of the Jersey Standard organization. While working for Dryenforth, Lee, Chritton and Wiles, Howard had purchased Ellis' patent rights on the hydrogenation of fatty oils for one of the meat-packing concerns. Clark and Robinson also knew of Ellis' research in the manufacture of alcohol from light petroleum cracked fractions. In 1915, Ellis had organized the Melco Chemical Com-

[32] G. S. Gibb and E. H. Knowlton, *op. cit.*, p. 533.

[33] *Ibid.*, pp. 534, 535. Ellis had a broad grasp of petroleum engineering and, with one colleague, wrote a textbook of the early processes. (Carleton Ellis and J. V. Meigs, *Gasoline and Other Motor Fuels*, New York: D. Van Nostrand, 1921.) Although he describes many of his own patents in the field of refining, Ellis does not dwell on his early work in pressure distillation, apparently feeling that it was not significant. He does, however, note the fact that a gasoline consisting primarily of unsaturated material is "more responsive to the throttle when used in an automobile, than a saturated gasoline" (*ibid.*, p. 25). He was therefore one of the first to notice the superior combustion characteristics of cracked gasoline.

pany, in order to produce alcohol. A factory was built in Bayonne, close to Jersey Standard's refinery. After observing the operation of Melco's pilot plant, Clark and Robinson purchased for Jersey Standard the patent rights to the process.

In 1920, however, Ellis was promoting neither the hydrogenation patents nor the alcohol patents but his early patents and patent applications in the field of distillation and cracking.[34] Ellis pointed out that the applications antedated Jersey Standard's own cracking patents. Moreover, he argued that the product claims covered the gasoline manufactured by the Burton process as well. Ellis was willing to sell his patents to Jersey for $225,000, which Howard at first thought to be a ridiculously high price.[35] Looking more carefully at Ellis' claims, which were based on experiments carried out over a period of several years prior to 1913, Howard changed his opinion of their worth. In December 1920, he told Teagle that Ellis' patents and applications would indeed cover all the cracked gasoline manufactured by Jersey Standard. This, of course, was Ellis' claim, and on this basis his fee was very modest. But Howard considered Ellis' patents to be even more strategic because they disclosed the principles which underlay the Tube and Tank process. Ellis was not aware of this coverage, and Howard feared that if he became aware of the value of his patents to Jersey Standard he would be certain to ask for more money. Howard therefore recommended that Jersey Standard purchase the patents immediately, giving Ellis the $225,000 that he desired.[36] Teagle accepted this recommendation, and a few weeks later, on January 18, 1921, the Ellis patent applications became the possession of the Standard Oil Company (New Jersey).

Although the acquisition of Ellis' patents gave Jersey Standard a relatively strong patent position, Teagle and Howard did not feel that all the legal difficulties of the Tube and Tank process had been solved.[37] As a tentative measure they decided to license two refining companies of their own choosing but not to solicit any additional licensees. The companies selected were the Beacon Oil Company, operating in Massachusetts, and

[34] Among the patents Ellis held or was subsequently granted were U. S. No. 1,249,278 (applied for April 29, 1913; issued December 4, 1917), 1,396,999 (applied for October 1, 1913; issued November 15, 1921), and 1,415,232 (applied for November 30, 1920, as division of application filed October 4, 1913; issued May 9, 1922). See E. H. Leslie, op. cit., p. 381; C. Ellis and J. V. Meigs, op. cit., pp. 277–280; and David McKnight, Jr., A Study of Patents on Petroleum Cracking, University of Texas Publication No. 3831, Austin, Texas: University of Texas, August 15, 1938, pp. 80–84.

[35] G. S. Gibb and E. H. Knowlton, op. cit., p. 535.

[36] Ibid.

[37] Ibid., p. 536; also interview with F. A. Howard, October 17, 1955.

the Owl Oil Company in Oklahoma.[38] The royalty rate charged these two companies was 10¢ per barrel of fresh feed stock, 5¢ a barrel less than the proposed royalty on the Dubbs process and approximately 7¢ less than the going Burton royalty. The first Tube and Tank unit was constructed at Beacon's refinery in Everett, near Boston, and went into service in 1921. Approximately 23,600 barrels of cracked gasoline were produced during the year.[39]

Few Tube and Tank installations were made in 1921 and 1922 for a number of reasons. The first Tube and Tank unit apparently did not yield so high a percentage of gasoline as had been hoped,[40] and hence had little to recommend it as a replacement for the Burton units. Besides, in 1922, Jersey had $20,000,000 invested in Burton stills, and in the recession following the end of the war these seemed adequate to take care of the immediate demand for gasoline.[41]

Personal antipathy to the Tube and Tank process was widespread in the Jersey organization. The majority of the company's refinery managers refused to accept the new cracking technique, preferring to operate the Burton process, with which they were familiar. Clark was not particularly tolerant of anyone whose views differed from his, and, in the course of promoting his own process, he had offended these men. Jersey's largest refinery, at Bayonne, had no Tube and Tank installation because the manager, W. C. Koehler, was not sympathetic to the ideas of the Development Department. At Baton Rouge, Louis Link, the refinery's able but egocentric manager, refused to accept continuous cracking, concentrating instead on his own research and development program of batch-type units. The Baytown refinery of the Humble Oil and Refining Company, newly opened in April 1921, had been equipped with Burton stills in spite of their imminent obsolescence. The decentralized nature of the Jersey refining organization and the support of Charles G. Black, the chairman of the Manufacturing (refining) Committee, aided these men in their persistent efforts to avoid installing Tube and Tank units.

The organizational structure of Jersey Standard was partly responsible for the widespread disagreement.[42] Operating for the most part as separate corporate entities with memories of former independence, scattered geographically, and facing different local conditions, the refining managers

---

[38] G. S. Gibb and E. H. Knowlton, op. cit., pp. 535, 536. Beacon was subsequently acquired by Jersey Standard.

[39] J. H. Westcott, Oil, Its Conservation and Waste, 4th ed., New York: Beacon Publishing Co., 1930, Table 62, p. 129.

[40] In 1921, only 14.2% gasoline was recovered from the charge stock (J. H. Westcott, op. cit., p. 128). In contrast, the maximum gasoline yield on Burton stills was above 30%.

[41] G. S. Gibb and E. H. Knowlton, op. cit., p. 536.

[42] Ibid., pp. 526–533.

did not function harmoniously. The responsibility for co-ordinating the refineries fell to the Manufacturing Committee, composed mainly of the refinery managers, which was supposed to translate the general policies enunciated by Jersey's board of directors into action. As manager of the Bayway refinery, Clark was a member of the Manufacturing Committee, as well as having the additional duties of analyzing operating problems and presenting his solutions to Jersey's board. Unfortunately, even after becoming a member of the board in 1920, Clark did not enjoy their complete confidence.[43] The Development Department also suffered from the confused pattern of responsibility and authority. Some of the refinery managers thought it was a division of the Manufacturing Department, others an appendage of the Bayway refinery. Few were informed of its aims and progress, and able to evaluate its achievements. Before 1927, when Jersey Standard was reorganized, the strength of the Development Department lay mainly in the personal vigor of Teagle, Clark, and Howard.

The Bayway refinery, under Clark's personal direction, therefore became the center of the continuous cracking operations in the Jersey organization. Late in 1922, three Tube and Tank units were placed in operation at Bayway, and by the end of the following year three more units had been installed.[44]

Profitability of the Tube and Tank Process

It is now possible to compare the profitability of the Tube and Tank process with that of the improved Burton process.[45] Based on processing similar raw materials,[46] the Tube and Tank units yielded 39.0% gasoline on charge, compared with 41.3% for the Burton units (see Appendix Table 8). Although the yield of gasoline from the Tube and Tank unit was lower, the yield of middle distillates, some of which could be treated and sold as kerosene, was considerably higher, 36.0% compared with 10.7%. Finally, the Tube and Tank units had a lower output of heavy fuel, producing only 15.0% on charge compared with 40.6% for the Burton units. Neglecting the possibility of producing kerosene, the prod-

[43] *Ibid.*, p. 528.

[44] Standard Oil Company (Indiana); W. M. Burton, W. W. Holland, and R. E. Wilson, "Comparison of the Burton vs. Tube and Tank Process," *Whiting Lab Report*, April 11, 1923, p. 3.

[45] *Ibid.*

[46] The Standard Oil Company (Indiana) was charging a midcontinent light virgin gas oil of approximately 32° API gravity to their Burton-Clark tube stills (*ibid.*). The raw material for the Tube and Tank units was also a midcontinent (80–90%) virgin gas oil of 30.5° Baumé (equivalent to 30.7° API) gravity (*ibid.*, also interview with N. E. Loomis, March 31, 1956).

uct revenues were $3.54 from a barrel of gas oil processed in the Tube and Tank units and $3.69 in the Burton units (Appendix Table 9).

The processing costs, including royalties, of the two cracking units were approximately equal, $2.63 per barrel of charge for the Tube and Tank compared with $2.71 for the Burton (Appendix Table 12). The Tube and Tank unit economized on fuel but consumed more labor. Subtracting costs from revenues, we obtain a profit per barrel of cracking charge of $0.91 for the Tube and Tank Unit and $0.98 for the Burton unit (Appendix Table 13).[47]

On the basis of processing equal quantities of raw material, the Burton units would still be the more profitable, but such a calculation would not take into account the main advantages of the Tube and Tank units: first, that they could crack heavier charge stocks, and, second, that they had a larger capacity. Because of a lack of data on cracking fuel oils, we cannot calculate the value of the first advantage, but we can state the quantitative improvement that resulted from increasing the capacity of cracking plants. In 1922 a Tube and Tank unit could process 570 barrels of gas oil per calendar day, whereas each Burton unit could only handle 221 barrels per day. Since the capital cost of a Burton unit was 50% of the Tube and Tank and its capacity only 39%, its profit per dollar of investment was less, 180% per year compared with 210%. Capital invested in a cracking unit would therefore be recovered more quickly if Jersey Standard's new process were incorporated.

Summarizing, on the basis of raw material processed, the Tube and

[47] For the Burton process, this is equal to 5.7¢ profit per gallon of gasoline. If we look at Appendix Table 14 from which the estimated annual average profit per gallon of gasoline for all Burton cracking operations can be derived from profit per unit of charge, we find the figure for 1922 to be 3.1¢. At first it might seem improbable that in this one test the profitability of operating the Burton process would be nearly twice the average profitability of all the units over the year. There are, however, two reasons for this better-than-average showing: First, the Burton unit selected for the test was a tube bubble-tower unit, the most efficient variation of the Burton process. Only a small percentage of all the Burton units in operation in 1922 were tube bubble-tower units; the majority were of the older shell-radiator design. Therefore 3.1¢ per gallon is the average of the lower figure for the shell-radiator stills and the higher figure for the tube bubble-tower stills. Secondly, the charge stock used in the comparison between the Burton and the Tube and Tank process was one very amenable to cracking. It yielded 41.3% gasoline per gallon of charge, which was far greater than the average from the many charging stocks used in the regular operations. In 1922 it was the custom to charge to the Burton units not only light virgin gas oil (the sole charging stock in 1913) but also large amounts of heavy naphtha (that fraction just lighter than gas oil). Heavy naphtha was harder to crack, and the cracking cycle took longer because of the slower cracking rate (Standard Oil Company [Indiana], W. M. Burton, W. W. Holland, and R. E. Wilson, *op. cit.*, p. 34). Instead of obtaining 41.3% gasoline from each gallon of charging stock as they did during the comparison, the best that Indiana could obtain on the regular charging stock was 31.7% (*ibid.*, Table 1).

Tank process was less profitable than the Burton; on the basis of capital invested, it was more profitable. The margin between the two cracking processes was not wide. Apparently when a new process fulfilling approximately the same functions as an existing one is introduced, there is at first little to choose between the two. If a firm decides to invest in the new process, it will usually be on the basis of future prospects, which will be reflected in subsequent installations but may not accrue to the initial one. The first commercial unit could be regarded as a tryout of the drama of process development. When the equipment of the unit is designed, the process is complete, as a play is complete when the author has written the last word. But the merits of the work can only be judged when it is given a performance. The analogy can be carried further: subsequent performances will improve upon the first, and, if successful, the work will become part of the established repertoire.

The first installation of the Burton process would not fit this analogy, however, for there was nothing resembling it in the refining industry at the time. The Burton process was like a new art form, departing radically from the past and utilizing an entirely new medium. The innovation in the Burton process was the utilization of pressure so that gas oil might be used as a raw material in the production of gasoline. In other words technological progress broadened the definition of the inputs to gasoline manufacture. To the extent that the Tube and Tank process was able to crack stocks heavier than gas oil, it too provided innovation.[48] Moreover, the Tube and Tank development, as ultimately perfected, permitted the same factors of production used in the Burton process to be combined in a more efficient manner.

The Legal Struggle over Cracking Patents

Although Jersey Standard proceeded with caution in installing the Tube and Tank process, it advanced with alacrity in proving that the process had incontestable patent backing. On May 12, 1922, three days after Ellis' patent No. 1,415,232 was granted, Jersey brought suit against the Pure Oil Company, which was using the Cross process.[49] The owner of the Cross process, Gasoline Products Company, did not have the financial resources necessary to fight such a suit. Forced to obtain outside assist-

---

[48] Both the Burton and the Tube and Tank processes yielded higher-quality products, although this additional result was not appreciated until several years after their introduction.

[49] G. S. Gibb and E. H. Knowlton, *op. cit.*, p. 550. Jersey Standard and Pure Oil had clashed before, during the 1890's, when the two companies were competing bitterly in the domestic and export markets (J. G. McLean and R. W. Haigh, *The Growth of Integrated Oil Companies*, Boston: Harvard Graduate School of Business Administration, 1954, p. 70).

ance, Gasoline Products, in June 1922, began talks with The Texas Company, which had just introduced the Holmes-Manley process.[50] On January 26, 1923, these two companies created a patent pool.

The Standard Oil Company (New Jersey) now faced the united opposition of Gasoline Products Company and The Texas Company, and, because of an earlier pooling arrangement, the Standard Oil Company (Indiana).[51] In its suit with Pure Oil, the Standard Oil Company (New Jersey) thus faced not one but four adversaries. Through their agreements Jersey Standard's opponents had created a powerful legal and technical alliance. They seemed quite willing to fight the battle in the courts, and each could have been counted upon to have put all of its resources into the struggle, for at stake were all the royalties from cracking, representing millions of dollars. But several incidents occurred which so changed the situation that the battle was never fought.

The first of these incidents provided Jersey Standard with an unexpected but extremely powerful legal weapon. On the advice of one of Teagle's business friends from his native city of Plainfield, New Jersey, George T. Rogers offered his assistance to Jersey Standard. Rogers had formerly been a partner of Joseph H. Adams, whose patents underlay Texaco's continuous cracking process, at the time when Adams was doing his early experiments in distillation.[52] Rogers had lent his partner $5,000 in 1907, in exchange receiving a share in the process amounting to 40%. Shortly after that he and Adams had separated.

Howard thought that it would be worth while for Rogers to sue Texaco on the basis of his contractual relationship with Adams in order to see what information the action would reveal.[53] Jersey Standard was to back Rogers' action and in return for his claims paid him the sum of $50,000. At first, the Jersey company did not reveal its own interest in the case. Texaco responded by offering Rogers $10,000, which was immediately refused. As the suit progressed, Jersey Standard's role came to light.

When the decision was published on June 5, 1923, by the Appellate Division of the Supreme Court of New York, it was obvious that Jersey

[50] Named Holmes-Manley after two of Texaco's refining executives, the process is described in E. H. Leslie, op. cit., pp. 366–368.

[51] The Texas–Indiana Standard patent pool was established in an agreement on August 26, 1921 (G. S. Gibb and E. H. Knowlton, op. cit., p. 548). The agreement had been mutually advantageous, for Texaco had not yet perfected its own cracking process and Indiana Standard was happy to benefit from the technological advance. (See P. H. Giddens, Standard Oil Company [Indiana]: Oil Pioneer of the Middle West, New York: Appleton-Century-Crofts, Inc., 1955, pp. 257–259.)

[52] The patents relating to the Holmes-Manley process are discussed in David McKnight, Jr., op. cit., pp. 65–78. Adams' patent applications preceded Burton's and Ellis' although like Dubbs's they were altered during the course of their voyage through the Patent Office (ibid., p. 68).

[53] G. S. Gibb and E. H. Knowlton, op. cit., pp. 551, 552.

Standard had won. The decision contained four main points, startling in their breadth and grave in their significance. First, Texaco was bound by the Adams-Rogers agreement. Second, Rogers (and therefore Jersey Standard, since it had purchased Rogers' claim) was entitled to 40% of all the revenues received by Texaco under its cracking patents. Third, in their original agreement Adams had stated that he would not use his inventions without Rogers' consent. Since this consent had not been obtained, the use of Adams' inventions in the Holmes-Manley process was a violation of contract. All the licenses issued were also violations of Rogers' right. Fourth, Indiana Standard, because of its agreement with Texaco and because it had taken licenses under the Adams patents, was liable to Rogers (that is, to Jersey Standard) for 40% of its profits from cracking. This was interpreted to mean that it was liable for the patent royalties and operating profits from all of the cracking processes (not just the Holmes-Manley but the Burton process as well) for the entire time that these had been in use. Indiana Standard, however, would not have borne such a staggering judgment because in their agreement in 1921 Texaco had warranted the Adams patents. In the event that the rights to the Adams patents were questioned, and the decision was certainly clear on this point, Texaco was ultimately responsible.

At this point, the Jersey Standard's managers were faced with a momentous decision. They could have instituted a suit against Texaco and Indiana Standard, in order to recover the past royalties due to Rogers, with every likelihood of success. This would clearly have been followed by another, directed by Indiana Standard against Texaco, in which Indiana would attempt to relieve itself of the responsibility of Rogers' claim. Since the sums involved were enormous, a favorable decision for Jersey might well have the ultimate result of putting Texaco out of business.[54]

Under these circumstances, Texaco would be fighting for its life. A long and costly suit in the courts was inevitable. There was a possibility of great winnings for Jersey Standard, were it to be successful, and a certainty of large legal expenses regardless of the outcome.

Another certain result of the suit would be a great deal of ill will directed at Jersey Standard. Should the Jersey company win, it would receive royalties from the operation of three processes — the Burton, the Holmes-Manley, and the Cross — in whose development it played no part. It was hardly in Jersey Standard's interest to appear in the light of the sole collector of royalties from the oil industry's cracking processes.[55]

If Howard and Teagle had not had these views on their own part, they

---

[54] We recall that in the ten years following the introduction of the Burton process, Indiana made profits of about $100,000,000.
[55] Interview with F. A. Howard, October 17, 1955.

would certainly have them forced on them by public opinion. First of all, there was dissatisfaction with Jersey Standard's role in its initial suit against the Pure Oil Company as the operator of the Cross process.[56] Any claims arising from the suit would have to be paid by the Gasoline Products Company, the owner of the Cross process. Despite his backing, Walter Cross, one of the developers of the process, admitted that the assets of Gasoline Products Company would be sorely taxed in meeting the damage claims asked by Jersey Standard. It would have looked as if Jersey Standard were trying to prevent outside firms from entering the refining industry.

The public was kept aware of the altercations between the petroleum refiners by the LaFollette Committee, which was investigating concentration in the petroleum industry.[57] The committee seized upon every opportunity to discredit the large oil companies, particularly Jersey Standard. In giving testimony, E. M. Clark had admitted that Jersey was suing the Pure Oil Company in order to give notice to the rest of the industry that it would attempt to prevent further installations of the Cross process.[58] To the legislators, and to the public with the memories of the Standard Oil "trust" still fresh in their minds, Jersey Standard was still the ogre of the industry.

A second factor responsible for public antagonism to the Jersey company was the rise in gasoline prices which followed World War I.[59] With the widespread fear that because reserves of petroleum were being exhausted rapidly, gasoline prices would rise, the public was quick to attribute the major blame for the shortage to Jersey Standard. Jersey's management was therefore forced to decide whether or not to promote the suits against Texaco, Indiana Standard, and Gasoline Products in an atmosphere of public hostility.

To Howard, carrying the suit to completion or dropping it entirely were not the only alternatives; there was also a possibility of negotiating a settlement with the disputants.[60] Politically, this would have the advan-

[56] G. S. Gibb and E. H. Knowlton, op. cit., p. 550.

[57] U. S. Senate, Committee on Manufactures, 67th Congress, 4th Session, Report No. 1263, "High Cost of Gasoline and Other Petroleum Products," March 3, 1923.

[58] G. S. Gibb and E. H. Knowlton, op. cit.; Jersey was not the only company to warn the refining industry against installing cracking plants. On October 5, 1922, Indiana Standard sent to all the independent refiners letters "threatening action without further notice . . . to . . . independent refiners . . . operating processes involving pressure . . . warning them that the Standard owns the Burton and other patents." (Testimony of Russell Wiles, attorney for the Standard Oil Company [Indiana], quoted by Paul Truesdell, "Standard Attorney Says Nothing Was Basically New in Burton's Patent," National Petroleum News, Vol. XIV, No. 41, October 11, 1922, pp. 21–22.)

[59] U. S. Senate, op. cit., p. 63; see also Appendix Table 2.

[60] Interview with F. A. Howard, October 17, 1955.

tage of being quick and quiet. Economically, it would have the advantage for Jersey Standard of ending its obligation to pay royalties on the Burton units which it was still operating. In the eight years that Jersey and its affiliates had been licensed under the Burton process, the company had paid approximately $8,000,000 in royalties. Unless the royalties ceased, an average yearly payment of $1,000,000 would be necessary until Jersey could replace all the Burton stills with its own Tube and Tank units.

Moreover, because of the overlapping patent claims, not even Jersey Standard's Tube and Tank process could be considered perfectly protected. Just as Jersey Standard was able to sue Gasoline Products Company on the basis of the Ellis patents, so Indiana Standard might well sue Jersey on the basis of Burton and Clark's inventions. A negotiated settlement, in which each company's patents would be respected, would leave Jersey Standard free to install the Tube and Tank process in its own refineries and to promote it among other refiners.

Since all highways leading toward the federal courts were hazardous, a clear path in the other direction seemed more attractive. On this basis, Howard recommended and Teagle approved entering into negotiations with their adversaries. The companies first met together in the summer of 1923, and within the period of a few weeks had settled their differences. On September 28, 1923, Texaco, Indiana Standard, Jersey Standard, and Gasoline Products signed an agreement which permitted "a limited exchange [of licenses] giving to each party the opportunity to proceed with the logical development of his own method without interference from others." [61]

The agreement among Texaco, Indiana, Jersey, and Gasoline Products not only cleared up their own problems but also freed other refineries from any fear of investing in new cracking facilities. [62] The rest of the industry rejoiced, for the suits had shown "the impossibility of straightening out, by ordinary court procedure, the tangled skein of conflicting patents." [63] Installations went ahead rapidly, and within two years the output of cracked gasoline had nearly doubled (see Appendix Table 1a). The agreement thus promoted competition in refining by making the cracking process available to all. Because firms without cracking were afraid of jeopardizing future earnings and because companies which had developed

[61] U. S. vs. Standard Oil Company (Indiana) et al., 283 U. S. 163, Petitioners' Book of Exhibits, Agreements Nos. 72 and 74 between Jersey Standard, The Texas Company, and Standard Oil Company (Indiana), September 28, 1923; as quoted in G. S. Gibb and E. H. Knowlton, op. cit., p. 553.

[62] The only company which had vigorously promoted its invention during the period of legal strife was Universal Oil Products.

[63] Paul Truesdell, "Suit to Annul All Basic Cracking Patents Would End Confusion That Retards Progress," National Petroleum News, Vol. XIV, No. 37, September 13, 1922, pp. 17–18.

new cracking processes were unwilling to license their inventions, few cracking plants had been installed between 1919 and 1923. In spite of the fact that several continuous cracking processes had been developed by 1921, the Burton process continued to provide most of the cracked gasoline until the settlement. Since the Burton process had been licensed almost solely to the former members of the Standard Oil "trust," the cracking facilities were still concentrated in the hands of the various Standard Oil companies. The only independent oil company with ample cracking capacity was Texaco. As late as 1924, three firms alone produced about 80% of all the cracked gasoline in the United States.[64] After 1924, however, the rest of the industry, particularly the large integrated firms, began to catch up.[65]

The Department of Justice did not rejoice at the formation of a "patent club." On June 25, 1924, it filed suit in the Federal Court for the Northern District of Illinois against Indiana, Texaco, Jersey, Gasoline Products, and forty-six other corporations. The government claimed that the agreements constituted a combination in restraint of trade in violation of the antitrust laws, Specifically, it challenged the validity of many of the patents, the legality of the patent-pooling agreements, and certain other

[64] The individual companies and their shares of the output of cracked gasoline in 1924 were:

Company	%
Standard Oil Company (Indiana)	34.82
Standard Oil Company (New Jersey)	24.29
Texaco	21.94
Subtotal	81.05

(G. S. Gibb and E. H. Knowlton, *op. cit.*, pp. 554, 555.)
Other companies with significant output of cracked gasoline were:

Company	%
Pure Oil Company	5.5
Standard Oil Company (Ohio)	3.7
Continental Oil Company	1.5
Standard Oil Company of Kentucky	0.9
Subtotal	11.6
Total	92.7

(J. H. Westcott, *op. cit.*, pp. 231–241.)
These percentages may be overestimated, however, for the figure used for the industry's total output of cracked gasoline was questionable. The hearing examiner in the cracking-patents suit refused for this reason to accept the above percentages as evidence.

[65] By 1938, Jersey's share of the industry's cracked gasoline output had declined to 10.2%; Indiana's and Texaco's to 9.0% each (R. C. Cook, "Control of the Petroleum Industry by Major Oil Companies," *TNEC* Monograph No. 39, Washington, D. C.: Government Printing Office, 1941, Chart VIII, p. 72).

agreements between single members of the "patent club" and their licensees regarding market territory. Late in 1927, the master taking the testimony exonerated the defendants.[66] The District Court reversed the decision, declaring the agreements to be in restraint of trade.[67] The companies appealed to the Supreme Court, which in April 1931 in turn reversed the decision of the District Court and found for the defendants.[68] The court felt that removing the fear of legal action for adopting new cracking processes was beneficial to all enterprising refiners, large or small.

On the whole, this decision ended most of the conflicts over patents in the cracking art. The legal altercations had occupied fifteen years, from 1916, when UOP initiated its suit against Indiana Standard, until 1931, when the Supreme Court brought in its decision.[69] During the first seven years of this period, resources which otherwise might have been put into the development of the cracking art went into legal squabbles. Those companies most fitted by means of their experience and economic power to carry out the research in cracking were either embroiled in the controversy or, like scavengers, standing hopefully outside the fray. Those companies which did not have the talent necessary to carry out the research were denied the opportunity to license the new and profitable refining processes. The consuming public, purchasing gasoline in ever greater quantities, was faced with steadily rising prices.[70] In part the conflict over patent rights was the result of competition between the various refiners. In part it was the result of granting an extremely large number of patents in the area of cracking by the patent office. The decade following 1910 was one of great activity in research on cracking, and many significant process inventions were made. Since the problems faced by those doing research in cracking were similar, it was natural that many of them should come up with the same answers. The patent office had the responsibility of deter-

[66] United States vs. Standard Oil Company (Indiana), et al., Report of Honorable Charles Martindale, Master in Chancery, pp. 351–384.

[67] Standard Oil Company (Indiana) et al. vs. The United States of America, Transcript of Record, District Court for the Northern District of Illinois, Eastern Division, 1930 (33 F. [2d] 617).

[68] Standard Oil Company (Indiana), Standard Oil Company (New Jersey), Standard Development Company et al. vs. The United States of America, Supreme Court of the United States, October Term, 1930, No. 378 (283 US 163–183).

[69] A few suits were initiated after 1931, principally by Universal Oil Products Company and the Standard Oil Company (Indiana). These were directed primarily against a process development concern, the Winkler-Koch Engineering Company (David Knight, Jr., op. cit., pp. 112–113). The bulk of this litigation ended with an agreement between UOP and the other licensing companies on December 1, 1937 (ibid., p. 113).

[70] Gasoline prices rose from 1915, when a gallon of gasoline at retail cost approximately 13¢, through 1920, when a similar gallon cost 28.5¢. Between 1920 and 1933, however, with the increase in cracking capacity, gasoline prices exhibited an equal decline to 12.4¢.

mining which of the inventors should have prior claim. In some cases the patent office seemed to bestow the rights promiscuously. The decision in the conflicting Dubbs-Behimer applications for the hot-oil pump is an instance of this. In other cases, and these seem more prevalent, the patent office seems to have granted two or more patents with almost identical claims. For example, broad patents covering the use of pressure in cracking were given to Burton, Dubbs, Ellis, Adams, and others. It was proper that the oil companies should turn to the courts for an interpretation of the claims, but given the existing network of patents it seemed impossible to carry out this adjudication without disrupting the industry.

Process Improvement

After the patent-pooling agreement, Jersey Standard began to install more Tube and Tank units at its various refineries. By the end of 1926, Jersey and its affiliates had 118 units in operation and another 46 under construction. Eighty per cent of Jersey Standard's output of cracked gasoline now came from the Tube and Tank units.[71] The charging capacity of all the Tube and Tank units installed in the refineries of Jersey Standard and its licensees was 260,100 barrels a day in 1926; by 1936, it had grown to 407,600 barrels a day.

While Jersey Standard's refineries were busy constructing and putting into operation new Tube and Tank units, the Standard Oil Development Company continued its research on continuous thermal cracking. By 1923, the original complement of the Process Development Division, under Dr. N. E. Loomis, had increased in size by at least nine men. Since they were located at the Bayway refinery and under Clark's jurisdiction, close to the scene of the actual refinery operations, the employees of the Development Division were always aware of the potential applicability of their research.

Their combined efforts in cracking research were toward higher pressures and better heat utilization. There were two incentives for cracking at higher pressures, now permitted by the cross-licensing arrangements of the cracking pool. Of first importance was the indirect effect of pressure in permitting higher cracking temperatures. The higher the pressure, the higher the temperature that could be retained in the coil without vaporization of the oil; and the higher the temperature, the faster the rate of cracking.

In the Burton process, the operating pressure had been approximately 95 lb./sq. in. since shortly after the initial operation of the units. The first to use higher pressures were Walter M. and Roy Cross, who built their

[71] G. S. Gibb and E. H. Knowlton, *op. cit.*, Appendix 2, Table IX, p. 680. David McKnight, Jr., *op. cit.*, p. 79.

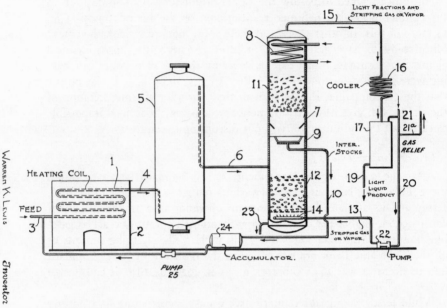

Illustration from W. K. Lewis' process improvement patent.

initial units to operate at 600 lb./sq. in.[72] With the example of the Cross process to spur them on, the process development group worked concertedly on utilizing higher pressures.

The second stimulus to the work in high pressures was their effect upon the quality of the cracked gasoline produced. Howard knew of Kettering's experiments on gasoline quality at General Motors and had reproduced some of them at the Bayway laboratory.[73]

High pressures were tried first in the laboratory. There it was found that the higher the pressures, the greater the yield of gas and fuel oil, products of less value than gasoline. The higher the pressure, however, the better the antiknock characteristics of the gasoline. Most important, at higher pressures, the rate of cracking was much more rapid. When the laboratory materials finally permitted it, experiments were made at pres-

[72] The Cross brothers were able to achieve this high pressure by careful construction of the furnace and by the use of a forged reaction chamber, 40 feet long and 40 inches in diameter, with walls 3 inches thick. These forgings were made from a single ingot by the Midvale Steel and Ordnance Company, using the same techniques that it had applied to the manufacture of naval guns (E. H. Leslie, *op. cit.*, p. 375).

[73] G. S. Gibb and E. H. Knowlton, *op. cit.*, p. 540.

[*Esso Research and Engineering Company*]

Two Tube and Tank units at the Camden works of the Standard Oil Company (New Jersey), Parkersburg, West Virginia, September 1926.

sures as high as 3000 lb./sq. in., and it was found that at these very high pressures the yields became stabilized.[74] In the refineries, pressures of 250 lb./sq. in. were used at first, although by the 1930's they had been raised to 1000 lb./sq. in.

Simultaneously, research was carried out on the problems of heat transfer, both in furnaces and in heat exchangers. The cracking temperature within the body of the oil was approximately 700°F. in the Burton process. With the higher pressures that accompanied the development of continuous cracking, the temperatures were built up to between 875 and 925°F. At the Baton Rouge refinery of the Standard Oil Company of Louisiana, experiments at still higher temperatures were carried out in a furnace designed by Professor H. C. Hottel of M. I. T. Utilizing thermocouples set in the oil stream at the outlet of the coil, the research group increased the combustion until the oil temperature reached 975°F. and the tube temperature 1100°F. This was the highest temperature that could safely be attained, for at temperatures above 1100°F. the strength of carbon steel

[74] Interview with Harold Sydnor, March 15, 1955.

tubes drops to about 1000 lb./sq. in. and the tubes are liable to rupture. The temperature ceiling was therefore set by the characteristics of the existing type of structural material.

Besides increasing cracking temperatures, the process-development group, aided by consultants such as Hottel, expended considerable effort on improving furnace design so as to reduce the cost of fuel. Except for the material itself, fuel was the most expensive input. Many furnace designs were developed so that it became possible to build efficient heaters for both general and specialized application.[75] Of all the development work being carried on, this caused most displeasure among the refinery managers.[76] Recognizing the danger inherent in elevating temperatures and conscious of their responsibility for providing safe working conditions, refinery managers were not happy to see higher temperatures used in experiments, let alone in standard operations.

Apart from the furnace, heat was transferred at several other spots in each cracking unit. Some of the product streams were condensed, and all were cooled, sometimes with water and sometimes by giving up their heat to incoming charge stocks. The engineers began to calculate the extent to which it was economical to recover this heat. To be sure, there was a cost involved in heat recovery, namely the cost of constructing and maintaining the heat-exchange equipment, and a balance had to be struck between fuel saved and equipment expense. A calculating method was derived, which took into account both the physical variables (such as the difference in temperature between the two fluids and the rate of heat transfer) and the economic variables (such as the cost of heat-exchanger surface, the cost of repair, and the cost of fuel) to determine the optimum size of the heat exchangers at the customary rate of return on investment.

These experiments in the transfer of heat made it obvious that large amounts of fuel were wasted when the recycle stream was cooled from approximately 620°F. to 150°F.[77] The recycle stream had to be cooled because the pump which forced it through the furnace was not able to withstand high temperatures in the circulating fluid. Like other groups working on continuous cracking, Jersey Standard's engineers therefore turned their efforts toward the development of a hot-oil pump. The first pump tried was a push-pull pump, similar to the one used by Dubbs. The disadvantage of the push-pull pump was that it leaked continually. The process-development group tried every type of packing available, but came to the decision that a radically different type of pump would have to be

---

[75] For a description of the different furnace designs, see W. L. Nelson, *op. cit.*, pp. 525–528.
[76] Discussion with Professor H. C. Hottel, M. I. T.
[77] Interview with Robert Shepardson, March 15, 1955.

invented. About 1928, the news spread that Weiss, a German concern, was working on a centrifugal pump. Weiss's design was adopted by the Pacific Pump Company, a manufacturer of deep-well pumps in California. In 1929, Pacific centrifugal hot-oil pumps were installed in both the Cross and the Tube and Tank units and proved satisfactory.[78]

Once hot-oil pumps had been installed, the capacity of the cracking units could be increased considerably. The capacity had been limited by the ability of the furnace to raise the oil to the cracking temperature. Inserting the hot-oil pump eliminated the recycle cooler, with the result that the furnace no longer had to make up for the heat lost in cooling the recycle stream. Since the ratio of recycle to fresh feed was approximately 3 to 1, and since the temperature drop in the cooler had been approximately 500°F., the increase in fresh feed obtained was considerable. From a capacity of 570 barrels of gas oil a calendar day in 1922, the capacity of the original Tube and Tank units was raised to 900 barrels merely by the addition of the hot-oil pump.[79]

The development group, now aided by a formidable engineering staff, designed new Tube and Tank units to operate at higher pressures. In 1928 units were built which would operate at 750 lb./sq. in. These were designed to charge between 3,000 and 4,000 barrels a day, but within a few years were being operated at from 7,000 to 8,000 barrels a day.[80] Soon after, the pressure was raised still again to 1,000 lb./sq. in. The first cracking units to operate at this high pressure were installed at the Montreal refinery of Imperial Oil Company. Four 1,000-pound pressure units were also installed at the Bayway refinery approximately two years later. Like the 750-pound units, these cracking units were also designed to charge approximately 3,500 barrels a day. In subsequent years they were increased in capacity to approximately 6,000 barrels a day. The increase here was not so sizable as had been obtained in the 750-pound Tube and Tank units, probably because the units were not so overdesigned as the earlier ones had been. In the few intervening years, the engineers who designed cracking units had learned much about the performance of their equipment and therefore were able to keep closer tolerances.

Returns from the Tube and Tank Innovation

As we did for the Burton and Dubbs processes, we have attempted to measure the cost and profitability of the Tube and Tank innovation.

[78] Interview with Harold Sydnor, March 15, 1955.

[79] The later figure is based upon a total feed charge of 10,000 gallons per hour, of which approximately one-quarter was fresh feed (interview with Robert Shepardson, March 15, 1955).

[80] Design was stated in terms of 17,000 gallons per hour of total feed, of which 35% was fresh charge. The throughput later achieved was 35,000 to 40,000 gallons per hour (ibid.).

First an estimate of the cost by years, from 1918 through 1957, was constructed.[81] Research and development costs rose from about $9,000 in 1918 to a maximum of $180,000 in 1922, diminishing gradually from then on. The total for the forty-year period was $2,364,000. Legal costs and the purchase of patents consumed $460,000 between 1918 and 1923, and $663,000 thereafter, for a total of $1,123,000. All costs associated with the Tube and Tank innovation, therefore, came to $3,487,000.

Compared to the cost of development, the revenues that accrued to Jersey Standard were substantial. The estimate is nearly $300,000,000 (see Appendix Table 16), or over $80 for each dollar invested in research and development. The estimate is conservative on two counts: it assumes that Jersey Standard's own Tube and Tank units returned an amount equal to the royalty rate Jersey charged others; and it makes no allowance for any royalties or operating profits after 1942, although the estimate for that year was over $7,000,000.

On two other counts, however, the estimate is not conservative. First, it assumes that the Tube and Tank units were always operated at full capacity. Second, it assumes that all licensees paid the full royalty rate, which may not have been the case for members of the "patent club."

Returns rose each year from 1921 until 1932, when they reached a plateau of about $34,800,000 a year. The reduction in royalty rate in 1934 resulted in one decline, and the second reduction in 1938 resulted in another. When in the 1940's catalytic cracking began to supplant thermal cracking, estimated royalties and operating profits dropped still further, to the point where today they are negligible.

Even if we make allowance for a return on capital invested in cracking equipment, there is no doubt that the Tube and Tank development was extremely profitable. It was not so magnificently profitable as the Burton process, to be sure, but still it rewarded the Jersey company handsomely for its endeavors, and encouraged all other firms in the industry.

In summarizing the development of the Tube and Tank process, we find that the result was not one innovation but two. The first was the process itself. Beginning with the ideas of one inventor, Edgar M. Clark, the Standard Oil Development Company developed a continuous cracking process. After the initial installations had been made, Jersey Standard turned the talents of its substantial research organization to the improvement of the process. The end result was an efficient thermal cracking process, continuous in nature, with extended on-stream time, adaptable to operation in large-scale equipment, and capable of processing a wide

[81] J. L. Enos, *The History of Cracking in the Petroleum Refining Industry; The Economics of a Changing Technology*, unpublished Ph.D. thesis, M. I. T., June 1958, Chapter III, Tables 6, 7, and 8.

variety of raw materials. By the end of the 1920's, it was possible to charge any one of a large number of heavy oils to the cracking units and to take from them as products fuel gas, heavy fuel oil, and a light distilled product which required only slight chemical treatment to make it into a finished motor gasoline.

By the mid-1920's the quality advantages of cracked gasoline were becoming appreciated. In 1925, with the building of its "Red Flash" engine, Chrysler increased the compression ratios of its cars so as to utilize this higher-quality fuel. As compression ratios were further increased, improving still further the performance of the vehicles, the oil industry was called upon to turn out ever larger quantities of cracked gasoline.

The emphasis upon cost reduction led the Standard Oil Development Company to improve the design of the Tube and Tank units to take advantage of economies of large-scale operation. One by one, the main bottlenecks — inefficient furnaces, the lack of a hot-oil pump, inadequate fractionating equipment, and weak structural materials — were overcome. Although the development of improved pieces of refinery equipment would normally have been within the province of the equipment suppliers, the oil industry found that it had to take part in the auxiliary inventions, either through ownership or through contributions to research.

One result directly sought was the increased capacity of the individual cracking units. For the first time the minimum cost units were larger than a small refiner could afford. The Burton unit in its most advanced stage had a capacity small enough to be integrated with ease into the operations of a refiner charging as little as 500 barrels of crude a day. By 1928, however, 8000-barrel-a-day Tube and Tank units had been installed, and these could be supported only by a refinery charging more than 20,000 barrels of crude a day. In the late 1920's, few independent, or nonintegrated, firms had refineries capable of charging so large an amount. As a result, cracking capacity in large units tended to be concentrated in the major oil companies. In 1930 the independent refiners could claim 19.5% of the industry's total crude-oil capacity and 14.7% of the total cracking capacity. By 1935, their share of total cracking capacity had decreased to 9.3%. The major reason for their relative decline was the large addition to cracking capacity made by the major oil companies during these five years.[82] Partly as a result of their inability to install the latest cracking units, many of the independent refiners either left the industry or merged with the larger companies.

For the companies that could install the large units, cracking was a profitable operation. But, like the Burton process during the latter years of its reign, so the continuous cracking processes also returned a smaller

[82] J. G. McLean and R. W. Haigh, op. cit., p. 701.

average profit as time went on. The average profit per barrel of gas oil charged to the Tube and Tank units in 1922 and 1923 was 91¢. By 1938, the profit on a similar charge stock had decreased to 19¢.[83] The same trend is observed in the return on investment in cracking units. In 1922 and 1923, the yearly profit from operating a new Tube and Tank unit amounted to 210% of its capital cost; by 1938, it had diminished to 26%.

The continuous-cracking unit of 1938 was in all respects more efficient than its predecessor. It consumed less of each of the factors of production — raw material, fuel, labor, and capital — in manufacturing each gallon of motor gasoline. Yet it was less profitable to operate by almost any standard. The years chosen could explain part of the difference, because 1922 and 1923 were more prosperous for the oil companies than 1938.[84] But a greater part of the decline in the profitability of cracking could be explained, I believe, by the increase in competition within the refining segment of the industry in general and by the adoption of the cracking processes in particular. Before 1923, cracking was practiced by only a few companies. But the introduction of many continuous-cracking processes, the end of the patent litigation, and the widespread licensing that followed reduced the concentration of cracking facilities and promoted competition.

Although by 1921 the development of several continuous-cracking processes, the Tube and Tank among them, had advanced to the stage where they could be installed commercially, the morass of patent litigation kept things at a standstill for at least two more years. Because the basic patents underlying the cracking process had been granted with little regard to overlapping claims and because each company developing a process was eager to obtain the maximum benefits, not only from the application of its own techniques, but also from the application of its own principles in the processes of other firms, these companies spent large amounts of resources — legal, technical, and financial — on promoting their claims. It was only when the quantity of money involved became huge and the risks tremendous that the companies were forced to reach a settlement, forming a patent pool. The agency for settlement was not the formal mechanism of the court but informal negotiations between the interested parties. The

[83] See Appendix Table 13. The calculation for 1938 is based upon charging a virgin gas oil, 32° API, to a new (1938) Holmes-Manley cracking unit of 6,750 bpcd capacity. By this date, all thermal cracking processes were essentially identical (W. L. Nelson, *op. cit.*, pp. 605–609), and so a comparison of the Holmes-Manley with the early Tube and Tank unit is valid.

[84] The rate of return on net worth for the petroleum industry was 6.3% in 1923 and 4.9% in 1938 (American Petroleum Institute, *Petroleum Facts and Figures*, 9th ed., p. 442). An equivalent figure for 1922 is not available, but the experience of the Standard Oil Company (Indiana) and of McLean and Haigh's sample of companies (*op. cit.*, Exhibit V-15 and V-16, pp. 140–141) suggests that profits in 1922 were higher than in 1923.

public was not represented in the decision, and the government through its antitrust division questioned its legality. By then, however, the decision was beyond the public grasp although not beyond the public concern. Part of the blame for the tangled patent situation must be laid upon the patent office for its naïve acceptance of similar claims on the part of many of the inventors in the cracking art.

The second innovation carried out in the United States by Jersey Standard was the deliberate creation of a permanent research and development organization. Of those concerns which were engaged in research on a continuous cracking process, only two made a further contribution. Gasoline Products Company went out of existence when the Cross process became obsolete. Texaco did little in the area of cracking after developing the Holmes-Manley process. Indiana Standard did nothing. A similar fate befell all the other less successful inventive groups. Of the two remaining companies, Jersey Standard and Universal Oil Products Company, UOP's research activities were not to be considered a lasting feature until the concern had been in existence for several years. Although UOP later broadened its base and contributed widely to petroleum technology, its continuity at first was more a matter of good fortune than of deliberation. The sole American continuum was Jersey Standard's research group, the Standard Oil Development Company.[85]

This organization was not responsible for the genesis of the Tube and Tank process, but it did promote its development and most of the improvements. The Development Company also supplied the process with its title. Howard had noticed the effect of attaching to a joint effort the name of the one man most responsible for the creation. Although the Burton process bore the name of W. M. Burton, several other inventors had made significant contributions. Yet the majority of the credit went to Burton, and to Howard's mind this was in part responsible for the dearth of scientific activity at Indiana Standard following 1916. Similarly the Holmes-Manley process was the development of at least three men. Here most of the honor went to R. C. Holmes, again to the misfortune of nearly all concerned. Howard was therefore determined that Jersey Standard's new process should not bear the name of any individual. He hoped that with a generic name for the process, each man taking part would feel that he had played a vital role in its creation. In addition, as cracking technology became more complex, the numbers of scientists and engineers involved in research, development, operation, and improvement increased; as a result each individual's contribution became more difficult to meas-

---

[85] Shell's activities in Amsterdam continued, and its later successes compensated for a slow beginning.

ure. In Burton's time four or five men were able to carry out an innovation; by the mid-1920's many times that number were required. Specialists, such as mechanical, chemical, and construction engineers, physicists, chemists, refinery operators, lawyers, and managers all became necessary. With specialization came anonymity, at least as far as the outside world was concerned. Only within a group of scientists working toward a common goal could each individual's performance be recognized. Better a certain recognition than a problematical fame.

The Standard Oil Company (New Jersey) made two major innovations, the first a refining process, and the second a research organization. The Tube and Tank process provided the company with a profitable manufacturing technique. The research organization, the Standard Oil Development Company, provided a constant source of new ideas and developments, assisting the company in attaining its long-run goal of continued vitality and growth.

4

THE HOUDRY PROCESS

Even the advocates of thermal cracking recognized that subjecting the charge stock to high temperatures and pressures was, as Dr. Egloff of United Oil Products said, "a brutal way to treat hydrocarbons." In 1910, when Burton and Humphreys were working on the first thermal cracking process, they were aware that catalysts could accelerate the rate of reaction. But twenty-five years elapsed before Eugene J. Houdry, a French engineer, developed the first successful catalytic cracking process. The history of the Houdry process is the story of three companies and two continents. But above all it is the story of the imagination, enterprise, and persistence of one individual.

Eugene Houdry

Eugene Jules Houdry was born in Domont, near Paris, on April 18, 1892.[1] He received an engineering education at the École des Arts et Métiers, where he achieved an outstanding record both in his studies and in sports. Houdry's father, a wealthy manufacturer of structural steel, was anxious to have his son join the firm. After gaining some practical experience, Houdry was made a partner, responsible for engineering.

Three years later, in 1914, Houdry was called into military service. He began his training in the Artillery Corps, but after war broke out transferred to the French Tank Corps — *l'Artillerie d'Assaut*. One of the original members of that new fighting arm, he took part in the first battle in which tanks were employed. Later, at the Battle of Juvincourt, on April 16, 1917, he was seriously wounded. For his heroism in action, he was awarded the *croix de guerre*, with a citation for "having organized the repair of the disabled apparatus on the battlefield under heavy fire and in spite of particularly difficult conditions."

With the signing of the Armistice in 1918, Eugene Houdry returned to the family business, now Houdry and Son. In addition to his regular

---

[1] "Pioneer," *Catalytic News*, Houdry Process Corporation, April, 1944, pp. 1–5. The following data on Houdry's background came from this article and other biographical material collected by the Houdry Process Corporation, and from "Monsieur Houdry's Invention," *Fortune*, February, 1939.

duties, he became the director of several other companies; one, significantly, was a manufacturer of automobile parts. He seemed well on the way to success in the industry.

His main interests, however, lay in different fields. He was intensely patriotic, and he was fascinated with auto racing, particularly its technical aspects. In combination with an overwhelming curiosity, these interests were to dictate the course of his life.

[Houdry Process Corporation]

Eugene J. Houdry, 1948.

Racing puts great demands upon an automobile. It is a testing ground for present models which shows up defects that under normal conditions would become visible only after many thousands of miles and many months. Improvements in mechanical design are frequently tried out in racing vehicles on the course before being incorporated in new models of standard cars. It has long been the custom for European automobile manufacturers to use the major races as a means of popularizing their *marques* and testing their designs.

While visiting the United States in 1922, Houdry attended the 500-mile Memorial Day Race at Indianapolis and inspected Ford's assembly plant in Detroit. He was impressed by the fine construction of the automobiles and by the poor quality of the fuels they used. Houdry felt that further advances in engine design could not be made until a better fuel was found. He saw that progress in the field of automotive design was dependent upon simultaneous advance in the field of petroleum technology.

There was yet another force tending to interest Houdry in motor fuels: his desire for a stronger France. France's resources of motor fuel were inadequate. As an operator of a tank and as an observer of the increasingly strategic importance of the airplane, Houdry realized that in time of war great quantities of gasoline were necessary for national survival. France therefore had vital need of an indigenous supply of motor fuel. Houdry recognized that he could do a great service to his native land if he could develop an acceptable motor fuel from her natural resources.

Research in Catalysis

Also influencing the direction of Houdry's research was an earlier investment he and his father had made in a catalytic process for synthesizing gasoline. During and after World War I, many European scientists had tried to make liquid fuel out of abundant raw materials, particularly bituminous coal. In Germany and in France several alternative methods were tried; the low-temperature distillation of coal, the destructive hydrogenation of coal or lignite or of oils derived from these two raw materials, and the hydrogenation of carbon monoxide were the chief processes investigated. A group working in Italy in 1922 on the hydrogenation of carbon monoxide, the so-called water-gas synthesis, caught Houdry's attention. This work had been proceeding under the direction of a French chemist, E. A. Prudhomme. The Prudhomme process utilized nickel and cobalt catalysts to promote the reaction between carbon monoxide and hydrogen. The liquid hydrocarbons synthesized were, from all of Prudhomme's reports, an excellent motor fuel.[2] Houdry bought into the syndicate, hoping to profit when the process was used on a commercial scale.

As time went on, the chances that Prudhomme's process would be perfected seemed progressively slimmer. Rather than write off the investment as a total loss, Houdry and his father decided that they would take over its development. Houdry made a complete break with his profession, his business, and his many entrepreneurial activities, and devoted himself entirely to research in catalysis.

[2] Oil companies, investigating Prudhomme's process, were struck by the lack of conformity between his claims and his results. The Standard Oil Development Company found in making a material balance between the input and products from Prudhomme's equipment that the publicized yield of motor fuel was considerably higher than that actually obtained. (Interview with F. A. Howard, former president, Standard Oil Development Company, March 15, 1955.)

"According to Houdry, 'Prudhomme always thought of the catalysts as little animals. By putting a little gasoline in with them, he thought he could give them the right idea—help them along.'" ("Monsieur Houdry's Invention," *op. cit.*, p. 130.)

A man of great enthusiasm, his natural inclination was to throw himself completely into the project. He was well suited for the task: his experience in automotive design enabled him to recognize a superior motor fuel, and his background in mechanical engineering helped him in designing and fabricating the complex equipment needed in the cracking plants. Finally, his financial resources, and those of his family, were adequate to support an active development program for several years.

Thus committed, Houdry set out to gain assistance. Scientific aid came from three friends who had been trained as engineers. Alfred Joseph, a graduate of the École Polytechnique, was his chief collaborator, Eugene Dinorie, a graduate of the École des Mines, was the second, and René Le Grain, a civil engineer, was the third. On February 8, 1923, these men formed a process-development firm, whose aim was to produce motor fuels through the chemical processing of lignite.

Houdry himself started to study the chemistry of hydrocarbons and built a laboratory in Beauchamp, Department of Seine-et-Oise, in which he could conduct his own experiments. At this laboratory, he and his associates tested the Prudhomme process, and found that it was not so promising as they had originally believed. Varying the process, they attempted to obtain a motor fuel by distilling lignite and carrying the gaseous product through two other steps, one of which involved the use of dehydrogenating catalysts.[3]

Whatever the interest he may have had in the laboratory itself, Houdry's other activities — the formation of the syndicate, the establishment of a commercial company, and subsequently the disclosure of the potentialities of the process to the French government — forced him to spend most of his time as a promoter rather than an experimenter. In 1927, three years after the formation of the company and beginning of research, the French government agreed to investigate the lignite process. A favorable report from the Commission des Mines led to an official recognition of its merit. Since the laboratory experiments and pilot-plant operations at Beauchamp had been favorable, the French government directed that a larger pilot plant be built at St. Julien-de-Peyroles, Gard, France. The operation of the plant was demonstrated in 1929 and, as far as the chemical aspects of the process were concerned, was a success. The cost was very high, however.

[3] The reactions were probably of the following nature:

$$\text{lignite} \underset{\text{heat}}{\rightleftharpoons} CH_4 \text{ (methane)} + \text{other hydrocarbons}$$

$$2\,CH_4 \underset{\substack{\text{heat,}\\\text{catalyst}}}{\rightleftharpoons} C_2H_2 \text{ (acetylene)} + 3H_2$$

$$3\,C_2H_2 \underset{\text{polymerization}}{\rightleftharpoons} C_6H_6 \text{ (benzene)}$$

[E. J. Houdry]

Houdry's pilot plant at Beauchamp, France, 1925.

Although the French government had tentatively agreed to subsidize the operation, the amount of subsidy required turned out to be much greater than planned. The government withdrew, the plant at St. Julien was shut down, and lignite was abandoned as a raw material.

Fortunately, the emphasis had not been entirely upon producing gasoline from a suitable raw material. The phenomenon of catalysis had also intrigued the group. Catalysis might not solve the problem of producing gasoline from lignite, but it might be useful when applied to other raw materials. An obvious choice of raw material was crude oil, then as now the chief source of liquid hydrocarbon fuels. The fear of a worldwide shortage of crude oil, which had been widespread in 1909, in Burton's time, gripped Europe after the war. To be sure, thermal cracking had increased the yield of gasoline from each barrel of crude oil. But even this was not satisfactory, because the demand for higher-quality motor gasoline at the existing price was increasing faster than additional motor gasoline could be produced by the thermal cracking process. Even though it would not utilize a native raw material, Houdry realized that a process which would produce a larger yield of gasoline from a given amount of crude oil would have great merit. Two years before the experiment at St. Julien, Houdry had therefore broadened the scope of his research to include transforming crude oil into gasoline by the use of catalysis.

In 1925, when the work on the catalysis of crude oil and its fractions began, next to nothing was known about catalysts themselves. The only two well covered in the literature were the hydrogenating catalysts and aluminum chloride, but these retarded the cracking reaction. The activity of certain metals in the iron group, such as nickel, cobalt, and iron itself, were recognized; these, too, were useless to Houdry, for their principal effect was to set free large quantities of carbon, which adhered to the catalyst and destroyed its effectiveness. This experience with catalysts tended to frighten away many researchers in the field.

But Houdry persisted. A successful catalytic process, he realized, would require a catalyst which could promote the cracking reaction and which could be maintained at a high level of effectiveness. The first part of the problem was to find a suitable catalyst. The second part was to discover a way to keep its effectiveness from diminishing.

In his search for a catalyst Houdry was persevering. Hundreds of different materials, chosen at random, were tried. Some had no effect upon the crude stock. Others showed some catalytic activity, but because the quality and yield of the gasoline were less than that obtained from thermal cracking, they were abandoned. The experiments proceeded much the way those of Edison had, forty years before, when he was trying to find a suitable filament for the electric lamp. Substance after substance was tested, only to be rejected along with the hope that had accompanied it.

After three years of this empirical activity, the fortunes of Houdry and his associates changed. Houdry frequently remained at his apparatus twenty-four hours a day, sleeping on a cot in the laboratory. At three o'clock in the morning of a day in April 1927, he discovered that one of the units charging a low-grade heavy crude oil was producing a clear distillate. Packed in the reaction chamber was a catalyst composed of oxides of silicon and aluminum.

The distillate was motor fuel whose quality and yield were sufficiently high to meet Houdry's most optimistic hopes. The catalytic gasoline was subjected to the two simple tests. Its color stability and gum-forming tendencies were checked by hanging bottles of the gasoline on a clothesline in back of the laboratory. There, by the changes in temperature brought about by the pattern of day and night, the cracked gasoline was found to be acceptable. The second test was the strategic one: the performance of the motor fuel in an automobile engine. In Houdry's Bugatti the cracked gasoline was compared in operation with that of racing quality already on the market. On a long hill close to the laboratory, where the greatest demands on the gasoline were made, the catalytic gasoline performed well.

Now that Houdry had found a suitable catalyst he turned to the second part of the problem — maintaining its effectiveness. During the cracking reaction the deposit of carbon on the silica-alumina pebbles grew thicker as the reaction progressed. The coating reduced the contact between the catalyst and the raw material. As contact was reduced, so was the catalyst's ability to promote the reaction. In order for the catalyst to be regenerated, the carbon would have to be removed.

How to remove the coating of carbon was the question. Houdry conceived of the simplest answer: burn it off. If the reaction chamber were evacuated of hydrocarbons and air admitted instead, the carbon would be oxidized. Burning the carbon off did not damage the catalyst, and it seemed to offer the additional advantage of bringing the process more nearly into a heat balance. The cracking reaction is endothermic, that is, it requires heat; whereas oxidation is exothermic — it liberates heat. Regenerating the catalyst, therefore, provided some of the heat consumed in cracking. Catalyst regeneration, technically necessary, proved also to be economically attractive.

Houdry Process Corporation

It was not in Houdry's nature to let the results of these experiments go unnoticed. He publicized the information widely, and within a year began to receive inquiries from companies in the oil industry. In the experiments in the manufacture of gasoline from lignite, which the French government had just initiated, Houdry depended upon public support. Now, for his catalytic cracking of oil Houdry felt that he could attract the private firms that processed crude oil.

Among the first to visit Houdry's laboratory at Beauchamp were representatives of the Anglo-Persian Company, the Royal Dutch Company, and the Standard Oil Company (New Jersey). These companies submitted their own charge stocks, which were catalytically cracked. In spite of the fact that a high yield of a new type of gasoline could be produced, none of the companies showed much interest in the process. There were two reasons. First, many major problems of the design and construction of the commercial equipment had not been solved: the cycles of operation had to be established; heat-transfer problems, which arose particularly during the regeneration of the catalyst, had to be solved; specialized equipment for the catalytic portion was needed; and the catalyst had to be manufactured on a large scale. Second, a competing process, hydrogenation, which had been developed by Bergius at I. G. Farben and which had received worldwide publicity, seemed to many to have more promising possibilities.[4]

[4] Jersey Standard, and later several other oil companies, chose to concentrate on hydrogenation (see Chapter 6).

Although confident of the ultimate success of his invention, Houdry was finding it increasingly difficult to justify further experiments. Six years, from 1923 to 1929, had been spent on research without any visible returns. A large share of his family's, and even his wife's family's, wealth had been consumed.

The stock-market crash in 1929 gave every evidence of being followed by a business recession. This might well produce a reduction in the demand for crude petroleum and its products, and therefore a lessening interest in the attainment of greater yields of gasoline from crude oil. Research with this aim was therefore increasingly difficult to finance. Since he had been unsuccessful at obtaining aid from French or even European companies, Houdry shifted his emphasis to America. At the Vacuum Oil Company he received a warm reception.

[Shelburne Studios, Socony Mobil Oil Company]

Harold F. Sheets.

The European representative of the Vacuum Oil Company in 1930 was Harold F. Sheets.[5] Impressed by the results of the laboratory experiments, Sheets persuaded his company to take out a license on the Houdry process. In order to get more detailed results and to demonstrate the process to the management of the company, he asked Houdry to bring his laboratory

[5] Sheets became the vice-president of the Socony Vacuum Oil Company (now Socony-Mobil Oil Company) and subsequently the chairman of its board of directors.

apparatus to the United States. Accompanied by a close associate, Raymond Lassiat, Houdry arrived in New York in October 1930 and immediately set up his equipment at the laboratory of the Vacuum Oil Company in Paulsboro, New Jersey. From then on, the United States was to be the scene of all his activities.

The next year, Houdry and the Vacuum Oil Company formalized their relationship by establishing the Houdry Process Corporation; Houdry and his French associates took two thirds of the stock, Vacuum the remaining third. Houdry was appointed president.

Gone were the days when Houdry's activities were mostly those of the entrepreneur. Although he was the head of the research company, Houdry spent all his time on laboratory experiments. In the early days of his work

[Houdry Process Corporation]

Houdry pilot unit at refinery of Vacuum Oil Company, Paulsboro, New Jersey (early 1930's).

at Paulsboro, he lived in a bricklayer's home close to the laboratory so as to be able to be present at any hour. After several months, the work was expanded to the pilot-plant stage, and Houdry and Vacuum Oil increased the total complement to fifteen men. During the three years, 1930–1932, that the research was carried out at Paulsboro, the main efforts were directed at cracking gas oil. Because they formed smaller amounts of coke on being cracked, hydrocarbons boiling in the gas-oil range could be processed more easily than heavier hydrocarbon fractions.

During the development stage the depression deepened. Vacuum Oil reduced the amount of capital to be spent on research and new equipment. This cutting back in research effort was felt particularly by Houdry and his associates. The pilot-plant results were not very promising, for the gas oil proved resistant to cracking. Consequently, the American backers lost their enthusiasm. In 1931, shortly after the formation of the Houdry Process Corporation, the Vacuum Oil Company merged with the Standard Oil Company of New York. As a result of the merger, there was a reshuffling of administrative duties among the top personnel of both companies. Just at the time when Houdry's research was in jeopardy, his main supporters became responsible for different activities. For some time it looked as if the fate of the lignite development was to be repeated.

Sun Oil Company

Houdry, his faith unshattered, was not willing to drop the work. Since Socony-Vacuum would not provide more funds, he decided to obtain financial assistance outside. So, once again, as he had done in Paris in 1928, Houdry started to canvass other oil companies. It was only after two years and several unsuccessful attempts that Houdry was able to find another backer. Two astute engineers and administrators, Arthur E. Pew, Jr., and Clarence H. Thayer, saw the potentialities of the process, and their company, the Sun Oil Company, joined with Houdry Process Corporation. In entering the management of the process company, Sun was authorized to buy one third of the total stock. This portion came entirely from the two thirds held by Houdry and his associates, so that the ultimate distribution was one third each to Houdry, Socony-Vacuum, and Sun.

With the addition of the new partners came a shift in the location and direction of research activity. The laboratory was moved across the Delaware River to Marcus Hook, Pennsylvania, where Sun had a large refinery and a research laboratory. The main direction of research was away from cracking gas oil and toward cracking stocks in the heavy fuel fraction. This desire was motivated by the fact that the market for heavy fuel oil had become glutted. With the American depression had come a reduction in industrial activity, and since heavy fuel is very sensitive to changes in industrial activity, a great decrease in its demand.[6] The price

---

[6] This sensitivity is illustrated in the table on the opposite page, which shows the relative changes in the prices for gasoline and heavy fuel oil, from 1924–29 to 1932.

had dropped to the point where it would be a cheap raw material for a catalytic cracking process. But as Burton had discovered many years before this, in cracking, heavier stocks deposit more coke than gas oil does. The regeneration cycles had turned out to be the critical phase, and the increased deposit of coke on the catalyst brought about by the selection of a heavier charge stock would increase the problems of design, construction, and operation substantially. Hence the shift in emphasis from a gas-oil to a heavy-fuel charge stock diminished the chances of success, but Sun was willing to take the risk.

During the depression the demand for motor gasoline was remaining remarkably stable. Competition within the oil industry was taking the form of improving gasoline quality. Given the gradual economic recovery of the United States, the increasing consumption of motor gasoline, and the drive for higher gasoline quality, the need for some process to replace thermal cracking was becoming obvious to the management of every oil-refining company.

In the light of the history of Sun Oil Company, it is not surprising that this independent firm, rather than one of the giants of the industry, took over the research on the Houdry process. To be sure, Sun's research staff was smaller and the funds that it had at its disposal were more limited. Yet two attributes of the Sun Oil Company more than compensated for these limitations. The first was the close connection between its ownership and management.[7] Sun was run by men whose position and personality were such that they were able to act quickly and decisively when it came to adopting a new process.

In the second place, Sun had for many years been marketing a single grade of gasoline that was superior in quality to the regular grade sold by its larger competitors. If it were to retain this advantage, it would of necessity have to be among the first in adopting any new process which could produce superior gasoline.

Product	Average Prices (¢ per gallon) 1924–29	1932	Price Decline (%) 1924–29 to 1932
Gasoline	16.03	10.08	37
Heavy Fuel Oil	2.91	0.85	71

Source: Appendix Tables 2b and 4:
    Gasoline — Dealers' net price
    Fuel Oil — Oklahoma fuel oil at refineries.

[7] In 1938, the Pew family owned approximately 71% of the common stock of the Sun Oil Company (R. C. Cook, "Control of the Petroleum Industry by Major Oil Companies," *TNEC Monograph No. 39*, Washington: Government Printing Office, 1941, facing p. 60).

Compared with the other companies in the industry, Sun was a late-comer where gasoline was concerned. Before the 1920's, when Sun entered the gasoline business seriously, the company had been primarily a manufacturer of lubricating oils. Its founder was J. Newton Pew, Sr., a former schoolteacher, who had entered the oil industry by way of the gas-transmission business.[8] He himself was an innovator, being the first to transport fuel gas over a long distance. Beginning in 1877, Pew purchased gas from wells in the Pennsylvania oil fields and piped it to Olean, New York. This experiment in gas transmission was followed in 1882 by a more substantial pipe line to serve the city of Pittsburgh, Pennsylvania.

In the 1890's, he became interested in the oil business and, with a friend named Emerson, formed the Pew and Emerson Company. Emerson later dropped out of the concern, at which time it became the Sun Oil Company. Its first refinery was located in Toledo, Ohio. In order to market petroleum products on the East Coast, it also built, in 1901, a refinery at Marcus Hook in Pennsylvania. Originally it intended to utilize Mexican crude oil in its refinery operations,[9] but just after the refinery was completed the famous Spindletop field in Texas came into play, and Mexico was abandoned as a source of supply.

The physical characteristics of the Spindletop crude oil had greatly affected the future course of the Sun Oil Company. It was a so-called "grade A" crude, whose high quality was evident in the lubricating-oil fraction.

Crude petroleum is composed of three types of hydrocarbons: aromatics, naphthenes, and paraffins. In the aromatics, the hydrocarbon molecules are unsaturated, and the carbon atoms are joined to each other in a ring formation. The naphthenes likewise are in the form of rings but are saturated. The paraffin hydrocarbons are saturated and are formed in long chains. Because of their molecular structure, paraffin hydrocarbons are the least valuable as motor fuel.

In addition to the chemical characteristics, the paraffins also exhibit certain physical characteristics. In the case of the heavier hydrocarbons, these show up as a tendency to solidify into wax at normal temperatures. The lower the concentration of paraffin in the lubricating-oil fraction, the less is the tendency toward the formation of waxy deposits at normal

[8] Interview with Clarence H. Thayer, vice-president, January 6, 1955. (The following brief history of the Sun Oil Company and its relations with the Houdry Process Corporation is derived primarily from Mr. Thayer.)

[9] In order to transport this Mexican crude oil to Philadelphia, it purchased a large tanker. The only disadvantage to this possession was that it was afloat on the Great Lakes at the time. In order to get it to the sea Mr. Pew was forced to cut it in half, a rather unusual undertaking.

temperatures. Spindletop crude oil, like other low-paraffin crudes, therefore, made excellent cold-weather lubricating oils.

The Spindletop crude oil did not yield its lubricants easily since, unlike the Pennsylvania crudes, the heavy lubricating oil fractions had to be separated from an asphaltic residuum. It was necessary to develop a new method of separation; the process adopted consisted of distilling the heavy fractions with steam. During the distillation a certain portion of the lubricating fraction vaporized; this was condensed, treated, and sold as "Sun Pale Neutrals." The physical distillation was accompanied by a very small amount of thermal cracking. The residual material which had been subjected to the cracking was sold as "Sun Red." Sun Red was a heavy oil, which provided good lubrication under severe conditions, and had the additional advantage, gained from its low paraffin content, of a low "cold test." But a special process had to be developed to purify it. Treating normally consisted of two operations, the first an acidification, and the second a neutralization. With the Sun Red, the first step was easily achieved, but neutralization was much more difficult. The refinery personnel at Marcus Hook found that if neutralization were stopped at just the right moment, the undesirable naphthenic soaps and sulfonates would form small balls and sink to the bottom of the treating tanks.[10] When the impurities had settled on the bottom of the tanks, they were drawn off, leaving the remaining oil essentially pure. These lubricating oils were sold successfully throughout the entire world.

Playing a prominent role in the development of these lubricating oil processes was one of J. N. Pew's three sons, J. Howard Pew. J. Howard Pew attended Grove City College in western Pennsylvania, as had his father before him, and M. I. T. He went to work in the Marcus Hook refinery and soon after became refinery manager.

In 1910, J. Howard Pew became president of the company, and together with his brothers, Arthur E. Pew and J. N. Pew, Jr., bought out a part interest of United Gas Industries in the Sun Oil Company. In his new position, J. Howard Pew became intimately concerned with the entire operation of the firm. During the decade from 1910 until 1920, he devoted his attention to lubricating oils, but after 1920 he shifted to motor gasoline, as it became a more important aspect of the business.

It was not surprising that the manufacture of gasoline was emphasized, for gasoline prices were very high after World War I, and the rapid development of the automobile presaged a continued increase in

---

[10] These naphthenic soaps and sulfonates were of no commercial value at first, but Sun decided to collect them in large tanks; by the middle of the 1920's it had several 50,000-barrel tankfuls. A few years later a market was developed for this former waste material, and the entire volume sold profitably.

[Sun Oil Company]

J. Howard Pew.

gasoline sales. But the form which Sun's efforts should take, the particular features which it should emphasize, was largely a matter of chance. The item which dictated the conditions of Sun's entry into gasoline manufacturing was the composition of the crude oil which the refinery was running, the Spindletop crude oil.

Not only did Spindletop crude provide an excellent lubricating-oil fraction, but it also provided an equally good gasoline fraction. The virgin gasoline cut from Spindletop crude has a very high octane number. This high-octane gasoline stock became one of the two chief constituents of Sun Oil Company's finished blend.

The other constituent was a cracked gasoline, obtained by the thermal cracking of the gas-oil fraction of the crude. Earlier, Sun had sold the gas-oil fraction to the gas-manufacturing companies, such as United Gas Industries, which used it to enrich fuel gas. Sun discontinued this arrangement with the gas companies, however, and in the period from 1923 to 1926 built several Cross cracking stills in which the company processed the gas oil into gasoline. The thermally cracked gasoline from the Cross stills was of a higher octane than the average gasoline that was marketed during this period. When combined with the high-octane virgin gasoline, the resulting blend was also considerably higher in octane than that manufactured by competitors.

The total output of gasoline from the Marcus Hook refinery then was approximately 3,000 barrels a day. While this was not a very large output compared with that of the major refiners, it was, by reason of its high octane number, considered worth marketing under the company's name. Sun dyed it blue to give it a distinctive color and in 1927 set up a distribution system and began to advertise Blue Sunoco for the first time.

The advertising campaign was very successful, and for the first few years sales doubled each year. The public was becoming conscious of the advantages of high-octane gasoline, and the automobile companies were beginning to design higher-compression engines to take advantage of the greater efficiency of the premium fuel. In 1926, just as Sun was deciding to advertise and market its own brand of gasoline, Chrysler had produced a relatively high-speed, high-compression engine. Blue Sunoco was an excellent fuel for this automobile.

Sun thus entered the gasoline market in the mid-1920's with a product of high quality. In order to maintain its position Sun in the early 1930's abandoned the Cross units and developed its own very high pressure thermal cracking equipment. The research and development work at very high pressures was carried on at Sun's Marcus Hook refinery by the supervisor of the cracking department, an engineer named Clarence H. Thayer. He had come to the Sun Oil Company in 1926, after having worked for the Standard Oil Company of California. In the early 1930's, in laboratory equipment, Thayer utilized pressures as high as 2,000 lb./sq. in. The laboratory results indicated that at these high pressures the quality of the motor gasoline produced in the cracking process was superior to that produced at lower pressures. He reported the results to Arthur E. Pew, Jr., J. Howard Pew's nephew and vice-president in charge of manufacturing.

The manner in which Thayer's report was treated illustrated the speed with which a relatively small and privately owned firm can react to changing conditions. Arthur Pew decided that it would be well to investigate further the advantages of going to very high pressures, and gave Thayer fifteen minutes in which to calculate how much it would cost to increase the current operating pressure of 1,200 lb./sq. in. to 2,000 lb./sq. in. In these fifteen minutes, Thayer was required to estimate the expense of changing over heat exchanger, pumps, tubes, and piping to withstand the severity of higher-pressure operation. Later the same afternoon, J. Howard Pew himself, who had been informed of the decision to adopt higher pressures, called Thayer to ask whether the new tubes had been ordered already. Thus in the space of a few hours the results of the laboratory experiments were presented, analyzed, and accepted as the basis for the decision to go ahead with a radical alteration in the major processing step in the manufacture of gasoline. Eight weeks later the equipment had been revamped and the operations at elevated pressures were taking place.

Success followed the brisk adoption of high pressures and led to the design and construction in 1933 of a 25,000-barrel-a-day unit. Sun wanted to maintain its lead in the octane race and also to take advantage of the economies of large-scale processing. The giant unit was the logical means to this end.

Possession of one of the most efficient processing schemes then existent in the industry did not blind the managers of the Sun Oil Company to the possible course of future events. Manufacturing a gasoline of quality equal or superior to that of any competitor was not enough. If Sun wished to retain its lead in the future, it would have to be the first to adopt new processes.

The Sun Oil Company was therefore keenly interested in the experiments which Eugene Houdry was conducting in his laboratory across the Delaware River. Sun first learned of the Houdry process through an employee of Sun's subsidiary, Sun Dry Dock and Engineering Company, which had been building the pressure vessels for Houdry. This employee, Perry Shaver, suggested to Eugene Houdry that he approach Sun for funds. By this time Houdry had been turned down by almost all of the major companies in the industry — those that refined petroleum and those that built the refining equipment. He therefore eagerly contacted Arthur Pew, who in turn called in Thayer and asked him "to go see the Frenchman's process."

In Paulsboro, Thayer observed Houdry's apparatus. At this time Houdry was operating a large pilot unit, processing between 50 and 100 barrels of gas oil a day. The gas oil was charged to the equipment for eight hours at a time, and then the catalyst was regenerated for another eight hours. This would have permitted continuous operation with two reaction vessels or cases; while one was on stream, the other one would be regenerating.

Thayer's emotions upon observing the apparatus were mixed: wonder that the quality of the gasoline produced was so high, and dismay that the physical construction of the equipment was so complicated and primitive.

From the gas oil, which had an end point of 720°F., Houdry claimed a gasoline yield of between 23% and 24% and an octane number of 91, according to the series-30 test, which was approximately fifteen numbers higher than the octane of most thermally cracked gasoline. The material yield of gasoline was somewhat less than that obtained from thermal cracking. The advantage of the catalytic process, therefore, seemed to lie in the greatly improved gasoline quality.

The apparatus left much to be desired; as constructed in the pilot plant, it could not possibly be expanded to the size necessary for a commercial installation. The catalyst case, which was being operated under pressure, was rectangular in shape, and the tubes which perforated it emerged in a maze of bends, angles, and joints, all of which had been necessary in the early experiments to allow for the expansion at high temperatures. Thayer saw immediately that in order to be commercially practical, the case would have to be cylindrical in shape, and the tubes would have to lie entirely in the vertical plane.

After investigating Houdry's apparatus, Thayer returned to Marcus Hook. He brought with him his impressions of the process and the sample of the catalytically cracked gasoline, which was sent to the laboratory for a routine chemical and physical analysis. The next day he drew a rough sketch of the Paulsboro unit and wrote a brief report in pencil, on some yellow notepaper, describing the Houdry process, emphasizing the high quality of the gasoline which could be manufactured and the serious limitations in the existing mechanical design of the equipment. Not having a secretary, he put this penciled report in a drawer in his desk until he could find someone who would be able to type it.

It was customary for the results of laboratory tests to be dispatched not only to Thayer and the other refinery personnel who were intimately concerned with the quality of the products, but also to the president of the company, J. Howard Pew. Pew exhibited an interest in and control over even the minor activities of the Sun Oil Company. He made it a policy to check over every gasoline test and every equipment requisition that originated within the firm.

The laboratory test from Marcus Hook substantiated Houdry's claims. The sample of gasoline which Thayer had brought back from Paulsboro did have an octane rating of 91. The splendor of this figure was immediately evident to J. Howard Pew. He summoned Arthur Pew, who in turn called in Thayer and relieved him of his penciled report. To the owner-managers of the Sun Oil Company, the process looked good. At the higher-octane numbers expected for the future, it would probably be profitable to operate the catalytic equipment. The mechanical problems might well be overcome if the company were willing to spend a sufficient amount of money.

Further Development

Sun made its investment in the Houdry process through the purchase of stock in the Houdry Process Corporation and also through financing the research. In order to hasten the development of the process, Sun requested the transfer of experiments to Marcus Hook. Eugene Houdry, accompanied by his closest associates, Raymond Lassiat and Dr. W. F. Faragher, moved his apparatus from Paulsboro. With the added help of Sun's engineers and scientists, pilot-plant work was carried out simultaneously with additional experiments in the laboratory.

For their pilot-scale operations the investigators selected two of the old Cross cracking stills. The reaction chambers of the Cross units, approximately 10 feet in height and 3 to 4 feet in diameter, were used as the catalyst cases. They were filled with catalyst manufactured by Houdry from an activated natural clay purchased from the Filtrol Company. The catalyst bed was pierced by small-diameter tubes whose purpose was to allow the circulation of cooling water.

Sun began charging heavy oil to the pilot plant, but the accumulation of coke was found to be quite heavy. Moreover, it was difficult to remove traces of the heavy oil from the catalyst after the cracking process had been carried out and before the coke was burned off the catalyst in the regeneration step. J. Howard Pew himself suggested trying a vacuum purge, that is, reducing the pressure so that the heavy oil remaining on the catalyst could vaporize more easily. Because there was no vacuum pump at Marcus Hook large enough to evacuate an entire catalyst case, an intermediate vessel of large capacity was kept constantly under a vacuum. The heavy oil vapors from the catalyst case were drawn into this vessel before the regeneration phase of the cycle took place.

The vacuum purge was an improvement but still was not entirely satisfactory. Steam had been thought of as a purging agent before, but it was believed that steam at high temperature destroyed the effectiveness of the catalyst. When it was found later that steam did not damage the catalyst, a combination of reduced pressure and steam stripping was used which turned out to be successful.

Although this process problem was solved, a new mechanical problem arose to take its place. This problem concerned the valves, the pieces of equipment which control the flow of materials through the pipes and vessels of the unit. In the Houdry process the valves had to act quickly, for they had to admit the raw materials, air, and coolants at just the proper time so that the process temperatures and pressures would not exceed their closely specified limits. Such fast action was severe on valves of any existing design. With conventional valves, the passage of material through the orifice at high velocities eroded the metal seriously. Moreover, the repeated heating and cooling of the valves caused the shell of the valve to shrink more than the gate. New valves and operating mechanisms, as well as two entire cycle-timing devices, had to be developed before an adequate control of the flow of materials was obtained.

While these improvements in the pilot-plant equipment were being made, studies of the fundamentals of the cracking reaction were being carried out in the laboratory. There the time-yield relationships of the catalytic cracking process were investigated. During the first few minutes after the oil vapors were admitted to the catalyst section, a large amount of gas and coke was formed. The formation of gas then decreased and, from this point until a time fifteen minutes from the beginning of the reaction, large amounts of catalytic gasoline were produced. After the first fifteen minutes or so, the activity of the catalyst was reduced because of the coke deposit, and the formation of additional gasoline was relatively meager. If the greatest part of the motor gasoline was produced in the first fifteen minutes of the process, then it seemed to be of little use to consume more time on this phase of the cycle. Shorter operating cycles than Houdry's sixteen hours seemed desirable.

Another fundamental discovery was that the yield of catalytic gasoline, expressed as a percentage of the volume of cracking stock, could be raised from the approximate value of 23%, which Houdry had been obtaining, to a peak of 43%. This was achieved by altering the operating conditions (such as temperature and pressure) and by improving the equipment. In the early 1930's, Sun was obtaining about the same fraction of gasoline on charge from thermal cracking operations by cracking both the virgin gas oil and the recycle stream, and could hardly be expected to substitute with any satisfaction a process which gave a lower over-all gasoline yield, in spite of its higher gasoline quality.

At this point, Houdry and his associates had developed a catalytic process that was successful in terms of the physical and chemical reactions involved. They had shown that it was possible, with the equipment they had designed, to break up the molecules of a gas-oil stock into smaller molecules, yielding a substantial fraction of high-quality motor gasoline. Economically, however, the Houdry process was not yet successful. One step, namely, the pumping of air into the catalyst cases during the regeneration step, remained extremely expensive to perform. Fortunately, and in direct contrast with Dubbs's experience on the hot-oil pump, the investigators were already aware of an invention of strategic importance: the turbo-compressor.[11]

The development of the turbo-compressor was first observed by a member of Sun's research department, Dr. Vose. Vose was particularly interested in regeneration because he had earlier made experiments in the laboratory in which the regeneration phase was carried out under a positive pressure. Pressure regeneration had satisfied the requirement of burning the coke off the catalyst relatively quickly, and Vose had recommended that a pressure of 50 pounds be used in the Houdry process. But this recommendation was made before the discovery of the turbo-compressor and had had to be dropped because of the excessive cost of compressing air by conventional means.

Two experts in the design of power-plant equipment, Harry Thomas and Henry Melton, were sent to Switzerland to observe the turbo-compressor. These men made a favorable report, and on the basis of their figures a new cost calculation was made. On the basis of this calculation, the installation of the Houdry process appeared to be an attractive proposition.

Not content with having a process which could crack light and medium charge stocks, Sun continued its efforts to crack the heaviest fractions of the crude oil. The amount of heavy material that could be cracked was limited by the amount that could be vaporized before it entered the catalyst cases and by the coke deposited in the catalyst. By first heating the residuum and then permitting the major portion of it to vaporize in a vessel (the tar separator), Sun was able to crack all the fractions boiling above $1000°$ F.; i.e., all but the last 10% of the crude oil. A large amount of superheated steam, however, as much as 25% by weight when running 35% East Texas reduced crude, was necessary to assist the vaporization. Moreover, the coke yield was so great that the cracking phase of the cycle had to be relatively short. The capacity of a unit cracking heavy fuel would therefore be less than the same unit cracking gas oil.

Because Sun had spent a considerable amount of money in the im-

---

[11] The turbo-compressor used in the Houdry process is described in an article by J. E. Evans and R. C. Lassiat, "Combustion-Gas Turbine in the Houdry Process," *Petroleum Refiner*, November, 1945. In brief the turbo-compressor works as follows: the gaseous combustion products created by the burning of the carbon off the coke during the regeneration phase are piped from the catalyst cases through the turbine. The gas, being at a temperature betwen $800°$F. and $850°$F. and at a pressure more than 40 lb./sq. in., can provide power to compress, in an axial compressor attached to the shaft of the turbine, enough air from the atmosphere to satisfy the requirement for regeneration in the next case. Thus the output from the regeneration phase could be used to provide the input for the next regeneration phase, without any additional consumption of power.

provement of the Houdry process and because Socony-Vacuum still owned one-third interest in the Houdry Process Corporation, Arthur Pew decided to try to interest Socony-Vacuum in the venture again. Pew and Thayer, armed with the results of the experiments at Marcus Hook, traveled to New York to present the case.[12]

In the closing months of 1936, Socony, Sun, and Eugene Houdry came to an agreement. The rationale for the agreement was as follows. Since the Houdry process seemed profitable, each company would wish to erect Houdry units in its refineries. The greater the refinery capacity of the company, the greater the benefits it would receive from the installations. Since the benefits were proportional to total refining capacity, the contribution to the expenses of research and development should also be proportional to the company's refining capacity. Prior to the close of 1936, Sun had spent more than Socony. On the basis of a formula that equated the two ratios (the capacity of Socony to the capacity of Sun; and the money that Socony had spent to the money that Sun had spent), Socony therefore agreed to contribute to the Houdry Process Corporation an amount that would balance Sun's development expenditures.

Adoption of the Houdry Process

Both companies did construct Houdry catalytic cracking units, although their plants were not identical. It was still Socony's intention, as it had been back in 1931 when the company initiated experiments with Eugene Houdry, to crack light gas oil. Because of its lack of experience in the design and operation of the process, Socony decided to build a relatively small commercial unit so as to be able to construct the equipment rapidly and to test the process thoroughly before building a larger-scale unit. As a result, Socony was able to bring on stream, in June 1936, the first commercial Houdry catalytic cracking unit, located at the company's Paulsboro, New Jersey, refinery and having a capacity of 2,000 barrels a day of light gas oil.[13]

Sun's first commercial Houdry unit, installed the following April at Marcus Hook, was larger than Socony-Vacuum's, charging 12,200 barrels a stream-day of heavy gas oil and costing $3,250,000.[14] This unit was followed in 1939 by two combination units, which performed on a single site the two functions of crude distillation and catalytic cracking. These

[12] Interview with Clarence T. Thayer, January 6, 1955.

[13] This unit was operated until March, 1940, when it was replaced by one with a capacity of 10,000 bpsd.

[14] *Ibid.*; also W. F. Faragher, H. D. Noll, and R. E. Bland, "Contribution of the Houdry Catalytic Cracking Processes to Petroleum Refining," World Petroleum Congress, the Hague, Netherlands, 1951, Section IV, Subsection II, Preprint 4, p. 4, and "Monsieur Houdry's Invention," *Fortune*, February, 1939, pp. 134, 135.

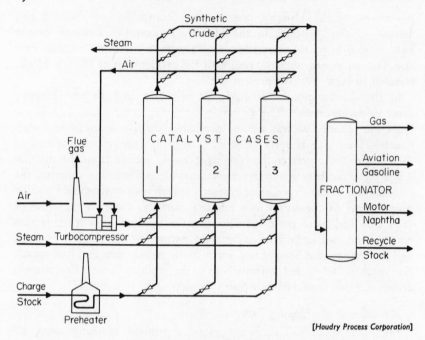

[Houdry Process Corporation]

Flow sheet, Houdry process.

two units were constructed simultaneously, one at Marcus Hook and the other at Sun's refinery in Toledo, Ohio. Although designed to process 28,000 barrels a day of crude oil and to crack 19,000 barrels a day of reduced crude, these units were quickly increased in crude capacity to between 40,000 and 45,000 barrels a day of crude oil. In the same year, Socony began to crack gas oil in five new units in various states. By 1939, Sun and Socony together had fifteen catalytic-cracking units in operation or under construction with a combined capacity of 221,675 barrels a day of charge; these catalytic-cracking facilities cost a total of $35,000,000.[15] In a little over three years these two companies increased the industry's total cracking capacity by 10%.[16] The situation was much as it had been twenty years before, when Burton invented the first cracking process: one company (in the case of the Houdry process, two companies), having developed a radically new process, and having control of that process as a

[15] O. W. Wilcox, "Houdry Catalytic Processes Opening New Era in Refining Operations," *World Petroleum*, Annual Refining Issue, 1939, p. 51. The cost of the separate units was not given.

[16] Total industry cracking capacity, operating and shut down, was 2,210,318 barrels of charge per day as of January 1, 1936 (American Petroleum Institute, *Petroleum Facts and Figures*, 9th ed., 1950, p. 263).

[Houdry Process Corporation]

Houdry fixed-bed catalytic cracking plant, catalytic reactors shown in foreground.

result of patent ownership and technical know-how, invested large amounts of money as quickly as possible in order to derive the greatest competitive advantage from the innovation.

In terms of benefits to the innovator, the situations were also similar; in each case the new process was more profitable to operate than the old. Based upon cracking units of equal capacity and prices of inputs as of 1938, thermal cracking cost approximately 31.5¢ per barrel of gas oil to operate and the Houdry process 24.5¢[17]

[17] See Appendix Table 12a. The cost of the gas oil is not included in this figure; it is equal for the two processes. Royalties are included. The capacity of each of the

The chief advantage of the Houdry process lay in the high quality of the products. The gasoline from the Houdry process had an octane number, according to the research test, of 88 compared with 72 for the thermally cracked gasoline. Similarly, the heavier-than-gasoline material from the Houdry process could be sold as No. 2 furnace oil, whereas the heavy material from the thermal cracking process could be sold only as heavy fuel oil. One oil company figured the octane advantage to be worth 0.62¢ per gallon of catalytic gasoline when the catalytic gasoline was blended with the rest of the refinery's motor fuel.[18] The price differential between No. 2 furnace oil and heavy fuel oil in 1936 was 1.76¢ per gallon.[19] Making allowance for the different product mix, the Houdry catalytic cracking process yielded an estimated profit of 23¢ per barrel of charge compared with an estimated profit of 19¢ per barrel for thermal cracking. The yearly profit on a 6,750-barrel-a-calendar-day Houdry unit, costing $2,191,200 would have been $560,000, representing a yearly return of 26% on the investment.[20]

Although attractive, the estimated rate of return on the Houdry process is less than were those on the Burton (approximately 50%) and on the Tube and Tank (210%) processes. Three reasons can be given for this difference. First, all refining operations were less profitable in 1936. The earlier process innovations were made when the spread between the prices of gas oil and gasoline was wide, whereas the Houdry process was introduced while the nation was still in the depression of the 1930's and the spread was narrower.

Second, cracking was now universal. By the end of the 1930's all of the major oil companies and many of the small refiners had adequate cracking capacity. Competition, based upon equivalent manufacturing

---

two units was 6,750 barrels per calendar day. By 1938, all the thermal cracking processes were essentially identical, so the results of a comparison between catalytic and thermal cracking would have been independent of the particular thermal cracking process selected.

A comparison between the direct costs of thermal cracking and of catalytic cracking was made by a representative of the Houdry Process Corporation. The figures were 12–14 ¢ per barrel of thermal cracking charge and 10–12 ¢ per barrel of catalytic cracking charge (O. W. Wilcox, *op. cit.*, p. 60).

[18] Standard Oil Company (Indiana), "Comparison of Houdry Process with Operations Now Used . . . ," Report of Subcommittee on Houdry Process Investigation, December 27, 1938, p. 36.

[19] At midcontinent refineries, No. 2 furnace sold for 3.31¢ a gal.; heavy fuel oil for 1.55¢ a gal. (*The Petroleum Data Book*, 1947, Dallas: Petroleum Engineer Publishing Company, 1947, p. F–12.)

[20] In this calculation, the charge stock was assumed to be virgin gas oil of 32° API gravity. On a charge stock of 50% East Texas reduced crude, the "payout" was claimed to be less than three years (O. W. Wilcox, *op. cit.*). "The "payout" is the reciprocal of the undiscounted rate of profit, stated as a fraction. Thus a "payout" of less than three years is equivalent to a rate of profit of greater than $33\frac{1}{3}$%.

processes, limited the return on cracking facilities. In 1913, and even in 1922, when only a few companies had cracking units, the high returns on the process innovations resulted in part from the restricted practice of the art.

Third, the main characteristic of the Houdry process, as contrasted with the earlier processes, was the high quality of the catalytically cracked gasoline. When the effect of a process is to increase the product yield, the advantage can be immediately and fairly accurately estimated through cost and revenue calculations. If, however, the effect is to improve quality, and if at the same time the higher quality cannot be fully appreciated until a later date, cost and revenue estimates are more likely to be in error.

Sun and Socony operated their Houdry units differently. To a great extent these differences were due to the choice of cracking stock, light gas oil in the case of Socony and heavy gas oil derived from reduced crude oil in the case of Sun. Light gas oil when being cracked produces less coke than does an equivalent volume of heavy gas oil. Thus, for a given amount of coke deposited on the catalyst, more light gas oil can be charged. Socony, processing light gas oil in its Houdry units, could therefore employ longer cycles and use an essentially simpler processing scheme. The large valves were operated manually; regeneration was carried out at atmospheric pressure, and the air for regeneration was supplied by the normal type of blower.

Sun's processing scheme was more complex. The tendency of the heavy gas oil to deposit more coke on the catalyst demanded that the operating cycle be short. Had the reaction phase of the cycle taken as long as 45 minutes, the valves could still have been operated by hand. But Sun's engineers had found that 45 minutes was too long and that the catalyst should be regenerated after 15 minutes. No human operator could turn the valves fast enough to ensure 15-minute cracking phases, so it became necessary to operate the valves by machine. The complex battery of valve-operating motors, co-ordinated by a cycle-timing device, added to the capital cost of Sun's Houdry units.

The short time interval that could be devoted to cracking set a similar limitation on the time devoted to regenerating the catalyst. Vose's development of pressure regeneration (as the only alternative to slower regeneration and a greater number of catalyst cases) and the discovery of the turbo-compressor allowed this phase of the cracking cycle to be accelerated. Still, it became necessary to have not two cases (one case cracking and the other regenerating) but three. The additional one was purged while the other two were going through their operations. The turbo-compressor and the extra catalyst case likewise added to the capital cost.

All of the Houdry units installed between 1936 and 1940 worked well for approximately their first two years. After this initial period, however, defects in the cooling system became evident. In these units, the excess heat liberated during the regeneration phase of the cycle was originally removed from the catalyst cases by the generation of high-pressure steam. The steam was produced in tubes running up through the catalyst bed by means of heat transferred from the body of the catalyst.[21] After being subjected to the intermittent heating and cooling, which placed stress upon the tube walls, and to the slightly corrosive action of the water, which tended to eat away the interior of the tubes themselves, several of the tubes ruptured. Since steam can be injurious to catalysts, a rupture in the catalyst bed would be serious. In solving this problem, Socony conceived the idea of using a heat-transfer medium; rather than subtracting the heat from the catalyst through the vaporization of water, the heat was to be removed by an intermediate material, salt, which would take the heat from the catalyst and then flow to a boiler in which it would generate steam. The double transfer of heat from catalyst to salt and from salt to water eliminated the need for passing a mixture of water and steam under high pressure through the catalyst cases.

This use of molten salt as a heat-transfer medium was the first in the petroleum-refining industry; originally it had been used by Monsanto Chemical Company for chemical operations. Its application to the cooling system of the Houdry process was a lengthy one. First it was necessary to determine whether the salt formed explosive compounds on being subjected to high temperatures, for molten salt flows very easily and would seep through the smallest crack. Under the stress of expansion and contraction, the cracks would enlarge and frequently some salt would reach the atmosphere, much as the oil vapors had in the Burton process. Eugene Houdry and engineers at du Pont worked together on this problem and ultimately were able to assure the operators of the equipment that molten salt was not dangerous. Once the salt had been declared safe, both Sun and Socony designed new cases suitable for salt cooling. Subsequent units incorporated the new case design, and existing units were altered.

After these developments the mechanical operation of the Houdry units was satisfactory, but there was always an incentive to obtain a higher yield of gasoline. Since the yield of gasoline from any given

---

[21] See R. C. Lassiat, H. G. Shimp, and A. G. Peterkin, "The Houdry Fixed-Bed Catalytic Cracking Process," in *The Science of Petroleum*, Vol. V, Part 2 (*Synthetic Products of Petroleum*), Oxford University Press, 1953, pp. 234–5.

charge stock was a function of the type of catalyst used, the direction in which the experimental activity took place was toward the development of better catalysts. A search was begun for a catalyst which had a higher activity and a longer life.[22] Higher activity would mean a higher yield of gasoline; longer life would mean uniform production of gasoline and a longer interval between catalyst changes, which were quite expensive to perform. The development of better catalysts led away from those occurring naturally in the earth to synthetic ones.

The manufacture of synthetic catalysts had its roots in work which J. Howard Pew initiated at Marcus Hook before World War I. There an employee of the Sun Oil Company, Maitland, developed a silica-alumina gel for decolorizing lubricating oils. This gel was formed through the coprecipitation of silicon and aluminum salts. Pew took out patents on the gel and on its method of manufacture, but by the late 1930's these had expired. Because of his familiarity with the synthetic silicon-aluminum salts, Pew suggested that they might provide a suitable catalyst for the Houdry process and encouraged Eugene Houdry to investigate it. For over a year experiments were carried out that resulted in the first successful synthetic catalyst. Later Socony, too, carried out research on coprecipitated synthetic silica-alumina catalysts and developed a variety which took the shape of small spheres known as beads. These were also well suited for catalytic cracking. The manufacture of "pelleted" synthetic catalyst was initiated by the Houdry Process Corporation, which constructed a plant at Paulsboro, and began supplying the units with cracking catalyst in 1940.[23] Socony later constructed a synthetic "bead" catalyst plant.

By 1942, a total of fourteen Houdry fixed-bed units had been put into operation by four major oil companies, Socony, Sun, Tidewater Oil Company, and the Standard Oil Company of California. Several others were under construction. These units were to do yeoman service during the war, for in addition to yielding a superior motor gasoline, the Houdry process could produce excellent aviation-gasoline blending stocks. At the time when the need for aviation gasoline was growing by leaps and bounds, the Houdry units were discovered to be the best possible source for quickly increasing the supply. All of the Houdry units were converted to the manufacture of aviation-base stock.[24] During the first two years of the war they provided 90% of all the catalytically cracked aviation gasoline.

[22] See W. F. Faragher, H. D. Noll, and R. E. Bland, *op. cit.*, pp. 3, 4.
[23] *Ibid.*
[24] D. B. Ardern, J. C. Dart, and R. C. Lassiat, "Catalytic Cracking in Fixed- and Moving-Bed Processes," reprint from *Advances in Chemistry Series*, No. 5, American Chemical Society, 1951, pp. 20–21.

For a number of reasons, one of which was the shortage of construction materials, particularly steel, the original Houdry fixed-bed catalytic cracking process was rather quickly superseded. From nearly 10% of the industry's cracking capacity the share of the Houdry process dropped to 6% in 1950 and 1% in 1956. Its success had led quickly to imitation (see Chapter 6), and the experience Houdry and Socony had gained in making the new process practicable enabled them, too, to discover more efficient ways to crack fractions by catalysis (see Chapter 5). Although no Houdry fixed-bed units were built after 1944, the Houdry process continued for several years to be competitive with the subsequent catalytic cracking processes. As recently as 1955 all of Sun's fixed-bed Houdry units were still being operated profitably.[25]

Having progressed to this degree with the fixed-bed process, the Houdry Process Corporation then shifted its interest to continuously moving catalyst beds. To emphasize and expedite this work, Arthur Pew of Sun and Wilbur F. Burt of Socony in 1944 brought in Arthur V. Danner as executive vice-president and chief executive officer of the Houdry Process Corporation. Eugene Houdry had continued to work on the improvement of his process until 1941, when he shifted to the problem of manufacturing raw materials, particularly butadiene, for synthetic rubber.[26] During the period from 1944 to 1948, Eugene Houdry, while president of Houdry Process Corporation, directed special research and development projects of primary interest to Sun.

In 1948, although maintaining his financial interest in the company he had founded, Eugene Houdry separated himself from management responsibilities in the Houdry Process Corporation. At this point, several years before the concern became general, Eugene Houdry recognized the seriousness of atmospheric pollution. With his typical foresight, he was attracted far more by problems and challenges of research than by those of administration, and he formed a new company to discover and harness catalysts which could transform noxious chemical gases into harmless

[25] Interview with Clarence H. Thayer, January 6, 1955.

[26] Sun Oil Company during World War II constructed at its Toledo, Ohio, refinery one of the two commercial-size units built in that period to produce butadiene from a normal-butane charge. This catalytic dehydrogenation process was to assume considerable importance after the United States government decontrolled the synthetic-rubber industry. (See R. C. Lassiat and F. D. Parker, "Butane Dehydrogenation by the Houdry Process," *Petroleum Refiner*, Vol. XXIII, No. 11, November, 1944; G. F. Hornaday and J. J. Cicalose, "Houdry Dehydrogenation Process," *Houdry Pioneer*, Vol. 6, No. 4, December, 1953; and G. F. Hornaday, "Economics of Houdry Dehydrogenation," *Petroleum Refiner*, December, 1954.) The development of the Houdry dehydrogenation process is described in three news releases from the Houdry Process Corporation, titled "Development of the Houdry Dehydrogenation Process," "How the Houdry Dehydrogenation Process Operates," and "The Industrial Role of Butane Dehydrogenation."

substances. Houdry firmly believed that the hydrocarbons and their derivatives produced by the incomplete combustion of fuels could be trans-
formed into carbon dioxide and water. His company, Oxy-Catalyst, Inc.,
in Wayne, Pennsylvania, has produced several catalysts for industrial and
domestic applications.[27]

Cost and Returns from Houdry Innovation

As we conclude the story of the Houdry fixed-bed catalytic cracking
process, let us attempt to measure how profitable the innovation was.
The cost of research and development was approximately $11,000,000, of
which Eugene Houdry and the members of his syndicate contributed
$3,000,000, and Sun and Socony each $4,000,000.[28] Any returns to the
Houdry syndicate would have arisen from their one-third interest in the
Houdry Process Corporation; in the years from 1935 to 1944, when the
last Houdry fixed-bed unit began operation, one third of the profits of
the company would have amounted to $2,230,734.[29]

From 1935 through 1944, the company declared dividends equal to
$14.81 a share on each of the Houdry group's 110,000 shares.[30] Thus a
total of $1,629,100 was paid out as dividends on an investment of
$3,000,000, not a very munificent return. Of all the cracking innovations
the one which was the most novel was also the one which was the least
profitable.

This comparison of costs and revenues does not make any allowance
for increase in the assets of the Houdry Process Corporation, towards
which the royalties from the Houdry process contributed. We can make
an estimate of the total royalties accruing to Houdry Process Corporation
from the installations of the Houdry process; according to Appendix
Table 17 these were a little more than $39,000,000. The share of Eugene
Houdry and his associates would have been one third, or $13,000,000.
The profits for the comparable period 1935–1944 comprised only 18% of
this amount; part of the remaining 82% was consumed in improvements in the Houdry process and in other research projects.

For Sun and Socony, the innovation was probably more beneficial. Not
only did each of the operating companies obtain dividends equal to those

[27] Eugene J. Houdry, "World's Biggest Cleaning Job," *Journal of the Franklin Institute*, Vol. 258, No. 3, September 1954, p. 175.
[28] "Monsieur Houdry's Invention," *Fortune*, February 1939, pp. 134–137. In addition Socony paid $1,500,000 to the Houdry Process Corporation for a license to operate the Houdry process (*ibid.*).
[29] Profits for the years 1935–1939, 1943–1944 are taken from *Moody's Manual of Investments*, New York; Moody's Investors Service; for 1940–1942, Houdry Process Corporation.
[30] *Ibid.*; 330,000 total shares were outstanding in 1937; slightly fewer in the other years. It is assumed that the syndicate's block remained constant at 110,000 shares.

received by Houdry and his associates, but each also profited from installing the process in its refineries. This is not evident, however, from a
comparison of the over-all profits of these two companies with those of
the petroleum corporations as a group. As may be seen in Table 3, from
1930 through 1945, Sun's profits after taxes as a percentage of net worth
were usually above those of the rest of the industry. Socony's profits were
somewhat lower than the average of the industry in the period after
1936. The contributions of the Houdry process to the activities of the
innovators were thus much less than those of the Burton or the continuous thermal cracking processes.

TABLE 3

Profits of the Sun Oil Company and of the Socony Mobil Oil Company
Compared with Average Profits of the Major Oil Companies, 1930–1945

Year	Sun Oil Company			Socony Mobil Oil Company			Major Oil Companies; Profits after Taxes: Net Worth
	Net Worth	Profits after Taxes	Profits: Net Worth	Net Worth	Profits after Taxes	Profits: Net Worth	
	(Mil. $)	(Mil. $)	(%)	(Mil. $)	(Mil. $)	(%)	(%)
1930	62.6	7.7	12.3	785.5	41.5	5.3	4.4
1931	64.0	3.1	4.8	860.9	−4.2	−0.5	−1.5
1932	65.2	4.2	6.4	843.1	37.3	4.4	0.9
1933	79.8	7.0	8.7	848.7	21.5	2.5	1.4
1934	83.7	6.7	8.0	612.8	24.4	4.0	2.6
1935	88.5	7.1	8.0	622.4	22.5	3.6	4.8
1936	93.5	7.6	8.1	633.4	42.9	6.8	7.8
1937	100.3	9.5	9.5	665.3	56.8	8.5	10.0
1938	100.5	3.1	3.1	689.3	40.1	5.8	5.0
1939	104.6	7.0	6.7	708.1	34.5	4.9	5.4
1940	109.4	8.0	7.3	649.4	36.4	5.6	5.4
1941	120.3	16.5	13.7	626.5	43.2	6.9	9.9
1942	124.9	8.7	7.0	641.1	30.8	4.8	7.0
1943	133.7	13.4	10.0	622.1	35.9	5.8	7.9
1944	173.8	13.4	7.7	701.1	62.3	8.9	9.3
1945	153.5	15.7	10.2	792.7	42.3	5.3	8.4

Sources: Sun Oil Company and Socony Mobil Oil Company—Moody's Manual of Investments, New York:
Moody's Investors Service, 1932, pp. 2643–2646; 1936, pp. 2246–2250, 2510–2514; 1939, pp. 2833–2837,
2898–2903; 1946, pp. 1906–1909, 2316–2319. In 1934 Socony-Vacuum wrote off good will and apprecia-
tion of properties to the extent of $228,125,581 (1939, p. 2901).
Major Oil Companies—National City Bank of New York, Monthly Letter on Economic Conditions,
August 1945, p. 96; April 1946, p. 46.

By 1936 the major oil companies had all expanded vertically into all
phases of oil operations, and the investment in catalytic-cracking facilities
represented a smaller relative addition to total assets than did the earlier
investment in thermal cracking. In 1939 the combined assets of Sun and
Socony were $1,076,500,000, and their investment in Houdry units was

$35,000,000, or 3.3% of the total. In 1916 the Standard Oil Company (Indiana) had had approximately $8,660,000, or 14.3% of its total assets of $60,600,000, invested in Burton units.[31]

The profitability of the Houdry process becomes evident if we calculate from engineering data the specific profit of catalytic cracking. A barrel of gas oil charged to one of Socony's Houdry units yielded approximately 2¢ more profit than did the same barrel charged to modern thermal cracking units. Sun's profit per barrel of charge may have been greater, for Sun charged heavy rather than light gas oil. The design capacity of Sun's four Houdry cracking units was 70,200 barrels a stream day, and the capacity of Socony-Vacuum's units was 74,500 barrels. Assuming an average operating rate of 90% of design and an incremental profit of 2¢ per barrel, the additional profits accruing to Sun Oil from Houdry operations would have been $600,000 a year, and to Socony $635,000. These estimated profits from catalytic cracking are about 8% of Sun's total net income and 2% of Socony's. In absolute amount, these are substantial sums, but in relative terms they are considerably less than the contribution to total profits made by the early thermal cracking processes. This is to be expected from a single process in an increasingly complex industry.

Sun enjoyed yet another benefit; the company was able to continue improving the quality of its motor gasoline without resorting to the addition of tetraethyl lead. Sun's competitive advantage lay in marketing at the price of regular gasoline an unleaded fuel of premium quality, and the high octane of the catalytic stock permitted the firm to utilize this tactic for several years more.

Although the Houdry process was not as profitable an innovation as the Burton process had been, its development closely resembled that of the first thermal cracking process. Both were major innovations, achieving an existing product, gasoline, by a radically new means: the use of pressure by Burton and of a catalyzing agent by Houdry. In making these two original contributions, Burton and Houdry essentially started from scratch. Each man worked with unfamiliar techniques and was forced to derive the fundamental principles governing the reactions of the raw material, as well as to design and construct the novel equipment. Both were several years ahead of other researchers in their fields, and in each case their success inspired others to build on the foundation provided by

[31] For total assets of the Standard Oil Company (Indiana), see *Moody's Analyses of Investments, 1916*, New York: Moody's Investors Service, 1916, pp. 1118–1119. By the end of 1915, Indiana was operating 330 Burton units and was constructing 100 more, having invested approximately $20,000 in each; see Standard Oil Company (Indiana), "Historical Summaries of Products and Manufacturing Processes," memorandum from J. K. Roberts to Dr. O. E. Bransky, October 7, 1938. For the assets of Sun and Socony see *Moody's Manual of Investments, 1939, op. cit.*

their work. Although each of the two processes represented significant improvements over the previously existing art, each was in turn superseded within seven years; the main reason for the rapid obsolescence was the lower unit costs achieved in continuous, rather than batch or semicontinuous, operations in any industry processing extremely large volumes of materials.

Any differences between the Houdry and the Burton developments can be explained by the differences between the two innovators. Burton was a man known to the entire petroleum industry, respected as a capable refinery manager as well as a petroleum scientist. Houdry was literally and figuratively an outsider; both he and his concept were foreign to the refining industry. The introduction of the Houdry fixed-bed catalytic cracking process therefore required, in addition to rare scientific and engineering competence, the activities of a promoter. The process had to be "sold" at each stage in its development.

But when we consider to whom the Burton and the Houdry processes were sold, we re-enter the region of similarity. Although all of the innovating firms, Sun, Socony and Indiana Standard, were large corporations, none dominated the industry. In 1913 Indiana Standard was a fragment of the former Standard Oil "trust," while in 1936 Sun was one of the smaller firms. Only Socony was a major concern, but its role in the crucial years 1933–1935 was minor. Neither Indiana Standard nor Sun was fully integrated; neither was national in scope. Yet each had competitive advantages. Indiana Standard's advantages have been discussed earlier. Sun had its aggressive private management, the construction facilities of its shipbuilding subsidiary, and the distinctiveness of its gasoline product. The firm was not magnificent, not secure, but its management was willing to take the large risks inherent in the research, development, and installation of a radically different process. Among the firms of the oil industry, the iconoclast is rarely the giant. And yet, if our calculations are correct, the iconoclast is certainly not the fool.

5

THE TCC AND HOUDRIFLOW
PROCESSES

Aₗₜₕₒᵤ Although the Houdry fixed-bed catalytic cracking process was to
become outmoded within the first decade after its introduction, the research groups which developed that method of gasoline manufacture were
themselves to invent two of the three superseding processes.[1] The TCC
(Thermofor Catalytic Cracking, "Thermofor" referring to the kiln in
which regeneration took place) and Houdriflow catalytic cracking processes, therefore, were not isolated innovations, but readily identifiable
links in the chain of cracking-process development. The common ingredient is catalysis. The principles enunciated by Eugene Houdry and developed in the Houdry fixed-bed process were to prove equally applicable to
continuous processes, and the strengths of the research groups lay in their
understanding of catalytic phenomena.

The shortcomings of the Houdry fixed-bed process were apparent even
to those who had developed it. There were three main drawbacks. First,
the equipment was expensive to construct.[2] Second, in the construction of
the units, metals and assemblies were required which with the advent of
World War II had a higher priority of use elsewhere. Third, the first catalytic process, like the first thermal cracking process two decades earlier,

[1] The third process, Fluid Catalytic Cracking, will be described in Chapter 6.
[2] "The salt case units had a high initial cost. The pressure regeneration and energy
recovery system which had been included in the unit involved problems, particularly
during the war, when it was difficult to obtain the flue gas-driven turbines and parts
for the same. In addition, the elimination of the most obvious problems associated
with the water-cooling system revealed other disadvantages in the fixed-bed process
which had previously seemed of minor importance. One drawback was the fact that,
even though several cases were assembled together to operate on staggered cycles,
there was still a marked fluctuation in the composition and quality of the synthetic
crude and in the amount of gas in the product stream passing to the product recovery system. This necessitated the provision of extra gas holders to handle the
peak gas load and the design of the product recovery towers and exchangers for peak
load, with necessary operation of the same far below capacity a substantial percentage of the time." Socony Mobil Oil Company, Inc., "The Catalytic Cracking
Story," May 27, 1957, p. 9. This paper, together with a TCC license agreement,
photographs, and a list of commercial units, were made available to the author by
Socony Mobil. All other information was drawn from sources outside Socony.

could not handle successfully the very heavy cracking stocks, nor could it tolerate high sulfur charge stocks.

Development of the TCC Process

The idea which permitted the solution of these difficulties was that of a "moving bed" of catalyst. In the fixed-bed process, the catalyst remained in one vessel, where it went through alternating phases of reaction and regeneration. In the moving-bed process, cracking and regeneration could be carried out simultaneously in separate vessels while the catalyst circulated continuously from one to the other.

Research on a moving-bed process was begun in 1935 at the laboratory of Socony-Vacuum Oil Company in Paulsboro, New Jersey, while Socony's associates, Eugene Houdry and Sun Oil Company, were concentrating on their fixed-bed project at Marcus Hook, Pennsylvania (see Chapter 4). Two years earlier, in 1933, Socony had cast off the major burden in the development of the Houdry fixed-bed process. By 1935, however, there was a renewed interest in research on catalytic cracking. But since, by this time, they had lost contact with Eugene Houdry and his group, Socony did not try to augment or reproduce Houdry's work, but began work in a wholly different direction.

Beginning very early in Socony's consideration of catalytic cracking, there were some who felt that the catalyst should be caused to move through separate conversion and catalyst regeneration zones. By 1935–36, thinking in Socony had progressed to the point where it was believed that low-pressure converter and regenerator operation would be necessary, at least at the outset, for a practical continuous catalytic cracking unit. Experiments were conducted in Socony's Research and Development Laboratories early in 1936 to explore the conversion yields and thoroughness of catalyst regeneration which might be expected for long path operations conducted at pressures near atmospheric. The results were very encouraging, and an experimental continuous catalytic cracking unit employing a pelleted clay-type catalyst of approximately 2.5-millimeter diameter size was built and operated. The catalyst was supplied to and withdrawn from the reactor through lock chambers which were sealed by means of steam employed in conjunction with mechanical plug valves.[3]

The moving-bed process thus was conceived of as consisting of two zones, the first in which the cracking reaction took place and the second in which the catalyst was regenerated. Each would be designed for its own purpose and each would function continuously for that purpose. Flowing downward through each zone would be a compact bed of cata-

[3] *Ibid.*, p. 10.

lyst, which would then be lifted mechanically to the top of the other zone, and so on. In 1937 patent application was made.[4]

Soon after research began on the moving-bed process, Socony was informed by the Houdry Process Corporation that the fixed-bed process was ready to be installed commercially. Rather than wait several years for a moving-bed process to be perfected, Socony decided to invest in the more fully developed Houdry technique. Over the next three years, Socony installed in its domestic refineries twelve Houdry fixed-bed units, totaling 112,100 barrels a stream day of cracking capacity.

Simultaneously, the scientists at Paulsboro continued their research on the moving-bed adaptation of the principles discovered by Houdry. They were faced with such problems as purging the hydrocarbon vapors from the deactivated catalyst before it entered the regeneration zone, preventing interflow of reactants between the zones, controlling the temperature and pressure drop in the regenerator, and regulating the flow of catalyst so as to provide a smooth and even distribution throughout the moving-bed.[5]

In the commercial units then envisioned, the rate of circulation of the catalyst was expected to be of the order of 100 to 150 tons an hour.[6] Two problems arose in controlling this avalanche of pebbles. In the first place, it was extremely difficult to distribute the catalyst evenly throughout the interior of the reactor and the regenerator. Complicated systems of grids and baffles had to be designed to obtain the proper flow. In the second place, catalyst ground into dust (called "fines") by abrasion had to be removed from the system.[7] Moreover, the moving catalyst itself caused erosion in the interior surfaces of any slanted pipes and vessels, so that baffles had to be inserted or special alloy steels had to be used. Strangely enough, it was farmers, facing the problem of the flow of corn through silos, who had first investigated these phenomena and contributed ideas toward their solution.

As in the catalyst cases of the Houdry fixed-bed process during the regenerating phase, so in the regenerator of the moving-bed process temperature control was a critical problem. The temperature in the moving-bed regenerator was regulated by varying the rate and temperature at which air was supplied to the burning zone and by circulating water through cooling coils woven through the catalyst bed.

It was from the regenerator that this moving-bed process took its name. Socony-Vacuum had at the same period gained experience in designing regenerators or kilns for burning carbon off the clay used in purifying lubri-

[4] U. S. Patents 2,419,507 and 2,419,508.

[5] Socony Mobil Oil Company, Inc., *op. cit.*, pp. 11–13.

[6] R. V. Shankland, "Industrial Catalytic Cracking," *Advances in Chemistry*, Vol. VI, New York: Academic Press, Inc., 1954, p. 295.

[7] *Ibid.*, pp. 292–301, 303–304.

cating oils.[8] This reaction had been called "thermofor," and it was natural for the cracking process to be named Thermofor Catalytic Cracking and abbreviated to TCC.

Spiral-finned Thermofor kiln, developed at Paulsboro, New Jersey (late 1930's).

As had become customary in the oil industry, the research and development was carried out by Socony's own research organization,[9] headed by Dr. J. B. Rather. Rather (later a member of the Houdry Process Corporation's Technical Information Committee) was also a member of Socony's

[8] Socony Mobil Oil Company, Inc., *op. cit.*, pp. 12, 13.

[9] Costs of research and development of the TCC process eventually were paid by Houdry Process Corporation, which by agreement became licensor of the TCC process.

Manufacturing Committee, a group composed of the heads of the various line and staff departments, reporting to the vice-president in charge of manufacturing. Another member of the Manufacturing Committee was Clark S. Teitsworth, who was assigned the job of co-ordinating the process development and of setting priorities on the various phases of the work.

Teitsworth was an engineer, but not a member of the research organization. To have a man in charge of the development whose experience lay outside the specific field of petroleum research was unusual. It can be explained in part by Teitsworth's reputation within the company for having good judgment, and in part as the tradition within Socony's organization. Both the Vacuum Oil Company and the Standard Oil Company of New York, before their merger, had had manufacturing committees, to whose individual members was delegated the responsibility of co-ordinating research programs. Most of the ideas, of course, came from the laboratories and from engineering groups, but the co-ordinator had the job of determining which paths seemed more attractive.

This type of organization is reminiscent of that of the Standard Oil Company (New Jersey) at the time when E. M. Clark was in charge of the development of the Tube and Tank process. In Jersey Standard's case, however, putting the development in charge of a man who had line responsibilities was not the normal procedure; it was done solely because Clark was the only man with sufficient experience in cracking to carry out the job. In the early 1920's, the link between the refinery executives and the scientists was tenuous indeed. The years between 1920 and 1936 marked a change in the attitude of refining personnel toward research. By the end of the period nearly all refinery managers were aware of the benefits accruing from research and development, and almost all were eager to install new processes in their refineries. There were several reasons for this change: the desire to cut costs and the recognition that new processes resulted in lower unit costs, the need to produce a higher-quality gasoline and the knowledge that the greatest increases in gasoline quality resulted from introducing new processes, the arrival of a new group of refinery managers all of whom had had technical training, usually in engineering, and the demonstrated success of the earlier cracking processes. When the first thermal cracking processes were developed, they were installed in the refineries in spite of the refinery managers. By the time the catalytic cracking processes were developed, the refinery managers were as eager as anyone else to apply them commercially.

Adopting the TCC Process

The moving-bed process was operated first in laboratory equipment capable of running 2 gallons an hour. The next step, in January 1941, was a semicommercial unit of 250–500 barrels a day at the Paulsboro, New Jersey, refinery. At the same time that the pilot plant was being tested, design was begun on the first commercial installation. Construction was started at the Beaumont, Texas, refinery of Socony's affiliate, the Magnolia Petroleum Company, and in October 1943, the installation of two units was completed.[10]

[Socony Mobil Oil Company]

Semicommercial TCC unit at Paulsboro, New Jersey (early 1940's).

Although first designed as two units each charging 5,000 barrels a day of gas oil, the capacity of Magnolia's TCC installation was increased to two 10,000-barrels-a-day units before completion.[11] It was unusual that the first commercial TCC units should have been as large as 10,000 barrels a day each. The more usual procedure would have been to build a unit of smaller size, upon which the process variables could have been tested and which would have involved considerably less risk. As in the case of

[10] *Ibid.*, pp. 13–20.
[11] R. V. Shankland, *op. cit.*, p. 290.

the first Fluid Catalytic Cracking unit, so in the first TCC unit the Allies'
needs in World War II and the United States' imminent entry therein
dictated that the intermediate step should be skipped.[12] It was known that

[Socony Mobil Oil Company]

**Commercial bucket-elevator and airlift TCC units (airlift TCC unit on
left).**

the TCC process, employing the principles established by the Houdry
fixed-bed process, would produce high-quality aviation-gasoline blending
stocks, and these were urgently needed. In addition, the federal authority
responsible for allocating supplies of refinery equipment recognized that it

[12] Socony Mobil Oil Company, Inc., *op. cit.*, p. 19.

would be well to find an alternative for the Houdry fixed-bed process because the steel requirements for the Houdry process, per barrel of aviation-gasoline output, were very high. Besides, the turbines which were used to compress air for the Houdry fixed-bed process were in short supply and Allis-Chalmers, the main supplier, was told to direct its output to the United States Navy for use in propulsion systems. For these reasons, the emphasis was on getting into operation as quickly as possible a TCC unit of large capacity.

The upper limit on the size of the unit was set by the capacity of the elevator which lifted the catalyst from the bottoms of the regenerator and the reactor to the tops of the opposite vessels[13] (see figure, p. 169). The chain of relationships was as follows: The capacity of the catalyst elevators set the external dimensions of the TCC unit. There was a maximum height to which the elevator could lift the catalyst, for at greater heights the weight of the chain used for lifting grew too heavy to support and move. This limitation on height imposed an equal constraint on the vertical dimensions of the reactor and regenerator, both of which had, therefore, to be somewhat less than the height of the elevator. Given the height of the kiln, its diameter was determined by the velocity of catalyst flow, the proper velocity being between ·5 foot and 1 foot a minute, or 100 to 150 tons an hour.[14]

In spite of the fact that the first commercial TCC unit was considerably larger than a peacetime unit would have been, it operated from the beginning with few technical difficulties. This was due in part to excellent equipment design, carried out by a group under the chief engineer, George Dunham; in part to the general experience in designing large units which Socony had gained from the installation of the Houdry fixed-bed units; and in part to the large number of engineers Socony assigned to the project.

At an early stage in its development, the TCC process was made available to other refiners.[15] The Houdry Process Corporation, which licensed the Houdry fixed-bed process, also licensed the TCC process, and continued to do so until 1948, when the Houdriflow moving-bed cracking process was introduced.[16] The royalty on the TCC process was established

---

[13] For a description of the elevators, see R. V. Shankland, *op. cit.*, p. 301. These elevators were manufactured by the Jeffrey Elevator Company.

[14] R. V. Shankland, *op. cit.*; and Socony Mobil Oil Company, Inc., *op. cit.*, p. 20.

[15] Public announcement of the moving-bed process and its availability for licensing was made on November 11, 1942, at the 23rd Annual Meeting of the American Petroleum Institute, Division of Refining (see *Petroleum Refiner*, Vol. 21, No. 11), nearly a year before the first commercial unit commenced operation.

[16] According to the Houdry Process Corporation, "The arrangement whereby Houdry Process Corporation paid the T. C. C. process research and development costs, and acquired status as its licensor, stemmed from prior contracts and is clearly

at $125 per barrel of charge on a paid-up basis, or 5¢ per barrel of charge on a running basis.[17]

The first outside licensee was Gulf Oil Corporation, which built three TCC units while Magnolia was constructing its two. Within the next two years, eleven more corporations constructed TCC units.

By June, 1944, less than one year after the first unit went on stream, eighteen large TCC units had been placed in operation in the refineries of eight major oil companies.[18] Four more units were under construction. The TCC process had already shown that it had specific advantages: "the simplifications of the process equipment [had] made possible substantial economies in initial investment, maintenance, and operating costs."[19] By the end of the war, thirty-four TCC units, with a capacity of 299,810 bpsd, were in operation.

It might normally have been expected that Socony, employing Houdry's principles to develop the TCC process, and Sun, associated with Socony through Houdry, would have installed many of the early TCC units. Only a few years before, however, both firms replaced nearly all their thermal cracking facilities with Houdry fixed-bed units. During the war, the government's criterion for allocating investment was ability to increase the industry's output of gasoline, and this did not permit replacing such equipment as Houdry fixed-bed units, which already yielded a product of acceptable quality. Any TCC installations would

---

set forth in correspondence exchanged in November, 1948, between Eugene Houdry and Wilbur F. Burt of Socony-Vacuum. Mr. Houdry, recalling that late in 1938 Houdry Process Corporation was heavily engaged in development of aviation gasoline facilities and unable to undertake any part of the work or cost of the moving-bed process development, discussed the subject at that time with Mr. Arthur Pew and Mr. Burt. For the record, Mr. Houdry wrote Mr. Burt as follows: 'At that time you suggested that, since H. P. C. would have certain licensing rights under this new moving catalyst process for petroleum conversion, H. P. C. should absorb the development expense. I agreed with this in principle and suggested that we make some arrangement for future reimbursement. . . . In order to make definite the amount that H. P. C. is obligated to pay Socony, you have informed us that the aggregate amount expended by Socony on the development of the T. C. C. process up to May 1, 1943, is approximately $1,150,000. H. P. C. agrees to reimburse Socony-Vacuum for the development cost.' Houdry's letter then states terms of payment, and other pertinent conditions and relationships, to all of which the Socony-Vacuum Board of Directors agreed as stated in Burt's reply of November 24, 1948. Burt had been Socony's senior representative in the Houdry organization until 1947, when he withdrew to be replaced by Clark S. Teitsworth, who had represented Socony on Houdry's Board since 1934."

[17] These were identical to the royalties for the Fluid Catalytic Cracking process, announced a few months earlier. (See Chapter 6.)

[18] R. E. Bland, A. W. Hoge, and G. F. Hornaday, Houdry Process Corporation, "Development of Houdriflow Catalytic Cracking," Houdry Pioneer, Vol. V, No. 1, February, 1950, p. 4. It was in that month, June 1944, that the last Houdry fixed-bed unit was completed.

[19] Ibid.

have had to be justified as providing increases in aviation gasoline output. Of the thirty-five TCC units that were built and put into operation during the war, Socony (together with its subsidiaries, General Petroleum and Magnolia Petroleum) and Sun accounted for ten units, or roughly 30%. In terms of capacity, Socony and Sun's TCC units were rated at 93,000 barrels a stream day, 31% of the total. Because of the restrictions on the construction of new refinery equipment imposed by the federal government, the TCC process gives us our first and only example of a case in which the oil company which developed the cracking process did not install the major fraction of the first new units.

The smallest of these TCC units was 8,000 barrels a day, which placed it well above the range of the average small petroleum refiner. As a result almost all of the capacity was installed by large oil companies. Since catalytic cracking reduced costs substantially, the small refiners "were faced with the prospect of being unable to meet the competition of the large refiners unless they, too, could install catalytic cracking facilities."[20]

On the one hand, the Houdry Process Corporation realized that the small refiners would not be attracted to the large units. On the other hand, they also realized that the smaller refiners would want catalytic cracking facilities of some variety.[21] They suspected that after the war many of the small refiners would be willing to invest in a TCC unit if the investment cost could be reduced. In their calculations prior to 1941, Socony's engineers had found that below 8,000 barrels a day, the capital cost of a TCC unit decreased very little as the size was reduced. These calculations were based upon using in the small TCC units equipment identical with that used in the large ones, reduced only in scale. Houdry decided, however, that in order to lower the capital costs for smaller units it would be necessary to redesign and simplify the process equipment.[22]

TCC Process Improvement

Houdry knew that the small refiners were eager to install catalytic cracking units and that many were able to afford small installations. There were three reasons for this demand. First, because of stable prices and guaranteed markets, many of the small concerns had had high earnings during the war[23] and had accumulated funds for future expansion. Second, some of the small refiners had benefited from government-con-

[20] R. E. Bland, A. W. Hoge, and G. F. Hornaday, op. cit., p. 5.
[21] "Refineries Must Have Catalytic Cracking to Meet Competition, Frame Tells A. P. I.," Petroleum Processing, July 1947, pp. 549–552.
[22] R. E. Bland, A. W. Hoge, and G. F. Hornaday, op. cit.
[23] "Gulf Coast's Independent Refiners Are Reorganized," Oil and Gas Journal, August 8, 1949, p. 176.

structed cracking plants located in their own refineries.[24] These fortunate companies presented an example which many of the small concerns were desirous of imitating. Third, the federal government and the industry, through their wartime program of disseminating technological information, presented all the firms in the industry with a considerable amount of data illustrating the profitability of catalytic cracking, both for wartime and for peacetime operations.[25]

The capital cost of building small TCC units was reduced primarily through redesign of the equipment.

The reactor, hot-catalyst storage drum, and reactor-feed hopper were built as one structure. Because of the lower catalyst circulation rate (50 to 75 tons/hour), it was possible to use a single bucket elevator of standard design except that three compartments were used in each bucket. Regenerated catalyst is transported in the center compartment, and the cooler spent catalyst in the two end compartments next to the chain. The reactor and regenerator are used as structures to support platforms and to furnish top guides for the bucket elevator, which is located between the two vessels.[26]

The preliminary designs were completed before the end of the war, and in October 1945, Houdry announced that TCC units of 2,000 to 3,000 barrels a day of charge capacity were available "at investment costs comparing favorably with those for larger units."[27] Costs and performance of these small TCC units were publicized in the trade journals.[28] The first small TCC unit was contracted for by Leonard Refineries, Inc., in 1946 and in March, 1947, a 3,000-barrel-a-day unit went on stream at Leonard's Alma, Michigan, refinery.[29]

[24] Of the $236,000,000 spent by the government for new plant facilities during the war, $153,000,000, or 65%, was expended on equipment located in the plants of small, non-integrated refiners (U. S. Petroleum Administrator for War, *History of the Petroleum Administration for War, 1941–1945*, Washington: Government Printing Office, 1946, p. 368).

[25] Petroleum Industry War Council, Technical Advisory Committee, *Wartime Petroleum Research*, May 8, 1945, Appendix VI; see also U. S. Petroleum Administration for War, *op. cit.*, p. 199.

[26] R. V. Shankland, *op. cit.*, p. 304.

[27] R. E. Bland, A. W. Hoge, and G. F. Hornaday, *op. cit.*, pp. 5, 6.

[28] H. D. Noll, E. V. Bergstrom, and K. G. Holdom, "New Integral T. C. C. Unit Makes Catalytic Cracking Available to Small Refiners," *Oil and Gas Journal*, April 6, 1946. The capacity of the TCC unit reported here was 2,450 barrels per calendar day, and the authors compared in quantitative terms the outputs of a small refinery with and without this catalytic cracking unit.

[29] R. E. Bland, A. W. Hoge, and G. F. Hornaday, *op. cit.*, p. 6. There were several small refiners in southern Michigan which were able to consider installing catalytic cracking units. With access to the nearby crude-oil field and with a local market for heavy fuel oil, these refineries had always been profitable to operate. In addition, the Michigan crude oil contained a large fraction of naphtha which found

In 1945, even before Houdry began to promote small TCC units, both Houdry and Socony were working to improve process design. In the original design, the flow of catalyst and oil in the reactor had been in opposite directions; the oil vapors flowed upward and the catalyst pellets downward. This mode of operation was called countercurrent. In the improved TCC process, the flow of reactants and of catalyst was in the same downward direction. This was called concurrent operation.

The advantage of concurrent operation was that it mixed the incoming oil with the catalyst when it was at its highest temperature, just after leaving the regenerator. Since catalyst temperature was higher, the sensible heat in the catalyst could vaporize some of the oil as well as promote the cracking reaction. The oil could thus be fed partly in liquid form, either saving on preheating or permitting the use of a heavier gas-oil charge. In laboratory experiments Socony had discovered that product yields and qualities were as good for liquid as for vaporized feeds. The only disadvantage was a larger deposit of coke, but this could be eliminated by increasing the proportion of catalyst to oil. Since the proportions of catalyst to oil were still within the range which had been explored in pilot-plant units and which was incorporated in the design of existing commercial units, concurrent flow was easily adopted.

In the spring of 1946, concurrent flow was thus installed by Socony and Houdry engineers on Socony's TCC unit at the Paulsboro refinery.[30] As Socony's processing scheme did not provide heavy gas-oil charge, however, the concurrent flow operation was applied to vaporized feeds only. Soon all other TCC units were revamped to facilitate concurrent operation.

Even though Socony itself did not immediately charge heavy gas oil to its TCC units, the main effect of the change in the process was to permit charging the heavier feed. Both the Houdry fixed-bed and the early TCC processes had been unable to charge gas oils having a boiling point above approximately 1000°F. Stocks boiling at higher temperatures could not be used because the feed had to be completely vaporized upon entering the reactor.[31] Even then, the vaporized oil had tended to condense on the catalyst, which in its trip through the reactor had already been cooled in promoting the cracking reaction. With concurrent flow, any unvaporized oil in the feed would be cracked during the time that it took for the catalyst to move down through the reactor.

Another effect of the change in the process was to increase the capacity

---

a market as a solvent in the manufacture of paints and varnishes. ("Cracking to Aid Michigan Refineries," *Refiner and Natural Gasoline Manufacturer*, October 1935, 457–459.)

[30] Socony Mobil Oil Company, Inc., *op. cit.*, pp. 26–28.

[31] R. V. Shankland, *op. cit.*, p. 390.

of existing TCC units. The higher-boiling feed stocks are more readily cracked, and therefore require less severe operating conditions than the light gas oils.[32] This permits an increase in the rate at which the reactant can be propelled through the reactor, which is equivalent to an increase in capacity of the units. Still another advantage gained by the switch from countercurrent to concurrent operation was a reduction in the amount of fuel consumed per barrel of charge.[33]

In November 1947, shortly after the development of small TCC units and concurrent flow, "Socony withdrew from management and other participation in the affairs of Houdry. Thereafter, Houdry, on the one hand, and Socony, on the other, pursued separate catalytic-cracking development programs."[34]

[32] *Ibid.*, p. 391.

[33] *Ibid.* The changes in equipment design that were required in the shift from countercurrent to concurrent operation are described by Shankland on pp. 305–309.

[34] Socony Mobil Oil Company, Inc., *op. cit.*, p. 30. Relations between Socony and Houdry did not remain cordial—"In March, 1953, after some negotiations back and forth with Socony, Houdry Process Corporation brought suit against Socony. The suit was a very broad and complicated one, and included a large number of issues, including the charge that certain of Houdry's patents were infringed. Pre-trial work on the suit was pursued for over two years. In December, 1955, a settlement agreement was reached between the companies, thereby putting an end to what might have proved to be a very long and complicated litigation. The following press announcement was released in connection with the settlement of this litigation:

'Pending litigation between Houdry Process Corporation and Socony Mobil Oil Company, Inc., involving certain catalytic cracking processes in petroleum refining will be terminated by agreement before December 31, the two companies jointly announced today.

'The principal processes involved are the Air-lift Thermofor Catalytic Cracking (TCC) process and the Houdriflow process.

'Managements of the two companies have approved an agreement providing for amicable settlement before the end of the year of all issues existing between them. Under the terms of the agreement:

'(1) The two companies will exchange full and complete immunities in the field of moving-bed catalytic cracking (including certain improvements in synthetic cracking catalyst, the so-called Houdresid technique, and the like) for their own operations and for those of their respective licensees, and the right to receive, use, and pass on to licensees technical information and know-how owned or controlled before December 31 by either company.

'(2) The two companies will grant to each other for themselves and their respective present and future licensees an irrevocable non-exclusive royalty-free immunity under patent rights for certain inventions in the field of moving-bed catalytic cracking made during a five-year period beginning next January 1.

'(3) In acquisition of certain patent rights and in settlement of patent claims, Socony Mobil will pay $3,000,000 to Houdry. In addition with respect to any new TCC licenses granted by Socony during the five-year period beginning next January 1, Socony will pay Houdry $12.50 per barrel of licensed capacity with respect to each paid-up license and three-quarters of a cent per barrel out of running royalties received until such payments amount to $12.50 per daily barrel of capacity.' " (*Ibid.*)

The Development of Pneumatic Lifts

There was a demand not only for TCC units smaller than 8,000 barrels a day, but also for TCC units of capacities greater than 10,000 barrels a day. We recall that the upper limit on the capacity had been set by the amount of catalyst that the elevator could lift to the top of the regenerator and the reactor. If some alternate means of elevating the catalyst could be found which would lift more than 150 tons of catalyst an hour, moving-bed units of considerably larger capacity could be constructed. Both the large Houdry fixed-bed units and the even larger thermal cracking units had proved more profitable to operate than smaller units incorporating the same processes.

> The possibility of employing a pneumatic lift to replace the bucket elevators, which possibility had been periodically considered over the years, was again considered [at both Houdry and Socony]. Also considered was the possibility of increasing the size of the bucket elevators. At an early date, Houdry, Socony, and Lummus had contacted elevator manufacturers, particularly Jeffrey Manufacturing Company of Columbus, Ohio, on this problem. The first reaction was that a larger elevator was not feasible. Upon further consideration, at a later date, the elevator manufacturers suggested that, if such a design were to be developed, the cost would have to be borne by the user of the equipment. This position was a factor in the final decision to develop a pneumatic conveyor.[35]

So some time prior to 1938, research began on elevating the catalyst with an upward-flowing stream of gas. It was found that large volumes of catalyst could be blown upwards, much as a little ball can be elevated by a jet of water.

The main problem in employing pneumatic lifts was the breakage and attrition of catalyst particles. Both Houdry and Socony attacked the problem. Their experiments ranged from using small laboratory lifts to using commercial lifts 16 to 20 inches in diameter and 200 feet in height.[36] Houdry's lift employed flue gas from the regenerator as the transporting fluid; Socony's employed air.

Since Houdry and Socony had separated their research and development activities, it was natural also for them to separate their licensing activities. Houdry's catalytic cracking process, employing the gas lift, was named Houdriflow, and was promoted by the Houdry Process Corporation. Socony's process, employing the air lift, retained the name Thermofor Catalytic Cracking and was licensed by Socony. Thus we have after 1947 two similar processes, stemming from the original TCC inventions.

[35] Socony Mobil Oil Company, Inc., *op. cit.*, p. 31.
[36] *Ibid.*, pp. 32, 33.

Houdriflow Process

Let us look first at the elements of the Houdriflow process. With the bucket-elevator TCC process, the amount of catalyst by weight which could be introduced to the cracking zone could be just a little more than the amount of vaporized oil injected, giving a ratio of about 1.5 pounds

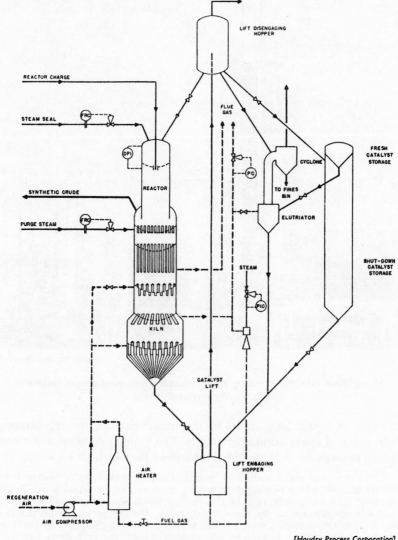

[Houdry Process Corporation]

Houdriflow catalytic cracking process, flow sheet.

of catalyst to 1 pound of oil; whereas the Houdry pneumatic-transport system permitted an increase in the catalyst-to-oil ratio up to at least 7:1. As a result, with more — and much hotter — catalyst coming into the reactor chamber, more heat was provided so that the fraction of oil

[Houdry Process Corporation]

Houdriflow catalytic cracking plant, reactor-kiln vessel shown in center foreground.

injected in liquid form could be increased.[37] Second, the regenerating kiln required fewer burning-off stages. The higher rate of catalyst circulation through the kiln provided additional heat without exceeding the

[37] In developing the Houdriflow Process, Houdry worked on a reactor feed-nozzle assembly which would permit feed to be entirely in the liquid phase. In the elevator TCC units, only 15% of the feed could be liquid. Subsequently, along with the development of the Houdriflow process, Houdry perfected and installed on all Houdriflow units a system which would permit the charge to be 100% in the liquid phase. (This liquid-feed system made possible the later development of the Houdresid Catalytic Cracking process which charges residual stocks almost entirely in the liquid phase.)

temperature limit for the catalyst. Third, simplification of the kiln made it possible to superimpose the reactor above the kiln in a single unit, using gravity flow rather than mechanical means to introduce the moving catalyst from the reactor to the regenerator stage. Heat loss from the

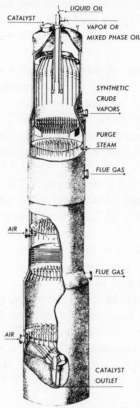

[Houdry Process Corporation]

Houdriflow integral reactor-kiln vessel.

catalyst was diminished, thereby reducing the cost of heat input to the reactor. Fourth, pneumatic lifting of the regenerated catalyst to the top of the reactor chamber provided a continuous moving-bed catalytic cracking process that was competitive with the "Fluid" process.

The spring of 1948 found Houdry Process Corporation negotiating with prospective licensees. The process was announced publicly in December of that year,[38] and the first plants — a 6,750-bpsd unit at the Tide-

[38] R. E. Bland, A. W. Hoge, and G. F. Hornaday, *op. cit.*, p. 6.

water Oil Company refinery at Drumright, Oklahoma, and four units totaling 30,000 bpsd at Sun's refinery in Toledo, Ohio — went on stream in 1950.

The first Houdriflow units were somewhat smaller than the original TCC units. For example, each one of the four units erected at the Toledo refinery of the Sun Oil Company[39] had a nominal charging capacity of 7,000 bpsd, including recycle.[40] There was, however, a common fractionating system.

In the Houdriflow process, with the catalyst to gas-oil ratio increased and the hot catalyst providing the heat required for the endothermic cracking reaction, it was possible to substitute a greater amount of catalyst for the feed preheater used in the original TCC process. The Houdriflow unit could be designed to be in balance with respect to heat, that is, as much heat was generated in the kiln as would be consumed in the reaction. In addition, the higher catalyst circulation rates led to a simplification in the design of the regenerator.[41] Two burning zones are sufficient in the most recent Houdriflow kilns, whereas seven to ten had been required in the early TCC bucket-elevator units. With the installation of the gas lift, and the combined arrangement of the vessels, the capital cost of the Houdriflow units was about 20% less than the earlier TCC units.[42] Likewise, operating costs were reduced, the main reduction resulting from the saving of fuel.

Since the installation of the first Houdriflow unit, the design has been improved. The over-all height of the unit has been lowered by having the reactor and the regenerator contained within a single shell.[43] Houdriflow units both larger and smaller than the first plant have been built. Capacities range from 5,000 to 27,000 bpsd, and still smaller units are under construction.[44] The capital cost of small Houdriflow units is kept

[39] Paul D. Barton, "Sun's New Houdriflow Unit," *Oil and Gas Journal*, March 29, 1957.

[40] The reasons for having four 7,000-barrel-per-day units rather than one 28,000-barrel-per-day unit were as follows: the reactors and kilns could be fabricated in the shops of the constructing company; one reactor and regenerator could be shut down for repairs, and the other three could charge nearly the same amount of gas oil. The advantage of shop fabrication was a lower investment cost. The advantages accruing from the operating flexibility were less fluctuation in plant output, less raw material and finished product tankage, and a smaller refinery maintenance crew. (*Ibid.*)

[41] R. E. Bland, A. W. Hoge, and G. F. Hornaday, *op. cit.*, p. 7.

[42] R. V. Shankland, *op. cit.*, p. 313.

[43] *Ibid.*, pp. 313–316. Other less significant improvements are also described in this article.

[44] D. B. Ardern, "If You Can't Modernize All At Once—Do It In Steps," *Petroleum Processing*, November 1953.

as low as possible, but there is every indication that the investment per unit of input or output is still higher in the smaller units.[45]

Air-Lift TCC Process

The first TCC unit designed by Socony to utilize the air lift for the catalyst was installed in the Beaumont, Texas, refinery of the Magnolia Petroleum Company, and placed on stream on October 6, 1950. This air-lift TCC unit had a capacity of 15,000 barrels a day, 50% greater than the TCC bucket elevator. The air was heated before entering the lift line so as not to cool the catalyst unnecessarily. In a 15,000-barrel-a-day unit, 12,000 cubic feet of air per minute were required in order to lift the 270 tons of catalyst that the unit circulated each hour.[46] In order to confine the catalyst, a pipe about 2 feet in diameter at the bottom and 3 feet at the top was required; the lift line had to be widened to compensate for the expansion of the air as it was heated by the catalyst. The elevator in the earlier TCC units had limited the height of the equipment. This, in turn, had required separate structures for the reactor and the regenerator, and two lifting stages. With the air-lift TCC process, the height of the units was no longer limited, and therefore (as in Houdriflow) the reactor and regenerator no longer had to be placed on separate structures. With the TCC reactor on top and slightly to one side of the regenerator, both vessels were supported by the same structural framework. Since the catalyst flowed by gravity from reactor to regenerator, only one lifting stage was required, to raise the catalyst from the regenerator to the top of the reactor. At the same time that the air lift was developed, the kiln was redesigned in order to improve the heating efficiency of the TCC unit.[47] The economic results of the adoption of the air lift and of the consequent redesigning of the TCC process were lower investment cost, greater flexibility of operation, and a slight increase in variable costs owing in part to a greater attrition of catalyst in the moving air stream.

Many TCC air-lift units have been installed. With the limitation to

[45] "Houdriflow Catalytic Cracking Applied to Current Economics," *Petroleum Processing*, May 1949. In this article, the charge capacity and capital cost of five different-sized Houdriflow catalytic cracking units were given:

Capacity (barrels per day)	Capital Cost	Capital Cost per Daily Barrel of Input
4157	$1,505,000	$360
4272	1,550,000	360
4767	1,600,000	340
8544	1,900,000	220
9534	1,960,000	210

[46] R. V. Shankland, *op. cit.*, pp. 316, 318.

[47] *Ibid.*, p. 316–319.

higher capacities removed, TCC units incorporating the air lift have been designed with capacities up to 30,000 barrels a day.[48] The air-lift principle has also been applied to small TCC units for the independent refiners. Units with capacities as low as 1,500 barrels a day have been constructed, in which investment costs have been reduced by a standardizing of design.[49] In the standardized or "packaged" units, most of the equipment is fabricated in the factory of the construction company, rather than at the site of the installation.[50] The supporting structure for the small TCC units is a derrick similar to those used in the drilling of oil. Not only is a derrick a standard item, but it can also be used as a crane to hoist the equipment into place during construction. All of these economies of design and construction tend to offset, at least in part, the disadvantages of building small-scale cracking units.

Development work directed towards improvement of the TCC process has continued . . . improvement of lift design and operation with resultant decrease in attrition, elimination of plume from kiln stack gas, improvement in kiln internals permitting very substantial increase in coke burning capacity, improvement in reactor bed temperature pattern with resultant substantial increase in product revenue and improvement in the fresh catalyst make-up system and in catalyst hardness with further resultant catalyst attrition decrease. The increasing scarcity of light gas oil charge stocks has gradually increased the demand for catalytic cracking units capable of handling as much as fifty per cent liquid feed in the reactor charge. This demand has stimulated development by Socony engineers of a new injection-type liquid feed system capable of handling larger quantities of liquid feed. . . . Modifications of this newly developed liquid feed system have been installed in a number of the most recently constructed commercial TCC units, as well as in the commercial Paulsboro Air Lift TCC, where Socony's most recent version was successfully demonstrated. This system not only permits handling of large quantities of liquid feed, but also permits elimination of the usual phase separator and injection of the liquid into the catalyst in the upper section of the reactor in the mixed phase.[51]

[48] Socony Mobil Oil Company, Inc., *op. cit.*, p. 38.
[49] R. V. Shankland, *op. cit.*, p. 316.
[50] The larger "packaged" units utilized two small regenerators rather than one large one in order to retain the advantage of shop fabrication. (*Ibid.*)
[51] Socony Mobil Oil Company, Inc., *op. cit.*, pp. 37, 38. Concern with the disposal of the very heavy fractions of crude oil, which cannot be treated in a conventional catalytic cracking unit, has led to the development of yet another catalytic cracking process by Houdry Process Corporation. This process is known as Houdresid ("Houdresid Catalytic Cracking," *Oil and Gas Journal*, March 19, 1956, p. 143). With the Houdresid process it is now possible to crack the heaviest 60% of crude oil, twice the amount that the Burton stills were able to handle.

Cost and Returns for the Innovation

The TCC process was licensed to the refining industry from the date of its introduction. The royalty rate established by the Houdry Process Corporation, 5¢ per barrel of fresh charge, was deferred during the war, but was collected afterwards. The Houdriflow and air-lift TCC units have been licensed at lower rates: for the TCC process on a running basis it has been 3¢ per barrel of fresh charge; on a paid-up basis, $50 per barrel of daily capacity.[52] Royalties for the bucket-elevator TCC units, all of which were licensed by Houdry, totaled $18,200,000 through 1956.[53] Houdriflow royalties, from 1950, when the process was introduced, through 1956, amounted to $4,050,000.[54] Returns for the air-lift TCC process, which has been licensed by Socony, were estimated by the author to be $12,108,000 for the same period (see Appendix Table 18). Implicit in the last calculation is the assumption that Socony has made a profit on each of its air-lift TCC units equal to the royalty rate it charges others. Together, therefore, royalties and operating profits accruing to the innovators of the initial TCC process and its derivatives through 1956 were about $34,000,000. Since this sum does not include all of Socony's profits from operating the TCC process, it is most likely an understatement, perhaps by as much as 50%.

We do not have a good estimate of the costs of the TCC and Houdriflow developments. We do know that by May 1, 1943, Socony had spent a total of $1,150,000 on the TCC process. Assuming that in each of the preceding seven years an equal amount was spent, the annual expenditure would be $165,000. Making the additional assumptions that the rate of spending remained the same for Socony through 1956 and that Houdry spent an equal amount each year from 1945 through 1956 on the Houdriflow process, we can estimate the development of the TCC and Houdriflow processes to have cost approximately $5,000,000.[55] If this figure is accurate, the development of the TCC and Houdriflow processes has been very profitable for the innovating firms; on an investment of roughly $5,000,000 they had recovered through 1956 in royalties and operating profits at least $34,000,000, or seven dollars for each dollar invested.

Some of the returns from the development of the TCC and Houdriflow processes might well be allocated to the earlier Houdry fixed-bed

[52] Socony˙Mobil Oil Company, Inc., *TCC Process Agreement*, Sections 14, 31 and 32, pp. 4, 7.
[53] Houdry Process Corporation, letter from W. P. Reed, November 27, 1957.
[54] *Ibid.*
[55] This is a very rough figure; we might better say that it lies in the range of $3,000,000 to $10,000,000.

process. Much that was learned during the innovation of the fixed-bed process — the general understanding of catalysis and regeneration, the attributes of an acceptable cracking catalyst, and the flow characteristics of large volumes of hydrocarbon vapor — were applicable in the moving-bed process. The total development costs of both innovations were at least $16,000,000. Together the revenues that have accrued from the innovations are at least $83,000,000. This is a return of somewhat over four dollars for each dollar invested. The profits of the second innovation when added to those of the first yield an average return that was quite attractive. It was in the TCC and Houdriflow processes that the Houdry fixed-bed process paid off.[56]

Conclusions

The original Houdry fixed-bed process was the first commercially practical catalytic cracking process, and from 1936 to 1942 was the only significant process in this field. Within a few years, however, three continuous cracking processes, two of which utilized the principle of the moving bed, were to be developed. The moving-bed process was seen to have many advantages.

> With the moving-bed system it is no longer necessary to construct all vessels to withstand the most severe conditions encountered during both cracking and regeneration. This advantage is especially important in plants for processing high-sulfur feed stocks.
> Heat is removed from the regenerator by means of the circulating catalyst, supplemented by water-cooled tubes. This technique eliminates the need for the complex and expensive temperature-control system used in the Houdry process (the closely spaced, perforated inlet and outlet pipes, and the circulating molten-salt system).
> Catalyst replacement is greatly simplified.
> Operations in both the reactor and regenerator are continuous, so there is no need for the complicated system of valves, control mechanisms, and safety devices required in the Houdry process.
> Composition of the cracked product stream is constant, whereas in fixed-bed processes it varies during each cycle.[57]

One of these moving-bed processes was Thermofor Catalytic Cracking. In 1944, Socony Mobil Oil Company, which with the Houdry Process Corporation had developed the TCC process, made the first TCC instal-

---

[56] The Houdry Process Corporation wishes to dissociate itself from the assumptions and conclusions of the author in the foregoing paragraphs discussing economics.

[57] D. E. Ardern, J. C. Dart, and R. C. Lassiat, "Advances in Chemistry, Series Number 5," *Progress in Petroleum Technology*, Washington: American Chemical Society, 1951, p. 13, as quoted in R. V. Shankland, *op. cit.*, p. 289.

lation, two units totaling 20,000-barrels-a-day capacity, in the refinery of its subsidiary in Beaumont, Texas. Within two years thirty-two more units were added so that by the end of the war a total of 299,810 barrels a day of TCC capacity had been installed. The majority of the TCC units were built not by Socony and Sun but by other concerns. Having previously installed enough Houdry fixed-bed units to satisfy the cracking requirements of most of their refineries and being restricted on new investments, Socony and Sun accounted for no more than 30% of the wartime additions to capacity.

The Thermofor Catalytic Cracking process differed from the Houdry fixed-bed process in several ways. First, the reactor and regeneration zones were separate; each was designed specifically for its own purpose. Second, each zone functioned continuously. Third, a compact bed of catalyst moved continuously through the two zones in endless cycle, the catalyst being elevated mechanically from one zone to another. The TCC process had the inherent advantages of the Houdry fixed-bed process, that is, it produced a high percentage of high-octane gasoline blending-material from gas-oil stocks. The product quality was considerably superior to thermally cracked gasoline, and the product yield was as great as that of the thermal cracking processes.

As is usual in the petroleum industry, the TCC process was improved shortly after the installation of the initial bucket-elevator units. The first major improvement was the shift from countercurrent to concurrent flow in the reactor, which reduced fuel consumption of the unit and permitted the charging of heavier cracking stocks. The second major improvement, reflected in both the TCC and the Houdriflow processes, was the substitution of a pneumatic for a mechanical means of conveying the catalyst. This change in the physical handling of catalyst permitted the equipment to be redesigned and considerably simplified, and so lowered investment cost.

Simplifying the process equipment — the vessels, the structure, and the mode of construction — permitted small TCC and Houdriflow units to be built for the independent refiner. The development of the air and gas lifts also permitted the building of very large units, which had not been possible when mechanical elevators conveyed the catalyst.

For its developers, the Socony Mobil Oil Company and the Houdry Process Corporation, the TCC and Houdriflow process innovations have been quite profitable, yielding several dollars for each dollar spent. Building upon their experience in catalytic cracking gained in the development of the Houdry fixed-bed process, the companies were able to develop a superior, continuous process. In this respect, Socony and Houdry are unique, for they are our only example of companies which made two consecutive innovations in the cracking process. Previously, first one company, then another, had been the innovator. Following their initial success, earlier innovating firms (although not necessarily individuals) had either slackened their research efforts or had shifted to different problems. Socony and Houdry, however, were able to see the limitations as well as the merits of the fixed-bed process, and to break away from their earlier pattern. It should be noted, however, that different men developed each innovation.

Continuous moving-bed catalytic cracking continues to be a profitable process. Units recently constructed have increased the total capacity of the two moving-bed processes to roughly 1,256,000 bpsd. TCC and Houdriflow installations have represented an increasing share of the total cracking capacity of the industry in the United States; the TCC process constitutes a larger percentage of the total, but both show an equally rapid rate of growth (see Appendix Table 1c).

Since the first installation of cracking units, forty years ago, American petroleum refiners have consistently worked toward cracking greater and greater portions of each barrel of crude oil. When combined with the simultaneous trend toward the production of higher-octane gasoline, the results of the industry's efforts have been to produce a product of ever-increasing quality while utilizing lower and lower quality raw materials. The changes in technology have thus resulted both in improving the quality of the product and in extending the range of raw materials suitable for gasoline manufacture. The TCC and Houdriflow catalytic cracking processes have been among the most important steps in this long sequence of advances.

6

THE FLUID CATALYTIC CRACKING
PROCESS

Until 1942, the Houdry process remained the only significant catalytic process. In that year a competitive process, Fluid Catalytic Cracking, was introduced through the combined effort of Standard Oil Company (New Jersey), M. W. Kellogg Company,[1] Standard Oil Company (Indiana), British Petroleum Company, Ltd., the Royal Dutch/ Shell group, Texaco Corporation, and Universal Oil Products Company. Research on catalytic cracking was undertaken by each one of these firms with the common aim of developing a process which would not infringe on any of the Houdry patents. For each of them this deliberate attempt to improve upon and circumvent the Houdry process resulted primarily from the high price which Houdry asked of its licensees. In the course of developing the Fluid Catalytic Cracking process, these firms improved the cracking technique, mainly by making the process continuous. The replacement of the semicontinuous Houdry process with continuous processes reduced costs at all outputs up to the capacity of the largest Houdry unit and extended economies of scale to outputs beyond that.

The pattern of the development of the Fluid Catalytic Cracking process differed markedly from preceding innovations. It was a joint effort by several firms working amicably and co-operatively rather than the independent, secretive effort of a single firm. The research was carried out by many scientists and engineers, each specializing in an area in which he was most expert, rather than by a single man or a small group. In contrast to the development of continuous thermal cracking, there was a pooling of patents and information at an early stage rather than protracted litigation. Also in contrast, the chief problems were limited to the

---

[1] Kellogg was a construction company which began building refining equipment in the 1920's. In 1928, it became the sole licensor for the Cross thermal cracking process and in the following decade designed and installed many thermal cracking units. The development of catalytic cracking threatened to make Kellogg's experience in thermal cracking valueless — hence the urge to contribute to the new technique.

realm of technology instead of encompassing a wider area which included finance, administration, and promotion as well.

The development of the Fluid Catalytic Cracking process also showed that benefits can be gained from the steady accumulation of knowledge and a continuously functioning research and development organization. In the decades between 1920 and 1950, the major oil companies one after another established permanent research and development organizations.[2] Institutionalizing research made technological progress endemic to the oil industry. During the same period, the independent process-development companies strengthened their position so that they too became institutions for improving technology. All these organizations provided vast amounts of knowledge and large pools of scientists and engineers, who could be assigned wherever there was a need, for knowledge and skill gained for one purpose were frequently of value in entirely different projects. In this sense, technical knowledge and skills are like certain capital goods which can be used to produce not one but many different products.

The final feature of the Fluid Catalytic Cracking process that we shall notice is its rapid adoption by the refining industry. Because of the desperate need for their products and because they required less steel and other critical materials in their construction, Fluid Catalytic Cracking units were authorized by the federal government during the early stages of World War II. In order to create large-scale units in the shortest possible time, the stages of development — from laboratory to pilot plant to small-scale commercial unit to larger commercial units — were compressed. The second stage — the transition from pilot plant to a small commercial unit — was completely eliminated. Where economic factors might have pressed for a less rapid development, the overriding importance of military factors was to increase the pace.

Early Research in Catalysis

The early development of catalytic cracking had proceeded in much the same way as thermal cracking nearly twenty years before. The companies which produced the first commercially successful process, the Burton process in thermal cracking and the Houdry process in catalytic cracking, each held a monopoly on the practice of the art for approximately six years. In each case, research on competitive processes began before the original innovation had been widely adopted.

The major firm in the group of eight innovating companies, Standard

---

[2] See J. L. Enos, "The Mighty Adversaries: Standard Oil Company (New Jersey) and Royal Dutch/Shell," *Explorations in Entrepreneurial History*, Vol. X, No. 3, April 1958, p. 142.

Oil Company (New Jersey) became interested in catalysis during the 1920's. Aware of the alternatives, its initial line of endeavor led it not toward cracking alone but toward hydrogenation combined with cracking.[3] Catalysis can be utilized to promote both of these reactions, even though they are of a different nature. Jersey Standard chose the destructive hydrogenation process because it seemed to offer greater prospects. In the first place, the basic raw materials for the hydrogenation process — coal, heavy oils, tar, and hydrogen — were in abundant supply; whereas the better grades of crude petroleum — the existing source of similar hydrocarbons — were then thought to be close to exhaustion. In the second place, a considerable amount of research, primarily in Germany, had already been done on hydrogenation. Germany, with abundant coal resources and very little crude petroleum, offered an even greater promise for the future of hydrogenation than did the United States. With a sizable incentive to the development of the hydrogenation process and with able scientists and a strong chemical industry to carry out the development, Germany was able to achieve some success. During World War I, Dr. Friedrich Bergius was able in the laboratory to produce oil by the hydrogenation of coal, relying upon heat and high hydrogen pressure to carry out the reaction. During the middle 1920's, a hydrogenation process was developed which utilized a catalyst, and which seemed superior to Bergius' process.

The results of this research were known by the Standard Oil Development Company (now Esso Research and Engineering Company), the subsidiary of the Standard Oil Company (New Jersey), whose function is research and development, and whose origin we discussed in Chapter 3. The German company which owned the catalytic hydrogenation process, Badische Anilin und Soda Fabrik (which later merged with other German chemical companies to become I. G. Farbenindustrie) was approached by Standard Oil Development in 1926. Discussions began concerning the possibility of a co-operative research program on hydrogenation, and this was extended in 1927 by the visit of a technical group from the Development Company to Badische's plant. The investigation led to the conclusion that the hydrogenation process was potentially very significant, but that a large amount of research would still be necessary

[3] Hydrogenation consists in the joining of additional hydrogen atoms to unsaturated hydrocarbon groups. Although two commercial plants have been operated in the United States since the early 1930's, hydrogenation first became important in the U. S. oil industry only in World War II when the process was applied to the manufacture of iso-octane, an aviation gasoline blending stock (W. L. Nelson, *Petroleum Refinery Engineering*, 3rd ed., New York: McGraw-Hill Book Co., 1949, pp. 654–656).

before it could become commercially profitable.[4] With coal as the raw material, the hydrogenation process showed less immediate promise than the hydrogenation of certain fractions of crude petroleum. The manufacture of gasoline by hydrogenating the residual oils was considered to be the most attractive of all.

One member of the group sent to Germany by the Development Company was Robert T. Haslam, a specialist on fuels who had formerly been a member of the Department of Chemical Engineering at M.I.T. When Jersey Standard had decided to proceed with research in hydrogenation, it sought for the services of capable chemists and chemical engineers. Upon the recommendation of Dr. Warren K. Lewis, long a Jersey Standard consultant and then chairman of M.I.T.'s Chemical Engineering Department, it hired Haslam. At the same time, it also induced several men from the same department to accompany Haslam to Baton Rouge, Louisiana, where a new research laboratory had been erected. This laboratory was to be the center of research in catalysis for the Jersey organization.

With the aim of continuing the research on hydrogenation, rather than actually purchasing the rights to the process as then defined, the Development Company in the fall of 1927 signed an agreement with I. G. Farben whereby the former undertook to carry out large-scale development of heavy oil hydrogenation and to exchange the information with I. G. Farben.[5]

By 1929, after an extensive program of experimentation, the Development Company had become convinced of the future profitability of the hydrogenation process. Negotiations with I. G. Farben were renewed; the Development Company wanted the right to practice the hydrogenation art. I. G. Farben was quite willing to sell the process to a company in the oil industry rather than try to license it themselves. For a sum of $35,000,000, paid in Jersey Standard stock, I. G. Farben sold the hydrogenation process and other processes relating to the petroleum industry, plus the relevant patents, for all the world except Germany,[6] while it retained a 20% interest in any royalties collected.

---

[4] C. S. Popple, *Standard Oil Company (New Jersey) in World War II*, New York: Standard Oil Company (New Jersey), 1952, p. 8. The relationship between Jersey and I. G. Farben was explained at the hearings instituted by the antitrust division of the Department of Justice, which had accused Jersey Standard of violation of the Sherman Act (United States of America vs. Standard Oil Company [New Jersey], United States District Court for the District of New Jersey, Consent Decrees March 25, 1942, and April 7, 1943 [Commerce Clearing House Trade Regulation Service, Court Divisions Supplement, 1941–43, paragraphs 52,768 and 52,927]).

[5] *Ibid.*, pp. 8, 9.

[6] Although Jersey was subsequently to take part in the development of a new

With the rights to the hydrogenation process in its possession, Jersey Standard went ahead to construct several hydrogenation plants at Linden, New Jersey, Baton Rouge, Louisiana, and Baytown, Texas.[7] These plants were small installations, aimed at manufacturing specialized products. Although the process functioned well from a technical standpoint, it was extremely expensive to operate and with the existing product price structure and ample supplies of high-grade crude oil was not generally adopted by the refining industry.[8]

Although the hydrogenation process was not to play a significant role in refinery operations for many years, its development had enabled Standard Oil Development Company to build up a sizable research staff skilled in catalysis. The development also led to an awareness of the properties of catalytic reactions by other firms in the industry, and subsequently to an exchange of information between several of these firms under the aegis of the Hydro Patents Company. Hydro Patents was organized by Jersey Standard in 1930 for the purpose of making the hydrogenation process available to the rest of the industry.[9] The hydrogenation patents were given to this company, and Jersey Standard received payment through the sale of Hydro Patents stock. All companies large enough to consider

---

catalytic cracking process in order to avoid paying royalties to Houdry, the company in 1929 apparently did not consider it worth while to try to invent around I. G. Farben's hydrogenation process, even though the payment involved was substantial. Several reasons can be given for this difference in behavior. First, companies were more ready to dispose of large sums on speculative ventures in 1929, when the hydrogenation patents were purchased, than in 1938, when the Houdry process was available for license. Moreover, in 1929, I. G. Farben had a strong and unchallenged coverage on process features essential to the operations of the hydrogenation process, whereas by 1938, Jersey Standard had satisfied itself that there were serious doubts as to the strength of Houdry's patent position. Second, hydrogenation involved a technique wholly new and beyond the experience or capabilities of the oil industry. In 1929, the Jersey company was not yet equipped with a skilled research and development group operating in the field of catalysis, whereas by 1938, such an organization existed.

[7] The first plant to incorporate the hydrogenation process charged 100 barrels per day (interview with C. E. Starr, Jr., March 15, 1955). This pilot plant was followed in 1930 and 1931 by two larger units of 2,500 to 7,500 barrels per day each (H. W. Sheldon, "Twenty-five Years of Progress in Petroleum Refining," *Twenty-five Years of Chemical Engineering Progress*, New York: D. Van Nostrand, 1933, pp. 55–57; also comment by Dr. Miller of the Baton Rouge refinery).

[8] Much of the process equipment had to be imported from Germany, for the process operated at 3000–4000 Psia (pounds per square inch absolute), and only in Germany were high-pressure valves and compressors being manufactured (interview with C. E. Starr, Jr., March 15, 1955). Moreover, the East Texas oil field was discovered at this time, and advances in geophysics promised further discoveries. (C. S. Popple, *op. cit.*, p. 24; also F. A. Howard, *Buna Rubber*, New York: D. Van Nostrand, 1947, pp. 53, 54).

[9] C. S. Popple, *op. cit.*, pp. 10, 11.

hydrogenation plants were invited to purchase the stock;[10] Ultimately seventeen joined, including Texaco Corporation, Pure Oil Company, Standard Oil Company (Ohio), Skelly Oil Company, Gulf Oil Corporation, Shell Oil Company, and Standard Oil Company (Indiana).[11] Three of these stockholders, Texaco, Shell, and Indiana Standard, were later to share in the development of the Fluid Catalytic Cracking process.

All the time that Jersey Standard was investigating hydrogenation, it was aware of Houdry's research. The data that it gathered from Houdry tended to be inconsistent, and the process was deemed unpromising.[12]

During the 1930's, Jersey Standard continued its research in the field of catalysis. The development proceeded in two directions; the first was the application of the hydrogenation process, which was now directed toward re-forming heavy naphthas (the low-octane portion of straight-run gasoline) to improve their chemical characteristics, and the second was directed toward catalytic cracking.[13]

Jersey Standard's extended experiments in catalytic cracking utilized a powdered catalyst, which, when mixed with oil vapors, promoted the cracking reaction.[14] This process was later called "Suspensoid" cracking. Powdered catalyst was propelled into a stream of vaporized oil by means of a rotating screw. The mixture was then fed to a cracking coil, similar to those used in the Tube and Tank units. In a later processing stage, the

[10] Like cracking, there were economies of scale to hydrogenation. Jersey calculated that 5,000 barrels per day was the minimum size that a hydrogenation unit could be in order to return a profit, and that a unit of this size would not fit in any refinery with a crude capacity less than 20,000 barrels per day ("Pooling of Patents," Appendix to Hearings . . . on H. R. 4523, Committee on Patents, House of Representatives, 74th Congress Washington: Government Printing Office, 1936, testimony of Frank A. Howard, Vol. IV, pp. 3668–3669). All companies with refineries this size or larger were given the opportunity to join Hydro Patents Company. If further research and development reduced the minimum economic size, smaller refiners were to have been solicited (*ibid.*).

[11] P. H. Giddens, *Standard Oil Company* (*Indiana*), New York: Appleton-Century Crofts, Inc., 1955, pp. 452–453; R. C. Cook, "Control of the Petroleum Industry by Major Oil Companies," *TNEC* Monograph No. 39, Washington: Government Printing Office, 1941, p. 31; and "Perfect Permanent Organization for Hydro Patents Company," *Oil and Gas Journal*, August 4, 1953, p. 28. Some of these companies built hydrogenation plants; the initial unit, which was designed to process naphtha stocks, was installed in 1939 at the Texas City, Texas, refinery of the Pan-American Refining Company, a subsidiary of Indiana Standard. See J. V. Hightower, "First Hydroformer Unit Put on Stream," *Petroleum Refiner*, May 1941, p. 63; H. G. McGrath and L. R. Hill, "Intermittent and Fluid Catalytic Reforming of Naphthas," *Progress in Petroleum Technology*, Washington, D. C.: American Chemical Society, 1951, pp. 39–57; and E. V. Murphree, C. L. Brown, and E. J. Gohr, "Hydrogenation of Petroleum," *Industrial and Engineering Chemistry*, Vol. XXXII, 1940, p. 1203.

[12] See Appendix B, Reference 1.
[13] See Appendix B, Reference 2.
[14] See Appendix B, Reference 3.

light cracked material was separated from the heavy; the catalyst was subsequently filtered from the latter stream and discarded. The main advantages ascribed to the process were a slightly higher yield of gasoline than under the thermal cracking process and a higher octane number for the finished product. Serious disadvantages were the difficult removal of the catalyst from the heavy cracked oil and the relatively small contribution made by the catalyst to the over-all reaction.[15] By 1934, a 12,000-barrel-a-day unit incorporating this process had been designed, and its profitability calculated. Even with no credit for the higher octane number of the catalytically cracked gasoline, the unit would have given as good a rate of return on capital as most of the other units in the Jersey refineries.[16] But because of the problem of catalyst separation and disposal, and the inauspiciousness of any capital investment during the depths of the depression, no installation was made. In 1940, Imperial Oil Company, Ltd., a Jersey Standard affiliate, at its Sarnia Refinery, Canada, did convert a Tube and Tank unit to Suspensoid cracking.[17] Subsequently, at Sarnia, three other Tube and Tank units were converted and a fifth new plant was built during World War II as part of the war effort. These plants were operated until they were replaced by a Fluid cracking unit in 1953.

The Concept of Circulating Catalyst

The Suspensoid process was not the Jersey company's only effort in catalytic cracking during the middle 1930's. Patent searches were made and research carried out on different types of catalysts and different means of promoting contact between the catalyst and oil. The most significant activity was to be that directed toward a moving catalyst. A moving catalyst was believed to be preferable to a stationary catalyst because there was greater contact between the catalyst and the oil. The patent literature revealed several moving-catalyst systems, one of which, W. W. Odell's, anticipated the Fluid process.[18]

During the 1930's, research in catalysis was also being carried on by other companies active in the oil industry. After Jersey Standard, the major effort was that of Universal Oil Products Company, in the fields of cata-

---

[15] In the Suspensoid process, where the oil was in a liquid state, the ratio of catalyst to oil was very low; and so the catalyst had little opportunity to promote the reaction. R. V. Shankland, "Industrial Catalytic Cracking," *Advances in Catalysis,* Vol. VI, New York: Academic Press, Inc., 1954, pp. 319–320; also W. L. Nelson, *Petroleum Refinery Engineering,* 3rd ed., New York: McGraw-Hill Book Co., 1949, pp. 701–702.

[16] Interview with L. S. Bonnell, June 13, 1955.

[17] R. V. Shankland, *op. cit.*

[18] See Appendix B, Reference 4.

lytic polymerization[19] and catalytic cracking. By 1938, UOP had developed a fixed-bed catalytic cracking process, which utilized catalyst granules in the shape of pills,[20] but this work was put aside in 1939 when the company's resources were allocated to research on Fluid cracking. Simultaneously, Texaco was also attempting to develop a fixed-bed catalytic process, and Indiana Standard was carrying out research on a pelleted cracking catalyst.[21] Kellogg's initial work was on a moving granular bed.

Availability of the Houdry Process

While four companies were carrying out their initial research on catalysis in general and on catalytic cracking in particular, Eugene Houdry, with a perseverance that approached fanaticism, was perfecting the fixed-bed process. In 1936, Socony Mobil brought the first commercial Houdry unit on stream, and in 1937 the Sun Oil Company began operating its first unit. The rest of the industry watched with some concern as Socony and Sun, pleased with the high quality of the catalytically cracked gasoline, initiated an extensive construction program. The oil industry expected an increase in competition, especially from Sun, which had always been a problem to the more orderly companies, when these two companies brought out gasoline of improved quality. In such a situation, any company unable to manufacture unleaded gasoline of a quality as high as that sold by Sun would be at·a disadvantage. Soon after learning about the achievements of the process, most of the large refiners therefore approached the Houdry Process Corporation to investigate the fixed-bed process.

Houdry was quite aware that without catalytic cracking the other refiners could not manufacture as high a quality gasoline as Sun and Socony.[22] Eugene Houdry himself must have felt that this was divine

[19] See Chapter 2; also P. A. Maschwitz and L. M. Henderson, "Polymerization of Hydrocarbon Gases to Motor Fuels," *Progress in Petroleum Technology*, Washington: staff of *Industrial and Engineering Chemistry*, August 7, 1951, pp. 83 ff.

[20] J. G. Alther, Universal Oil Products Company, "Gasoline, Yesterday, Today, and Tomorrow," address given February 2, 1943, p. 30.

[21] Interview with Pike H. Sullivan, Standard Oil Company (Indiana), November 24, 1954.

[22] The octane number of thermally cracked gasoline was approximately 72 (research method), that of catalytically 87. In the mid-1930's, cracked gasoline constituted half of the total volume of stock blended into motor fuel (American Petroleum Institute, *Petroleum Facts and Figures*, 9th ed, 1950, New York: American Petroleum Institute, p. 225). An octane differential of 15 numbers on half the total blend could not be overcome by extra refining on the other half because the different companies had no refining processes not available to Sun and Socony.
Sun actually chose not to maximize its gasoline octane but to avoid adding tetraethyl lead. Because one of its main ingredients was catalytic distillate, Sun's gasoline was equivalent in octane number to that of its competitors, even though it lacked the antiknock fluid. Since tetraethyl lead tends to leave deposits inside

retribution. Those companies which had been uninterested in furthering his development during the early 1930's were now eager to apply the finished result, and it seemed only fitting that they should be required to pay a high price for their negligence. The problem was just how much could be obtained from the potential licensees; from Houdry's point of view the ideal figure would be one which was high enough to bring him sizable royalties and yet not so high that it would encourage the more agile firms to develop competitive catalytic cracking processes.[23]

One of the first companies to approach the Houdry Process Corporation about the possibility of purchasing a license to operate the fixed-bed process was Jersey Standard. Negotiations started in the latter part of 1937. Jersey Standard was represented by F. W. Abrams, president of Standard Oil Company of New Jersey (the Jersey subsidiary concerned with refining and marketing along the East Coast, now Esso Standard Oil Company), H. C. Wiess, president of Humble Oil and Refining Company (Jersey's producing and refining affiliate in Texas), and Frank A. Howard, president of Standard Oil Development Company.[24] Representing Houdry was Arthur E. Pew, vice-president in charge of manufacturing for the Sun Oil Company. In discussing the terms of a license agreement with Houdry and Sun, Howard was informed that the royalty rate would involve a payment of about $50,000,000 if Jersey Standard adopted the process as its basic cracking method.[25] Howard felt that this was too much to pay, particularly since he believed that the Houdry patents covered only one catalytic cracking process, not the whole field of catalytic cracking.[26] Jersey Standard made an offer which they calculated would eventually cost them $15,000,000.[27] Houdry would not accept the reduction, and negotiations were dropped. Jersey Standard, recognizing that it was vitally important to develop a catalytic cracking process of its own, increased its research efforts.

---

the combustion chamber of the automobile engine, which have been claimed to be harmful, marketing an unleaded gasoline gave Sun a competitive advantage. Socony also attempted to minimize purchases of tetraethyl lead, for neither company liked buying this ingredient from the Ethyl Corporation, half-owned by Jersey Standard.

[23] See Appendix B, Reference 5.

[24] C. S. Popple, *op. cit.*, pp. 12–13.

[25] See Appendix B, Reference 6.

[26] C. S. Popple, *op. cit.*, also interview with F. A. Howard, October 17, 1955.

[27] When the Houdry fixed-bed process was finally licensed to the refining industry, the stated royalty fee was $150 per daily barrel of cracking capacity, roughly midway between these two extremes (J. S. Carey and H. W. Ortendahl, "Catalytic Cracking Economics Complicate Comparisons," *National Petroleum News*, October 16, 1940).

The Development of the Fluid Process

While Jersey, Sun, and Houdry were disagreeing with one another as to the size of the royalty payment, Kellogg began to promote its moving-bed process. It approached British Petroleum and I. G. Farbenindustrie in order to enlist their co-operation. When I. G. Farben informed Kellogg that Jersey Standard owned all of I. G. Farben's petroleum patents, Kellogg asked Jersey to join the group. A third company, Standard Oil Company (Indiana), was also invited. Together in London on October 12, 1938, these four companies — Jersey Standard, Indiana Standard, Kellogg, and I. G. Farben — organized a group which was later known as Catalytic Research Associates.[28] Their aim was to develop a catalytic cracking process that would be commercially profitable and would not infringe on the Houdry patents. Areas of research were assigned to the various members, and each agreed to exchange information. British Petroleum (then the Anglo-Iranian Oil Company) joined within a week and was followed by Royal Dutch/Shell, Texaco, and Universal Oil Products. In the year 1939, this group of eight corporations controlled most of the research facilities in the petroleum industry. This was a formidable grouping and, with four hundred men at Jersey and about six hundred in the other companies, represented probably the largest single concentration of scientific manpower in the world. It was also probably the greatest scientific effort directed at a single project, and would be surpassed only by the development of the atomic bomb. By 1942, the group of companies composing Catalytic Research Associates had spent collectively $15,000,000 for research and development.[29] They anticipated spending an additional $10,000,000 to $15,000,000 in the next three years, and amounts of similar magnitude for many years thereafter. The largest expenditure by a single firm was made by Jersey Standard, which allocated to Fluid Catalytic Cracking nearly $30,000,000 from 1935 through 1956.[30] There was no lack of men or of money and, since the main alternatives were paying large

[28] C. S. Popple, *op. cit.*, p. 13. The question might well be asked, Why did the companies co-operate, rather than proceed independently? For Kellogg, the initiator of the union, co-operation with companies skilled in catalysis would yield access to a research organization and to a fund of knowledge, both of which it lacked. To Indiana Standard, which was then faced with the decision of whether or not to invest in the Houdry process (see Standard Oil Company [Indiana], "Report of the Subcommittee on the Houdry Process Investigation," December 27, 1938), a joint project designed to develop a competitive process might well be a more economical means of obtaining catalytic cracking. Jersey Standard, having already entered into one agreement with I. G. Farben, was presumably not averse to broadening the membership.

[29] A. V. Danner, "Memo for the Deputy Administrator," Petroleum Administration for War, October 12, 1943, p. 135.

[30] Esso Research and Engineering Company, letter from B. L. Bragg to the author, December 10, 1957.

royalties to Houdry or defying the Houdry patents in the courts,[31] there was no lack of incentive.

Prior to the meeting which resulted in the formation of Catalytic Research Associates, Jersey Standard had made a comprehensive review of the entire patent art related to catalytic cracking. Jersey believed that Houdry's contribution lay in his ability to combine known principles, in his patent strength, and in his engineering design. The Jersey company received from outside counsel the opinion that its own proposed fixed-bed type of catalytic cracking with tray reactors would not infringe any valid Houdry patent. In spite of this, however, it was felt that a continuous process would be both cheaper and better, and still farther distant from possible patent infringement.

A continuous process employing a moving catalyst was thought to have several advantages. The technical argument was the desirability of very short contact time, which would be achieved in a process with a high ratio of catalyst to oil. Savings would be made if separate vessels were specifically designed for reaction and regeneration.

The [aim] . . . was to avoid the problems in cyclic reaction and regeneration in a fixed bed. These problems included the need to supply heat by expensive heat exchange surface during the endothermic process of reaction, and of removing heat from the bed in the exothermic process of burning off the carbon. There was also a large expense involved in making multiple vessels to carry out this cycle so that the flow of oil through the unit as a whole could be maintained by switching it from one vessel to another when the appropriate time came for those vessels to undergo the corresponding cyclic changes. The swing valves had to be suitable for high temperature and were expensive. Further, they had to be carefully controlled to avoid mixing oxygen containing vapors with oil vapors and causing an explosion. The problems of uniformity of flow of vapors through the catalyst mass and of localized hot spots were moderately well solved, but at great expense through the use of carefully designed heat exchange tubes buried in the catalyst mass, through which was pumped a molten salt heat transfer medium.

On the other hand, it was well appreciated that at even the earliest date the use of powdered catalyst would permit flowing the catalyst through some form of reactor in a continuous stream. This would permit flowing the oil vapors likewise through the same reactor in a continuous stream without swinging to other vessels and would give a constant yield and quality of products. Similarly, the spent catalyst from the reactor could be regenerated by burning in some other vessel through which it flowed continuously. Heat exchange equipment within the reaction and regeneration vessels could be avoided by making enough catalyst, or vapors, or both flow through the

[31] See Appendix B, Reference 7.

vessel so that the total heat content of the flowing streams would not permit the temperature to fall or rise excessively when reaction or regeneration took place.

During the period of pooled research efforts it took some time to appreciate fully the properties of these flow streams. At first, for instance, it was thought that it might be necessary to burn part of the carbon off the catalyst at a time. Then the catalyst would have to be cooled before more air could be added. Later the possibility arose of holding the temperature uniform during regeneration by keeping the catalyst flowing through the regeneration vessel thoroughly mixed while it was in the vessel. At first, it was thought that mechanical mixing would be required, but later it was realized that the fluid dense bed would give this uniformity.[32]

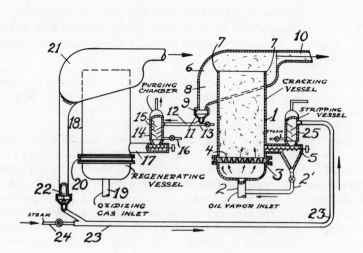

Illustration from Lewis and Gilliland's fluid-process patent.

A catalyst could be moved by a wide variety of means — canisters, conveyor chains, grates, blower fans, and so on — and a great number of these were considered through the design and estimating stage and discarded before coming to the "fluid bed."[33] The mechanism of the fluid

[32] Esso Research and Engineering Company, memorandum on "History of Cracking — Fluid Catalytic Cracking," by D. L. Campbell, December 9, 1957, pp. 2, 3.
[33] The term "fluid bed" first appeared in the Odell Reissue Patent; the name "Fluid Catalytic Cracking" was given to the process by F. A. Howard later on in

UNITED STATES PATENT OFFICE

2,498,088

CONVERSION OF HYDROCARBONS WITH SUSPENDED CATALYST

Warren K. Lewis, Newton, and Edwin R. Gilliland,
Arlington, Mass., assignors to Standard Oil Development Company, a corporation of Delaware

Original application January 3, 1940, Serial No.
312,200. Divided and this application October
23, 1945, Serial No. 624.044

7 Claims. (Cl. 196—52)

1

This invention relates to an improved method and apparatus for the treatment of gaseous fluids with solid materials and more particularly to a method and apparatus adapted for the conversion of hydrocarbon oils in the presence of solid catalysts.

This application forms a division of application Serial No. 312,200, filed January 3, 1940, now abandoned.

It has long been recognized that if a gas be made to flow upwardly through a bed of granular, finely subdivided solid particles, the bed is converted into a kind of quicksand, with the surface of the solid mass having the appearance of a boiling liquid; i. e., the lifting effect of the rising gas imparts to it a high degree of mobility, making it resemble a liquid to such an extent that the analogy between it and the liquid state has been heavily stressed. (See Martin, Chemical Engineering, 1928, Crosby, Lockwood and Sons, London, section 31, p. 1; et seq.). Furthermore, it has been recognized that the maintenance of this condition of mobility in a bed of solid granules offers excellent conditions for interaction of a gas with a solid, as in the conversion of coal into producer gas, the catalysis of various gas reactions by solid catalysts, etc. It offers the advantages of (1) an enormous surface of contact between solids and gases per unit volume of reaction vessel, (2) a correspondingly large reaction capacity per unit volume of reactor and (3) the dampening effect on any heat liberated or absorbed by the reaction of the high heat capacity of the suspended particles, minimizing the temperature changes that would otherwise occur. However, it has been found that this condition of operation has the following disadvantages which are so serious that it is useful only under exceptional circumstances.

(1) The velocity of the gas rising through the bed must be kept relatively low, as otherwise the gas will blow the bed up and out of the reactor. It is true, that this gas velocity can be increased by using a bed of particles of large size, but this inherently defeats one of the major advantages of the method, i. e., the provision of large surface area of the particles per unit volume of the reactor. This fact means that the gas-treating capacity per unit volume of the reactor is of necessity low. The attempt has been made to correct the condition by the introduction of a considerable portion of the gas above the surface of the bed of granules, but directed downward toward it and into it. Obviously, however, this is merely an ameliorating expedient. Because of

2

these difficulties the use of such a unit is advantageous only in those cases in which the reaction rate desired requires an enormous solid surface per unit volume of gas reacted and the capacity of the equipment is limited by the amount of this interfacial surface.

(2) This condition of operation almost necessitates the use of granules of substantially uniform particle size. Otherwise, there is a marked tendency for the heavier particles to settle to the bottom and the lighter ones to rise on top. Moreover, the gas velocity must be kept down to a value which will prevent the blowing over of any signicant portion of even the finest particles in the mass, since this would not only reduce the solids in the bed but eliminate those particles with the largest surface per unit volume.

(3) It is true that the bed of granules can be rendered mobile by air velocities well below those at which the bed can still be maintained without serious "evaporation" into the gas stream, i. e., blowing overhead with the gas, but this obviously results in low gas treating capacity per unit volume of the reaction space and this condition also tends to give poor mixing of the bed, due to formation of chimneys through which the gas rises, surrounded by dead areas of bed.

In the effort to secure the advantages of this general type of interaction of gas with solid particles, but to avoid these limitations, the operation has been modified by constricting the cross section of the reaction chamber and flowing the gas at a correspondingly higher velocity through it. Doing this eliminates the presence of a "liquid" bed of particles, the particles being carried at a fairly high rate overhead with the gas and necessitating separation from it. Furthermore, the particles travel through the apparatus so quickly that they almost never have time to secure the desired stoichiometrically complete interaction with the gas, so that the separated particles must often be returned to the reaction zone. This general condition of operation can greatly increase the gas throughput per unit volume of reaction space, but it also results in a very great decrease in concentration of solid granules in the reaction space, because these granules, instead of resting in it as a quite compact mass, are blown out with the gas. It is true that on the average the gas always moves somewhat faster than the solid particles, so that the concentration of solids in the reactor is higher than that in the gas stream entering the reactor, but none the less under ordinary conditions of

Specification from Lewis and Gilliland's fluid-process patent.

bed was not well known. In 1938, Drs. W. K. Lewis and E. R. Gilliland of M.I.T.'s Chemical Engineering Department, in their role as consultants to Standard Oil Development Company, suggested that the tube in which the reaction took place should be vertical rather than horizontal.[34] They were asked to investigate the behavior of finely divided particles in vertical tubes and so initiated a research program at M.I.T. Two graduate students, John Chambers and Scott Walker, carried out the experiments and derived some of the engineering relationships underlying the fluid technique.[35]

Under certain conditions, finely divided solids and vapors in intimate contact behave like a fluid. The mixture of components has the same flow characteristics as a fluid, characteristics which solid particles alone do not have. The fluid bed will flow in any direction with a slight differential in pressure; it is relatively compressible; and through physical agitation of its constituents, it will tend to exhibit uniform temperatures throughout its mass. With these features, the fluid bed would seem to be an ideal mechanism for carrying out the cracking reaction. The solid particles would be the catalyst, ground up into a fine powder. Oil vapors, when mixed with the catalyst in the right proportion and with the proper pressure differential, would cause the mass to flow like a fluid. Since it could be propelled from one spot to another as the cracking reaction took place, the physical conditions in any one zone in the equipment would remain constant, thus fulfilling the requirements of a continuous process. After cracking had taken place, the catalyst could be separated from the oil vapors more easily than it could have been if the oil had condensed into a liquid stream. Finally, since the catalyst flowed like a fluid, it could follow contorted paths with relative ease.

The Standard Oil Development Company realized that the fluid technique offered an excellent mechanism for manipulating the catalyst and oil streams and quickly took over the research. The students at M.I.T. had worked with air and catalyst mixtures alone, but within six months the Development Company was cracking oil in the presence of a fluid

---

its development. See E. J. Gohr, "Background, History and Future of Fluidization," in D. F. Othmer, ed., *Fluidization*, New York: Reinhold Publishing Corporation, 1956, pp. 103–147. See also Appendix B, Reference 8.

[34] Interview with E. R. Gilliland. In the cement industry, the reaction chamber was closer to horizontal, and the early experiments in the use of fluidized catalysts had followed this example.

[35] J. M. Chambers, "Flow Characteristics of Air-fine Particle Mixtures in Vertical Tubes," M.I.T., Department of Chemical Engineering, M.S. Thesis, 1939; S. W. Walker, "Flow Characteristics of Air-fine Particle Mixtures," M.I.T., Department of Chemical Engineering, M.S. Thesis, 1940; and Lewis and Gilliland patent 2,498,088 filed on January 3, 1940. See also Appendix B, Reference 9.

catalyst. The first cracking apparatus was a vertical tube 1 inch in diameter, located in the laboratory at Bayway.[36]

The problem now arose of how best to transfer the fluid bed from the reactor to the regenerator and back again. After several different means were tried,[37] the standpipe valve and riser system was developed.

The principle of the fluidized standpipe ... consisted of three elements intended to carry out the purpose of causing the powdered catalyst to flow from one place to another. This had to be carried out even when taking the powdered catalyst from one vessel and discharging it to another vessel at the same or higher elevation and at the same or slightly higher static pressure. In the standpipe the powdered catalyst first flowed downward through a substantially vertical column within which it was kept fluid (by the addition of vapor, if necessary), but the amount of vapors that mixed with the catalyst was kept small so that the flowing stream would be relatively dense. Then the direction of flow of the stream was reversed into a substantially upward riser and a considerable amount of vapors was added to make the flowing stream less dense. The difference in density in the two columns provided the driving force and the energy of course could be put in by supplying the vapors to the riser under pressure. No moving parts in contact with catalyst were required to cause the catalyst to flow. However, there was one other important element; namely, a variable restriction [a valve] in the lower part of the downcomer to regulate the flow.[38]

The fluidized solids transfer system involving the standpipe was tested in 1940 in a 100-barrel-a-day pilot plant, which had been built at Baton Rouge in order to gather data for the construction of large-scale equipment.[39] It was found to work well, and was therefore incorporated in the design. The Fluid Catalytic Cracking process was now essentially complete.

The other companies allied in the research in catalytic cracking observed this pilot plant and were persuaded that the fluid bed was the best mechanism for obtaining a continuous flow of processing materials. The majority of them had been orienting their research toward catalyst pellets, but the success of the fluid pilot plant led them to redirect their efforts.

[36] See Appendix B, Reference 10.

[37] See Appendix B, Reference 11.

[38] Esso Research and Engineering Company, memorandum in "History of Cracking — Fluid Catalytic Cracking," op. cit., pp. 3, 4. See also R. V. Shankland, op. cit., pp. 323, 324. This system was described in two patent declarations. See also Appendix B, Reference 12.

[39] Esso Research and Engineering Company, letter from H. J. Hall to W. M. Craig, October 24, 1957, p. 10.

Administering Research and Development

At Standard Oil Development Company, where the majority of the research was being done, the Fluid Catalytic Cracking process moved in 1938 from the first to the second of Jersey's five procedural stages of process innovation. In the first stage, the initial research is carried out, usually by various groups working on process development. An over-all supervisor is assigned to the project, who co-ordinates the activities in the laboratory and at the pilot plant, as well as the process, product, and equipment engineering sections. When the process shows indications of being commercially feasible, according to the economic calculations of the development engineers, the second stage is inaugurated. At this point, the Engineering Department enters the picture. While process development continues,[40] the Engineering Department designs the process equipment and makes more detailed estimates of the cost of construction and operation. In the third stage, the refinery personnel are brought in, in order to familiarize the development engineers with the characteristics of the site and the existing plant equipment with which the new process must be synchronized.[41] When it is time to proceed with an actual commercial unit, a proposal is made to the board of directors of the operating company, and if accepted, final design and construction begin.[42] This fourth stage is followed by the fifth and final one, namely, the initial operation and subsequent improvement of the process. Throughout this entire period, a patent committee closely follows the development in order to give advice on patentability, licensing, and infringement.[43]

This procedure is followed in the hope that it will institutionalize innovation. In an industry where innovation becomes a common feature, there exists the need to rationalize its "production." The techniques applied are

[40] Among the variables investigated at this point were the type of feed stock, the boiling range of the charge stock, the effects of temperature and time, and the quality of the products (interview with C. E. Starr, Jr., March 15, 1955). The catalyst was also studied carefully in order to determine its effect upon the cracking reaction, its attrition during the cycle, its optimum physical composition and form, and its heat characteristics.

[41] Because the first Fluid unit was to be installed at Baton Rouge, Louisiana, in the refinery of Esso Standard Oil Company (Jersey's refining and marketing branch), it was the Baton Rouge organization with which the development engineers worked.

[42] Ideally, the process design is now complete, but when a process innovation is accelerated, as was the Fluid, changes may later be made during the construction. The principle of the standpipe as the catalyst feed mechanism was adopted during the fourth stage, and was demonstrated in the first commercial unit at the same time that it was being studied in the laboratory.

[43] Paul O. Dunham, patent attorney on Development's staff, was chairman of the Fluid Catalytic Cracking Process patent committee. Dr. H. J. Hall acted as technical secretary, suggesting any useful features that had been uncovered in the catalytic cracking patent search.

the same as those used in the manufacture of any mass-produced items: a factory establishment with capital equipment, specialization of labor, "roundabout" production, emphasis on synchronization, and a standard method of accounting. The factory establishment is the research laboratory. Labor is specialized at the outset through the educational process in the universities and is further specialized within the research organization by assignment to a particular area of interest or a particular development stage. The research engineer is not just a chemical engineer; he is a chemical engineer specializing in some particular field, as for example, the design of fractionating towers. In recent years, the laboratory has been equipped with complex and accurate analytical devices such as mass spectrometers and digital and analog computers. The production process is synchronized through careful scheduling of tasks, assignment of areas of responsibility, and continuous liaison between groups. The projects are assessed periodically and are continued only if they meet certain profit criteria. By having a standard method of measuring the potential merits of an innovation, the research organization remains impersonal. By being emotionally uncommitted, it is able to drop any project that begins to look unrewarding, rather than throw good money after bad.

Adopting the Fluid Process

At about the beginning of 1941, the Fluid Catalytic Cracking process had been brought to the stage of development where it could be incorporated in a commercial unit. Standard Oil Company (New Jersey) was the first to install a Fluid unit. Had Jersey Standard been motivated solely by pecuniary profit, it might well have chosen the established path of development, which called for the first commercial unit to produce approximately 10,000 barrels a stream day. But by 1941, national security was high on the list of considerations, and it was decided to build larger-scale units immediately. With larger units, there would be a greater total volume of products. The advantage of a greater yield of cracked distillates would more than compensate for any operating problems caused by making the larger-than-normal step in the the development procedure. In 1941, the catalytic distillates were being considered not as motor gasoline but as aviation-gasoline blending stock. According to Jersey Standard's projections of demand for 100-octane aviation gasoline, a substantial shortage was predicted beginning in 1942. Showing more foresight than the United States government, the Jersey company rushed through the construction of the first Fluid Catalytic Cracking unit as one phase of its over-all program for increasing the production of aviation gasoline.[44]

[44] C. S. Popple, *op. cit.*, pp. 31–32. The government's estimates of aviation gasoline needs were as follows:

On May 25, 1942, the first Fluid unit was placed on stream at the Baton Rouge refinery of the Standard Oil Company of Louisiana, a Jersey Standard affiliate. To this unit were charged initially 12,000 barrels a stream day (equivalent to 10,200 barrels a calendar day) of fresh gas oil.

Even before the Baton Rouge unit was completed, construction was started on two other units of the same size, one at Bayway, New Jersey, and the second at the Baytown, Texas, refinery of Humble Oil and Refining Company (then an affiliate, now a subsidiary company). Here again, national necessity was an overriding factor; the normal procedure would have been to operate the initial Fluid unit to discover any errors and then to design the second unit to incorporate the improvements. In the rush to get the units built and operating, these considerations were neglected. The next two units were, therefore, almost exact duplicates of the original Baton Rouge plant. Fortunately, the same technical skills which could be applied to designing improved units could also perform the function of technical service, that is, investigating and adapting the existing units in order to operate them most efficiently.

The first three Fluid Catalytic Cracking units were similar in size and physical appearance. Each consisted of two major vessels, a regenerator and a reactor, within a steel skeleton. The oil vapors were cracked in the reactor, where the rate of reaction was promoted by the fluidized catalyst. The mixture of cracked oil vapors and catalyst rose from the reactor to smaller vessels encasing cyclone separators, which separated the oil vapors

---

United States Military Demands for Aviation Gasoline

Date of Estimate by Joint Aeronautics Board	Aviation Gasoline Needs from Domestic Plants	Required Date for Fulfillment
December 23, 1940	33,000 bpd	July 1, 1941
September 17, 1941	80,000 bpd	July 1, 1942
January 27, 1942	180,000 bpd	July 1, 1943
February 16, 1942	200,000 bpd	n.a.
October 20, 1942	367,000 bpd	n.a.
October 26, 1942	507,000 bpd	n.a.

Sources: Figures abstracted from C. S. Popple, op. cit., pp. 31–38.

As early as the middle of 1940, Dr. R. E. Wilson, then president of Pan-American Petroleum Corporation and an advisor to E. R. Stettinius, estimated wartime requirements of aviation gasoline at 71,300 barrels per day, more than twice the Joint Aeronautics Board's estimate of 33,000 barrels a day (C. S. Popple, op. cit., p. 31). Later in the year, W. S. Farish, president of Jersey Standard, wrote to the presidents of fifteen major oil companies urging them to operate their aviation-gasoline facilities at full capacity, even though there was a temporary surplus of the product. The government, however, showed no inclination to purchase the excess, nor did it during the next nine months facilitate any expansion of capacity (ibid., p. 32). Jersey Standard went ahead on its plans to construct Fluid units in spite of the lack of official encouragement.

from the catalyst particles through centrifugal action. The oil vapors flowed from there to a fractionating tower, where the cracked material was separated into gasoline, heating oil, heavy gas oil, and a small amount of residual material. The catalyst, now separated from the cracked oil, but carrying on its surface the coke formed in the cracking reaction, flowed into the spent-catalyst hopper, where it was stored until it could be directed to the regenerator. In the regenerator, the carbon was burned

[*Esso Research and Engineering Company: Photo by Rosskam*]

The three catalytic crackers of the Baton Rouge refinery. The Model I unit is on the left; two Model II units are on the right.

off the catalyst particles; the temperature within the regenerator was controlled primarily by the amount of carbon being burned. The mixture of flue gas and carbon-free catalyst rose from the top of the regenerator to a cyclone system, similar to the one at the top of the reactor, where the two materials were separated. The regenerated catalyst flowed from the cyclone system to its own hopper, from which it was withdrawn to supply fresh catalyst to the reactor. A sizable fraction of the heat generated when the carbon was burned off the catalyst was stored as sensible heat in the catalyst itself, that is, the catalyst was hotter when it left the generator than when it entered. This heat, liberated in the reactor, was more than the cracking reaction required; the excess was therefore used to generate steam and to preheat the oil feed. The proper flow of catalyst from the hoppers to the reactor and to the regenerator were assured by the difference in hydrostatic pressure between the dense catalyst in the standpipe and the dilute catalyst in the processing vessels.[45]

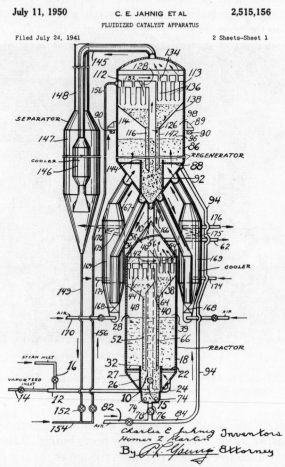

July 11, 1950   C. E. JAHNIG ET AL   2,515,156
FLUIDIZED CATALYST APPARATUS

Filed July 24, 1941   2 Sheets—Sheet 1

Illustration from C. E. Jahnig and H. Z. Martin's " downflow " design patent (Model II).

Process Improvements

The three Fluid units which incorporated the initial process design were called Model I. Yet, even before they came on stream, the Model I

[45] For a more detailed description of these units see R. V. Shankland, *op. cit.*, pp. 323–326; and E. V. Murphree *et al.*, *Industrial Engineering Chemistry*, Vol. XXXV, 1943, p. 768.

units were out of date. On the basis of the operation of Jersey Standard's pilot plant in 1940 and 1941, improvements were made in the design.[46] The first major development, as well as the most significant change in the operation of the process, was to withdraw the catalyst from the bottom rather than the top of each of the two main vessels.

Three major advantages resulted from this change in the design: greater ease of catalyst recovery, simplification in plant layout, and an improvement in operating flexibility.[47] This resulted in lower investment and maintenance costs.[48] The "downflow" design (as contrasted with the

COMPARATIVE ELEVATIONS · FLUID CATALYTIC CRACKERS · EQUAL CAPACITY

[M. W. Kellogg Company]

Comparative elevations of different Fluid units. These units all have a capacity of 8,300 barrels per day. The height of the wartime unit (Model I) was approximately 160 feet.

original "upflow") reduced the problem of catalyst recovery by removing most of the catalyst that had been formerly entrained in the vapors leaving the reactor and the regenerator. In the upflow units, all of the catalyst had to be separated, from the oil vapors or from the flue gas, in the cyclone separators. In the downflow unit, however, only 1% of the catalyst remained in the exit stream, for the other 99% had been withdrawn from the dense catalyst near the bottoms of the reactor and the regenerator. By this change in design, the catalyst hoppers were eliminated, and the size of the cyclone system materially reduced. The major items of equipment could be built lower to the ground, because the smaller pressure drop in

[46] See Appendix B, References 13 and 14. For a description of the improvements, see R. V. Shankland, *op. cit.*, pp. 326–356.

[47] *Ibid.*, pp. 327, 390–391.

[48] On-site investment costs for an "upflow" (Model I) Fluid unit of 12,750 bpcd (equivalent to 15,000 bpsd) were roughly $2,280,000, in 1939 dollars. This is equal to $179 per barrel of charge. In converting from "upflow" to "downflow" operation, it was possible to increase the capacity of the units at a cost, in 1939 dollars, of only $76 ($100 in 1945 dollars) per barrel of charge (E. V. Murphree, E. J. Gohr, H. Z. Martin, H. J. Ogorzaly, and C. W. Tyson, "High Capacity Operations on Fluid Cracking Units," *Proceedings of the American Petroleum Institute*, Vol. 25, Part III, 1945, p. 64).

the catalyst circulation stream reduced the need for long standpipes. This in turn reduced the cost of the steel framework supporting the vessels.

Greater operating flexibility was obtained through increasing by one the number of variables which controlled the cracking reaction. In the upflow design, the catalyst circulation rate was limited by the capacity of the catalyst recovery system. With the downflow design, the catalyst recovery system was no longer limiting and the amount of catalyst circulated through the reactor could be varied at will. If the flow of oil vapors is maintained at a constant rate, a change in the amount of catalyst circulated through the reactor changes the ratio of catalyst to oil, which changes the intensity of cracking.

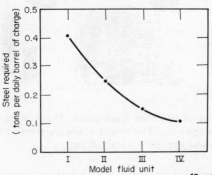

[Esso Research and Engineering Company]

Steel requirements for Fluid Catalytic Cracking units.

Still another advantage that came with the development of the downflow design was that wide-range feedstocks could be cracked. In the early Fluid units, it was necessary to vaporize completely the gas oil charged to the reactor. This set a temperature of approximately 750°F. as the upper limit of the boiling range of the gas-oil charge. With the downflow design, more heat was carried by the catalyst from the regenerator to the reactor. Now, in the reactor, all of the feed could be vaporized by the latent heat of the catalyst. With more heat available, it was possible to crack catalytically the heavy gas-oil fraction, that is, the portion boiling between 750°F. and approximately 1,000°F. Since the alternate use of this material was as heavy fuel oil, the heavy gas oil had a low alternate-use value and made a profitable cracking stock.

Accompanying the changes in the design of the Fluid process were many improvements in the manufacture of the individual items of equipment. The first catalyst had been a naturally occurring material, but synthetic catalyst was found to improve the process yields. Erosion was

[Esso Research and Engineering Company]

Model III Fluid cracking unit at the Bayway refinery.

reduced by better design of the transfer lines, and corrosion was mini-
mized by the use of alloy steels.[49] Catalyst recovery was improved by an
increase in the size and efficiency of the cyclone separators.[50] The careful
programming of maintenance activities reduced the amount of time necessary for "turnarounds," and so increased the capacity of the units.[51] Other

[49] F. L. Resen, "Revamped Cyclone System Features Humble's Cat Cracker Expansion," *Oil and Gas Journal*, May 25, 1953, pp. 220–228.
[50] R. V. Shankland, *op. cit.*, p. 341.
[51] *Ibid.*, p. 352. Normally, catalytic cracking units are run continuously, day and
night, for an extended period of time. At first the period was 2–6 months, but it has
now been extended to 1–2 years. At the end of this period, the unit is taken off
stream and inspected carefully for corrosion. At the same time, repairs which were
postponed are carried out, and any obsolete pieces of equipment are replaced. In the
first Fluid installations, the turnaround took on the average 55 days a year, whereas
by 1955 the period had been reduced to 37 days. If we consider two Fluid units of
equal charging capacity on a stream-day basis, one of which was built in 1942 and
the other in 1955, the first could be operated 85% of the time, and the second 93%
of the time. If both units were of 10,000 bpsd capacity, the average charge rate of
the first would be 8,500 bpcd, the second 9,300 bpcd. Capital cost depends upon the
stream-day rate, the economic worth upon the calendar-day rate; in this case the
more advanced Fluid unit has an 800-bpcd advantage.

improvements were made by reducing catalyst contamination and increasing its fluidity, as well as by combating erosion, and by increasing gas-solids contact. Finally, investigations into the chemical nature of the cracking reaction and the design of the equipment gave a greater understanding of the Fluid process. This increased knowledge of the engineering relationships, combined recently with high-speed computing equipment, enables the refiner to determine rapidly and accurately the conditions under which his unit can be operated most profitably.

[M. W. Kellogg Company]

Orthoflow Fluid Catalytic Cracking units.

Many of these improvements have been made since 1945, for with the end of the war there was a greater opportunity for experiment in the design of the Fluid units. UOP and Kellogg, the two process-design companies, now had to cater to the demands of large and small refiners alike. Each of these two companies modified the downflow design to reduce investment and operating costs, particularly for smaller units. Both companies now place the reactor directly above the regenerator, which reduces the amount of structural steel and simplifies the appearance.

The first Fluid unit incorporating UOP's design began operation on June 10, 1947, in the refinery of the Aurora Gasoline Company in Detroit,

[*Esso Research and Engineering Company*]

Model IV Fluid Catalytic Cracking unit.

Michigan. According to R. V. Shankland, the improvements in the UOP unit include:

> Elimination of the customary regenerator riser. Use of a shorter regenerated catalyst standpipe. Simplification of piping. Operation of the regenerator under pressure.[52]

For a regeneration vessel of given size, increasing the pressure increases the rate at which carbon can be burned off the catalyst. This advantage, however, must be weighed against such disadvantages as the need for an expensive air compression system and heavier construction materials.

[52] *Ibid.*, p. 352.

The first unit designed by the M. W. Kellogg Company to have the reactor directly above the regenerator was put on stream in 1951 at the Edmonton, Alberta, refinery of the British-American Oil Company. This unit, like UOP's, was very small, of 2000-barrels-a-day capacity.[53] The advantages of Kellogg's "Orthoflow" design, according to Shankland, are:

> Elimination of all external catalyst piping. Use of straight vertical pipes for catalyst circulation. Elimination of expansion joints. Use of special plug type valves for control of catalyst circulation.[54]

Standard Oil Company (New Jersey) has also brought out a new unit, called "Model IV," improving upon the downflow design. Jersey Standard's Model IV design was developed as a low-investment unit to compete with smaller units promoted by competitors, mainly in range of capacities from 5,000 to 20,000 bpd.[55] The first Model IV unit, of 15,000 bpd, was placed on stream in November, 1952, at the Destrahan, Louisiana, refinery of the Pan-Am Southern Corporation (a subsidiary of Indiana Standard). The advantages of this design are a reduction in height, an improved catalyst transfer system, a greater stability of operation, easier process control, reduced erosion in the catalyst carrier lines, and elimination of slide valves for the control of catalyst circulation.[56]

The Model IV design proved to be well adapted for large as well as small units. Model IV units of 40,000 bpd fresh feed have been built and operated successfully.

Improvements in the design and operation of the Fluid units have been

[53] The improvement in the design of small Fluid units did not reverse the economies of scale; large units were still, per barrel of charge or of product, cheaper to construct. W. L. Nelson estimated continuous catalytic cracking (process not specified) to vary in capital cost from $800,000 (1946 dollars) for a 2,000 bpd unit to $4,700,000 (1946 dollars) for a 20,000 bpd unit (W. L. Nelson, "Over-all Plant Costs — Cracking," *Oil and Gas Journal*, November 24, 1949, p. 149). Per barrel of charge, the smaller unit cost $400, the larger $235. Nelson's relationship between capital cost and capacity was logarithmic. Leslie Cookenboo, compiling figures for Fluid units three years later, found essentially the same pattern (Leslie Cookenboo, Jr., *Crude Oil Pipelines and Competition in the Oil Industry*, Cambridge: Harvard University Press, 1955, pp. 121–123, especially Chart 12). He reported capital costs, per barrel of charge, of $800 (1952 dollars) for a 3,000 bpd unit versus approximately $250 (1952 dollars) for units between 20,000 and 60,000 bpd. Cookenboo's data show a logarithmic relationship between capital cost (per barrel) and capacity for sizes up to 20,000 bpd. Above 20,000 bpd the observations are not numerous, but on the basis of those that are given we would conclude that further economies of scale in Fluid unit construction did not appear to exist. My own figures, valid for 1955, and thus three years subsequent to Cookenboo's, indicate substantial economies of scale up to at least 40,000 barrels per day.

[54] R. V. Shankland, *op. cit.*, p. 354.

[55] See Appendix B, Reference 15.

[56] R. V. Shankland, *op. cit.*, p. 354.

accompanied by increases in maximum plant size. This growth in capacity has been obtained both from existing units and from new units. By better knowledge of the operating relationships and by minor modifications in equipment, the charge rates of some of the Fluid units have been increased to a point where they are four times the rate of the original design.[57] For example, the first Fluid unit at the Humble Oil and Refining Company's Baytown refinery, which was designed for 12,000 barrels a stream day, now processes 55,000 barrels a stream day.[58]

Since 1942 the size of the largest unit in existence has steadily been rising. The first three Fluid units had capacities of 12,000 barrels a day; the next were 14,000. Within the last few years, three huge units of 63,000, 72,000, and 102,000 barrels a day have been built, the last for the Tidewater Oil Company.[59] At the other end of the scale, a 1,250-barrel-a-day plant is now in operation.[60]

Costs, Royalties, and Profits from the Fluid Process Innovation

In operation, the first Fluid units of 1942 proved to be as efficient as any cracking units then in existence. The product yields were approximately the same as those obtained in Houdry fixed-bed operation, but the quality of the gasoline obtained in the Fluid process was higher. The costs of operating the Fluid units were slightly greater, approximately $1.51 per barrel of gas oil charged compared to $1.42 per barrel for the Houdry units (both cost figures excluding royalties).[61] However, even without allowance for the higher quality of the gasoline, the product revenues from the Fluid process were greater, $1.77 a barrel of charge compared to $1.70. Profit per barrel, the difference between revenues and costs, was roughly 26¢ for the Fluid process, 28¢ for the Houdry. Given the degree of accuracy of the estimates, the profits can be assumed to be equal. In addition, it seemed likely that Fluid units could be built in sizes greater than those possible for fixed-bed units, which would result in economies of scale over a wider range.

These facts were apparent not only to Jersey Standard, which installed the earliest units, but also to many other companies, both those which

---

[57] Interview with C. E. Starr, Jr., March 15, 1955.

[58] F. L. Resen, op. cit., p. 220. This startling increase is not entirely attributable to improvements in technique; a certain amount of excess capacity was built into this unit as a precautionary measure. (E. V. Murphree et al., "High Capacity Operations in Fluid Cracking Units," op. cit., p. 63.)

[59] R. V. Shankland, op. cit., p. 320; Oil and Gas Journal, March 19, 1956, p. 257. These figures are a little misleading, for they measure the total feed charged to the reactor, both fresh feed and recycle. Earlier Fluid units did not recycle appreciable amounts of material.

[60] R. V. Shankland, op. cit., p. 320.

[61] See Appendix Tables 9, 12, and 13.

had taken part in the Fluid development and those which had not. As a result there was an instantaneous demand for Fluid cracking licenses. Since the products from the Fluid units were desperately needed for the war effort, construction was started on several Fluid units, even though the terms of the licenses had not been agreed on.[62] No opportunity was given for a repetition of the controversies that took place among the owners of the continuous thermal cracking processes.

Since the Fluid Catalytic Cracking process was a commercial success, the six parties in the Catalytic Research Associates (I. G. Farben was now *ausgeschlossen*) were faced with the problem of setting a royalty rate and of dividing the royalty payments among themselves. These deliberations could not be made in the privacy of the corporate office, however, for the United States government had entered upon the scene. In order to increase the speed with which the country mobilized for war, the President had formed the Office of the Petroleum Coordinator for National Defense (later the Office of the Petroleum Coordinator for War, and finally the Petroleum Administration for War), with Harold Ickes as director. The functions of the PAW were to collect material and recommend actions to the petroleum companies and government agencies to ensure that the supply of petroleum products would be sufficient for needs of the civilian economy and the military forces.[63] In carrying out these duties the PAW became involved in determining the terms of the Fluid cracking license, as well as who should be given an opportunity to install the process.

The six companies that developed the Fluid process decided on a running royalty of 5¢ a barrel of fresh charge. If the licensee wished to meet the royalty obligations in one lump-sum payment, the fee was to be $125 per daily barrel of fresh charge, averaged throughout the year.[64] At this time, the paid-up royalty for the Houdry process was $150 per daily barrel of fresh charge. There was no running royalty rate for the Houdry process, but the running rate on the less efficient thermal cracking processes was also equal to 5¢ a barrel.

The PAW was satisfied with these royalty charges. The royalty rates

[62] "Royalty Rates for Fluid Catalytic Cracking and Hydro Catalytic Reforming," memo for the Deputy Administrator, Petroleum Administration for War, October 1943, quoted in *Selected Documents in Connection with Licensing and Cross-Licensing Arrangements Pursuant to PAW Recommendation Number 41*, August 7, 1942, p. 140.

[63] U. S. Petroleum Administration for War, *History of the Petroleum Administration for War, 1941–1945*, Washington: U. S. Government Printing Office, 1946, Appendix VII, Exhibit 1, pp. 374–375.

[64] "Royalty Rates for Fluid Catalytic Cracking and Hydro Catalytic Reforming," *op. cit.*, p. 136.

for the Fluid process were set "at the lowest rate ever granted by the owners of the older thermal cracking process patents. . . . Ordinarily patent royalties on a new and superior process are much higher than the royalty rates on older processes which they are superseding. . . ."[65]

The Fluid Catalytic Cracking royalties were low by two other standards. In the Burton process licenses, the royalty rate was 25% of the estimated savings. "In applying this test to the rates for Fluid Catalytic Cracking . . . , it will be found that the rates . . . are substantially less than 25 per cent of the savings obtainable by their use."[66] According to our calculations, the profit (neglecting royalty) from operating the Fluid process would have been about 31¢ per barrel of charge. Subtracting the royalty payment of 5¢ per barrel of charge reduces the profit to 26¢. Thus the royalty was about 16% of the savings.

The second standard consisted of stating the royalties as a certain percentage of the value of the products manufactured by the process. Legal precedent had established 5% to 10% of the market value as an acceptable basis.[67] The Fluid Catalytic Cracking royalty amounted to only 2½% to 3% of the value of the products when used to produce motor fuel.[68] Compared either with the past experience in the petroleum refining industry or with industrial practice in general, the royalty rates on the Fluid Catalytic Cracking process were favorable to the licensees. But we cannot ascribe this result entirely to a deliberate generosity on the part of the licensors. In the first place, the government might not have permitted a greater return on the investment in research.[69] In the second place, in absolute amounts royalty rates on cracking processes had declined as cracking installations became more numerous. From a peak of about 17¢

[65] R. K. Davies, Deputy Administrator, Press Release Number 430, Petroleum Administration for War, April 19, 1944, on basis of Recommendation 41 (July 24, 1942).

[66] Memo for J. H. Marshall, Chief Counsel, Office of the Petroleum Coordinator for War, December 1, 1942, in *Selected Documents in Connection with Licensing and Cross-Licensing Arrangements Pursuant to PAW Recommendation Number 41*, August 7, 1942, p. 156.

[67] *Ibid.*, p. 157. The memo quotes as precedents United States vs. Berdan Firearms Company, 26 Ct. U.S. 48 and 156 U.S. 552 (5% of the cost of manufacture); Autographic Register Company vs. Sturgis, 110 F. (2d) 883 (10% of selling price); and others.

[68] *Ibid.* Given our estimated product revenues, a 5¢ royalty rate would amount to 3% of the total value. On operations to produce aviation gasoline for the government, the royalty rate of 5¢ per barrel of charge would have amounted to 1½% to 2% of the total value of the products manufactured (*ibid.*).

[69] The government took into account expenditures on research and development of $25,000,000 to $30,000,000 and total estimated royalties of $2,500,000 per year. "Based on the above considerations the Refinery Division of PAW has accepted the 5¢ per bbl. royalty rate as an element in the cost of aviation gas . . ." ("Royalty Rates for Fluid Catalytic Cracking and Hydro Catalytic Cracking," *op. cit.*, p. 136).

per barrel of charge for the Burton process in 1913, royalty rates on thermal cracking had been lowered in three steps to 5¢ before the war. Moreover, the original royalty rates on the Dubbs and the Tube and Tank processes were no higher than those on the less efficient Burton process. Hence it could be argued that there was no precedent for raising the royalty rate even though the Fluid process was more profitable to operate than any of its predecessors.

The historical pattern of dropping royalty rates is being repeated in the Fluid Catalytic Cracking process. In October 1952, the royalty rate was reduced to 4¢ per barrel of fresh charge.

Just as the decision on the royalty rate was somewhat arbitrary, so was the decision on the division of the royalties among the innovating firms. The fairest rule would seem to be that each company should receive an amount in proportion to its contribution. But in applying this rule there arises the familiar problem of estimating the relative value of products produced jointly. When several concepts, contributed by different individuals, are combined to produce a viable design, and when each one is necessary to the efficient functioning of the design, it is impossible to specify the value of a single contribution. In such a situation, something that can be measured must be substituted. Such a criterion is the number of patents. There is a close relation between a company's share in royalties and the number of patent applications pertaining to the Fluid Catalytic Cracking process that its employees made (see Table 4). The deviations can be explained if we take other factors into account; first, the concept of the fluid bed, which was Jersey Standard's contribution, was generally agreed to be the most important single idea, and therefore Jersey Standard would receive a larger share than would be indicated by the number of its patent applications. Moreover, Jersey Standard had spent considerably more money on research on the Fluid process than any of the other companies, and argued that the division should also be influenced by the relative expenditure.[70] Second, Kellogg and UOP and, outside the United States and Canada, Jersey Standard and Shell had the duties of administering the licenses and therefore would be expected to receive relatively more than Indiana Standard and Texaco.

Learning of the Fluid process through the trade journals[71] and the war-

[70] Interview with Frank A. Howard, October 17, 1955.
[71] E. V. Murphree, H. G. M. Fischer, E. J. Gohr, W. J. Sweeney, and C. L. Brown, *Proceedings of the American Petroleum Institute*, Vol. 24, Part III, 1943, p. 91; and E. V. Murphree, C. L. Brown, H. G. M. Fischer, E. J. Gohr, and W. J. Sweeney, *Industrial and Engineering Chemistry*, Vol. 35, 1943, p. 768.

TABLE 4
Division of Fluid Catalytic Cracking Royalties and Patent Applications

Company	Patent Applications		Distribution of Royalties (after 10% commission) (%)			
	Number	Per-centage	Kellogg license in U.S.A. or Canada	U.O.P. license in U.S.A. or Canada	ICOP[a] license outside U.S.A. or Canada	Simple arithmetic mean
Standard Oil Development Company	296	38	50	30	36.1115	38.7
Universal Oil Products Company	239	31	17.5	52.5	27.0830	32.4
M. W. Kellogg Company	57	7	17.5	17.5	16.2500	17.1
Standard Oil Company (Indiana)	96	12	5	0	2.2220	2.4
Texaco Development Company	55	7	5	0	2.2220	2.4
Shell Development Company	38	5	5	0	16.1115	7.0
Total	781	100	100	100	100	100

[a] International Catalytic Oil Process Corporation.

Sources: Patent applications: Ralph K. Davies, Press Release, Petroleum Administration for War, April 19, 1944 (on basis of Recommendation Number 41, July 24, 1942). The date as of which this compilation was made is not stated.

Distribution of royalties: Esso Research and Engineering Company, letter from F. R. Loofbourow to the author, May 5, 1958:

. . . there are about eight different splits of net royalty after the 10% commissions. I enclose a Table showing the three most typical splits of "net royalties." From this you will see that the mean percentage in the net royalties is in the neighborhood of 32% for Universal and 39% for Standard Oil Development (after taking into account SOD's share in ICOP). [*Ibid.*]

The mean percentage received by Universal Oil Products Company may be understated, for that company has granted over half the total number of Fluid licenses (although the average size of UOP licensed units tends to be smaller than the average Fluid plant).

The parties felt that it would be a good idea for Universal and Kellogg to have an incentive to compete against each other in this licensing business rather than to be in a position where it would make no difference to either of them whether it got the business or the other got the business. . . . Universal was courageous enough to moderate its royalty share in cases where it did not get the business in return for very substantial increases in its royalty share in cases where it did get the business. [Esso Research and Engineering Company, letter from F. R. Loofbourow to B. L. Bragg, July 8, 1957.]

time government agencies, many companies of all sizes sought to install the process. But during the war it was the government which made the decision as to where investment funds should be allocated, and the government was motivated primarily by the desire to obtain the greatest output.[72] During the early years of the war, steel and transportation were very scarce resources. In order to conserve steel, large units were authorized rather than small ones, because doubling the size of the unit did not double the amount of steel that was required in its construction. Shortage of transportation equipment decreed that the Fluid units should be placed in well-integrated refineries, so that large amounts of semiprocessed material would not have to be transported from one location to another. For these reasons the new units were allocated to the firms with large refineries, which usually meant the major oil companies.[73]

Twenty-four Model II units were constructed in the United States, four of which were installed by Jersey Standard and its affiliates. Two of Jersey's units were at Baton Rouge, one at Baltimore, and one at Baytown. These four units had a capacity of 14,000 barrels each, which represented an increase of 2,000 barrels a day over the Model I design. As of February 1944, when the last unit went on stream, Jersey Standard and its affiliates had Fluid Catalytic Cracking units designed to process a total of 92,000 barrels a day. In less than two years, therefore, Jersey Standard had increased the nation's total catalytic cracking capacity by about 20%.

Nine of the other twenty-three Model II units were built for the three operating oil companies which, besides Jersey Standard, were members of Catalytic Research Associates. Standard Oil Company (Indiana) itself and through its subsidiaries Pan-Am Southern Corporation and American Oil Company, built three; Texaco built three; and Shell built three. The remaining fourteen Model II units were constructed for large integrated companies (eight units) and smaller independents located near crude-oil fields (six units). For reasons of national security therefore the new facilities tended to become concentrated in the hands of the large concerns. This initial concentration tended to aggravate the disadvantageous position of the small refiner. Many of them were denied crude oil because they were not able to process it to achieve the required product distribution. The single product that was in greatest demand during the war, aviation gasoline, required in its manufacture facilities which few small refiners possessed. What might have been a questionable national policy in peacetime was a necessity in time of war.

Of the six companies which carried out the Fluid Catalytic Cracking process innovation, it is Jersey Standard which has spent the most and

---

[72] "... PAW ... made its decision(s) at all times harmonizing ... often-conflicting factors, and ... doing so in such a way as to get the most 100-octane quickest." (U. S. Petroleum Administration for War, *op. cit.*, pp. 205–206.)

[73] In 1940, the average capacity of the plants of the 30 largest oil companies was 23,940 bpd, whereas the average of the remaining refiners was only 2,397 bpd. (J. G. McLean and R. W. Haigh, *The Growth of Integrated Oil Companies*, Boston: Harvard Graduate School of Business Administration, 1954, Table 23, p. 701.)

undoubtedly received the most in return. From the beginning of the research effort in 1935 through 1956 the Jersey company spent nearly
$30,000,000 on research and development of Fluid Catalytic Cracking.[74]

Jersey Standard's revenues from the Fluid process have been derived
from two sources, royalties and operating profits. We have a measure of
the first: from 1942 through 1956 Jersey's royalties from the Fluid process
were just slightly over $30,000,000.[75] Counting royalties alone, Jersey has
just about broken even.

When we attempt to account for the second source of returns, profits
from operations, we find the amount difficult if not impossible to determine. According to our two sets of calculations, the one for 1942 and
the other for 1955, the ranges of profits from applying the Fluid process
were about 20¢ to 30¢ and 30¢ to 60¢ per barrel of charge, respectively.[76]
These figures are much higher than the royalty rate of 5¢ per barrel, so if
we assume that Jersey Standard received as profits from its own cracking
operations the same amount as the royalty rate others paid, we would in
all likelihood be understating Jersey's returns. According to Appendix
Table 20, at 5¢ per barrel charged through 1952 and 4¢ thereafter, the
total profits to all users of Fluid Catalytic Cracking units would have been
a little more than $266,000,000. As of mid-1955, the design capacity of
Jersey Standard's (that is, Esso's, Carter's, and Humble's) Fluid units was
447,000 barrels a stream day, representing 17.5% of the domestic total of
2,563,760. Assuming Jersey Standard's share of total estimated profits to
be equal to its share of total Fluid Catalytic Cracking capacity, Jersey's
profits from 1942 through 1957 would have been about $46,000,000. This
further understates the Jersey company's returns because the majority of
Jersey's Fluid units were built in the early 1940's and so have been in
operation, yielding profits, for a longer time than the average. Added to
the royalties, however, this yields a total return of over $76,000,000, or
nearly two and a half dollars for each dollar invested.

If operating profits were assumed to be 20¢ per barrel rather than 5¢,
the sum for all Fluid units for the seventeen-year period would be four
times as great, about $1,060,000,000, and Jersey Standard's share
$188,000,000. The Jersey company's total return would then be almost
$210,000,000, or about seven dollars per dollar spent on research and de-
velopment.[77] The actual amount probably lies closer to the higher figure.

[74] Esso Research and Engineering Company, letter from B. L. Bragg to the author,
December 10, 1957.
[75] *Ibid.*
[76] See Appendix Table 13b.
[77] This is greater than Jersey Standard's average return on all research and development expenditures (Esso Research and Engineering Company, *Leadership through
Research*, 1955, p. 7).

For Jersey Standard and probably for the other innovating firms, developing the Fluid process was a very profitable act.

Conclusions

In glancing back over the development of the Fluid Catalytic Cracking process, we can make several observations. With the consumer desiring a gasoline of ever higher quality, there existed a need for a process which would manufacture economically gasoline of octane number higher than that possible with thermal cracking. In response to this need, the Houdry process was developed. Because of the high value set by the owners of the Houdry process upon its practice, and because of certain inherent disadvantages attributable to a semicontinuous process, several of the larger oil companies and process engineering firms attempted to develop a competitive technique. The Fluid Catalytic Cracking process was the result. A close similarity exists here between the development of the Fluid process on the one hand and the development of the continuous thermal cracking processes on the other. In each case there was an earlier, similar process in commercial use, but either it was not available to others than the owners of the patents or else it was available only at a substantial royalty. The desire to own a competitive process was the stimulus to research activity. The inventions that followed from this research were superior to the patented processes that were already in existence. In each case they represented an advance in technology.

Here ends the similarity between the development of the Fluid process and that of the continuous thermal cracking processes. Because of changes in the state of the economy from peace to war and in the organization of research activity, the two developments do not entirely resemble each other. With the war, the whole pace of research and development was accelerated in order that the fruits of the invention might be gathered as quickly as possible. This meant that the second and third Fluid units were begun so soon after the construction of the first that the experience gained from its operation could not be put to use in their design.

But just as the war changed the pace of the Fluid development, so the growth of the industry and the progress it had already made in improving its technology changed its pattern. Perhaps the major change was from an individualistic to a co-operative approach.[78] As petroleum technology advanced, more and more skills were needed to improve upon existing

[78] In the Fluid process, for example, ". . . entirely separate groups were deployed on the problems of better synthetic catalysts, operating conditions for the catalytic reaction, control of catalyst regeneration, the general study of fluidized solids, and the study of possible patent conflicts; in addition to engineering designs, cost estimates, and product evaluations." (Note by H. J. Hall.)

processes. This required specialists in many fields, all working with an awareness of one another's work.

Another change in the pattern of research and development was the continuation of research on alternative patterns to a late stage. During the middle 1930's, Jersey Standard, with its substantial research and development organization, was able to experiment along several different lines simultaneously, concentrating on the fluidized bed only when the company had proved to its own satisfaction that it was the best technique. A smaller firm with fewer resources could not have been so flexible, could not have distributed the risks inherent in technological development over so many projects.

To engage in research and development requires large amounts of money. The amounts expended illustrate the fact that as the industry has progressed it has cost more to develop and improve a new cracking process. The amount was $200,000 for Burton's invention, increased to $6,000,000 for the Dubbs process and $3,500,000 for the Tube and Tank, to $11,000,000 for the Houdry, and finally to well over $30,000,000 for the Fluid process.

Although it has cost more to develop each new process, the span of years spent on research has not changed significantly in one direction or the other. The development of the Burton process occupied four years, from 1909 to 1913. UOP was active for nine years, from 1913 to 1922, before the first Dubbs unit went into operation. The development of the Tube and Tank took about four years. The Houdry process took the longest to be perfected, the thirteen years from 1923 to 1936. Nine years of research underlay Socony Mobil's first Thermofor Catalytic Cracking unit. The time necessary to develop the Fluid Catalytic Cracking process, from the discussions inspired by Dr. Lewis in 1938 to the completion of the first unit in 1942, was four years. For our six observations, we have an arithmetic mean of seven years. But with so few observations, we cannot generalize as to how long it takes to develop a new process in the petroleum-refining industry. We might venture several hypotheses: as an industry advances, each new process becomes more complex than its predecessor; also as the industry grows and the firms become larger, a greater number of scientists will be employed on a single development. The greater number of scientists tends to compensate for the increase in complexity, with the result that each development takes approximately the same amount of time.

If a company decides to allocate a large amount of resources to research and development, it will most likely succeed in improving its products or its manufacturing techniques. If the company does this consistently year after year, it will be developing new products and processes constantly. In the petroleum industry many companies have adopted this pattern with the result that innovation has become institutionalized. Research and development are an integral part of the day-to-day operations of the major concerns. To a certain extent, this institutionalizing of research has changed the environment within which it takes place. In the early days of the industry, to be an innovator a man had to be independently wealthy or have a patron. The first situation occurs relatively infrequently, and the second requires that the innovator have the confidence of the financier. Besides capital, the early innovator also needed an overriding passion to do research, in order to compensate for the lack of appreciation (Burton's case) or of immediate financial reward (Houdry's). When innovation is made a normal business activity, the innovator becomes the manager, who can draw upon the talent of all scientists, not just the self-chosen few. In other words, entrepreneurs can enlist borderline inventors, those who will invent out of profession rather than out of vocation. Research now offers a career rather than an outlet. By working for a large corporation, as most of the inventors in the oil industry do, and assigning to it the patents which they receive, the inventors are precluded from making any very large monetary profit out of their inventions. They receive in compensation security of employment and recognition. By institutionalizing research, the petroleum industry has supplemented genius with intelligence and knowledge, aggressiveness with perseverance, and dedication with money.

When we consider that research has become an integral part of the activities of each of the large oil companies, we recognize that the return from the introduction of a new process cannot be calculated upon the basis of the research and development that produced this process alone. The proper relation is between the improvement in all processes and products and the cost of all research and development. For Jersey Standard, the largest firm in the industry, we do have such a figure. On the average, for each dollar invested in research the undiscounted return has been somewhat greater than five dollars.[79] A return of this size is an encouragement to research.

Another observation that arises out of the development of the Fluid process is the great increase in the range within which economies of scale operate. The largest Houdry unit was 19,000 barrels a stream day.[80] With the perfection of the Fluid unit, the maximum capacity of a single cracking unit has been increased to 102,000 barrels a day, a fivefold increase.

[79] Esso Research and Engineering Company, *Leadership through Research*, 1955, p. 7.
[80] Houdry Process Corporation, "Houdry and TCC Catalytic Installations," table enclosed in personal communication from G. F. Hornaday, March 7, 1955.

Few refineries could support a unit of this size.[81] With no exceptions, those that do exist belong to the major oil companies. In fact, few of the nonintegrated refiners could afford to install a unit of one-tenth this capacity. To build a 100,000-barrel-a-day catalytic cracking unit would cost approximately $20,000,000, which, even in an age of billion-dollar corporations, is an extremely large amount.[82] The day has now passed when the small firm, even by applying the most modern techniques, can hope to achieve processing costs as low as those of its large competitors. It was the development of the Fluid Catalytic Cracking process that tipped the scales irrevocably in the direction of the large refiner.

The most recent installations of continuous catalytic cracking processes — the Fluid process, in particular — show vividly how great the increases in productivity over the last forty-two years have been. To the measurement of successive improvements in cracking technology we shall devote a portion of Chapter 7, so no more than a few figures will be cited here. Table 5 (p. 224) lists the input requirements for 100 gallons of gasoline in each of three years: 1913, when the first Burton units were installed; 1942, when the Fluid process was introduced; and the present. By developing new cracking techniques, the industry has been able to increase the productivity of its cracking stock by 230%, of its capital by 700%, of its process labor by 8,000%, and of its energy utilization by 800%. These figures would be incredible if one were not aware of the anticipations, the resources, and the enterprise of the oil companies.

[81] As of January 1, 1956, there were only seven refineries running 200,000 or more barrels of crude oil per day in the United States ("Report on United States Operating Refineries...", *op. cit.*, pp. 215–240):

Company	Refinery Location	Capacity (bpsd of crude oil)
Esso Standard Oil Company	Baton Rouge, La.	343,000
Humble Oil and Refining Co.	Baytown, Texas	313,000
Gulf Oil Corporation	Port Arthur, Texas	272,000
Texaco Corporation	Port Arthur, Texas	256,000
Standard Oil Co. (Indiana)	Whiting, Indiana	220,000
Magnolia Petroleum Company	Beaumont, Texas	205,000
Gulf Oil Corporation	Philadelphia, Pennsylvania	204,000

[82] J. G. McLean and R. W. Haigh (*op. cit.*, pp. 558–571) show the effects of increases in equipment size upon refining costs and profits, and come to the conclusion that the largest refinery considered, one of 200,000-bpd crude-oil capacity, would be the most profitable. In order to yield the desired product mix (*ibid.*, p. 559), the 200,000 bpd refinery would need as part of its facilities a Fluid Catalytic Cracking unit of approximately 100,000 bpd. The 200,000 bpd refinery would have cost $109,000,000 to construct in 1950 (*ibid.*, Exhibit XX–2, p. 560). The process facilities alone would have required a capital expenditure of $50,300,000, of which the catalytic cracking unit would consume roughly two-fifths.

TABLE 5

Comparison of the Productivity of the Burton and Fluid Cracking
Processes

Input	Consumption of inputs (per 100 gallons of gasoline)		
	Burton process	Fluid process, original installation	Fluid process, present installations
Raw material (gallons)	396	238	170
Capital (1939 $)	3.6	0.82	0.52
Process labor (man-hours)	1.61	0.09	0.02
Energy (millions of BTUs)	8.4	3.2	1.1

Notes: Capital costs include construction, maintenance, royalty, and, for the Fluid process, catalyst. The unit capacities are 88.5 bpcd for the Burton process, 12,750 bpcd for the original Fluid installation, and 36,000 bpcd for the most recent one. In this table, no allowance has been made for quality improvement; for the effect of changes in quality, see Chapter 7.

In no case that we have studied, however, does the innovation savor less of the miraculous than Fluid Catalytic Cracking. The Standard Oil Company (New Jersey) and its associates in the development deliberately set about to invent a continuous catalytic cracking process, superior to and not infringing upon the fixed-bed process. With their purpose clearly envisioned, the companies allocated to the project the major part of their large research staffs. Four years and $15,000,000 later they had achieved their goal. No greater compliment can be given to the companies than to conclude that the Fluid Catalytic Cracking process was a normal development, flowing automatically from their research organizations. Today, process innovation is truly institutionalized.

7

INNOVATION IN PETROLEUM PROCESSING

W HAT have we learned from the six innovations in refining technology? First, they were process innovations, new ways of treating a particular raw material — gas oil — to produce a particular product — gasoline. To be sure, the product changed in its chemical composition, but the changes were largely incomprehensible to the consumer and therefore little appreciated. More significant were the changes in manufacturing methods. The innovation achieved by the Burton process was the introduction of a commercial process to crack heavy petroleum oil to produce gasoline. The Dubbs and the Tube and Tank processes represented innovations because they permitted the thermal cracking process to be carried out continuously. The Houdry process was an innovation in applying the principle of catalysis to cracking. Finally, the TCC, Houdriflow, and Fluid processes were innovations because they made possible continuous catalytic cracking.

The six innovations which we observed were similar not only in that they all incorporated new techniques, but also in that each one competed keenly with its predecessor. The Dubbs and the Tube and Tank processes supplanted the Burton, and were themselves in turn supplanted by the Houdry process. Finally the Houdry process yielded to the TCC, Houdriflow, and Fluid processes. The innovations were not a series of unrelated events but a developmental sequence. The forces underlying them were similar, but because they were introduced by different firms at different points in time, we would not expect complete uniformity. On balance it would appear that the similarities are on a grand scale while the dissimilarities arise in the details.

Objectives of the Innovators

The first major similarity is that each innovation was made to answer a specific need. In each case there was an overt economic *motive* — to achieve better results for a given cost and thereby increase profits. Each process in turn was seen as more profitable than its predecessor.

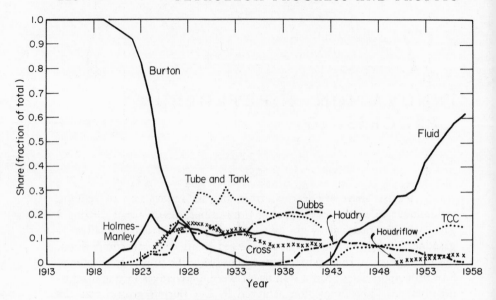

Share of cracking capacity by process, 1913–1957.

Source: Appendix Tables Ia–Ic. For the period 1913–1926, the data relate to percentage of total cracked gasoline output.

In each instance the *means* by which better processing was to be obtained was different. In the development of the Burton process it was the desire to reduce the consumption of crude oil that motivated Dr. Burton and his associates. The supply of crude oil in the Midwest had been adequate for the local refineries until about 1905, but production was declining and the refiners recognized that there was little likelihood that the trend would be reversed. As the demand for products from crude oil increased, Midwest refiners had to import crude oil from other regions. The refiners in other parts of the country were not under the same pressure to reduce their consumption of crude oil, either because their local production was adequate or because they had never been wholly dependent on local production. Thus it was the Midwest refiners who had the greatest inducement to reduce the consumption of crude oil without reducing the output of the higher-valued light products such as gasoline, kerosene, and solvents. One way to achieve this economy was to alter — or crack — the heavy components of crude oil. The means utilized in the Burton process was therefore a reduction in raw-materials input.

By means of a prior claim the owners of Jesse A. Dubbs's patent tried to appropriate the profits which Indiana Standard had made on the Burton process. When this legal tactic failed, the owners formulated a new plan: to improve on the Burton process so as to reduce substantially its costs. They were aware of the advantages a continuous process would have over the discontinuous Burton process. The Dubbs process was never conceived of as an imitation of the Burton process; it was always considered both technically and economically superior.

Similarly in the Tube and Tank innovation, the urge was to reduce the costs of cracking and thus increase profits. At first the reduction in costs following the development of the Tube and Tank process was expected to result from eliminating the royalties the Standard Oil Company (New Jersey) was paying to Indiana Standard. Very soon, however, it was found that an equally important reduction in costs was derived from the technical superiority of the Tube and Tank process.

The perfection of the Houdry process may be explained by the Sun Oil Company's desire to maintain the superiority of its gasoline product. Had the already-existing thermal cracking process been used to improve the quality of gasoline, the costs incurred would have been considerable. In catalytic cracking the Sun Oil Company saw a cheaper way of obtaining the same results. An additional inducement was offered by the possibility of fabricating the equipment in the company's own shipyard.

The TCC and Houdriflow processes, extensions of the earlier Houdry process, were developed because of the difficulty of operating the Houdry units, the widespread awareness of the merits of continuous over semicontinuous operation, and the competition offered by the Fluid Catalytic Cracking process. Similarly, one of the factors underlying the Fluid innovation was a desire to overcome the deficiencies in the Houdry process to reduce the cost of operation. In addition, Jersey Standard and its associates in the Fluid development did not have a favorable alternative to inventing their own process; they felt the price that Houdry was asking for the right to practice his art was extremely high. Given the existence of Jersey's research and development organization and similar groups under the control of the other participants in the Fluid development, combined with the financial incentives, it would almost be more difficult to explain the absence of innovation than its achievement.

When we look at the men who are responsible for innovations, men such as Burton and Humphreys, Dubbs and Halle, Clark, Howard, and Teagle, Houdry and Pew, it is hard to imagine that these men could not have been successful. They had all three necessary traits in abundance: vision, energy, and perseverance.

The innovators themselves were able to define the goals that they were seeking, to see them as profitable, and to realize the resources that would be necessary to achieve them. Dr. Burton recognized the need to economize on crude oil in the manufacture of gasoline, the petroleum product for which demand was growing most rapidly, and he saw that the gas-oil portion of the heavy petroleum fraction might be more amenable to cracking than the remaining components. He recognized that a large investment would be necessary to reap the benefits of innovation, and that once the investment had been made the returns would be substantial. He knew that an innovation required more than an invention. His contribution was not just the application of heat and pressure to the gas-oil fraction but a new technique, a new product, and, through the processing of purchased gas oil and the licensing of the Burton process, new business activities.

Burton expended a great deal of energy working simultaneously on two jobs: technical innovation and supervision of Indiana Standard's largest refinery. Clark's responsibilities were identical. Similarly we observe Teagle's capacity for work, Dubbs's dual research activities, and Houdry's complete dedication to his job. Those who worked with these men or observed them from the outside never ceased to be impressed by their vigor and their vitality. Perhaps the original ideas came easily, but in the petroleum industry they were all implemented only by an amazing amount of work.

Whenever the innovation was attributable to one or to a few men, the task was no easy one. Burton ran into difficulties both within the Whiting refinery and before Jersey Standard's board of directors. While he was employed by Indiana Standard, Clark faced the conservatism of Burton; while he was at Jersey Standard, he was confronted by the antagonism of several of the refinery managers. For several years, until the Dubbs process was widely installed, Halle and Dubbs had financial difficulties which became particularly acute at the time of the construction of the first commercial unit. Houdry faced probably the greatest obstacles of all; he lacked funds, skilled assistants, and credence. Only when research becomes institutionalized do many of the barriers to innovation disappear. A large research organization seems to be able to substitute its own existence and continuity for the persuasiveness and perseverance of its individual employees.

It is difficult to determine the personal goals of these innovators, although we can state confidently that financial gain was not the most important. With the possible exception of Carbon P. Dubbs, none of the innovators seemed to be driven by a desire to make money for himself. Nor did any of them make large fortunes; in general they seemed content to be paid at the standard managerial rate of the large corporation. Again, except for Carbon P. Dubbs, none of the innovators expected to share in the profits earned by their inventions.

It is surprising that the oil companies did not go to greater lengths in hiring extremely capable employees from their competitors. By inducing a genius to change his job a company could, with the expenditure of a few thousand dollars eventually save many millions; Jersey Standard accomplished this when it induced E. M. Clark to leave Indiana Standard. Possibly the companies did not wish to disturb the existing salary pattern. This is not a very persuasive explanation, however, for potential innovators seem less concerned with increases in salaries than with working in an organization that they find hospitable. Possibly the company managers felt that they would lose as many able employees as they could gain if their competitors became predatory, too. Perhaps they were unable to recognize genius or unwilling to suffer its disruptive force in their own organizations. We can only hypothesize as to what really motivated these innovators; from our evidence it appears to be a combination of curiosity and creativeness. They were driven to satisfy an observed need. They sought recognition and respect resulting from technical achievement and financial profit. These appear to be more important characteristics than acquisitiveness.

Besides these general traits, each of the innovators had additional personal attributes, both Burton and Humphreys had impressive technical backgrounds. In an era when petroleum refining was an art rather than a science, these two chemists had a knowledge of petroleum technology as great as any in the industry. Were technical knowledge the sole criterion of success, we would have predicted that the first cracking innovation would have issued from the Standard Oil Company (Indiana).

Another advantage Dr. Burton enjoyed, because his over-all ability was recognized, was his status in the organization. During most of the time when the Burton process was being developed, Burton himself was the manager of Indiana Standard's Whiting refinery. His rank was sufficiently high to enable him to control the research carried out in the laboratory, co-ordinate the pilot-plant operations with the rest of the refinery's activities, absorb the financial burden in the general refinery accounts, and, once the process was installed, assure its integration into the rest of the refinery's activities.

All of these advantages accrued to Burton through his position; had he been lower in the organization, he would have found it more difficult to focus on the development himself, and his efforts would have been directed toward immediately more but ultimately less profitable areas of research. Had he been higher in the organization, Burton would not have been able to keep informed of the day-to-day results of his research. Moreover, it would not have been easy for him to take time off from his managerial activities to carry out his own experiments. When Burton became vice-president and moved from the Whiting refinery to Indiana

Standard's headquarters in Chicago, research efforts first slackened and then dropped off almost entirely. The laboratory failed to grow, and its endeavors were increasingly directed toward achieving minor improvements in what was by then an obsolete cracking process.

Like Burton, the innovators in the Dubbs process were located at strategic places in the organization. Halle, president of the Universal Oil Products Company, was in the ideal position to promote the Dubbs process. Having almost complete control of the firm's financial and external affairs, Halle was able to mobilize the resources necessary to achieve the development, and to formulate the attractive licensing policy that made the Dubbs patents and process know-how available on equal terms to all refiners.

Carbon P. Dubbs, as the chief engineer in Universal Oil Products, was also in an ideal position. Given freedom by Halle, Dubbs was able to force the adoption of his inventions, particularly "clean circulation." The two men worked harmoniously; Halle concentrated on the legal and financial aspects of the development and Dubbs on the technical.

When we look at the innovators of the Dubbs process, we are more aware of their temperaments than we were of those who developed the Burton process. Perhaps this is the result of the differences between the two organizations. With the power of the Standard Oil Company (Indiana) behind him, Burton did not need the particular traits required by the employees of the struggling Universal Oil Products Company. At Indiana Standard there was no need for a man with Halle's combativeness and willingness to take risks, or Dubbs's audacity.

To the list of character traits that aided the innovators of the Dubbs process must be added the unusual personality of the financial backer of Universal Oil Products Company, J. Ogden Armour. Armour had complete confidence in the ability of Halle, and a willingness to implement this with a considerable financial investment. A more active investor would probably have thwarted the development of the Dubbs process at the time when it was decided that Jesse A. Dubbs's patents did not underlie the Burton process. A sensible man might have decided that patents which had no legal value could have no technical value. It was only Halle's stubbornness and Armour's support that made it possible for the development to continue.

When we come to the Tube and Tank process, we find it difficult to discover any attributes for success that the innovators did not have. All of the individuals who were necessary to support and control process development believed continuous thermal cracking to be the most efficient concept. Walter Teagle, president of the Standard Oil Company (New Jersey), knew both the advantages and, probably more important, the disadvantages of the Burton process. He was persuaded that a research and development organization would be a profitable addition to Jersey Standard's activities, and thus assured its permanence. Both he and Frank Howard, head of the Standard Oil Development (now Esso Research and Engineering Corporation) were farsighted, seeing beyond the immediate project on continuous thermal cracking and recognizing that a permanent research and development organization could deliver a steady stream of new processes and products. Frank Howard was a particularly versatile man, making contributions in the organization of the Development Company, in the solution of the legal problems that accompanied the development of the early continuous cracking processes, and in the technical aspects of the process development. There is, however, no evidence that Howard immersed himself in the details of the organization, or in the legal or the technical phases of the development. His talents were used to evaluate major developments rather than to predetermine minor ones.

In the development of the Tube and Tank process, Jersey Standard relied for technical skill almost entirely upon the employees whom it hired away from Indiana Standard: Clark, Loomis, and Carringer, at that time the most inventive and least contented men in Indiana's organization. Clark's position and talent remind us of Burton's; he was a refinery manager, carried out research on his own ideas in his spare time, gathered together a few loyal and capable assistants, and, during the middle period of the development, found obstructions to his further progress. For Burton, the obstructions were removed with the dissolution of the Standard Oil "trust"; for Clark the barriers to the reception of his process were removed only when he himself left to work for Jersey Standard.

With the Tube and Tank development, the abilities needed for the innovation were distributed over at least three individuals; when we come to the Houdry process, we find that Eugene Houdry incorporated all of them in himself. Even more than Burton, who did not suffer such a multitude of misfortunes and disappointments, Houdry should be given credit for the single-handed introduction of a significantly new cracking process. Houdry's characteristics — vision, perseverance, and strength of purpose approaching fanaticism — and his resources — his own, his wife's, and his family's money — account for his success. Those talents which he lacked — perspective, flexibility, and ability to manage a large organization — account for his frequent setbacks. Nevertheless, Houdry is our last heroic figure: the last man of genius, the last man with superb abilities and numerous but never debilitating faults.

The Institutionalizing of Research and Development

In the innovations following the Houdry process, we lose sight of individuals and their contributions. We become involved in aggregations —

fifty chemists, one hundred chemical engineers, and so on — each member of which probably embodies at least one of the attributes for success in research and development. A process no longer bears the name of one or more men; it no longer has the idiosyncracies that one powerful intellect imposes upon it. Gone are the heightened emotions, the violent controversies, and the auras of dedication and excitement. It becomes much simpler to classify the resources devoted to any process development and more difficult to categorize character traits. The focus shifts from the individual himself to the individual in relation to his associates, from the personality and talents of an individual to interactions of different individuals in a common environment and to the policy and structure of the organization. Understanding research and development becomes more difficult, for innovators can no longer be examined in isolation but only in the context of the group within which they work. Observing them alone is not enough; it becomes important to observe them working with their associates. Since even the most dedicated group is likely to break up willingly, if not deliberately, when an innovation is accomplished, historical investigations of the conditions of innovation are not particularly fruitful. One can see what was accomplished; nevertheless one finds it difficult to see how.

Considering the TCC and Fluid developments together, we notice that as research and development are institutionalized the activities become more standardized. Each organization deals with patents, laboratory research, pilot-plant operations, equipment design, investment analysis, licensing, and process improvement. Each employs chemists, physicists, mathematicians, chemical engineers, mechanical engineers, technicians, lawyers, and administrators. Each adopts similar policies: patents are assigned by the inventor to the employer; salaries vary within a rather narrow range; projects are evaluated periodically by the administrators and expanded, contracted, or eliminated according to how they meet uniform, economic criteria, and so on. The similarity comes partly from imitation, partly from the common nature of the problems and the common background of the scientists and engineers. The character or personality of an oil company that results in part from different locations, founders, and size becomes less vivid and less varied when one moves from its operating departments to its research and development organization. Gone are many of the eccentricities. The uniformity of science has produced a similarity of approach. Research itself becomes a process, following the same pattern, the same sequence of events, as did the continuous cracking processes.

In the continuous cracking process developments, several innovations took place almost simultaneously. Then as improvements were made, the processes tended to become more nearly alike. Similarly each of the various research organizations started quite differently, only through time to become more nearly alike. Burton, Humphreys, Rogers, Clark, and Loomis, with their technical training, carried out research under their own initiative and with no consistent policies or encouragement from Indiana Standard, their employer. Jersey Standard's Development Department, with its centralized and articulated organization focused on development rather than invention. Halle, Belknap, and C. P. Dubbs, with their research activities confined within the narrow scope of Jesse A. Dubbs's patent, emphasized exploitation. Houdry, with his dedication to catalysis, was forced into a continuing search for financial support. From these diverse beginnings emerged the Research and Development Department of the Standard Oil Company (Indiana), Esso Research and Engineering Company, Universal Oil Products Company, and Houdry Process Corporation – four large, autonomous, skilled, diversified, stable, almost identical research and development organizations. Moreover, as other oil companies have observed the benefits of research and development and have reached the size where they could support these activities year after year, this homogeneous group has been augmented. Later aspirants have all adopted research and development as necessary and permanent activities at approximately the same stage in their growth, in the period when they have maintained a crude-oil throughput in the range of 150,000 to 200,000 barrels a day.[1] In petroleum cracking processes we observed two radical departures, that of moving from no research at all to research carried out by a few individuals, and that of shifting from a few individuals working independently and sporadically to large groups of individuals working in combination and in perpetuity.

These shifts imply that the change from single individuals to innovating groups as the industry grew was a profitable one. We might question, however, the implication that combining a group of specialists would have been worth while during the early stages of the industry's growth. On the one hand, it would certainly have required funds, funds which might not have been available given the limited extent of the market. On the other hand, any firm which dominated the industry's early research might have secured for itself future supremacy. This argument admits some confusion, however, between benefits to the industry and benefits to the firm. From the point of view of the single firm, if it could rely upon

[1] See J. L. Enos, "The Mighty Adversaries: Standard Oil Company (New Jersey) and Royal Dutch/Shell," *Explorations in Entrepreneurial History*, April 1958, p. 142.

an absence of reaction from its competitors, then large-scale research — tantamount to institutionalized research — might have been profitable.

The more perplexing problem is whether or not the rate of technological progress in the industry would have been more rapid if all resources for innovation were combined within one firm. Unfortunately, since we looked only at successful innovations, we could not gather much of an impression of the total resources devoted to research and development by the petroleum-refining industry and by individuals outside. We do know that the Standard Oil Company (Indiana) controlled much of the research talent of the industry during the reign of the Burton process. For a few years this paid off for Indiana, as the high profits accruing from the practice and licensing of the Burton process illustrate. But the idea of continuity and the ethic of perpetual change had not been instilled into Indiana Standard's research organization, and it became ineffectual. Had there been in the industry no other firms with resources sufficient to carry out research and development, technological progress might well have ceased. In demonstrating the profitability of research, the Burton process stimulated the industry; in dazzling the scientists and engineers at Indiana Standard, it prevented them from seeing into the future and thus limited the contribution of the industry's most powerful aggregation of talent. We can only conclude that the problem of whether or not technology progresses more rapidly when all the resources are concentrated in the hands of one group has not been answered. We leave the question open.

Let us shift from economics to psychology and examine the psychic returns to the scientist and the engineer. Invention and innovation are by their nature disturbances, departures from convention. An individual who can consider innovating is an iconoclast, a person who does not cherish existing institutions and is able to consider himself a disruptive force. Yet the inventor or the innovator cannot be too far removed from the environment into which his creation is to be fitted. Each new product or process must be integrated with those already in existence or else it will not be a success.

It is the rare individual in which all of these qualities are combined. Where invention is concerned, the habitat of this rare individual has been mainly on the periphery of the petroleum industry. The most novel ideas — cracking by the application of heat and pressure, continuous processing, fractionation, catalysis, regeneration of catalysts, moving and fluidized beds — occurred to independent inventors, men like Dewar and Redwood, Ellis, Adams, Houdry, and Odell, who occasionally have contributed their talents, but never their permanent employment or loyalties, to the oil companies. The most capable inventors, with the notable exception of Eugene Houdry, have stopped at invention.[2]

If the most radical departures in thought have been made by inventors on the periphery of the oil industry, the least radical have been made by inventors working for the large, integrated oil companies. Of all the major inventions in petroleum cracking only one — Burton's choice of a cracking charge stock with a narrow boiling range — was discovered by such an employee.

Deficient as they have been in inventiveness, the large oil companies have excelled in adopting and applying the ideas of others, that is, in innovating. The history of the development of the cracking processes reveals how demanding of resources, patience, and persuasion is process innovation.

If we examine the innovators of the thermal cracking processes — the Burton, Dubbs, Tube and Tank, Holmes-Manley, and Cross — we find that they had unusual attributes. They were young men, in their early thirties, when they started to innovate. They had the flexible minds and the lack of respect that one associates with youth. Yet most of these men were in positions of responsibility, positions attained primarily through their administrative rather than their technical abilities. Thus we cannot say with confidence that the early innovators would have been frustrated had they been members of large research and development teams.

In recent years, success in process innovation has followed the adoption of the large research and development corporation, whose function is to institutionalize innovation. Now we find the environment considerably changed. We would expect that the character of the men who take part in innovation would change also, in the direction of more uniformity. A group places restrictions on an individual; it exerts pressure to conform to the taste, the behavior, and the ideas of the majority within it. Unpredictable and extreme individuals, fanatics, tend not to be accepted by the group and therefore not to be hired by the research organization. Moreover, any departure from existing customs or techniques by a large group must be a common one. Since the departure is one that is agreed upon by the majority, it will therefore not be as radical as that which a single individual might take. The group orders its environment; a single innovator like Houdry creates and dominates his own environment.

[2] Although they may have been motivated primarily by their personal desires, these independent inventors did not suffer financially by remaining aloof. The sums paid to Ellis, Adams, and Odell for their patents were as grand as those received by any of the oil companies' inventors. A possible exception is Carbon Petroleum Dubbs. It might be argued, however, that the several million dollars received by Dubbs came not from his inventions but from prudent investment in the common stock of Universal Oil Products Company.

The rewards for the individual working as a member of a closely co-ordinated team are considerably different from those of a lone inventor. The group scientist or engineer cannot expect much outside recognition or great financial reward, since his own contributions are only a small part of the whole. He can expect, however, recognition by the individuals in his own group, men of the same persuasion as himself. To the innovator, this reward may be one of the most important. We have observed that financial returns do not appear to be a major force impelling the single innovator, although we must admit that the men we observed were all reasonably secure financially. The early innovators could count on stable private income, as the modern researcher can today.

This discussion has treated innovation as a single activity. Actually, there are big and little innovations, completely radical departures from existing technique and minor improvements. Of the two most radical departures one, the Burton process, was the creation of an individual man from within the industry. His training had followed unconventional lines, however, and he had accumulated a unique technical knowledge. Eugene Houdry, who was almost singly responsible for the second major departure, was even more unconventional than Burton. From the two innovators who departed most from the existing mode came the most significant steps. Yet recently, the most radical departure in cracking technology, using radiation as the means of promoting the cracking reaction, appears to have been made by the largest company in the industry, the Standard Oil Company (New Jersey). It is of course difficult to anticipate what the next new process will be, but from the superficial evidence, the author would expect it to come from one of the large concerns which has institutionalized research.

At the other extreme, the Sinclair Oil Company has had remarkably little success subsidizing individual inventors. In May 1951, Sinclair initiated a program to "encourage and assist outside inventors who have worthwhile ideas for better petroleum products or their uses but who lack research laboratory facilities to test out such ideas."[3] Since 1952, however, the program has not been mentioned in its annual reports, an indication that it has not resulted in any substantial achievements. We do not know the reasons. It is conceivable that the program floundered because the company placed too many constraints on the inventors it did attract, or because the independent inventor may wish to remain independent and so few capable men were attracted.

It is even possible that in the petroleum refining industry the day of the lone inventor has passed. Aware of the complexity of the technology, of the great resources necessary to carry out innovation, and of competi-

[3] Sinclair Oil Corporation, *Annual Report*, 1951, p. 10.

tion from the large institutionalized research groups, the Eugene Houdry of the present day may be experimenting in an allied field such as petro-chemicals or in areas further removed from the petroleum industry.

Costs of Research and Development

Regardless of whether the innovations are carried out by individuals or by groups, the costs of developing new cracking processes have always been substantial. Even the Burton process, of all the cracking processes the least expensive to develop, required an investment of approximately $236,000 before it was perfected. As Table 6 (p. 238) shows, the cost of developing and improving new cracking processes has varied from this minimum figure to a maximum of over $30,000,000 in the case of Fluid Catalytic Cracking.

With as few as six examples it is difficult to have much confidence in the trend of costs of innovation. Any trend we do observe is toward higher costs with time. Of the two most radical departures, the Burton and the Houdry innovations, the second was considerably more expensive. Similarly, of the two pairs of major process improvements, the second pair — the TCC–Houdriflow and the Fluid — was more expensive than the first pair — the Dubbs and Tube and Tank. This conclusion does not apply to these innovations separately, however, for the Dubbs develop-ment probably exceeded the TCC–Houdriflow in cost, particularly when changes in price level are considered.

Time is another resource, one that can be significant when several firms are attempting simultaneously to develop similar processes. The time spans of the six cracking innovations are listed in Table 6. The first col-umn gives the time consumed in research before the innovators had any specific idea of the ultimate process. The eight years of preliminary activi-ties in the Dubbs process were consumed by Jesse A. Dubbs's experiments in emulsion breaking and by the early legal altercations of the Universal Oil Products Company. The five years preceding the Tube and Tank development include both E. M. Clark's work while he was still at Indi-ana and the research underlying Ellis' cracking patents. Houdry concen-trated on lignite for two years before turning to petroleum for his raw material. The ten years of work in catalysis carried out by Jersey Standard was in connection with hydrogenation.

This preliminary period was assumed to end when the innovators vis-ualized the new process, that is, when they had an idea of their goal and of the precise direction their research was to take. The terminal date of the development period (column 4) is the date at which the first successful cracking unit incorporating the new process achieved commercial opera-tion. The periods of development were rather similar in length, averaging

TABLE 6

Estimated Expenditure of Time and Money in Developing New Cracking Processes

Process	Preliminary Activities		Development of the New Process		Major Improvements in the New Process		Total	
	Time Interval	Estimated Cost	Time Interval	Estimated Cost	Time Interval	Estimated Cost	Time Interval	Estimated Cost
Burton	None	None	1909–1913 (5 years)	$92,000	1914–1917 (4 years)	$144,000	1909–1917 (9 years)	$236,000
Dubbs	1909–1916 (8 years)	n.a.[a]	1917–1922 (6 years)	6,000,000	1923–1931 (9 years)	1,000,000+	1909–1931 (23 years)	7,000,000+
Tube and Tank	1913–1917 (5 years)	$275,000[b]	1918–1923 (6 years)	600,000[c]	1924–1931 (8 years)	2,612,000	1913–1931 (19 years)	3,487,000[d]
Houdry	1923–1924 (2 years)	n.a.[e]	1925–1936 (12 years)	11,000,000	1937–1942 (6 years)	n.a.	1923–1942 (20 years)	11,000,000+
Fluid	1928–1938 (10 years)	n.a.	1938–1941 (4 years)	15,000,000	1942–1952 (11 years)	15,000,000+[f]	1928–1952 (25 years)	30,000,000+
TCC and Houdriflow	g	g	1935–1943 (9 years)	1,150,000	1944–1950[h] (7 years)	3,850,000	1935–1950 (16 years)	5,000,000

Notes to Table 6:

a A sum of $25,000 was paid to Jesse A. Dubbs for his asphalt and emulsion-breaking patents. There is no record of the amount spent by Universal Oil Products in challenging the Burton process patents, but it was probably several times this amount.

b This sum is the amount paid for the Ellis patents and for Rogers' claim against Adams and the Texas Company. Not included are the expenses incurred by E. M. Clark while he was working for the Standard Oil Company (Indiana).

c This consists of $498,000 for development expenditures and $102,000 for legal expenses.

d This amount is Jersey Standard's estimate of total expenses through 1931. Approximately $850,000 more was spent primarily on technical services from 1932 through 1957.

e The amount which Houdry and his associates spent on the development of the process of obtaining motor fuel from lignite is not known. The $11,000,000 given in the column under the development of the new process is the total for both the lignite and the successful Houdry process.

f The Model IV Fluid unit was introduced in 1952. This is assumed to be the last major improvement in the Fluid process. In 1942 the seven firms working on the Fluid development expected to spend $10,000,000 to $15,000,000 in the next three years. The higher figure is taken; this almost certainly understates the total for the entire ten-year period from 1942 to 1952 because expenditures for 1945 through 1952 were also substantial. Jersey Standard alone spent nearly $30,000,000 from 1935 through 1956.

g The time and expense in developing the Houdry process might well be included here, as the TCC and Houdriflow processes were based upon Houdry's earlier work.

h 1950 was chosen as the terminal year because it was then that the first air-lift TCC unit and the first Houdriflow unit were both installed.

seven years per process with a minimum of four for the Fluid and a maximum of twelve for the Houdry.

The periods during which major improvements in the new processes continued to be made likewise show some uniformity, averaging six years, with a narrower range from a low of four years to a high of eleven. Looking at the entire period of research, development, and improvement, we see that five of the six processes consumed about twenty years each. Only the Burton process — the first chronologically and the one which took the shortest time, cost the least, and returned proportionately the most — departed greatly from the average.

Regardless of variations in the cost of innovation, in absolute amounts the sums were large, representing sizable expenditures on laboratory equipment and on scientific, engineering, legal, and administrative personnel. If all process innovations were equally expensive, innovation by petroleum refiners or by process-development firms would be limited to the few companies able to command the necessary resources. There are not very many companies of this size. Historically, the integrated oil companies have not organized process-development departments — an indication that they were not ready to initiate much research and development — before they achieved outputs of 150,000 barrels a day. In addition to the big oil companies, there are a few important process-development companies, four of which could be considered large firms. All of these firms have long been established, for almost no firm has entered the process-development industry in the last thirty years.[4]

The number of competing processes existing at any time has been greatly reduced over the years. To be sure, neither the Burton nor the Houdry process had close competitors for several years. but once these techniques had been supplanted by continuous processes, there were many more competing processes in thermal cracking than in catalytic. In thermal cracking we were able to identify at least seven, whereas there have never been more than three continuous catalytic cracking processes — the Fluid, the TCC, and the Houdriflow.

How can we explain this reduction in the number of competing processes? One possible explanation is the existence of other attractive uses for

[4] The Lummus Company (founded prior to 1930, now 43.8% owned by Combustion Engineering, Inc. [1956 sales $169,015,000, assets $141,086,000] and 45% owned by Babcock and Wilcox Company [1956 sales $281,485,000, assets $200,679,000]); Universal Oil Products Company (founded in 1914, 1956 sales $32,207,000, assets [1958] $51,584,000); M. W. Kellogg Company (incorporated in 1920, now subsidiary of Pullman Inc., which purchased Kellogg in 1944 for $18,250,000); and Foster Wheeler Corp. (established in 1900, 1956 sales $173,032,000, assets $90,182,000). Another process development firm, Gasoline Products Company, which introduced the Cross continuous thermal cracking process, has since departed from the industry.

resources. In any petroleum or process-development company, there are always alternative uses for funds invested in research and development. For the petroleum companies, the alternatives are chiefly plants incorporating existing processes, investments in other branches of the industry, or product promotion. For the process-development firms, the immediate alternatives are to enter into refining, which none have done, or to concentrate on construction activity. The attractiveness of the alternatives has probably varied from company to company and from industry to industry, but because the decisions were made before the results were obtained, there is little that can be concluded quantitatively. Only when the potential innovation can be clearly visualized — which is difficult because of inability to predict and because of habitual optimism — or when so many innovations have been carried out that a potential innovation need not be considered singly, can the alternatives be clearly stated.[5]

The firm which brings out a new process has two ways of achieving a return, through operating the process itself or through licensing or selling it to others. Whichever way it chooses, it must be prepared to invest more funds before a financial return is obtained. Single inventors with patent claims backed by experiments have usually chosen to sell their art, at amounts in our case ranging up to the maximum of $275,000 received by Ellis for his continuous cracking patents. The process-development companies have elected to license the art.

We do not know what the costs of promoting a new process are. In the case of the first commercially successful cracking process, the Burton, the costs of the promotion and administration of licenses must have been extremely small. The Burton process was sufficiently attractive to the rest of the industry that it was the other petroleum companies that approached Indiana Standard for licenses. It appears that the larger the number of competing cracking processes available, the larger the amount of money spent in promoting each one. This would be necessary because, although the processes seem to be similar at first, significant differences do become evident when individual situations are considered. For example, there were several continuous thermal cracking processes available in the 1920's and the 1930's to all appearances very much alike. Yet given certain cracking stocks, fuel prices, capital availability, product quality, and so on, one

[5] The Standard Oil Company (New Jersey), the petroleum company which has been the most active in research, calculates that each dollar invested in research and development returned five dollars in profits. (Esso Research and Engineering Company, *Leadership Through Research*, no date, p. 7.)

DuPont has found that only one in twenty research projects ever results in a commercial application, and that "not more than one out of five research dollars ever pays off." (Testimony of President Greenewalt, quoted in "Mergers and Acquisitions," Subcommittee on Patents, Trademarks, and Copyrights, 85th Congress, 2nd Session, Washington, Government Printing Office, 1958, p. 14.)

process would prove most advantageous. In order to publicize differences, the firms with competing processes felt it worth while to examine special situations and design certain facilities for limited application.

Costs of Commercial Equipment

Although we do not have any measure of the cost of promoting a process, we do have a measure of the cost of installing the equipment in which it is incorporated. In Table 7 are given construction costs, both in

TABLE 7

Construction Costs for the First Commercial Cracking Units
Incorporating New Processes, 1913–1955

Process	Date	Capacity of Unit (Barrels per Calendar Day)	Construction Cost (of on-site facilities)		
			At Time of Construction	Construction Index, 1939=100	In 1939 Dollars
Burton	1913	88.5	$6,750	52.1	$12,950
Tube and Tank	1922	570	90,000	82.7	108,900
Houdry	1938	6,750	2,191,000	100	2,191,200
Fluid	1942	12,750	2,060,000	109	1,889,000

Sources: See Appendix Table 13.

current and in 1939 dollars, for the first units incorporating new processes. The cost of installing the first commercial cracking unit rose rapidly from the date of the installation of the Burton process in 1913 to that of the Houdry process in 1938. Between 1913 and 1922, installation costs rose tenfold; between 1922 and 1938 they rose twentyfold. Very little of this rise can be attributed to an increase in complexity of equipment, however, for the capacity of the units increased in very nearly the same proportion. The first Tube and Tank unit had approximately six times the capacity of the first Burton unit, and the first Houdry unit was approximately twelve times the capacity of the first Tube and Tank unit. As described earlier, the capacity of the pilot plants for the catalytic cracking processes was substantially greater than that of a commercial Burton still. Moreover, refinery capacities had increased so much between 1913 and the mid-1930's that cracking units with a capacity of less than 500 barrels a day could not be integrated into the over-all processing scheme of most refineries. Because of the growth in the capacity of individual refineries and in the economies of scale in individual cracking plants, therefore, the amount of money necessary to build the first commercial unit has increased substantially. We see now one possible explanation of the decline in the number

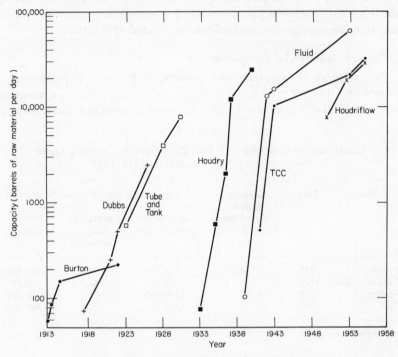

Growth in size of single cracking units, 1913–1957.

Source: Chapters 1–6.
Note: Includes pilot plants.

of competing processes. Few companies are willing or able to invest large sums in research and development with the knowledge that installing a new process will require an additional investment of several million dollars on capital equipment. The additional expenditure on equipment large enough to fit into existing facilities increases the magnitude of the risk.

Returns from the Innovations

We have looked at the cost of developing new cracking processes and at the cost of installing the first commercial unit; let us now examine the returns from the innovations. Innovations yield royalties and operating profits. If we assume that the innovators who utilize their own process receive the same profit per unit of output as competitors pay to license it, we derive the returns to innovation listed in Table 8.

This method of estimating undoubtedly understates the total return for innovators who are able to use their process in their own refineries.

TABLE 8

Cost of and Returns from Cracking Process Innovations, 1913–1957

Process	Cost of Innovation		Returns from Innovation		Approximate Ratio of Returns to Cost ($ per $)
	Period over which Expenses Incurred	Estimated Amount	Period over which Returns Calculated	Estimated Amount	
Burton	1909–1917	$236,000	1913–1924	$150,000,000+	600+
Dubbs	1909–1931	7,000,000+	1922–1942	135,000,000+	20
Tube and Tank	1913–1931	3,487,000	1921–1942	284,000,000+	80+
Houdry	1923–1942	11,000,000+	1936–1944	39,000,000	3.5
Fluid	1928–1952	30,000,000+	1942–1957	265,000,000+	9
TCC	1935–1950 ⎫	5,000,000+	1943–1957	71,000,000+ ⎫	16
Houdriflow	1935–1950 ⎭		1950–1957	12,000,000 ⎭	

Sources: Costs: see Table 6.

Revenues (undiscounted): Burton; see Appendix Table 14. If Indiana's estimate that one-half of the total company profits during the period 1913–1922 were derived from the Burton process is used, the ratio of returns to cost would be one and one-half times that estimated in the final column.

Dubbs: see Appendix Table 15. Royalties have undoubtedly continued to flow to Universal Oil Products since 1942, although we have no way of estimating their amount. In 1942, the last year for which figures are available, Dubbs process royalties were estimated at $7,540,000.

Tube and Tank: see Appendix Table 16. Like Dubbs royalties, Tube and Tank royalties continued after 1942, but again we have no measure. The estimate of royalties for 1942 was $7,008,000.

Remainder: see Appendix Tables 17–20.

Although royalties are wholly attributable to the process itself, operating profits must be allocated in some way to the operating firm in its role of innovator and to the operating firm in its role of processer. This allocation is arbitrary. Since licensors usually ask that only a fraction of operating profits be paid as royalties, equating the rate of return to the royalty rate understates considerably the operating profits.

A further bias toward understatement lies in neglecting the chronology of adoption. As we have observed in the Burton process, the innovating firm which installs its own technique may, by its early presence on the scene, earn a rate of return considerably higher than others. As the industry has matured, however, the time that elapses between the introduction of the new process by the innovating firm and its installation by other petroleum refiners has been reduced. The advantage accruing to the innovator from early processing has probably diminished to the same extent.

Granting the bias in the estimates, the first thing that we observe from Table 8 is a marked decline in the return on investment in process innovation. The Burton cracking process, the first to be introduced, returned over $600 for each dollar that was spent on research and development. The next innovations chronologically, the Dubbs and Tube and Tank, returned approximately $20 and $80 respectively. The Houdry process, having been introduced in the mid-1930's and then cut off by the exigencies of the war, was the least successful, returning somewhat less than $3.50 for each dollar spent. The three continuous catalytic cracking processes, the Fluid and the TCC and Houdriflow, have fared better than the Houdry, but still considerably less well than their predecessors. The general trend evident from our small sample is one of long-run decreasing profitability of innovation.

The figures in Tables 6 and 8 must be qualified. In the columns that are devoted to dollar amounts, the direction of bias in the estimates is indicated. A plus sign (+) means that the actual figure may be higher. For the Burton and Houdry processes the returns from the innovations are all that will be obtained during the life of the process. For the other five, the Dubbs, Tube and Tank, Fluid, TCC, and Houdriflow, we have only a partial accounting of the total. In the case of the first two, this is the result of not having output or capacity statistics for thermal cracking by process after 1942; for the remainder, it is the result of their not yet being obsolete.

Licensing and Royalties

In absolute amounts the returns to process innovation have been quite substantial, none less than $12,000,000. Yet part of these returns come from royalties other refiners pay. When the royalties are stated on the basis of a unit of charge, such as 4¢ per barrel (42 gallons) for the Fluid and 3¢ per barrel for the TCC and Houdriflow units, they do not appear to amount to much. But the petroleum-refining industry processes such large volumes of material that what seems like a low royalty rate can over time result in extremely large royalty payments.[6] In petroleum refining, paying and receiving royalties is a big business. There are few other industries within which such large transfers of money between competing companies — from those who adopt to those who innovate — take place.

More revealing than absolute figures are the fractions of total costs and profits represented by royalties. In Table 9, these fractions are estimated for each of the cracking processes: between 1913 and 1955, both fractions became considerably smaller. We conclude that in petroleum refining the

---

[6] In 1954, roughly $35,000,000 was incurred in royalties for the three catalytic cracking processes (see Appendix Tables 18–20). Assuming that half of this amount represented payments from licensees to licensors (the other half being internal transfers resulting from the licensors' own operations) the yearly transfer was $17,500,000. This represents a little less than 1% of the value added by manufacture in the petroleum-refining industry, $1,901,333,000 (U.S. Bureau of the Census, *U.S. Census of Manufactures*, 1954: Vol. II, Part 2, Washington: Government Printing Office, 1957, p. 29–2).

cost of licensing a process has declined in relation to all the other elements of cost.

It is difficult to relate changes in royalty rates to competition in process licensing. If absolute amounts are used as the measure of royalty rates, then there is a direct relation between the number of competing processes and the decline in royalty rates. When the Burton and the Houdry processes were in vogue there were no closely competing processes and no

TABLE 9
Royalties as a Percentage of Total Costs and Profits, 1913–1955

Process	Year	Royalty Rate (Cents per barrel of charge)	Royalties as Percentage of	
			Total Costs	Profits
Burton	1913	17	8.8	33[a]
Tube and Tank	1922	10	3.8	11
Houdry	1936	4.1[b]	2.4[b]	18[b]
Fluid				
(15,000 bpsd unit)	1942	5	3.0	19
(40,000 bpsd unit)	1955	4	1.2	5

Source: Appendix Tables 12, 13.
Notes:
[a] The royalty rate for licenses of the Burton process was 25% of the gross profit (profit plus royalty); this is equal to 33% of the net profit.
[b] Probably an understatement. The license to operate the Houdry process was available only to those who paid the royalty in a lump sum. In translating this into a running rate, no time-discount factor was allowed.

reductions in royalty rates. With the coexistence of three competing processes, Fluid, TCC, and Houdriflow, there has been one moderate reduction. When there were several competing continuous thermal cracking processes, during the 1920's and 1930's, three substantial reductions were made. The greater the number of processes available, the greater the decline.

When relative rather than absolute measures are used, however, there is little connection between the number of competing processes and changes in royalty rates. As fractions of total costs and profits, royalty rates were stable from 1913 to 1922, dropped precipitously with the almost simultaneous introduction of the Dubbs, Tube and Tank, Cross, Holmes-Manley, and other continuous thermal cracking processes, remained steady during the 1920's, rose substantially during the early 1930's, and have fallen equally substantially since then. It is not the number of processes available but general business conditions that seem best to explain fluctuations in the burden royalty payments impose. Only when several new processes are introduced at the same time may the burden suddenly become lighter.

Since the 1920's the only barrier to adopting a new process has been the financial one of paying the royalty; before then there were other, more serious restraints. The Standard Oil Company (Indiana), owner of the Burton process, formulated a restrictive licensing policy. Only those refiners operating outside Indiana Standard's markets were permitted to practice thermal cracking, and even they had to learn the technique themselves, for a Burton license was merely permission to operate under the process patents; know-how was not included. Finally, fellow Standard Oil companies were favored in the granting of licenses and the supplying of technical assistance.

Discrimination was eliminated by Hiram Halle when he established Universal Oil Products' licensing policy. Geography and, later, size were not to be considerations. Know-how was to be made available. To the credit of later innovators, some of whom have been oil companies rather than process-development firms like UOP, they have adopted Halle's policies. Licenses in the petroleum industry are now universal, uniform, and all-inclusive: they give not only permission to operate but access to the technology.

Changes in Productivity

A new process is adopted when it promises to reduce costs. To do this it must economize on at least one input. Conceivably it could economize on all of them; in other words, it would raise the productivity of all of the inputs. For each innovation, we have calculated the consumption of inputs; therefore, from this empirical evidence we can determine the extent of the changes in productivity.

In making the calculations, we defined the inputs to cracking quite broadly, for we wanted the categories of inputs to be few enough to permit easy comparison yet numerous enough to separate competing items. If a kilowatt-hour in a pump were replaced by a kilowatt-hour in a blower, this did not concern us, but if a barrel of gas oil were replaced by a dollar of capital, this did concern us. Ultimately, we specified four inputs: labor, capital, raw material, and energy.

The task of measuring the first productive input, labor, is not easy. We can identify at least four types of labor according to the skills involved and, more important economically, according to the conditions of employment: process labor, maintenance labor, supervision (at all levels of administration), and technical service. The first two are hourly-paid employees with loyalties to unions, while the latter two are salaried and part of the managerial class. Fluctuations in employment would be expected to be more severe for hourly-paid labor than for management. The problem that this division of labor creates is not too serious for us, however, as the petroleum-refining industry has grown steadily and employment in it has been quite insensitive to the business cycle. Engineers in the industry recognize this implicitly when they estimate supervisory and technical service costs (overhead) as a certain fraction of direct (process) labor costs.

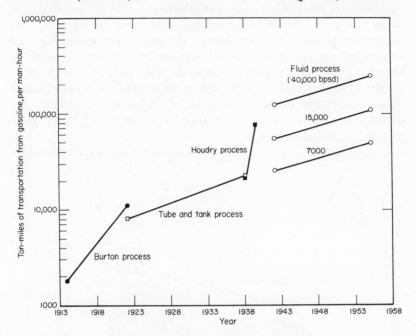

Productivity of process labor in cracking.

Source: Appendix Table 21.

We focused on process labor because it is the only type of labor for which inputs were reported in physical terms. Plotted on the graph is the quantity of process labor used in each of the processes, expressed as man-hours per 100 ton-miles of transportation.[7] Ton-miles of transportation is used as the unit because it allows for improvements in gasoline quality as well as in yield.[8] The vertical scale in the graph is logarithmic; a straight line on the

[7] The underlying data are tabulated in Appendix Table 21.

[8] In order to relate gasolines of different quality it was necessary to find a quantitative measure of quality. This measure is developed in Appendix A. The major assumptions are that historically the quality of all the other products has increased parallel to that of gasoline, that octane number is an adequate measure of gasoline quality, and that the gasoline is burned in an engine of the proper design, that is, one with a sufficiently high compression ratio.

Relating quantities of inputs to *total* ton-miles of transportation attributes all the credit for improved performance from higher-octane gasoline and higher-compression-ratio engines to the gasoline.

graph represents equal percentage changes. The four segments of the curve represent labor inputs appropriate to the Burton process (1913 and 1922), the Tube and Tank process (1922 and 1938), the Houdry process (1938 and 1939), and the Fluid process (1942 and 1955). For 1942 and 1955, we have three observations representing different scales of operation. The bigger the plant, the less process labor it required per barrel of raw material or product. For each process the points representing the two observations are joined by straight lines; the lines are merely to aid in identifying the points and do not imply that the yearly increases in productivity have been uniform. If we look at the terminal dates and calculate the rate of change in the consumption of the input, we find that the productivity of process labor has increased at a rate of 12% a year compounded, a substantial figure.

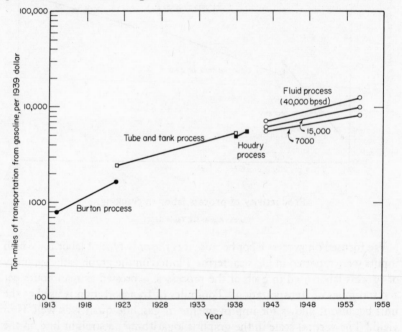

Productivity of capital in cracking.

Source: Appendix Table 21.

If allowance were made for the entire range of plant sizes, the plots on the graph would change from lines to blades, narrow in the early years when the size range was narrow and growing wider as time progressed and the range of possible plant sizes grew.

If we add estimates of administrative and technical costs to process-labor costs, we discover that the cost of the total labor input to cracking per unit of output has fallen less rapidly than the cost of the process-labor component alone.[9] The reason for this difference is the proliferation of technical personnel. Since we were not able to determine average wage rates for administrative and technical employees, we could not compare the two classes on a physical (man-hours) basis. Because of the long-run rise in wage rates, however, we can surely conclude that the average productivity of all labor has increased over time, although at a slower rate than process labor alone.

After labor the next input is capital. We are interested in determining the amount of capital required to construct equipment to process a certain amount of raw material or to produce a certain amount of finished product. Included in this sum are the amounts necessary to build the cracking plant, to provide the catalyst in the catalytic processes, to practice the art, and to maintain the plant in operating condition.[10] In order to eliminate fluctuations in the price level, all the costs are stated on the basis of 1939 dollars.[11]

The trend of capital inputs over time can be seen on page 248. The consequence of an advance in technology is generally a decline in the consumption of capital per unit of output. Any tendency toward a substitution of capital for the other factors of production is more than compensated for by an economizing in capital through technological progress. When we considered a gallon of gasoline as the unit of output, a reduction in capital input was not always obtained with each succeeding process innovation; the introduction of the Houdry catalytic cracking process actually resulted in a doubling of the input. But this result came about primarily because in relating capital input to a given *quantity* of gasoline output, we failed to recognize the main achievement of the Houdry process, that of improving gasoline *quality*. When we allowed for changes in

[9] See Appendix Table 24. On the basis of raw-material charge, given in this table, the decline is negligible. Only when gasoline or performance output is considered would the total labor component decline.

[10] See Appendix Table 23 for the data. Maintenance-labor inputs are customarily defined by the industry as a component of capital costs. When one finds estimates of maintenance-labor costs, they are usually stated as a certain per cent a year of the total capital cost of the cracking plant.

For all but the Houdry process, royalties were assessed on the basis of so many cents per barrel of charge, and paid as the raw material was processed. The Houdry Process Corporation did not set a running royalty rate but rather sold licenses for a fixed fee. In order to compare royalties for the Houdry process with those for the others, we were obliged to transform paid-up royalties to a running basis. By assuming that the paid-up royalty would be depreciated over ten years, the cost of the royalty payments were allocated to current output at the same rate as construction costs.

[11] The construction index is developed in Appendix Table 6.

quality as well as quantity (that is, when we computed our capital input on the basis of 100 ton-miles of transportation), we found that the introduction of the Houdry process resulted in a much less marked increase in input. In all the other cases the introduction of a new cracking process or the improvement of an existing one has reduced capital inputs; the overall reduction over the forty-two-year period was from 0.126 to 0.008 dollars per 100 ton-miles, or 6.8 per cent per year compounded.[12] The increase in the productivity of capital has been substantial.

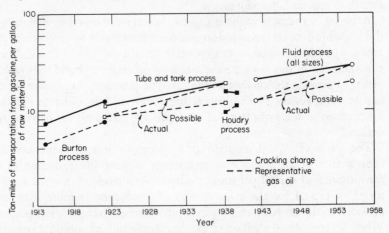

Productivity of raw material (cracking charge) in cracking.

Source: Appendix Table 21.

These capital inputs are stated in dollars of fixed value; even if we were to use current dollars we would find the trend of capital inputs generally unchanged in direction although considerably less in slope. When current prices are used, the yearly reduction in the amount of capital necessary to construct and maintain cracking equipment has been 2.6% (from 0.066 dollars per 100 ton-miles in 1913 to 0.021 dollars in 1955).

The third input considered is raw material. Fortunately the sole raw material of any importance to the cracking process is gas oil, which makes measurement relatively simple. From the graph, we find that when allowance is made for quality changes, new processes generally conserve raw materials just as they do capital. Based on a given output of transportation the average increase in the productivity of raw material has been 3.7% a year. The Houdry process again was the exception to the trend.

[12] See Appendix Table 21. This is approximately equal to the author's crude estimate for the whole refining industry arrived at in "A Measure of the Rate of Technological Progress in the Petroleum Refining Industry," *Journal of Industrial Economics*, June 1958, p. 196.

If only the light gas-oil faction of crude petroleum is considered, as cracking charge, it would prejudice the late (1930's) continuous thermal processes and today's continuous catalytic cracking processes, for these two groups of processes at these points in time could accommodate a much larger portion of each barrel of crude petroleum than the others. The graph allows for this by also illustrating the productivity of the processes when a representative (light plus heavy) gas oil is available.

Cracking units have usually been the most profitable destination for most fractions of crude petroleum that are heavier than kerosene, but the departure in recent years from the policy of maximizing gasoline production from available cracking stocks merely illustrates the subservience of technology to economics. Although the yield structure in the short run is determined by technical factors, in the long run the technology adapts to the economic environment. This may be seen clearly from the fact that the yield structure between different processes is far greater than the possible variation within a single process. When it becomes desirable to alter the yield structure (that is, to emphasize one of the products in a multiproduct mix), it is more profitable to achieve this alteration by developing a new technique than by modifying an existing one. The *lingua franca* for different technological states is economics.

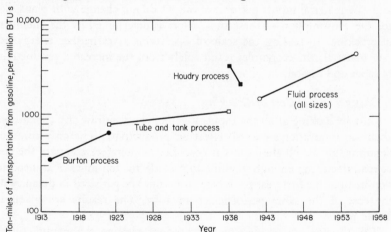

Productivity of energy in cracking.

Source: Appendix Table 21.

The fourth and final output that we specified is energy. Included in this category are fuel (used to elevate gas oil to the cracking temperature), steam (used for power and for facilitating vaporization or separating products), electricity (used for power), and, for the catalytic cracking processes, coke (deposited on the catalyst and burned in the regenerator). All the energy requirements are stated in similar terms, millions of British Thermal Units. The results are summarized on the graph (p. 251). We notice the same long-run decrease in energy input per unit of output. The rate of increase of productivity of energy, based upon ton-miles of transportation, has been 6.5% a year compounded, just slightly greater than the rate for capital, nearly double that for raw material, and about half that for process labor.

Again it is the Houdry process which departs from the trend, but from the examination of the other inputs this result is to be expected. Because process temperature and pressures varied throughout the reaction phase of the cycle, more coke was formed than there would have been under steady operating conditions. When burned during regeneration, coke liberated heat, which was recovered by generating steam. Steam generation represented a contribution to, rather than a consumption of, energy and thus reduced substantially the over-all energy input. Thus in the Houdry process raw material was substituted for energy.

Our final observation on the productivity of inputs is that energy consumption, like raw-material consumption but unlike capital and labor consumption, is independent of the scale of the cracking plant. Energy and raw-material inputs per unit of output do not change with plant size, for the consumption of these two factors is determined by the chemistry of cracking. Increasing the scale of operations saves neither energy nor raw material; the economies result solely from the increased productivity of labor and capital.

Changes in the Cost of Cracking

Only by looking at all the inputs together can we draw any conclusions about an innovation's over-all effect on productivity. The only common denominator for all the inputs is cost. Let us therefore compare the cost of manufacturing enough gasoline to provide 100 ton-miles of transportation in 1914, the first year for which costs could be gathered in detail, with the cost of the same performance in 1955. The results are given in Table 10.

If the Burton process were used to produce gasoline, the manufacturing cost would have been $1.47 per 100 ton-miles of engine performance; if the Fluid process were used, $0.26. The difference is substantial, equivalent to an average yearly cost reduction of 4.3% compounded over the forty-two years from 1913 to 1955. If we had used 1913 prices instead of 1955 prices, the cost of the Fluid process would have been one-fifth instead of one-sixth of the cost of the Burton.

By equating cost reduction with productivity, we may say that the

TABLE 10

Comparison of the Cost of Gasolines of Equal Performance (100 ton-miles) Manufactured by the Burton Process (1914) and the Fluid Process (1955)

Input	Consumption of Inputs		Price of Input in 1955	Manufacturing Cost (1955 $)	
	Burton Process 1914	Fluid Process 1955		Burton Process	Fluid Process
Gas Oil	13.63 gal.	3.47 gal.	$0.07 per gal.	0.954	0.231
Energy	0.2895 MMBTU	0.0224 MMBTU	$0.18 per MMBTU	0.052	0.004
Process and Supervisory Labor	0.0624 man-hours	0.00133 man-hours	$2.53 per man-hour	0.158	0.003
Maintenance Labor	0.00414 man-hours	0.000726 man-hours	$2.53 per man-hour	0.011	0.002
Catalyst	None	0.0495 lb.	$0.1875 per lb.	—	0.009
Royalty	$0.17 (at 1914 prices) per barrel of charge	$0.04 (at 1955 prices) per barrel of charge	—	0.250	0.003
Depreciation	—	—	10% of construction cost per year	0.031	0.007
Taxes and Insurance	—	—	5% of construction cost per year	0.015	0.004
Total				1.471	0.263

Sources: Appendix Tables 10, 11, and 21.

increase in productivity also amounted on the average to 4.3% a year. This rate may be too high in that we have not allowed for the other products of the cracking reaction, in which the Burton process might not be at such a severe disadvantage. If the over-all increase in productivity does amount to 4.3% a year, however, it approaches the yearly increase in the quantity of gasoline sold since the 1920's.[13] If it were equal (that is, if the rate of productivity increase were to equal that of sales), the quantity of resources allocated to production need never be augmented. Technological progress would make possible a bank or fund of resources, which, once established, would be capable of satisfying forever all the product needs.

The Gains of Process Innovation

How are these gains from process innovation distributed? How much has each participant benefited from technological progress? To answer these questions we must find out first how big the gains were and then how they were distributed. We shall again take as our basis enough gasoline to provide 100 ton-miles of transportation. Granting in each case that we had automobiles whose engines had a high enough compression ratio to utilize the gasoline, in 1914, 3.46 gallons would be required; in 1955, 2.04 gallons. The appropriate costs and unit prices of inputs are listed in Table 11.

Several assumptions were made in arriving at the figures in Table 11. In order to estimate the physical consumption of labor, we divided total labor cost by the hourly wage rate for process labor, thus assuming that all labor was paid at the same rate. In order to arrive at an estimate of the cost of energy, we valued all energy at the price of heavy fuel oil. We allocated to capital the sum left over after subtracting the costs of labor, raw material, and energy and after royalty owners had been reimbursed. Payment to capital is thus the remainder, and includes not only the return on the investment in equipment but also the return on the investments associated with the equipment (that is, in catalyst and maintenance).

The over-all return on capital was equal in 1914 to $8.70 per dollar invested. In 1955, the return was $2.30 per dollar invested. The calculations are based upon the assumption that cracking units have a useful life of ten years. The return therefore represents the undiscounted sum of a series of payments over the ten-year period. On a yearly basis the payment

[13] In 1918, the first year for which figures are available, the total U.S. output of motor gasoline from crude oil was 82,556,000 barrels (American Petroleum Institute, *Petroleum Facts and Figures*, 9th ed., 1950, p. 225). In 1955 it was 1,204,481,000 barrels (*ibid.*, 12th ed., 1956, p. 202). The average yearly rate of increase of motor-fuel output over the thirty-seven-year period was 7.4%. If we used a year in the 1920's as our initial point, we would derive a yearly rate of increase of demand closer to that of productivity.

TABLE II

Costs and Prices of Cracked Gasoline Equivalent to 100 Ton-Miles of Transportation, 1914 and 1955

Inputs	Consumption of Inputs		Cost of Inputs		Unit Price of Inputs	
	1914	1955a	1914	1955	1913	1955
Labor	0.0624	0.00133	0.0199	0.0034	0.32	2.53
	man-hours				$ per hour	
Raw material	13.63	3.47	0.3108	0.2429	0.0228	0.070
	gallons				$ per gallon	
Energy	0.2895	0.0224	0.0211	0.0040	0.073	0.18
	MMBTU				$ per MMBTU	
Royalty			0.0551	0.0029	0.17	0.04
					$ per daily barrel of charge	
		Subtotal	0.407	0.253		
Price of Gasoline plus Associated Products			0.494	0.294		
Capital less royaltyb (residual)	0.010	0.018	0.087	0.041	8.70	2.30
	Current dollars				$ per $ of investment over the life of the equipment	

Source: Appendix Tables 9,10, 11.

Notes:
a 36,000 BPCD Fluid unit.
b Includes maintenance and, for the Fluid process alone, catalyst cost. The definition of capital is thus broader than investment in equipment alone.

would be one-tenth; for 1955, this is $0.23 or 23% on investment before taxes. In 1955, the petroleum industry actually earned somewhat over 14% on its total investment.[14]

Between 1913 and 1955, the royalty rate declined from 5¢ to 0.3¢ per 100 ton-miles of performance. This represents a substantial decline in the price received by the process innovator. Earlier we estimated the returns on the investment in research and development; for the Burton process it amounted to a total of somewhat over $600 for every dollar expended,

[14] In 1955 total net fixed assets (depreciable and depletable assets, less depreciation, depletion, and land) of firms reporting balance sheets in the petroleum and coal products industry were $14,278,423,000. (U. S. Treasury Department, Internal Revenue Service, "Statistics of Income, 1955, Preliminary Corporation Income Tax Returns," IRS Publication No. 159, Washington: March 3, 1958, Table 2, p. 13). Total income before taxes was $2,038,250,000 (ibid.). Income was therefore 14.3% of net assets. Petroleum refining represents over 95% of the totals, the other minor industrial category — "other petroleum and coal products" — accounts for the remaining 5%.

and for the continuous catalytic cracking processes about $10 per dollar expended during the first fourteen years, with more to be received in the future. The trend in returns to research and development is the same for either method of calculation, but the rate of decline is greater when it is expressed on the basis of investment.

Over the forty-two years from 1914 to 1955, the prices (stated in current dollars) paid for three of the five inputs — labor, raw material, and energy — have risen: the price of labor has risen most, that of energy least. The prices of the other two inputs, capital and royalty rate, have actually fallen.

In terms of contribution to cost, not only capital and royalty rate but all of the inputs declined. For labor, raw material, and energy, the decreases in consumption have more than compensated for the increase in price. For capital (and for royalty if the calculation has any meaning) the reverse was true; consumption (in current dollars) increased, but the increase was more than compensated for by the decrease in the return. These results are summarized in Table 12.

It appears that the greater the relative rise in the price of a given input, the greater the restriction on its use. The relationship is not perfect, but it at least indicates that those inputs whose relative prices are falling are substituted for those whose prices are rising. Given the evidence on cracking innovations, however, we cannot state with any assurance that a relative increase in the price of one input has caused another input to be substituted for it. The only clear example of deliberate substitution we observed was in the developement of the first cracking process, the objective of which was to save on raw material. In order to save on raw material it was necessary to expend other inputs — labor, energy, and capital. Looked at after the fact, this was not a proper example of substitution, for the price of labor was actually rising faster than that of raw material. But we should not consider price trends after the fact; presumably, if cracking had not been adopted, the price of raw material would have risen much more steeply than the price of any of the other inputs. It was *expected* rather than the *actual* price trends that determined the substitution of inputs in the design of the Burton process.

The only input in Table 12 whose price and productivity changes were in the opposite direction was capital. Payments to capital typically fluctuate. Had a different process or even a different year been chosen, the over-all change in the return to capital might have been positive rather than negative. Even an adroit choice of years, however, could probably not provide a long-run increase in the price paid to capital that would approximate the increase in the price of labor. Although the productivity of capital has increased year by year, no such increase has been observed in the return to capital.

TABLE 12

Comparison of Yearly Rates of Change of Prices and Productivities
of Inputs, 1914–1956

Input	Average Rates of Change, 1914 to 1956 (% per year compounded)		Productivities
	Prices		
	Current Prices	Stable Prices[a]	
Process Labor	+5.0	+2.4	+12
Raw Material	+2.8	+0.3	+3.7
Energy	+2.2	−0.1	+6.5
Capital[b]	−2.6	−2.6	+6.8

Notes:

[a] Current prices were deflated by the consumer-price index (BLS) in order to obtain stable prices. For capital, both price and unit of quantity are the same, so the numerator and denominator were deflated by equal amounts, leaving the price unchanged.

[b] Capital excludes royalties.

In order to observe the changes in the prices that distributors and consumers have paid for gasoline we shall refer to the next two graphs, where the amount of transportation (ton-miles) that a dollar would purchase in the wholesale and retail markets is plotted for 1913 and for each year from 1925 through 1956.[15] (See pp. 258 and 259.)

When gasoline price is measured on the basis of equal volumes of product (that is, per gallon) the price first goes down, from 1913 to 1933, and then up, from 1933 to 1956. Compared with 1913, today's consumer of gasoline pays only a little more for the same quantity of product.

But this makes no allowance for the increase in gasoline quality. Taking the terminal years 1913 and 1956, we find that the value of the consumer's dollar, in terms of the transportation that his gasoline will provide, has increased from 145 to 202 ton-miles.[16] This gain is calculated at current prices; had we allowed for changes in the price level, the increase would have been from 145 to 546 ton-miles. Based on current prices, the price of

[15] The amounts are calculated from data on the price and quality of gasoline (see Appendix Table 2). Given the gasoline octane, the performance of one gallon was determined by the method developed in Appendix A. The total performance that a dollar will buy is found by multiplying the performance from one gallon by the number of gallons that could be purchased for a dollar. Gasoline prices are quoted including excise taxes. This assumes that the tax paid by the motorist is an integral part of the purchase of gasoline.

[16] This is for Regular gasoline. If Premium were considered, the increase would have been a little greater.

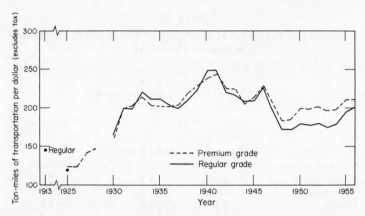

Performance from a given expenditure on gasoline purchased at retail, 1913, 1925–1956.

Source: Appendix Table 2b.

performance fell each year by about 0.75%; based on a stable price level, the annual rate of decline was about 3.2%.[17]

Thus the consumer has benefited substantially from advances in technology. From 1913 to 1956 the value of the consumer's dollar with respect to the performance which is provided by motor gasoline has increased, whereas the opposite must be said for its value with respect to commodities as a whole.

The amount of performance for a given expenditure on gasoline in both the wholesale (refinery) and the retail markets has followed a cyclical pattern during the thirty-one years which our observations cover. This can be seen in the graphs. The amount rose during the late 1920's and early 1930's. The peak amount was reached in the wholesale market in 1933. In the retail market, where prices were less sensitive to economic fluctuations, the 1933 value was surpassed in the late 1930's, and the peak was not reached until 1941. Since these two dates, 1933 and 1941, the amount of performance that a dollar could buy has decreased substantially in the wholesale market and mildly in the retail market.

Economies of Scale

Since the consumption of labor and capital, per unit of output, decreases with bigger cracking plants, while raw material and energy stay constant,

[17] In 1913, the consumer-price index (BLS) was 70.7 (1935–1939 = 100) (U. S. Bureau of the Census, *Historical Statistics of the United States, 1789–1945*, Washington, 1949, Series L-41, p. 236). In 1955, it was 114.5 (1947–1949 = 100) (*U. S. Department of Commerce, Business Statistics,* 1957, Washington, 1957, p. 26). The latter figure is equal to 191.5 on the 1935–1939 basis. The ratio of 1955 to 1913 is 2.71 to 1.

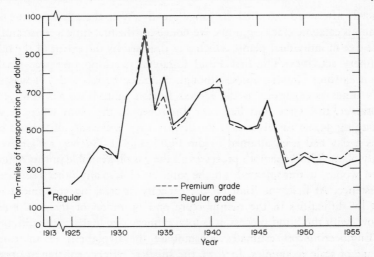

Performance from a given expenditure on gasoline purchased at the refinery, 1913, 1925–1956.

Source: Appendix Table 2a.

economies result from large-scale operation. It might be profitable to look at the ranges over which economies of scale have been effective.

The first Burton unit processed on the average 88.5 barrels of gas oil a day, producing from this raw material 22.5 barrels a day of gasoline.[18] Units smaller than this could have been built but, as we saw in Chapter 1, units larger than this could not. Hence, at the time of the first cracking innovation there were economies of scale up to a charge rate of 88.5 barrels a calendar day.

When continuous cracking was introduced, the Burton process had been improved sufficiently to raise the charge rate of a single unit to a maximum of 221 barrels a calendar day. The continuous thermal cracking units which supplanted the Burton units were larger from the beginning: the first Tube and Tank unit processed 570 barrels a day, and the first Dubbs unit processed 250 barrels. Subsequent continuous thermal cracking units grew in scale to the point where there were, in 1936, units capable of processing 25,000 barrels a day. Moreover, the yield of gasoline per unit of gas-oil charge had risen since the time of the Burton process so that the increase in the range of economies of scale was even greater when measured in terms of output.

The introduction of the Houdry process did not result in any extension of the range of scale economies, but the introduction of the Fluid process

[18] See Table 8, and graph on p. 242.

shortly afterward extended the range greatly. With the advent of the continuous catalytic cracking units, we notice for the first time a constraint on the size of individual plants which was imposed by the extent of the other refinery activities. The first Fluid Catalytic Cracking unit was smaller than existing Houdry units, although at 12,000 barrels a day it was still 135 times as capacious as the largest Burton unit. Within a few years, however, this same unit had been improved to the point where it was charging 55,000 barrels a day. Finally, by 1957, a capacity of 102,000 barrels a day had been attained in the Fluid unit at Tidewater's Delaware City plant. This behemoth processes all the gas oil available in this refinery and would, if transplanted, do the same in almost any other refinery in existence. At first, the limit on the capacity of cracking equipment was set by difficulties in the manufacture and operation of the equipment. Now, with the Fluid process, it is total refinery size that sets the ceiling.

Engineering-cost estimates substantiate the hypothesis of increasing range of scale economies. In 1939, the smallest refinery capable of operating at minimum cost was estimated to be one which would process 30,000 barrels (42 gallons each) of crude oil per day.[19] By 1951, the size had risen to approximately 125,000 bpd.[20] A plant of 30,000 bpd, the minimum efficient size in 1938, would have operated in 1951 at a cost disadvantage of between 5% and 6% compared with the 125,000 bpd plant. Considering that the over-all profit margin on sales before taxes in 1951 for petroleum refining was 9.5%,[21] this represents quite a serious liability. A firm whose costs were from 5% to 6% higher than the average at each stage of the petroleum industry would forgo over half the average profit.

Technological progress in cracking has undoubtedly influenced the structure of the petroleum-refining industry. The extension of the range

[19] U. S. Congress, Temporary National Economic Committee, "Investigation of Concentration of Economic Power," Hearings, Part 15, Testimony of Robert A. Wilson, pp. 8351–8353, 8661. This plant would have consisted of one combination distilling and cracking unit, and would have cost about $18,000,000 to construct.

[20] J. S. Bain, "Economies of Scale, Concentration and the Condition of Entry in Twenty Manufacturing Industries," *American Economic Review*, March 1954, p. 23. Bain estimated "minimal efficient plant scale" (equals lowest production costs) for petroleum refining to be 1¾% of the national industry capacity. As of January 1, 1951, the latter figure was 6,964,000 bpd (*Petroleum Facts and Figures*, 12th ed. New York: American Petroleum Institute, 1956, p. 217). To build and operate this refinery would have required an investment in equipment and working capital of about $200,000,000 (J. S. Bain, *op. cit.*, Table VII, p. 36).

[21] U. S. Internal Revenue Service, *Statistics of Income for 1954*, Part 2, Table 2, p. 47. Total sales of the minor industrial group petroleum refining were $23,367,492; profits before taxes were $2,210,446, and profits after taxes $1,257,139. For a group of the larger petroleum producers and refiners, the average profit margin *after taxes* was 11.5%. (National City Bank of New York "Monthly Letter on Business and Economic Conditions," April 1953, p. 42). This is 6.1% higher than the average rate for the refining industry calculated from the figure above.

within which economies of scale operate has favored refiners with large plants over those with small plants. The profitability of new techniques has favored innovators and those quick to adopt the innovations at the expense of the dilatory firms.

Chronologically, the most influential years were the earliest. It was then that cracking was denied to some refiners, first because of Indiana Stand-

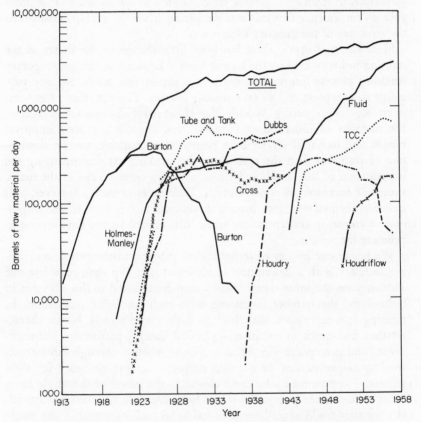

Growth in U. S. cracking capacity, total and by process, 1913–1957.

Source: Appendix Tables 1a–1c. For the period 1913–1926, it was necessary to convert the data from cracked-gasoline output to raw-material capacity. The assumptions were that the equipment was operated at full capacity and that the yield of gasoline from raw material was 22.4%.

ard's licensing policy and later because of the risks that were created by the legal struggle over the cracking patents; only after 1923 could cracking be universally adopted. It was during the early years that the investment necessary to build a small cracking unit increased substantially; since the 1930's, capital costs for units of minimum size, on a real dollar basis, have remained fairly stable. It was in the early years that royalty payments were most onerous. All of these factors benefited the eastern, Gulf Coast, and California refiners at the expense of midwestern refiners (that is, those operating in Indiana Standard's territory), large refiners at the expense of the small, and the strong and knowing at the expense of the weak. From 1913 to 1933, therefore, technological progress in the refining of petroleum tended to increase concentration in the industry. It is probably no coincidence that this was the period when the greatest changes in the structure of the industry took place.

Since the mid-1930's, there has been little change in the shares of the refining industry held by the largest firms.[22] Looking at the contemporary cracking process innovations we would expect this result. Royalty payments have represented an ever smaller burden. The net effect of government regulation during World War II was not discriminatory against the majority of independent refiners. New processes, process improvements, and technical service have been readily available, for the elimination of restrictions on the practice of the cracking art accompanying the introduction of the Dubbs and Cross processes removed one of the major causes of increases in concentration. Economies of scale, however, still manifest themselves. Since 1930, technological factors have tended to promote increases in concentration, while institutional factors have tended to promote the reverse.

We began our history of technological progress in the petroleum-refining industry with a description of an innovator. We shall complete our summary on the same theme. Many men contributed to the advances in technology, the number increasing with each successive innovation. In training and experience, their backgrounds varied widely, but in character they had much in common — physical energy, persistence, self-confidence, and perception. An access to funds, whether through inheritance, wealthy acquaintances, or a going corporation, was necessary for their success. The two men who came closest to the image of the single innovator were extremely versatile; it was fortunate that they were not specialists, for they could never have afforded to become immersed in any single task. If we were to devise a recipe for innovation, we would find diversity to be a necessary ingredient. All types of enterprise — small firms and large ones, firms within the industry and outsiders — made innovations in petroleum refining. Perhaps, because technological progress is so beneficial, its sources are manifold.

[22] L. J. Cookenboo, *Crude Oil Pipe Lines and Competition in the Oil Industry*, Cambridge: Harvard University Press, 1955, p. 45.

APPENDICES

APPENDIX A: MEASURING QUALITY IMPROVEMENT

I<small>F</small> we are going to isolate the effects of changes in technology from the other changes that take place in any industrial process, we must state all the other variables in units that are commensurable. In the case of petroleum cracking, this involves the problem of allowing for improvements in the quality of the inputs and outputs.

In the simplest situation, the nature of the inputs would not change from one time period to the next, nor would the nature of the products. Under these conditions, the effects of different techniques could be observed merely by comparing their physical outputs.

Changes in the Quality of the Inputs

But this assumes that neither the inputs nor the outputs change in quality. Let us see how far our actual situation (that is, cracking in the petroleum-refining industry) deviates from this situation. First we must ask whether the units in which the inputs and products are measured from one period to the next are similar. By adhering in each case to a wide-range midcontinent gas-oil of 28.5 API gravity, we have assured ourselves of an identical raw material for each cracking process.[1] Capital cost can be expressed in constant dollars by means of a construction-cost index. Fuels — coal, fuel oil, and fuel gas — can be related through their heat content. By applying conversion factors between power and heat, the utilities — electricity and steam — can also be expressed in heat units. Thus both fuel and utilities can be conceived of as a single input, energy.

The sole remaining input is labor. Here wage rates do not offer any problem different from that faced in comparing capital costs, but human skills do cause us some concern. The skills needed to operate and maintain a modern catalytic cracking unit are very different from those needed for a Burton unit. In the early processes, simple procedures were established which when adhered to usually permitted routine operation. As new cracking processes were developed, however, the operations became more complex. To compensate for this, the data made available to the operating

[1] For the characteristics of this charging stock see Appendix Table 7. The limitations in selecting a raw material of a hydrocarbon composition represented by a *midcontinent* stock can be inferred from the discussion in each of the preceding six chapters of the relation between the nature of the charging material and the ability of the particular process to handle it.

personnel became more detailed and exact, and the jobs were redefined so that men could specialize on different aspects of the operation.

Our assumption will be that the skills needed today, while different, are no greater than they were in Burton's day, and that the quality of labor can be considered constant over time. This conclusion is borne out by the experience of the cracking industry: Although each new process required new skills, these skills could usually be assimilated by the operators and maintenance men after a few days or weeks of training. Never did the ability of the operators set a limit on the nature or the size of the equipment.

Changes in the Quality of the Products

Although the inputs can be assumed to be commensurable throughout the forty years that we are studying, the products cannot. Each product has been improved in quality as one process has supplanted another. Products have been improved through closer adherence to the distillation specifications, through improvement of combustion characteristics, and through the elimination of corrosive, gum-forming, and ash-forming constituents.

Unfortunately, for all the products except gasoline, we do not have any ready method of comparing different qualities. For gasoline, however, we do have a continuous and accurate measure of one characteristic, namely, the tendency of the fuel to pre-ignite, or "knock," in the cylinders of the internal-combustion engine. The measure of this tendency is indicated by the octane number of the fuel. The octane scale is bounded by two reference fuels, burned under specific conditions. One is normal heptane, which is a poor fuel and is assigned a rating of zero; the other is iso-octane (2, 2, 4 trimethylpentane), which is a very good fuel and is assigned a rating of 100. When a sample of a commercial gasoline from the refinery is tested, the two reference fuels are blended in the proper proportions to "knock" at the same point as the refinery gasoline. The proportion of iso-octane in the equivalent blend gives the octane number of the sample.[2] Through the use of this single measure, we shall attempt to find the increase in gasoline *quantity* that is equivalent to each improvement in gasoline *quality*.

Before we proceed to utilize the octane scale, we must ask three questions. First, in what way does achieving a higher octane rating improve the fuel? Second, is the reduced tendency to knock sufficient in itself, or are other developments necessary before quality can be improved? Third,

[2] A description of the development of the octane scale can be found in an article by Graham Edgar (formerly a director of the Ethyl Corporation) in *Ethyl News*, January–February 1955, pp. 12–14.

is the improvement in the antiknock rating of gasoline representative of all the quality improvements that have taken place in gasoline and in the other products?

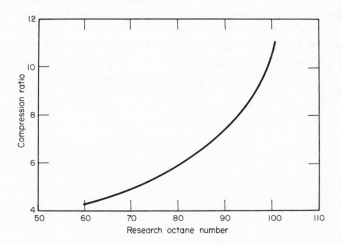

High-compression-ratio engines give more useful power per gallon of fuel.

Source: E. V. Murphree, A. R. Cunningham, J. P. Haworth, and A. F. Kaulakis, "The Trend to High Octane Number Gasoline Is Sound," paper presented before the Metropolitan Section, SAE, October 15, 1953.

A higher-octane fuel permits the use of a higher-compression engine, and a higher-compression engine in turn gives better performance. For example, an engine with a 4.3 compression ratio will be satisfied by a 60-octane fuel, and one gallon of this fuel will transport one ton at a speed of 40 miles an hour for a distance of 25.1 miles.[3] A 90-octane fuel, on the other hand, permits the use of a compression ratio of 7.3 and carries the same weight at the same speed for 43.4 miles. The increase in ton-mileage is 72.4%.

This example serves to introduce our second question: Do improvements in gasoline quality alone necessarily increase automobile efficiency? The answer is "No," because the design of the engine also determines performance. Only in an engine designed to use a high-octane gasoline will the full power of the fuel be applied. The answer would be "Yes" only if increases in engine-compression ratio could be obtained with lightning speed and at no cost; only then could all the potential increases in

[3] The third graph combines Murphree's two graphs, thereby eliminating compression ratio as a variable. (See p. 269.)

economy be realized, and only then could they be attributed to the higher-octane gasoline. This was not the case, however, for the two developments — higher-octane gasolines and higher-compression engines — have gone hand in hand.[4] We must therefore conclude that improvements in gasoline quality unaccompanied by improvements in engine design would not have given cheaper transportation.

The petroleum-refining industry has found the cost of developing new techniques which will produce higher-octane gasoline to be substantial.[5]

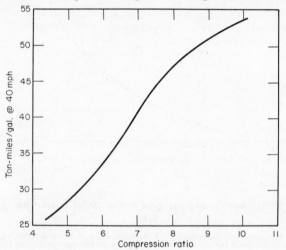

High-octane-number fuel is needed to satisfy high-compression-ratio engines.

Source: E. V. Murphree *et al., op. cit.*

Likewise, the cost to the automobile industry when it designs and manufactures new engines and related equipment is high. Since quality improvements have to be made in both gasoline and engines before the benefits can be realized by the automobile driver, only seldom has one industry consciously made an improvement without knowing that the other could follow.

This experience does not make our problem of measurement any easier. We are now faced with an indeterminate situation — we can attribute to higher-quality gasoline none, some, or all of the credit for improvement

---

[4] See Appendix Table 2c.

[5] In one recent study, it was estimated that an increase in octane number would cost a refiner between 3¢ and 20¢ per octane number per barrel of gasoline (R. C. Kersten and T. W. Warren, "That Octane-Improvement Headache," *Oil and Gas Journal*, July 30, 1956, p. 184).

in performance. We shall present the two extremes, and thus permit the reader to make the final decision.[6]

The third question asked was whether the increase in gasoline octane is indicative of the general improvement achieved in the over-all quality of gasoline and the other products of the cracking reaction. With regard to how closely octane improvement has approximated the over-all improvement in gasoline quality, we shall hypothesize that the other charac-

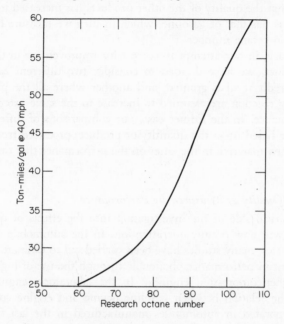

Relation between gasoline octane and performance, assuming efficient compression ratio.

teristics of motor fuel have been improved in the same proportion. There have been such improvements as closer control over volatility (resulting in easier starting in winter and less likelihood of vapor-lock in summer), lower tendency to polymerize and form gums (resulting in greater stability in storage), and less sulfur (resulting in less corrosion and better odor), to name a few. But the main emphasis in the petroleum and automotive industries has been on higher octanes.[7] For gasoline, then, the over-all

---

[6] Some individuals in the petroleum industry have claimed all the credit for gasoline; see, for example, D. P. Barnard, "Role of Gasoline in Engine Development," paper presented at SAE Annual Meeting, Detroit, January 9, 1951.

[7] See such articles as R. C. Kersten and T. W. Warren, *op. cit.*, D. P. Barnard, *op. cit.*, and E. V. Murphree, *et al.*, *op. cit.*

quality improvement will be assumed to be proportional to the improvement in antiknock tendency.

For the remainder of the products of the cracking process, we have no equivalent measure of the value of improvements. In volume, these products represent an amount greater than that of cracked gasoline, but in value they represent less, roughly from one-half to two-thirds of the revenues from gasoline.[8] Since some assumption will have to be made, let us assume that the quality of the other products has increased in the same proportion as has that of gasoline, which in turn we measure by the improvement in octane number.

In summary, in our attempt to correct for improvement in the quality of the product, we have decided to consider two different causes: one where no credit at all is granted, and another where all the products of the cracking reaction are assumed to increase to the same extent as gasoline performance. In the former case, our comparisons of different processes will be based upon the quantity of products produced from a given volume of raw material, in the latter on the performance that the products yield.

Gasoline Quality as Measured by Performance

The empirical side of the investigation into the effects of quality improvement will now occupy our attention. In the automobile and petroleum industries, many studies have been carried out to estimate the actual improvement in performance obtainable through the use of higher-octane fuel in higher-compression engines.[9] In the laboratory, engineers have examined the relation between gasoline octane and engine compression ratios incorporated in automobiles manufactured in the last forty years and expected in the future. Their purpose has been to illustrate the requirements and benefits of higher compression ratios, particularly with regard to the very high ratios to which the companies aspire. For our purpose, these analyses provide the correlations we desire (see the three charts) in order to relate improvements in quality to gains in quantity. Taking the octane numbers of the cracking gasoline from the various processes and assuming that the compression ratio of the engine is high

[8] See Table 9 in the Appendix.

[9] See for example C. L. McCuen, "1900 to 19XX," Detroit: General Motors Corporation (a reprint of a paper "Economic Relationship of Engine Fuel Research," given before the API's Division of Refining at Tulsa, Oklahoma, on May 3, 1951); D. P. Barnard, "Role of Gasoline in Engine Development," paper given at the SAE Annual Meeting in Detroit on January 9, 1951; W. M. Holaday, "What Can We Get From Higher Octane Fuels," paper presented at the SAE Annual Meeting in Detroit on January 11–15, 1954; W. M. Holaday. "Developments in and Economics of Motor Gasoline Refining," paper presented at SAE, Detroit Section, on October 4, 1950; and E. V. Murphree, *et al.*, *op. cit.*

enough to operate efficiently on the gasoline sample, we can obtain the performance figures in Table A.

TABLE A
Performance Characteristics of Various Cracked Gasolines

Process	Raw Material Boiling Range (Degrees Fahrenheit)	Gasoline Octane (Research)	Performance (Ton-Miles at 40 MPH)
Burton (1913, 1922)	430–750	55	24
Continuous Thermal Cracking (1922, 1946)	430–1000	73	29.2
Houdry (1936, 1939–1940)	430–750	87	39.5
Fluid (1942)	430–750	95	49.5
Fluid (1955)	645–1000	95	49.5

Sources: Burton: R. E. Wilson, "Pioneers in Oil Cracking," address delivered before the *Newcomen Society*, Chicago, October 29, 1946, p. 26.
   Continuous thermal cracking: W. L. Nelson, *Petroleum Refinery Engineering*, 3rd ed., New York: McGraw-Hill Book Co., 1949, p. 571, for stock with "characteristic factor" of 12.0.
   Houdry: *Ibid.*, p. 691; for midcontinent gas oil, 32.8° API gravity, yielding 10.0 pounds per square inch absolute (Psia) Reid Vapor Pressure Gasoline.
   Fluid (1942): Esso Research and Engineering Company, product yield information accompanying Cat Cracking Study, August 16, 1955, yield of 10.0 Psia RVP gasoline from gas oil of 32.0° API gravity (1942).
   Fluid (1955): *Ibid.*, yield of 10 Psia RVP gasoline from gas oil of 26.2° API gravity (1955).

The accuracy that can be imputed to the variation in these performance figures is $\pm 5\%$. Other methods of measuring performance tend to yield different results, because of changes in the units in which performance is defined and in the engine operating conditions.[10]

[10] In order to compare the results that different tests provide, let us try two other measures of performance: the Army-Navy performance number (developed originally for airplane-engine comparison and modified for use in automotive engines), and the Relative Density number (measuring the density of the air in the combustion chamber). A chart relating octane number and these two measures is shown in D. P. Barnard, *op. cit.*, p. 279, Figure 6. Taking the products listed in Table A, we can obtain the comparison given in Table B.

TABLE B
Comparison of Different Measures of Performance

	Performance Ratings			Performance Ratings (basis 100 = 55 octane)		
Octane Number	Ton-Miles	Army-Navy	Relative Density	Ton-Miles	Army-Navy	Relative Density
55	24	38	47	100	100	100
73	29.2	52	59	122	137	125
87	39.5	71	75	164	187	160
95	49.5	85	86	206	224	184

Our conclusion, based on the performance data, is that the improvement in gasoline quality has permitted sizable benefits in terms of better automotive performance. For example, each gallon of high-octane gasoline produced by Fluid Catalytic Cracking is roughly 80% more useful in an engine designed for it than was a gallon of gasoline from the Burton stills. The value of one gallon of catalytically cracked gasoline in a 7.8 compression-ratio engine could therefore be said to be worth, in terms of performance, the same as 1.8 gallons of Burton gasoline in the engine of a pre-World War I car. Thus we have expressed in quantitative terms the quality improvement.

Notes to Table B (p. 271):

The adherence of our measure to Relative Density numbers at low octane is all to the good. Barnard (*ibid.*, p. 280) mentions that "Relative Density Numbers (hereafter called RDN) are considered to give a more realistic appraisal of antiknock quality at the lower-octane-number levels than do AN performance numbers." He also says that the RDN do not take into account "the mechanical octane numbers which the automobile industry has built into its engines since 1925." A definition and description of mechanical octane numbers can be found in McCuen (*op cit.*, pp. 18–26).

Because we are working with actual automobiles, we wish to consider all the improvements in engine design when estimating the improvement in performance permitted by higher-quality gasoline. RDN would tend to underestimate the improvement at high octane numbers; so in measuring the benefits accruing from technological progress in petroleum cracking, the divergence between ton-miles and RDN at the upper end of the scale is desirable.

APPENDIX B: NOTES ON THE FLUID CATALYTIC CRACKING PROCESS

TH E following excerpts from documents of the Esso Research and Engineering Company relate to the development of the Fluid Catalytic Cracking process.

1. Dr. Homer J. Hall to W. M. Craig, October 24, 1957 (pp. 1, 2):

The first contact Jersey had with the Prudhomme process backed by Houdry was at an early stage, possibly 1924 (see 7/13/38 letter of W. E. Currie to M. E. Clark), when the process was proposed primarily as a means for removing sulfur from oil vapors. In March of 1926, Messrs. Ross Dickson and A. A. Wells made a trip to inspect the equipment in France. Mr. Dickson's letter of 3/16/26 to F. A. Howard (file TA 700.4291) reflects the conclusion reached during this visit:

"Mr. Wells feels convinced in his own mind that Prudhomme has a catalyst which will convert heavy product into lighter production from the above composition. The writer cannot entirely agree with this conclusion since there appears a possibility of some light ends having been inside the apparatus from the start. There is, however, a possibility that the catalysts do have the effect assumed by Mr. Wells."

The results of this demonstration were definitely unfavorable. In spite of this, the contract was kept alive and Mr. Howard visited the Houdry group again in France in 1927, as reported in Mr. Dickson's letter of 7/10/27 to C. A. Starr (file TA 700.4291):

"Mr. Howard offered to help them on the oil cracking again by either supplying plans or the apparatus (at cost) for carrying on their experimental work. He asked me to have Dr. Loomis prepare plans and also an estimate of cost f.o.b. New York for an experimental cracking outfit similar to the one Dr. Loomis has in use at Bayway. . . . The combination on the Houdry process was changed somewhat but that would not have anything of immediate interest to show us. Since they are again starting work on oil, we wish to keep in active contact. Prudhomme is out of the company and it is quite a mixed up affair."

2. *Ibid.* (pp. 2–4):

The attitude of most of the major companies in the U.S. toward the possibility of successful catalytic cracking at this time was largely a repeated story of theoretical promise and experimental failure. The reason for this had changed very little since U.S. patent 84,981 in 1868 outlined the fact that an adsorbent refractory agent once used "in previous processes" as a contact agent for cracking had little or no value, after it became coked in use. A wide variety of contact agents might be effective for a short time, but with a rapid loss in activity, after which they were useless. The only commercial example of catalytic cracking . . . [was] the McAfee process for making gasoline with aluminum chloride, which was tried extensively by Gulf without ever solving the problem of removing or disposing of the catalyst lost to sludge.

This attitude on the part of the major companies associated with Jersey in the exchange of thermal cracking research and patent rights—Texas, Indiana, and Gasoline Products (Kellogg)—led to a direct disagreement between these other companies and Jersey with respect to whether the Houdry type of catalytic cracking process was to come under their agreement. Jersey had successful experience with the use of catalysts in hydrogenation; the others had no real confidence in catalysts for the cracking process. They were quite willing and sought on many occasions to include catalytic cracking in the agreement, whereas Jersey consistently maintained that the use of a catalyst was distinct subject matter. Mr. Dearborn of Texas felt that the Gasoline Products patents would hinder Houdry from going ahead without restraint (Minutes for Subcommittee on Research, May 7, 1934. T.I.J.G.K. Folder No. 1), and in July, 1935, Sun told him they were planning for their licensing operations to be carried out by Gasoline Products (letter from R. P. Russell to F. A. Howard). Contracts involving the thermal cracking agreements finally reflected the definition that a process was to be considered thermal except where the presence of a catalyst made a difference in the product entirely distinct from that obtainable by changes in temperature and pressure.

This uncertainty was clearly reflected in the 1933 visit to Houdry's unit at the Socony Vacuum laboratories at Paulsboro, which followed immediately after Dr. W. F. Faragher of Socony had made the first public announcement of successful small scale results in catalytic cracking in the *Oil and Gas Journal* for October 19, 1933. At the very outset of this visit, Dr. Faragher and Mr. Houdry assured that the process was truly catalytic, giving 25 per cent conversion to gasoline with the catalyst, whereas without the catalyst, only 2 or 3 per cent was made. Laboratory units of the Houdry catalytic cracking equipment had been made up for trial runs and placed in the laboratories of the Sun Oil Company, Atlantic Refining Company, and Pure Oil Company. Almost immediately after this visit, however, it was apparent that the Sun Oil Company had become very much interested at their first opportunity, and further efforts of other companies to get information on the process were shut off during January of 1934.

The 1933 publication, however, was enough to stir up definite and widespread interest. Research in this field was included in the 1934 budget of the Standard Oil Development Company, and Dr. P. K. Frolich's letter of 5/8/34 to Dr. Maverick (Research Division file DA 722—General) identifies the group of Fulton, Cross, and Abate working on "speculative cracking." Summaries of the laboratory experiment programs of Texas, Indiana, Gasoline, Kellogg, and Jersey were being exchanged as part of the thermal cracking agreements, and the outline of the 1934 program is shown in P. E. Kuhl's letter of 8/10/34 to

H. G. M. Fis[c]her (file P-452). In line with the above position of the companies, there is no mention of catalytic work by Texas, Jersey, or Gasoline. Indiana volunteered an item on "effect of cracking gasoline oil by direct contact with potential catalysts, such as zinc chloride," and by January 4, 1935, they had done "considerable work" along these lines (letter of F. W. Sullivan to J. T. Ward, T.I.J.G.K. Research Program Folder No. 1).

Dr. Cross reviewed the bearing of earlier (1930–31) work at Baton Rouge on cracking over sulfo-active hydrogenation catalysts on his program, in a report to Dr. Frolich on April 17, 1934. His own initial work involved the use of catalysts in gas polymerization, which was considered an adjunct to the cracking process (reported in P. L. Young's letter of 1/24/34 to R. T. Haslam, in file "Gas Reversion and Polymerization," P-430, 1935). This work quickly developed, into direct research on catalytic cracking. Dr. Cross's laboratory results obtained during 1935 on the use of Marsil clay were filed later that year in the form of a patent application which issued in 1939 as U.S. patent 2,166,544. This was Jersey's first application in the field of catalytic cracking using a clay-type catalyst (see program review of 8/5/35, Maverick to Russell).

3. *Ibid.* (pp. 4, 5):

There were earlier hints of success, however, elsewhere in the operations of the Jersey company and affiliated research groups. Dr. R. K. Stratford of Imperial Oil Limited in Sarnia had developed a suspended clay process for treating naphtha vapors in 1925, and in 1931 he improved this process by adding a continuous clay-burning regeneration step. By 1934, in work leading to the issue of U.S. Patent 2,091,892, he found that the addition of a very small amount of clay to the coils in a thermal cracking process gave improved results with a product of higher octane number and less coking tendency, and he refers to this clay as a "cracking catalyst." This conclusion was not accepted readily, and there was considerable argument for some years after as to whether the clay in Stratford's "suspensoid process" acts as a catalyst or more nearly as a mechanical abrasive and coke carrier to permit the operation of the thermal cracking coil under more severe conditions than otherwise.

The renewed interest in catalytic cracking was also reflected in our discussions with representatives of the I.G. in Germany, whose background in the application of catalysts to the processing of petroleum hydrocarbons was available to us. Dr. E. B. Peck was our contact with the I.G. at that time. In these discussions, Messrs. Pier and Ringer emphasized their experience that it is very difficult to avoid killing vapor phase catalysts, especially in the absence of hydrogen, and that the complete regeneration of such a catalyst which has been coked in use is difficult, if not impossible, over a long period of time. Dr. Peck had confirmed this difficulty in earlier laboratory work on the "Catalytic Production of Blending Agents for Gasoline," checking in detail the results given in the I.G. report LU-498 of June 3, 1929. Several of the I.G. catalysts gave a product of exceptionally good knock rating for as long as 8 hours on stream, but after 96 hours, activity was reduced to about 3 or 4 per cent of the original value. Attempts were made to reactivate the coked catalysts by treatment with hydrogen, nitrogen, or steam and air at 700–1000°, without any success. In discussing these results (see 2/9/34 letter of P. J. Wiezevich to G. M. Maverick, file DA 700.43 I.G.) Dr. W. K. Lewis felt that satisfactory regeneration might still be accomplished at other temperature levels, based on his experience with a continuous system for charcoal reactivation developed for the Chemical Warfare Service during the First World War. He suggested that the catalyst might be introduced continuously at the top of a vertical tower and drawn off at the bottom.

The I.G. experts proposed a sump-phase or slurry type operation, with a cheap catalyst used once through and discarded, as in some of their work on coal hydrogenation. In reporting this, Dr. Peck's letter No. 762 of 12/15/34 to Mr. R. P. Russell suggested the possibility of a continuous process in which the solid acts both as a catalyst and heat carrier, which is separated from the product, burned, and recycled.

Experiments with a moving catalyst slurry were carried out shortly after the first successful fixed bed runs in the Research Laboratory at Bayway. Dr. A. E. Robertson, in October, 1936, (Notebook 320, pages 139–144) tried the use of a simple feed screw for slurry injection at low pressure, with a relatively large clay to oil ratio (equal volumes). The success of this work indicated that the catalytic effect which was questionable with very small amounts of clay in the suspensoid process might be realized when the amount of clay became large relative to the amount of oil. The work with slurry cracking was carried along for some time as a separate line of research, particularly at Sarnia and the Process Division, emphasizing systems using relatively small amounts of catalyst which could more easily be introduced and carried along with the oil.

4. *Ibid.* (pp. 6–8):

Definite interest continued in various means for moving the catalyst as well as the oil. This led, later in 1936, to the purchase of rights under U.S. patent 1,984,380 on a jiggling bed of fluidized solids, filed in the name of Mr. W. W. Odell, an independent inventor who had met Mr. Currie in earlier contract negotiations where he appeared as a chemical consultant. A reissue patent application to clarify the application of Odell's process to catalytic cracking was filed 12/17/36 and issued in 1940 as U.S. reissue patent 21,526. The original patent was noted in a preliminary research on ideas of Mr. Howard on the use of a jiggling bed, which were subsequently disclosed in the first moving catalyst case filed for him in January, 1937.

. . . During 1936, the Process Division carried out work on clay as a catalyst for gas oil cracking, but chose very high pressures, of the order of 1,000 psi, which was the usual range for experiments in thermal cracking. Under these conditions, the catalyst did not give outstanding results. The Research Division, working at more nearly atmospheric pressure, had more success. Their results during the latter part of 1936 gave a product of octane number in excess of 80. The first technical committee report showing successful results in this category was given in the spring of 1937 (Report EI-15-37 of 4/29/37 by S. C. Fulton, H. J. Hall and B. G. Baldwin). These results were obtained in a fixed bed reactor. Work continued along these lines at the Research and Process Divisions and also at Baton Rouge, where there was considerable emphasis on developing improved catalysts.

Contract negotiations, which were never really at a standstill, began in earnest as soon as the laboratory results made it clear that the gasoline yield and quality advantages claimed for catalytic cracking were real. Jersey's world-wide refining interests demanded attention, and Mr. Howard went to Paris and on to Germany in March of 1937. There were problems involved in working out a resolution of the conflicts between U.O.P. and Gasoline Products on the thermal cracking agreements, and between U.O.P. and I.G. on the Hydro process. Jersey's contracts with I.G. covered the world outside of . . . Germany for catalytic hydrocarbon conversions in the presence of hydrogen. There was another knotty problem with respect to the Kellogg Company, party to the Gasoline Products agreements, which was anxious to have these contracts extended or interpreted to cover catalytic cracking. This conflict might be resolved by including U.O.P. in a new catalytic cracking agreement, with Kellogg acting as engineering and contracting agent for the Hydro process (letter of 1/12/37 from F. A. Howard to R. P. Russell, file Catalytic Cracking No. 1).

. . . The experts at I.G. were reluctantly convinced that the results obtained in catalytic cracking experiments at the Esso Laboratories were strong enough to justify a major research effort (see letter from W. C. Asbury of 2/22/37 to E. V. Murphree). They were not particularly interested in entering any joint project with U.O.P., however, due to the past history of patent fights in both the Hydro and thermal cracking fields. They felt, furthermore, that the I.G. had or could acquire important patent assets in the field of catalyst manufacture (see cable from F. A. Howard to R. P. Russell, 3/19/37, file Cat. Cr. No. 2). As the beginning of a research program in this direction, therefore, they started out to prepare a synthetic catalyst better than Houdry's acid treated clay, as described in an issued British patent. Their first effort gave a catalyst as good as Houdry, but not better (letter from R. P. Russell to W. C. Asbury of 8/24/37, file Cat. Cr. No. 4). The press of internal affairs in Germany became continually more demanding, so that the proposed major research effort did not materialize, and the I.G. never did make a significant direct contribution to the development of fluid catalytic cracking.

The possibility of developing a moving catalyst system continued to be emphasized during this period (see program letter by R. Rosen "Conference on Gas Oil Cracking, November 11, 1936"). In May of 1937, Houdry received his U.S. patent 2,078,945 covering the use of a molded catalyst prepared from acid treated clay. This catalyst patent, as distinct from a large number of his earlier patents on specific engineering designs, compelled attention to the Houdry patent structure on fixed bed operations (see 1/4/37 "Summary of Report on Houdry Process," E. B. Peck and P. J. Whelan to R. P. Russell). Shortly thereafter, following a conference set up by Mr. Murphree on May 26,

1937, a comprehensive patent search was organized to develop a complete picture of the art relating to catalytic cracking (see E. V. Murphree memorandum of same date, file Cat. Cr. No. 2).

This patent search was carried out under technical direction and played a significant part in the research program for the next several years (see 6/17/37 letters on "Patent Search," W. J. Sweeney to H. J. Hall). Its object was twofold: to collect and systematize the extensive patent and literature art on cracking catalysts, methods and apparatus prior to Houdry, and to direct attention to all promising alternates which might avoid his patents. A major item was to develop the art on continuous systems for moving and recirculating a powdered catalyst independently of the process oil stream. One such patent immediately noted was Miller U.S. 1,799,858, originally owned by the Silica Gel Corp. (see Clay Catalyst Patent Survey, Weekly Progress Report for June 23, 1937, H. J. Hall to W. J. Sweeney). There were also a number of Silica Gel patents on synthetic siliceous materials suitable as potential cracking catalysts. This led to negotiations and later agreements with Davison Chemical Company, the patent owner, whereby Jersey acquired exclusive licensing rights under the Silica Gel patents and Davison supplied commercial quantities of the synthetic catalysts.

The time schedule in the Research Laboratories at the beginning of 1937 allowed the hope that an intensive development program would permit full scale plant design to start early in 1938, leading to the installation of a full scale fixed bed plant ready to start operation in 1939 (see 12/22/36 letter of R. P. Russell to G. W. Gordon, file Catalytic Cracking No. 7). The continued success of this program brought a rapidly increasing concentration of manpower into it, and the Jersey Board soon reached the radical decision to go ahead with both pilot plant work and plant design at the same time (letter of 3/2/37 from R. T. Haslam to R. P. Russell, file Cat. Cracking No. 2).

The first fixed bed results gave a definite indication that the best product distribution in catalytic cracking was realized at the beginning of the cracking cycle, when the catalyst was first put on stream. In correlating these results, E. D. Reeves reached the conclusion that a very short cycle time at high throughputs would be by far the best way of realizing good product distribution (letter of 4/16/37 to W. J. Sweeney, file EA 700.423). One way of accomplishing this would be by continuous operation with moving catalysts. This conclusion was confirmed by a variety of other experiments during 1937, with contribution both from the Development Division and from Baton Rouge.

By March of 1938, the Research Division started laboratory work in a continuous one-half B/D cracking unit using powdered catalyst. The Process Division continued the study of slurry catalyst systems. Baton Rouge was concerned with the development of synthetic catalysts, and at the same time, they began operations in the 100 B/D fixed bed pilot plant, PECLA. Before the moving catalyst work reached this stage, however, the Engineering Division had gone ahead with full-scale plans for a fixed bed plant with shallow layers of catalyst in a tray-type reactor. The patent search had progressed through a detailed analysis of the pertinent Houdry cases and voluminous earlier art to the point where Jersey were ready to ask for patent clearance from outside counsel for this design (see "Patent Art on Tray-Type Reactors," letter of 4/24/38, H. J. Hall to R. P. Russell). This was subsequently confirmed in the September, 1938, opinion of Mr. Merrell E. Clark that the proposed design would not infringe any valid Houdry claim (see summary letter of 6/22/38 on "Validity and Infringement of Houdry Patents," H. J. Hall to W. E. Currie).

5. Although Houdry's earlier cracking patents had only a few years left to run, a large number of process and equipment patents covering the fixed-bed operation had just been issued to the Houdry Process Corporation. These recent patents covered elements such as the turbo-compressor and the molten-salt system which were crucial to its profitable operation. *Ibid.* (p. 8):

The tray-type reactor was being seriously considered for installation at either Palembang or Aruba, both under Dutch jurisdiction. The refinery at Palembang was operated by Standard Vacuum, and thus owned jointly by Jersey and Socony. The question of whether or not to take a license from Houdry came up directly, therefore ("Visit to Sun Oil Company, Philadelphia," Memorandum of 10/19/37, R. P. Russell).

6. *Ibid.* (p. 8):

Jersey chose to approach the matter from the viewpoint of paid-up licensing rights for its world-wide operations outside the U.S., and the rate quoted amounted to a $50,000,000 royalty payment which Houdry refused to compromise. This rate seemed totally unrealistic in terms of all previous oil refining royalties (see 7/30/37 letter of R. P. Russell to N. E. Loomis, file Cr. Catalytic, Prudhomme-Houdry No. 2) and negotiations were discontinued.

7. After comprehensive patent review, occupying three men for three and one-half years, Jersey was ready to take court action against Houdry patents if necessary, and did so on a sort of preliminary basis by filing opposition proceedings in Holland starting in 1938. *Ibid.* (p. 9):

This situation directed attention to a special provision of the Dutch patent law permitting and requiring Dutch patents to be challenged as to validity only during the first five years after their issue (see cable of F. A. Howard to R. P. Russell, 9/4/37, file Cr. Catalytic Prudhomme-Houdry No. 3). The Dutch patent system is considered to be one of the strictest in the world, and this arena was chosen to challenge the Houdry patents in court. Ten Dutch opposition suits were ultimately filed, concentrating on the "basic" catalyst patents. These suits ran till after the war, but each of the Houdry patents opposed was finally declared invalid (see "Houdry Dutch Patents," letters of 9/3/37, H. J. Hall to W. E. Currie, 10/18 and 11/9/37, H. J. Hall to W. J. Sweeney; also separate search reports and memoranda, 1938–41, H. J. Hall to S. A. Kiss, file EA-030).

8. *Ibid* (pp. 9–10):

While patent clearance was obtained on the tray-type reactor, it was clear that a much better defense of noninfringement could be set up by going over to moving catalyst. There were also increasing indications of technical advantage to be realized in cost and product distribution by going this route (see H. J. Hall notes, discussion of 4/25/39 with M. E. Clark). The real question was how to feed the catalyst from cracking to regeneration and back without getting dangerous leakages between oil vapor and regeneration air supply, and how to keep the catalyst in motion or in suspension.

In starting the design of the continuous powdered catalyst unit, Dr. W. K. Lewis had visited the Research Division Laboratories in January, 1938, to discuss his earlier work with a "Jacob's Ladder" apparatus wherein solid flows down over alternately pitched baffles for intimate contact with a rising stream of gas. Units of this type were used as catalyst strippers in the laboratory units and are still used in many commercial designs. Mr. D. L. Campbell suggested the Fuller-Kinyon compression screw as a good means of injecting and circulating catalyst, and a pipe-type of apparatus was chosen for the reactor as probably the best method to ensure intimate mixing of the catalyst and gases (see Memorandum of C. W. Tyson on 2/28/38, Conference on Use of Powdered Catalysts, File DD 136.207). The reactor thus designed was built promptly and used in blocked operations, first to study the cracking reaction and then to study regeneration. Later that year, it was converted to continuous powdered catalyst operation with both cracking and regeneration tied together. By this time, Baton Rouge had converted their pilot operations to powdered catalyst in the PECLA unit. The reactor used in these units was of the coil type, feeding catalyst by means of Fuller-Kinyon screws or by star feeders.

Other methods of feeding the catalyst and keeping it in motion were recognized. After some experimenting with slurry cracking on heavy feeds, Kellogg was using a moving pilled or granular catalyst in a mechanical conveyor, and Anglo-Iranian had put up a 1500 B/D Kellogg-type pilot plant at Llandarcy, Wales (see Minutes of Cracking Research Committee, May 26, 1938, file EA-030). A number of other mechanical devices such as moving grates, Sirocco blowers and agitating chains or paddles were designed or actually installed for testing at the Research Division, but none of these ultimately showed any advantage over a simple reactor free of moving parts (see 3/28/38 "Memorandum Catalytic Cracking Using Powdered Catalyst," E. V. Murphree to F. A. Howard). The possibility of floating catalyst particles on a gas stream of suitable velocity was known from the patent art, usually in a cone-shaped reactor. It was estimated that catalyst floating thus in a vertical tube might carry only 5% of the powder over to a cyclone separator and Cottrell precipitator. However, high rates of catalyst supply were hard to get, and such systems used a very high concentration of catalyst which might almost be considered as gas entrained in solid rather than solid entrained in gas (see 4/14/38 letter of H. J. Hall to E. V. Murphree, "Patentable Ideas in Continuous Process Cracking," file EA-030). The conical reactor with solid moving upward more slowly than the concurrent gas was called a "hindered settler," to distinguish from a "jiggling bed" system with particles semi-stationary or moving countercurrent to the suspending gas. Some slippage was obviously taking place between the catalyst and vapor in the long coil reactors, but this was a complicating factor in engineering designs and was considered as a disadvantage (see 11/30/38 letter of D. L. Campbell—J. R. Schonberg to E. V. Murphree, file 130.726). When Dr. Lewis was called in to help evaluate this factor, he pointed out that the slippage was inherently desirable, and he was promptly authorized to do some fundamental work on how to take advantage of it (letter of 12/13/38 from E. V. Murphree to W. K. Lewis). This research led to the fluid bed reactor, was described in Lewis and Gilliland U. S. patent 2,498,088 and a number of later developments derived therefrom.

9. Paul O. Dunham to B. L. Bragg, December 18, 1957 (pp. 3, 4):

According to *prior* concepts, in order to maintain a fluidized bed within the reaction zone, it was considered necessary to (1) have the solid particles in the reaction zone of substantially uniform size, and (2) the velocity of the gases rising through the bed must be below the free falling velocity of the finest particles in the bed. Otherwise, it was believed that the finer particles would be selectively lifted out of the bed by the gases passing overhead.

The work done at M.I.T. demonstrated that these two prior concepts were unsound. It was found that a fluidized body of solids could be maintained in the reaction zone at velocities materially higher than the free falling velocity of even the coarsest particles in the bed, if the feed rate of solids into the bed was properly controlled. In other words, the work at M.I.T. under Dr. Lewis' direction, demonstrated for the first time that fluidized beds could be maintained under much higher velocities than would have been predicted by earlier investigators, such as Odell. For example, see the formula on page 5 of the Odell patent, setting forth the factors to be considered in determining the gas velocities. The work done at M.I.T. therefore, was an important step in the development of the fluid cracking process, because it made it unnecessary to use catalyst of uniform size and made it possible to pass the gases through the reaction zone at higher feed rates than was visualized by prior investigators. This important discovery is thoroughly described in the Lewis and Gilliland patent mentioned above.

10. C. E. Kleiber to C. E. Starr, Jr., December 12, 1956:

The early work in developing a competitive process was under the direction of Mr. Frank A. Howard as President of the Standard Oil Development Company, with Mr. R. P. Russell as Executive Vice-President, and Mr. E. V. Murphree in immediate executive charge of the research and engineering work on the project. Under . . . [Dr.] W. J. Sweeney, Mr. E. Duer Reeves directed . . . [continuing] laboratory research investigations, including small bench scale units, aided by Messrs. S. C. Fulton, P. H. Holt and M. E. Conn. A small one-half B/D semi-continuous unit, known as the CPC Unit, employed lead baths for heating.

. . . effort, slightly later, in somewhat the same direction, but first concentrating on feed preparation, was made by the Process Research group, under Mr. H. G. M. Fischer, with Mr. Paul E. Kuhl in immediate charge, aided by Messrs. A. B. Welty, Jr., A. C. Patterson, and W. O. Taff. . . . [Dr.] G. L. Matheson studied the fundamentals of fluidized solids behavior. Messrs. K. K. Kearby, R. W. Richardson, W. E. Spicer, and G. C. Connolly, although not all in the same laboratory, concentrated on catalyst development. Mr. E. J. Gohr . . . had charge of the chemical engineering aspects of the design work, aided by Messrs. C. W. Tyson, H. Z. Martin, and C. E. Hemminger; while, under Dr. N. E. Loomis, Mr. E. W. Luster directed the process design and mechanical engineering angles of the project, aided by Messrs. J. R. Schonberg, D. L. Campbell, and J. V. Marancik.

11. H. J. Hall, *op. cit.* (p. 10):

Plant designs in 1939 were shifted from the long coil to the hindered settling reactor, on the basis of Dr. Lewis' experimental results. The new design still used the compression-type feed screw, which was giving some trouble in pilot plant tests. Early in 1940, the laboratories discovered that one of these screws at the bottom of a pressured lock-hopper was acting only as an agitated orifice. If the catalyst was properly aerated, it would flow just as well when the screw was idle, with the lock-hopper acting as a blow case. This led to further work confirming suggestions in one of the 1939 plant designs that the best way to feed the catalyst by far was to leave out the screw, using the fluistatic pressure of the aerated solid in a simple standpipe as the driving form for catalyst circulation (see Minutes of C.R.A. Meeting of May 28, 1940, file RA-080, also Campbell, Martin, Tyson and Murphree U.S. patents 2,451,803-4).

12. Paul O. Dunham, *op. cit.* (pp. 4, 5):

The first patent, 2,451,803, covers the use of a fluidized standpipe for developing and restoring the pressure necessary for circulating the solids through the reaction and regenerating zones. One of the pressing problems in the early stages of the development of the fluid cracking process was to find a procedure for generating the necessary pressure for circulating the catalyst powder through the reactor and regenerator. It was initially thought that the pressure could be readily developed by conventional type of compression screws commonly used in the cement industry. The first pilot plant at Baton Rouge included such compression screws. However, it developed that in passing through the screws the solids were agglomerated into small pellets known at that time as "poppy seed" and the activity of the catalyst rapidly fell off. However, in carrying out the initial work in the pilot plant, it was noted that when the hoppers containing the catalyst were properly aerated, they would develop a hydraulic pressure at the base of the hoppers. This led to the suggestion of using a fluidized column of solids for generating the necessary pressure on the catalyst. Since it requires from 3 to 6 feet of fluidized solids to generate 1 lb. of pressure, it will be obvious that in order to utilize the hydraulic principle, the pressure drops through the unit must be relatively small, or otherwise the apparatus would be of impractical height. The use of fluidized beds of catalyst in the reactor and regenerator made it possible to design a unit with a relatively low pressure drop which brought the height of the standpipes down to more practical dimensions. The first patent, 2,451,803, covers the use of a fluidized standpipe for developing the pressure for circulating solids to the reaction system; and the second patent, 2,451,804, is directed to the combination of the fluidized standpipes and the fluid type reactor and regenerator.

13. C. E. Kleiber, *op. cit.* (p. 3):

As a result of the PECLA pilot operations, the Standard Oil Company of Indiana, and M. W. Kellogg and Company, who were close observers of the pilot work, and Jersey Standard received patents covering the fluidized dense bed with bottom dense phase catalyst drawoff. The design simplified plant construction in providing a heat balance unit with greater catalyst circulation capacity to permit liquid instead of vapor feed injection to the catalyst circuit, as incorporated in Model II of the process. Jersey's C. E. Jahnig obtained our best claims under U.S. Patent 2,518,693 (filed July 24, 1941, granted October 15, 1950) under this phase of the development. A companion patent issued to Messrs. C. E. Jahnig and H. Z. Martin, U.S. No. 2,515,156 (filed July 24, 1941, and granted July 11, 1950) was a valuable addition.

14. Paul O Dunham, *op. cit.* (p. 5):

These patents should be considered together since they cover certain details in the "downflow" design as the first major development in the fluid process. I might mention at this time that the 100 bbl./day pilot plant operated by Jersey at Baton Rouge was the only pilot plant in operation and its performance was observed by other members of the Recommendation 41 Agreement. It was early observed in operation of this plant, and in some of the Laboratory tests, that there was a relatively dense phase of solids in the bottom portion of the reactor and a relatively dilute phase near the top, with a surging level corresponding somewhat to the level of a boiling liquid. The true explanation of why such a density break occurred in the reactor was not understood at the time and is not clearly explained perhaps even today. In any event, this led to the suggestion by inventors working for Standard Oil of Indiana, the M. W. Kellogg Company, and Standard Oil Development Company, that substantial improvement could be obtained by withdrawing the catalyst directly from the dense phase, thus avoiding passing the bulk of the catalyst through the cyclone separators as required in the original "upflow" type unit. This idea was conceived independently by inventors of the three companies mentioned above, and each of the parties has patents covering specific details of this design. (See, for example, the Indiana Scheineman patent 2,562,225.)

15. C. E. Kleiber, *op. cit.* (p. 4):

During the subsequent years of commercial plant operations, many improvements in the art were made, such as in the fields of spent catalyst stripping, catalyst quality and contamination, catalyst fluidity, process efficiency as regards gas-solids contacting and mixing, combating erosion, and other mechanical problems to permit run length extension from the early 2–6 month runs to the present 1 to 2 year runs at high process and operating efficiency. In this work many individuals, including H. W. S. Nicholson, A. F. Kaulakis, H. D. Codet, H. G. Ogorzaly, F. H. Blanding, C. E. Kleiber, F. J. Feely, Jr., and J. S. Clarke, and others contributed.

The early designs covered by Models I, II, and III of the fluid cracking process utilized the original standpipe, valve and dilute phase riser technique of catalyst transfer between the reactor and regenerator vessels of the process. A major improvement in the process was made by Mr. J. W. Packie with his concept of the U-bend transfer system of catalyst employing the original standpipe concept but with a curved lateral transfer section and a dense phase riser with gaseous injection to control catalyst circulation rate. This is now commonly known as the Model IV type unit (U. S. Patent No. 2,589,124, filed May 1, 1950, granted March 11, 1952). Messrs. L. A. Nicolai and D. S. Borey contributed in this phase of the work.

APPENDIX C: TABLES

Appendix Table 1a

U. S. Output of Cracked Gasoline by Process
1913–1929

Year	Total cracked gasoline (000 bbls.)	Share of the Major Processes					
		Burton	Dubbs	Tube and Tank	Holmes–Manley	Cross	Other thermal processes
1913	1,218	1.000	--	--	--	--	--
1914	2,024	1.000	--	--	--	--	--
1915	4,141	1.000	--	--	--	--	--
1916	6,950	1.000	--	--	--	--	--
1917	10,035	1.000	--	--	--	--	--
1918	12,180	1.000	--	--	--	--	--
1919	16,200	1.000	--	--	--	--	--
1920	17,412	.971	--	--	.029	--	--
1921	22,441	.946	--	.001	.053	.000	--
1922	27,554	.924	.000	.006	.065	.005	--
1923	30,459	.824	.012	.026	.125	.013	--
1924	38,497	.665	.040	.050	.204	.041	--
1925	68,583	.412	.036	.056	.150	.087	.259
1926	93,756	.284	.041	.152	.125	.127	.271
1927	101,226	.156	.043	.195	.139	.158	.309
1928	122,584	.115	.059	.347	.174	.155	.150
1929	143,727	.094	.057	.334	.178	.174	.163

Sources: Total Cracked Gasoline: 1913–1919 – Standard Oil Company (Indiana),
C. J. Barkdull, "Figures on Production of Gasoline . . .," February
10, 1928. 1920–1924 – Sum of outputs from individual processes
(Burton, Dubbs, Tube and Tank, Holmes–Manley, and Cross. Because
there was no enumeration of gasoline output from other thermal
cracking processes the total is probably understated, less so in the
early years than in the later.). 1925–1929 – American Petroleum
Institute, Petroleum Facts and Figures, 9 ed., 1950, New York:
American Petroleum Institute, 1951, p. 225.
Burton: 1913–1926 – Standard Oil Company (Indiana), C. J. Barkdull,
op. cit. 1927–1929 – J. H. Westcott, Oil Its Conservation and Waste,
New York: Beacon Press, 4 ed., 1930, p. 119.
Dubbs: 1922–1929 – Listed in Appendix Table 15 are the royalties
collected by Universal Oil Products Company for the operation of the
Dubbs process. These were paid on the basis of 15 cents per barrel
of gas oil charged. Therefore dividing total royalties by $0.15
gives the total number of barrels charged in each year. If we assume
that each barrel of charge yielded 0.21 barrels of gasoline, then the
total production of cracked gasoline would be obtained by multiplying
the total charge by this fraction.
Tube and Tank: 1921–1929 – J. H. Westcott, op. cit., p. 129.
Holmes–Manley: 1920–1929 – J. H. Westcott, op. cit., p. 126.
Cross: 1921–1929 – J. H. Westcott, op. cit., p. 129 (these figures
omit ". . . a substantial production by other companies . . . not
included in the foregoing list of licenses." [28 licenses are
listed] ibid.).

Appendix Table 1b

U. S. Cracking Capacity by Process
1927-1942

Year	Total cracking capacity (thermal + catalytic in 000 bbls./day)	Share of the Major Processes						
		Burton	Dubbs	Tube and Tank	Holmes-Manley	Cross	Other thermal processes	Houdry
1927	1,246	.198	.128	.170	.170	.135	.199	---
1928	1,359	.154	.132	.219	.146	.168	.181	---
1929	1,476	.097	.124	.293	.141	.164	.181	---
1930	1,720	.065	.133	.283	.128	.159	.232	---
1931	1,829	.052	.157	.244	.117	.140	.290	---
1932	2,011	.032	.110	.316	.121	.131	.290	---
1933	1,882	.032	.120	.261	.130	.145	.312	---
1934	1,887	.008	.120	.267	.134	.132	.339	---
1935	2,153	.006	.166	.234	.127	.097	.370	---
1936	2,169	.005	.176	.215	.130	.087	.387	---
1937	2,195	---	.193	.210	.125	.071	.400	.001
1938	2,348	---	.207	.198	.117	.075	.397	.006
1939	2,138	---	.215	.194	.109	.079	.392	.011
1940	2,284	---	.206	.192	.102	.074	.370	.056
1941	2,352	---	.214	.182	.100	.081	.357	.066
1942	2,456	---	.213	.157	.099	.076	.385	.070

Source: Oil and Gas Journal, Annual Refining Issues (1927-1942). Total capacity
includes shut down plants. Shares are calculated by dividing total cracking
capacity by the capacity of each process.

Appendix Table 1c

U. S. Cracking Capacity by Process
1943-1957

Year	Total cracking capacity (thermal + catalytic in 000 bbls./day)	Share of the Major Processes					
		Thermal processes	Houdry	Houdriflow	T. C. C.	Fluid	Other catalytic processes
1943	2,541	.901	.079	---	---	.020	---
1944	2,544	.786	.092	---	.030	.092	---
1945	3,075	.715	.084	---	.065	.133	.003
1946	3,199	.700	.087	---	.069	.141	.003
1947	3,483	.678	.080	---	.069	.168	.005
1948	3,781	.660	.074	---	.071	.189	.006
1949	3,749	.626	.069	---	.079	.222	.004
1950	4,130	.583	.060	.005	.075	.277	---
1951	4,163	.562	.057	.013	.085	.283	---
1952	4,444	.533	.051	.018	.087	.310	.001
1953	4,104	.388	.040	.023	.124	.421	.004
1954	4,190	.325	.039	.025	.139	.468	.004
1955	4,442	.253	.033	.029	.155	.527	.003
1956	4,625	.207	.012	.040	.160	.576	.005
1957	4,754	.181	.009	.038	.152	.616	.004

Source: Oil and Gas Journal, Annual Refining Issues (1943-1957). Total capacity
includes shut down plants. After 1942 thermal cracking capacity is not
broken down by process. From 1953 through 1957, thermal cracking
capacity is included in the category "thermal operations." The
remainder of the "thermal operations" (vis-breaking, coking, etc.) are
excluded from this tabulation.

Appendix Table 2a

Gasoline Prices and Octanes at the Refinery
1901-1957

			Refinery			
	Cracked gasoline (cents per gallon)	Average refinery price (cents per gallon)	Midwestern (Group 3)			
			Premium grade		Regular grade	
Year			Price (cents per gallon	Octane (Motor)	Price (cents per gallon	Octane (Motor)
1901						
2						
3						
4		7.3				
5						
6						
7						
8						
9		7.4				
1910						
1						
2						
3	10.5					
4		8.4				
5						
6						
7						
8						
9		18.2				
1920		16.4				
1						
2	} 15.0	11.8				
3						
4						
5		11.2	12	61	11.75	59
6			10	59	9.75	57
7		8.2	7.25	59	7.00	57
8			6.22	59	6.00	57
9			6.88	59	6.63	57
1930			7.56	61	7.41	59
1			3.88	59	3.75	57
2			4.00	67	3.50	61
3			2.88	67	2.62	61
4			4.88	67	4.50	62
5			4.38	67	3.38	60
6	5.86		5.88	67	5.00	60
7			5.75	69	4.63	60
8	3.637		4.88	71	4.63	68
9	5.88		4.38	71	4.13	68
1940			4.25	71	4.00	68
1			4.38	73	4.00	65
2			6.5	78	5.75	73
3			6.75	78	5.88	73
4			6.75	76	6.00	72
5			6.75	76	5.88	72
6			5.75	79	5.00	74
7			7.75	78	7.00	74
8			11.25	78	10.50	74
9			10.63	79	9.88	74
1950			10.25	88(Research)	9.50	82(Research)
1			11.38	88 "	10.38	82 "
2			11.13	88 "	10.25	82 "
3			11.50	88 "	10.50	82 "
4			12.25	90 "	11.25	84 "
5	10.5		11.50	92 "	10.50	84 "
6			12.50	94 "	11.00	86 "
7						

Appendix Table 2b

Gasoline Prices at Wholesale

1901–1957

Year	Wholesale			
	Average price at export (cents per gallon)	Midwest price (cents per gallon)	Chicago Tank Wagon price (cents per gallon)	Dealers' net price (cents per gallon
1901	8.8			
2	7.1			
3	9.3			
4	10.7			
5	8.4			
6	8.0			
7	10.4		10.8	
8	11.0			
9	9.1			
1910	8.1			
1	8.5			
2	9.0			
3	13.3	16.0		
4	14.3	12.0		13.0
5	11.2	9.9	9.5	11.7
6	16.3	17.2	18.5	18.9
7	20.8	19.6	20.0	20.9
8	26.3	21.7	22.5	23.92
9	23.8	21.9	23.0	24.11
1920	26.6	27.8	26.0	28.05
1	23.1	21.4	18.0	24.09
2	21.9	21.6	23.0	22.63
3	16.3	17.4	20.0	18.66
4	14.1	15.9	18.0	16.86
5	15.3		19.0	17.46
6	14.8		n.a.	17.44
7	11.5		n.a.	15.00
8	10.7		15.0	14.83
9	10.6		16.0	14.58
1930	9.4		15.0	12.48
1	5.9			9.65
2	5.6			10.08
3	5.3			9.42
4	5.6			9.81
5	5.7			9.73
6	6.1			10.21
7	6.7			10.53
8	6.0			10.04
9	6.2			9.58
1940	7.7			9.08
1	8.5			9.49
2	9.9			10.44
3	11.8			10.45
4	15.2			10.49
5	13.5			10.33
6	6.6			10.40
7	8.7			12.33
8	11.7			14.55
9	12.0			15.05
1950	12.5			15.10
1	13.2			15.33
2	14.5			15.27
3	15.2			15.95
4	16.5			16.19
5	16.2			16.18
6	16.1			16.34
7	16.0			16.69

Appendix Table 2c
Gasoline Prices and Octanes at Retail, and Engine Compression Ratios
1901-1957

| Year | Retail | | | | Engine compression ratios |
| | Premium grade | | Regular grade | | |
	Price (cents per gallon)	Octane (Research)	Price (cents per gallon)	Octane (Research)	
1901					
2					
3					
4					
5					
6					
7					
8					
9					
1910					
1					
2					
3					
4					
5					
6					
7					
8					
9					
1920					
1					
2					
3					
4					
5	23.09	71.0	20.09	55.0	
6	20.97	71.0	20.79	n.a.	
7	20.28	72.0	18.28	n.a.	
8	19.90	73.0	17.90	n.a.	
9	19.92	n.a.	17.92	n.a.	
1930	18.16	74.0	16.16	63.0	
1	14.98	75.0	12.98	63.0	5.23
2	15.30	77.0	13.30	64.0	5.29
3	14.41	77.0	12.41	68.0	5.57
4	15.64	78.0	13.64	72.0	5.72
5	15.55	78.0	13.55	72.0	5.98
6	16.10	79.0	14.10	72.0	6.14
7	16.59	81.0	14.59	73.3	6.25
8	16.07	83.0	14.07	74.5	6.32
9	13.31	83.0	13.31	74.5	6.32
1940	14.75	83.0	12.75	77.9	6.41
1	15.30	85.3	13.30	80.4	6.63
2	16.46	85.3	14.46	78.0	6.60
3	16.56	85.0	14.56	77.8	--
4	16.62	81.2	14.62	75.5	--
5	16.48	82.9	14.48	75.9	--
6	16.69	86.3	14.69	80.4	6.77
7	18.93	86.5	16.93	80.4	6.73
8	21.54	87.0	19.54	80.9	6.78
9	22.27	88.6	20.27	82.2	6.93
1950	22.08	90.6	20.08	84.0	7.00
1	22.31	90.8	20.31	83.9	7.09
2	22.24	91.2	20.24	84.7	7.14
3	23.28	92.0	21.28	85.4	7.31
4	24.06	93.7	21.56	86.6	7.31
5	23.92	96.0	21.42	88.8	7.87
6	24.51	97.0	21.51	90.1	8.47
7	--	--	22.1	--	8.75

Sources to Appendix Table 2:

Refinery:

Cracked gasoline: 1913, 1922–3, 1938; Standard Oil Company
(Indiana), price at refinery in Indiana. 1938 gasoline octane
equal to 72 (Research); 1936; Petroleum Data Book, Dallas,
Petroleum Engineer Publishing Company, 1947, average price in the
Mid-continent region; 1939; Houdry Process Corporation, price at
refinery on the East Coast (?); 1955; Esso Research and Engineering Company, refinery price on the Gulf Coast for 10 #RVP gasoline
of 94.4 octane (Research).

Average refinery price: J. H. Westcott, Oil: Its Conservation and Waste; New York: Beacon Publishing Company, 4 ed.,
1930, p. 63 (calculated from Bureau of the Census figures).

Midwestern (Group 3): Prices and octane numbers; National
Petroleum News, gasoline prices in tank-car lots in Oklahoma
(1925) or in the Midwestern (Group 3: 1926–1956) markets as of
the first week in March of each year. When two or more prices
were quoted for each grade, the lowest was chosen. The price
differentials would have been the same had any other prices been
selected. When a range of octanes was quoted, the arithmetical
average was taken. For correlations between Motor and Research
octanes, see R. L. Nelson, Petroleum Refinery Engineering, 3 ed.,
New York: McGraw-Hill Book Company, Inc., 1949, pp. 571, 686.

Wholesale:

Average at export: for the group Motor Fuel, Gasoline, and
Naphtha (earlier, Light Products of Distillation). U. S. Department of Commerce, Bureau of Foreign and Domestic Commerce, Statistical Abstract of the United States, 1925, Washington: Government Printing Office (through 1918 for year ending June 30,
beginning 1919 for calendar year),   p. 326; U. S. Department
of Commerce, Bureau of the Census, Statistical Abstract of the
United States, 1950, p. 296; 1956, p. 333; 1959, p. 342.

Midwest: average price received for all gasoline shipped by
the Standard Oil Company (Indiana); U. S. v. Standard Oil Company
(Indiana) et al., District Court of U. S., Northern District of
Illinois, Eastern Division, In Equity No. 4131, Petitioners Book
Exhibits, vol. II, p. 1691.

Chicago Tank Wagon: 1907; Standard Oil Company (Indiana),
"Historical Summaries of Products and Manufacturing Processes,"
memorandum from J. K. Roberts to Dr. O. E. Bransky, October 7,
1938, p. 99 (this price is exclusive of freight charges); 1915–
1930; Standard Oil Company (Indiana), "Prices of Gasoline, Normal
Gasoline Tank Wagon Market in Chicago, Exclusive of Taxes." Tank
wagon price is the price for sales to large consumers or to retail outlets. The price for the year is taken as that in force

Sources to Appendix Table 2 (continued):

on July 1, except for 1925 (price after February 13), 1928 (price before August 1), and 1930 (price after April 12).

Dealers' net price: 1914-1917; U. S. Department of Commerce, Bureau of Foreign and Domestic Commerce, Statistical Abstract of the United States, 1925, p. 736; 1918-1955, American Petroleum Institute, Petroleum Facts and Figures, New York: American Petroleum Institute, 9 ed., p. 367; 12 ed., p. 305; 1956-1957, U. S. Bureau of Mines, Minerals Yearbook, 1957, vol. II, Washington: Government Printing Office, 1959, pp. 423, 4. From 1926, these are dealers' net prices for regular-grade gasoline, ex. tax, in fifty cities in the United States; prior to 1926 the figures are average tank-wagon price.

Retail:

Gasoline prices, regular grade: 1925-1949, American Petroleum Institute, Petroleum Facts and Figures: 9 ed., 1950, p. 367; 1950-1955, 12 ed., 1956, p. 305; 1956, American Petroleum Institute, communication from J. P. Buder, October 26, 1956. These are average service station prices, exclusive of taxes.

Premium grade; a 2¢ per gallon differential was assumed from 1925-1953. In 1954, the differential was assumed to have increased to 2.5¢ per gallon, and in 1956 to 3.0¢ per gallon (for the differential in 1925 see R. C. Cook, Control of the Petroleum Industry by Major Oil Companies, TNEC Monograph No. 39, Washington: Government Printing Office, 1941, p. 44).

Gasoline octanes—regular grade; 1925, 1930-1953, Stanford Research Institute, Chemical Economics Handbook, p. 694.73; 1954-1956, Ethyl Corporation communication with G. E. Bruhl, October 26, 1956.

Premium grade; 1926-1928, 1930 E. V. Murphree et al., "The Trend to High Octane Is Sound," paper presented before Metropolitan (New York) Section, SAE, October 15, 1953; 1931-1953, Stanford Research Institute, op. cit.; 1954-1956, Ethyl Corporation, op. cit..

Engine compression ratios:

Average compression ratios of new cars manufactured in the United States; Automotive Industries, March 15, 1956, p. 130; March 15, 1959, p. 130.

Appendix Table 3
Fuel Gas and Kerosene Prices 1900–1957

Year	Fuel Gas (FOE, cents per gallon)	Fuel Gas ($ per MMBTU)	Butane, Butylene (cents per gallon)	Kerosene Wholesale Refinery (cents per gallon)	Kerosene Wholesale Export (cents per gallon)	Kerosene Wholesale Chicago Tank Wagon (cents per gallon)	Kerosene Retail (cents per gallon)
1900							7.7
1				4.6	6.3		
2				5.3	6.3		
3				6.5	6.7		
4				6.4	7.8		
5				4.85	6.8		7.9
6				4.6	6.3		
7				4.1	6.3		
8				4.0	6.8		
9				3.85	6.6		
1910				3.2	6.2		7.3
1				2.5	5.6		
2				3.75	5.7		
3	1.42			4.05	6.3		
4				3.5	6.4		
5				3.1	6.0		
6				3.9	6.4		
7				5.2	5.4		
8				7.6	8.9		
9				9.3	12.2		
1920				13.9	15.3		17.1
1				6.0	12.5		
2	}4.0	}.203			9.3		
3					9.0		
4					9.7	11.5	
5					9.5	11.5	12.3
6					10.9	13.6	
7					9.8	12.4	
8					10.2	11.9	
9					10.1	12.8	
1930					9.0	12.5	12.1
1					6.6	9.3	
2					5.2	9.7	
3					5.2	9.1	
4					5.2	8.9	
5	(assumed) 2.25	(assumed) .114	(assumed) 3.0		5.6	9.4	
6					5.3	9.8	
7					5.7	10.0	
8	2.25	.114			5.3	10.3	
9		.131	3.0		4.7	10.0	
1940					6.1	10.0	
1					5.5	10.2	
2					5.5	10.3	
3					6.5	10.6	
4					6.3	10.6	
5					4.6	10.5	
6					5.9	11.4	
7					7.6	13.4	
8					9.5	15.9	
9					9.2	15.3	
1950					9.8	15.8	
1					10.0	15.8	
2					9.5	15.8	
3					9.4	16.1	
4					9.6	16.4	
5		.18	8.0		9.7	16.8	
6					10.2	17.1	
7					10.6	17.3	

Appendix Table 4
Distillates, Fuel Oil and Crude Oil Prices, 1900–1957

Year	Gas Oil Refinery (cents per gallon)	Gas Oil Cracking charge (cents per gallon)	Fuel Oil Refinery Indiana (cents per gallon)	Fuel Oil Refinery Oklahoma (cents per gallon)	Fuel Oil Cracked product (cents per gallon)	Crude Oil Refinery Indiana (cents per gallon)	Crude Oil Refinery Oklahoma-Kansas (cents per gallon)
1900	2.10		3.20			3.40	
1	2.40		2.25			3.35	
2	2.35		2.50			3.40	
3	3.00		3.25			4.05	
4	3.08		3.75			3.60	
5	2.60		2.20			3.20	
6	2.75		1.80			2.80	
7	2.30		1.70			2.55	
8	2.62		1.60			2.35	
9	2.60		1.55			2.25	
1910	2.13		1.50			2.30	
1	2.05		1.63			2.40	
2	2.13		1.80			2.80	1.98
3	2.28	2.5	2.00		2.063	3.50	2.45
4	2.25		1.80			3.10	1.31
5	2.40		1.85			2.80	2.86
6	3.80		2.70			4.30	3.33
7	5.15		2.60			5.70	4.75
8	6.00		3.40			6.70	5.35
9	6.30		3.15			7.05	6.55
1920	11.45		6.70			10.0	8.32
1	5.18		2.80			6.50	4.75
2	3.30	} 5.0	2.30		} 4.75	6.25	3.33
3							2.38
4				4.53			2.98
5				4.18			4.26
6				2.90			4.52
7				2.12			3.04
8				1.52			3.24
9				1.29			3.45
1930				1.26			2.26
1				0.70			1.83
2				0.85			1.64
3				1.00			2.38
4				1.54			2.38
5				1.58			2.38
6		3.31		1.54	1.56		2.62
7				1.93			2.90
8		3.3		1.80	3.0		2.43
9		2.86		1.72	1.84		2.43
1940				2.01			2.78
1				2.18			2.78
2				2.26			2.78
3				2.30			2.78
4				2.31			2.78
5				2.31			2.78
6				2.82			3.86
7				4.47			6.12
8				5.82			6.12
9				3.34			6.12
1950				3.89			6.12
1				4.27			6.12
2				2.86			6.72
3				2.75			6.72
4				3.12			6.72
5		8.0		4.13	3.93		6.72
6				5.10			6.72
7				5.36			7.31

Sources for Appendix Tables 3 and 4:

Fuel Gas:
1913, 1922-3, 1938; Standard Oil Company (Indiana), at refinery in
Indiana;
1939; Houdry Process Corporation, at refinery on East Coast (?);
1955; Esso Research and Engineering Company, at refinery on Gulf
Coast.

Kerosene:
Refinery:
Standard Oil Company (Indiana), Ford, Bacon and Davis, Inc.,
Engineers, "Report on the Fair Value of the Burton Process as of
March 1, 1913," Chart 21, p. 125. This is the average price at
Indiana's refineries.
Wholesale:
Export:
U. S. Department of Commerce, Bureau of Foreign and Domes-
tic Commerce, Statistical Abstract of the United States,
1920, p. 569 (through 1918, for year ending June 30; start-
ing 1919 for calendar year); 1925, p. 326; U. S. Department
of Commerce, Bureau of the Census, Statistical Abstract of
the United States, 1950, p. 296; 1956, p. 333; 1959, p. 342.
Chicago Tank Wagon:
American Petroleum Institute, op. cit., 9 ed., p. 375; 12
ed., p. 310; U. S. Bureau of Mines, Minerals Yearbook,
1957, vol. II, Washington: Government Printing Office,
1959, p. 429.
Retail:
Standard Oil Company (Indiana). The figures for 1900, 1905, and
1910 were obtained by adjusting the value declared at export to
the retail level. Subsequent figures compiled by J. E. Pogue.

Gas Oil:
Refinery:
Ford, Bacon and Davis, op. cit., Chart 22, p. 126.
Cracking Charge:
See sources under Fuel Gas. In 1922-3, when virgin gas oil was
valued at 5.0 cents per gallon, cracked gas oil was 4.5 cents
per gallon.

Fuel Oil:
Refinery:
Indiana:
Ford, Bacon and Davis, op. cit., Chart 22, p. 126.
Oklahoma:
American Petroleum Institute, op. cit., 9 ed., p. 375; 12
ed., p. 310; U. S. Bureau of Mines, op. cit., p. 439 (con-
verted from dollars per barrel to cents per gallon).
Cracked Product:
See sources under Fuel Gas. In 1922-3 petroleum coke, sold as
fuel, fetched $5.00 per ton, or 1.81 cents per FOE gallon; in
1938, 3 cents per FOE gallon.

Crude Oil:
Refinery:
Indiana:
Ford, Bacon and Davis, op. cit., Chart 22, p. 126; delivered cost at the refinery.
Oklahoma-Kansas:
American Petroleum Institute, op. cit., 9 ed., p. 363; 13
ed., p. 374; U. S. Bureau of Mines, op. cit., p. 394.
(price quoted in dollars per barrel at well-head, converted
to cents per gallon: 36° API gravity beginning with 1922;
no gravity scale used in pricing prior to that year).

Appendix Table 5

Refinery Labor Wage Rates, 1913–1957

Year	Process labor (dollars per hour)	Average hourly gross earnings, petroleum refining (dollars per hour)	Average hourly earnings, Bayway refinery (dollars per hour)	Composite index (1939 = 100)
1913				
4	0.32			
5			0.291	30.2
6			0.293	30.4
7	0.573		0.461	47.8
8			0.568	58.9
9			0.705	73.0
1920			0.801	83.0
1			0.820	85.0
2	0.80		0.748	77.5
3			0.758	78.5
4			0.762	79.0
5			0.753	78.0
6			0.753	78.0
7			0.764	79.1
8				
9				
1930				
1				
2				
3		0.648		67.1
4		0.752		78.0
5		0.793		82.1
6		0.817		84.7
7		0.933		96.7
8		0.968		100
9	1.00	0.965		100
1940		0.973		101
1		1.038		107
2		1.137		118
3		1.207		125
4		1.259		130
5		1.289		134
6		1.424		148
7		1.566		162
8		1.788		185
9		1.874		194
1950		1.929		200
1		2.08		216
2		2.20		228
3		2.32		240
4		2.37		246
5	2.53	2.46		255
6		2.65		275
7		2.76		286

Appendix Table 6

Construction and Equipment Cost Indices, 1913–1956
(1939 = 100)

Year	Nelson (1)	ENR (2)	Marshall and Stevens (3)	McLean and Haigh (4)	Composite of (2) & (3) (5)	Final index (6)
1913	–	42.4	71.5	–	52.1	↑
4	–	37.6	67.0	–	47.3	
5	–	39.3	68.8	59	49.2	
6	–	55.0	77.9	–	62.7	
7	–	77.0	101.0	–	84.9	
8	–	80.4	137.2	–	99.3	
9	–	84.3	148.4	–	105.6	
1920	–	116.8	184.1	–	139.1	(5)
1	–	85.6	141.3	–	104.0	
2	–	74.0	100.4	–	82.7	
3	–	91.0	117.0	–	99.7	
4	–	91.5	128.9	–	103.9	
5	–	87.7	127.7	–	101.0	
6	94.0	88.3	121.5	–	99.4	
7	–	87.6	117.3	104	97.5	
8	93.0	87.7	118.0	–	97.8	
9	94.0	88.0	111.8	–	95.9	↓
1930	91.8	86.1	104.7	–	92.2	↑
1	84.7	77.0	94.4	–	82.7	
2	73.9	66.7	85.2	–	72.8	
3	74.0	72.9	85.8	–	77.2	
4	81.8	84.1	92.4	–		
5	81.8	83.5	95.6	91		
6	87.9	87.8	100.3	–		
7	97.4	99.8	106.7	–		
8	100.2	101.0	101.2	–		
9	100.0	100.0	100.0	100		
1940	101.2	102.8	100.7	–		
1	104.3	109.3	107.1	–		
2	109.1	117.3	115.6	–		
3	112.9	123.1	117.4	–		(1)
4	114.9	126.9	121.5	–		
5	117.2	130.7	132.5	–		
6	130.5	147.0	147.7	160		
7	152.8	175.5	179.0	–		
8	173.0	195.6	195.3	–		
9	182.2	203	195.3	–		
1950	191.1	216	201.7	212		
1	205.3	230	215.4	–		
2	213.4	242	216.0	–		
3	226.5	255	218.2	–		
4	234.6	267	222.1	–		
5	240.4	280	228.4	–		
6	254.9	294	250.6	–		↓

Sources to Appendix Table 5:

Process labor. Wage rates quoted in studies made by the innovating firms at the time the processes were introduced; see
Appendix Table 3, source to Fuel Gas.

Average hourly gross earnings, petroleum refining (U. S. De-
partment of Labor). U. S. Department of Commerce, Office of
Business Economics, Business Statistics, 1959, Washington:
U. S. Government Printing Office, 1959, p. 78.

Average hourly earnings, Bayway refinery. G. S. Gibb and
E. H. Knowlton, History of the Standard Oil Company (New
Jersey), Vol. II, The Resurgent Years, 1911-1927, New York:
Harper and Brothers, 1956, Appendix 2, Table XV, p. 685.

Composite index. Combination of average hourly gross earnings, petroleum refining (column 3), and average hourly earnings, Bayway refinery (column 4).

Sources to Appendix Table 6:

Column (1): W. L. Nelson, Oil and Gas Journal, December 15,
1949, p. 91, and subsequent issues. This is the Nelson Index
of Refinery Construction Costs valid for the years 1926 and
1928 to the present, and has been changed from a basis of 1946
= 100 to 1939 = 100 by applying a ratio of the two yearly
indices.

Column (2): Engineering News Record, September 1, 1949,
pp. 421-432; and subsequent issues. This is a "Construction
Cost Index" and has been changed from bases of 1913 = 100 and
1947-49 = 100 to 1939 = 100 by the same method as above.

Column (3): R. W. Stevens, Chemical Engineering, November,
1947, pp. 124-5; and subsequent issues. This is the Marshall
and Stevens Index for Processing Equipment used by the Petroleum Industry. It has been changed from the basis 1926 = 100
to 1939 = 100.

Column (4): J. G. McLean and R. W. Haigh, The Growth of the
Integrated Oil Companies, Boston: Harvard Graduate School of
Business Administration, 1952, Exhibit XIX-10, p. 551. The
authors give a refinery construction cost index for a few
scattered years, based upon costs along the East Coast of the
United States. The base year is 1939.

Column (5): The Engineering News Record Index and the Marshall and Stevens Index have been combined from 1913 to 1933
in the ratio of two to one respectively.

Column (6): The composite index of Column (5) is spliced to
Nelson's in the year 1929.

Appendix Table 7

Characteristics of the Raw Material for the Cracking Processes,
1913-1955

Characteristics	Representative gas oil	Burton (all cases)	Tube and Tank (1922)	Holmes-Manley (1936)	Houdry (1936)	Houdry (1939-40)	Fluid (1942)	Fluid (1955)
				Process				
Source of crude	Mid-Continent	Mid-Continent	Mid-Continent	Mid-Continent	Mid-Continent	Mid-Continent	Mid-Continent	Mid-Continent
Gravity, °API	28.5° API	32° API	30.7° API	32° API	32° API	30.8° API	28.5° API	26.5° API
Distillation:								
Initial point, °F	400	400	400	400	n.a.	n.a.	400	645
10%	535	n.a.	n.a.	n.a.	n.a.	490	535	672
20%	590	n.a.	n.a.	n.a.	n.a.	n.a.	590	700
30%	645	n.a.	n.a.	n.a.	n.a.	n.a.	645	720
40%	680	n.a.	n.a.	n.a.	n.a.	n.a.	680	745
50%	720	n.a.	n.a.	n.a.	n.a.	660	720	773
60%	750	n.a.	n.a.	n.a.	n.a.	n.a.	750	810
70%	805	n.a.	n.a.	n.a.	n.a.	n.a.	805	844
80%	862	n.a.	n.a.	n.a.	n.a.	n.a.	862	890
90%	925	n.a.	n.a.	n.a.	n.a.	910	925	925
End point	1000	750	850	750	n.a.	n.a.	1000	1000
% Naphtha below 430°F	3	3	n.a.	n.a.	n.a.	0	3	0
% Sulphur (by weight)	.50	.25	n.a.	n.a.	n.a.	n.a.	.50	.50
Diesel index	56	n.a.	n.a.	n.a.	n.a.	n.a.	56	55
Conradson carbon	0.8	n.a.	n.a.	n.a.	n.a.	n.a.	0.8	0.8
% of representative gas oil	100	60	75	60 (100 possible)	60	75	100	70 (100 possible)
Remainder of representative gas oil sold as	--	Heavy fuel	Heavy fuel	--	Heavy fuel	Heavy fuel	--	Diesel oil or heating oil

Appendix Table 8a

Product Yields from the Cracking Processes, 1913–1955
(per barrel [42 gallons] charged to the process)

Product	Process				
	Crude dis-tillation, 1913	Burton, original in-stallation, 1913	Burton, false bottom plates, 1914	Burton-Clark with bubble tower, 1922	Tube and Tank 1922
Fuel gas (fuel oil equivalent gallons) (mil. of BTUs)	n.a.	n.a.	0.24	1.85 0.296	2.16 0.348
Butanes, butylenes (gallons)	—	—	—	—	—
Gasoline (gallons)	8.61	9.79	10.65	17.35	16.38
Octane (Re-search)	n.a.	55	55	72	72
Middle distil-lates[a] (gallons)	6.83	9.79	8.49	4.49	15.11
Fuel oil (gallons)	24.63	21.6	20.05	17.05	6.30
Coke	—	0.5% (by weight)	0.15% (by weight)	0.496 (FOE gal.)	1.60 (FOE gal.)

Appendix Table 8b

Product Yields from the Cracking Processes, 1913–1955
(per barrel [42 gallons] charged to the process)

Product	Process				
	Holmes-Manley, 1936	Houdry 1936	Houdry[b] 1939–40	Fluid[c] 1942	Fluid[c] 1955
Fuel gas (fuel oil equivalent gallons) (mil. of BTU's)	4.91 0.971	1.37 0.271	1.37 0.271	n.a. 0.68	n.a. 0.66
Butanes, butylenes (gallons)	—	—	—	5.25	4.91
Gasoline (gallons)	27.72	16.39	15.6	17.6	24.7
Octane (Re-search)	72	87.7	87.7	95.4	94.7
Middle distil-lates[a] (gallons)	—	23.60	25.8	16.4	11.3
Fuel oil (gallons)	11.04	—	—	0.93	1.35
Coke	n.a.	11.19 (pounds)	9.78 (pounds)	12.55 (pounds)	12.52 (pounds)

Notes:
  a. During 1913–1922, middle distillates were sold as kerosene. From 1936 to the present they have been sold as heating or furnace oil, for which the price received has generally been equal to that for virgin gas oil, i.e., the raw material for cracking.
  b. Yields for the Houdry process operating at a relatively low level of conversion but at a high rate of charge. If cracking had been more intense, the yield of gasoline would have been higher and the throughput lower.
  c. Product yields for the Fluid process are independent of the capacity of the units.

Appendix Table 9

Product Revenues from the Cracking Processes, 1913–1955
(dollars current prices per barrel charged to the process)

Product	Process							
	Burton, original installation, 1913	Burton–Clark with bubble tower, 1922-3	Tube and Tank, 1922-3	Holmes–Manley, 1936	Houdry, 1936	Houdry, 1939–1940[a]	Fluid 1939–1940[a]	Fluid 1955
Fuel gas	.00	.07	.07	.11	.03	.04	.09	.12
Butanes, butylenes	—	—	—	—	—	—	.16	.39
Gasoline	1.12	2.60	2.46	1.62	.96 +.10 (octane credit)	.92	1.03	2.59
Middle distillates	.21	.20	.68	—	.78	.74	.47	.91
Fuel oil	.41	.81	.30	.17	—	—	.02	.05
Coke	—	.01	.03	—	—	—	—	—
Total	1.74	3.69	3.54	1.90	1.87	1.70	1.77	4.06

Note:

a. Although the Fluid process was first installed in 1942 prices existing in 1939–40 were used in order to match the cost data.

Appendix Table 10a

Consumption of Inputs by the Cracking Processes, 1914-1955
(per barrel charged to the process)

Input	Burton, 1914[a]	Burton, July-Dec. 1917	Burton-Clark, 1922	Tube and Tank, 1922	Holmes-Manley 1936	Houdry 1936	Houdry 1939-40
Cracking charge (barrels)	1.00	1.00	1.00	1.00	1.00	1.00	1.00
Process labor (man-hours)	.1720	.1280	.0457[b]	.0584[b]	.0351	.0308	.0082
Maintenance (man-hours)	n.a.	n.a.	n.a.	n.a.	n.a.	n.a.	n.a.
Fuel (millions of BTUs)	.534	.777	.782	.594	.621	.159	.158
Steam (pounds)							
High pressure	—	—	—	—	n.a.	n.a.	10.6 (gain)
Low pressure	n.a.	n.a.	n.a.	n.a.	—	—	—
Water (000 gal.)							
Cooling	n.a.	n.a.	n.a.	n.a.	n.a.	n.a.	.607
Treating	n.a.	n.a.	n.a.	n.a.	n.a.	n.a.	.013
Electricity (KWH)	n.a.	n.a.	n.a.	n.a.	n.a.	n.a.	.149
Miscellaneous chemicals (pounds)	—	—	—	—	n.a.	n.a.	n.a.
Catalyst (pounds)	—	—	—	—	—	n.a.	n.a.
Instrument Air (standard cu. ft.)	—	—	—	—	n.a.	n.a.	n.a.

Notes:

    a. Although costs of cracking in 1913, the first year of Burton operation, were available on an aggregated basis, they were not broken down by input. Refinery records, from which data on inputs were obtained, commenced with 1914.

    b. Includes labor for cleaning out the stills and drums.

Appendix Table 10b

Consumption of Inputs by the Cracking Processes, 1914-1955
(per barrel charged to the process)

Input	Process					
	Fluid, 1942			Fluid, 1955		
	7,000 BPSD unit	15,000 BPSD unit	40,000 BPSD unit	7,000 BPSD unit	15,000 BPSD unit	40,000 BPSD unit
Cracking charge (barrels)	1.00	1.00	1.00	1.00	1.00	1.00
Process labor (man-hours)	.0343	.0160	.0067	.0229	.0107	0046
Maintenance (man-hours)	.0232	.0189	.0132	.0158	.0123	.0088
Fuel (millions of BTUs)	.309	.320	.318	.025	.025	.025
Steam (pounds)						
High pressure	75.3	76.8	78.0	63.0	63.1	63.2
Low pressure	—	—	—	—	—	—
Water (000 gal.)						
Cooling	1.36	1.33	1.35	1.29	1.29	1.29
Treating	.0051	.0048	.0051	.0051	.0052	.0054
Electricity (KWH)	3.43	3.61	3.54	8.64	8.64	8.64
Miscellaneous chemicals (pounds)	.16	.16	.15	.21	.21	.21
Catalyst (pounds)	.60	.60	.60	.60	.60	.60
Instrument Air (standard cu. ft.)	82.3	82.0	79.1	125.6	70.0	40.0

Appendix Table 11

Input Prices Used in the Cost Calculations,
1913–1955

Input	Location and Date					
	Indiana, 1913, 1914	Indiana, 1917	Indiana, 1922-3	Indiana, 1936	East coast, 1939	Gulf coast, 1955
Cracking charge ($ per barrel)	0.945	2.16	2.10	1.39	1.20	2.94
Process labor ($ per man-hour)	0.32	0.573	0.80	.817	1.00	2.53
Maintenance ($ per man-hour)	0.21	0.35	0.563	n.a.	n.a.	n.a.
(% of capital investment per year)	5	n.a.	5	5	varies	varies
Fuel ($ per million BTUs)	0.73	.111	.203	.114	.131	.18
Steam ($ per pound) High pressure	—	—	—	n.a.	.00025	.00031
Low pressure	n.a.	n.a.	n.a.	n.a.	—	—
Water ($ per 000 gal.) Cooling	n.a.	n.a.	n.a.	n.a.	.006	.012
Treating	n.a.	n.a.	n.a.	n.a.	.04	.04
Electricity ($ per KWH)	n.a.	n.a.	n.a.	n.a.	.0060	.0065
Miscellaneous chemicals ($ per pound)	—	—	—	n.a.	n.a.	n.a.
Catalyst ($ per pound)	—	—	—	n.a.	.0675	.1875
Instrument air ($ per standard cu. ft.)	—	—	—	n.a.	n.a.	.0001
Depreciation (% of capital investment per year)	10	10	10	10	10	10
Property taxes and insurance (% of capital investment per year)	10	10	10	5	5	5
Overheads (% of process labor cost)	11.6	13.2	50	150	200	250
Royalties ($ per barrel of charge)	.17	.17	.10	.05 (Holmes-Manley)	.05 (Fluid)	.04
(% of paid-up royalty per year)				10 (Houdry)	10 (Houdry)	

Appendix Table 12a

Cost of Inputs to the Cracking Processes, 1913–1955
(dollars [current prices] per barrel charged to the process)

Input	Process					
	Burton, original installation, 1913	Burton-Clark with bubble tower 1922-3	Tube and Tank, 1922-3	Holmes-Manley, 1936	Houdry, 1936	Houdry 1939–40[a]
Cracking charge	1.050	2.100	2.100	1.390	1.390	1.200
Process labor		.037	.047	.029	.025	.008
Fuel		.159	.120	.071	.018	.021
Steam		.014	.014	.010	.015 (credit)	.003 (credit)
Water		.001	.001	.000	.001	.007
Electricity	—	—	—	.002	.000	.001
Catalyst	—	—	—	—	.013	.008
Maintenance		.031	.031	.024	.030	.027
Depreciation	.041	.056	.043	.049	.061	.059
Taxes and insurance		.056	.043	.024	.030	.030
Overheads		.018	.023	.043	.038	.016
Royalty	.170	.170	.100	.050	.041	.041
Rerunning	.063	.069	.102	.010	.003	—
Treating, chemicals	.013	.002	.002	.003	—	—
Not specified	.153	—	—	—	—	—
Total	1.490	2.713	2.626	1.705	1.635	1.415

Note: a. Costs for the Houdry process as of 1942 were not available.

Appendix Table 12b

Cost of Inputs to the Cracking Processes, 1913-1955
(dollars [current prices] per barrel charged to the process)

| Input | Process | | | | | |
| | Fluid, 1942 | | | Fluid, 1955 | | |
	7,000 BPSD unit	15,000 BPSD unit	40,000 BPSD unit	7,000 BPSD unit	15,000 BPSD unit	40,000 BPSD unit
Cracking charge	1.200	1.200	1.200	2.940	2.940	2.940
Process labor	.034	.016	.007	.058	.027	.012
Fuel	.041	.042	.042	.005	.005	.005
Steam	.019	.019	.020	.020	.020	.020
Water	.008	.008	.008	.013	.013	.013
Electricity	.021	.022	.021	.056	.056	.056
Catalyst	.041	.041	.041	.112	.112	.112
Maintenance						
Depreciation	.170	.111	.070	.488	.333	.212
Taxes and insurance						
Overheads						
Royalty	.050	.050	.050	.040	.040	.040
Rerunning	—	—	—	—	—	—
Treating, chemicals	—	—	—	—	—	—
Not specified	—	—	—	—	—	—
Total	1.584	1.509	1.459	3.732	3.546	3.410

Appendix Table 13a

Profitability of the Cracking Processes, 1913–1955
(current dollars)

Measure of Profitability	Process					
	Burton, original installation 1913	Burton-Clark with bubble tower 1922–3	Tube and Tank, 1922–3	Holmes-Manley, 1936	Houdry, 1936	Houdry, 1939–40
Profit per barrel of raw material charged (dollars)	.25	.98	.91	.19	.23	.28
Profit per gallon of gasoline produced (dollars)	.026	.057	.056	.007	.014	.019
Profit per 100-ton-miles of performance (dollars)	.088	.20	.19	.023	.035	.046
Profit per year (dollars)	8,100	81,000	190,000	460,000	560,000	1,500,000
Cost of cracking plant (dollars)	16,700	45,000	90,000	1,778,000	2,191,000	3,120,000
Return on investment in cracking plant (per cent per year undiscounted)	49	180	210	26	26	48

Appendix Table 13b

Profitability of the Cracking Processes, 1913-1955
(current dollars)

Measure of Profitability	Process					
	Fluid, 1942[a]			Fluid, 1955		
	7,000 BPSD unit	15,000 BPSD unit	40,000 BPSD unit	7,000 BPSD unit	15,000 BPSD unit	40,000 BPSD unit
Profit per barrel of raw material charged (dollars)	.19	.26	.31	.33	.51	.65
Profit per gallon of gasoline produced (dollars)	.011	.015	.017	.013	.021	.026
Profit per 100-ton-miles of performance (dollars)	.021	.030	.035	.027	.042	.053
Profit per year (dollars)	408,000	1,190,000	3,820,000	746,000	2,520,000	8,510,000
Cost of cracking plant (dollars)	1,133,000	1,889,000	3,600,000	3,550,000	6,150,000	11,500,000
Return on investment in cracking plant (per cent per year undiscounted)	36	63	106	21	41	74

Note: a. Based upon 1939-40 product prices.

Sources to Appendix Tables 7 to 13:

For each of the cracking processes the costs, revenues, and profits from its operation were determined at two points in its history, when it was first introduced commercially and when it was supplanted by a more efficient process. Tables 7 to 13 develop these measures; in Table 7 there are reported the characteristics of the raw materials, in Table 8 the product yields, in Table 9 the revenues, in Table 10 the physical consumption of inputs, in Table 11 the price of each input, in Table 12 the cost of cracking, and, finally, in Table 13 the profit.

The data underlying these tables are derived primarily from refinery operating statements and technical reports. The major sources are:

Burton process, 1913 to 1922-3; Standard Oil Company (Indiana), Whiting Refinery, monthly records of cracking operations.

Tube and Tank process, 1922-3; Standard Oil Company (New Jersey), Bayway Refinery, plant records of Tube and Tank unit operations.

Holmes-Manley process, 1936; Standard Oil Company (Indiana), operation of typical Holmes-Manley units at the Whiting Refinery.

Houdry process, 1936; Standard Oil Company (Indiana), technical report comparing the Houdry process with the Holmes-Manley.

Houdry process, 1939-40; J. S. Carey and H. W. Ortendahl, "Catalytic Cracking Economics Complicate Comparison," National Petroleum News, October 16, 1940.

Fluid process, 1942, 1955; Esso Research and Engineering Company, "Catalytic Cracking Study," by David E. Cook et al., August 16, 1955; plus additional correspondence from the Engineering Economics and Process Research Divisions and additional information gathered there.

Appendix Table 14

Estimate of Burton Process Royalties and Operating Profits,
1913-1936

| Year | Cracked gasoline output by the Burton process | | | Royalties paid by licensees | | Estimated operating profits |
	Standard Oil Company (Indiana) (mil. gal.)	Licensees (mil. gal.)	Total (000 barrels)	Total (000 $)	Average (cents per gallon of gasoline)	from cracking in Indiana's refineries (000 $)
1913	51.18	---	1,218	---	---	2,087
4	72.80	12.36	2,024	74	0.60	1,732
1915	128.74	45.27	4,141	332	0.74	3,780
6	188.46	103.49	6,950	1,787	1.73	13,055
7	249.81	171.89	10,035	2,419	1.41	14,100
8	272.84	238.82	12,180	3,154	1.32	14,410
9	348.74	331.96	16,200	3,850	1.17	16,320
1920	344.66	365.87	16,910	3,442	0.94	13,000
1	423.18	469.46	21,230	1,991	0.43	7,200
2	504.91	565.27	25,460	4,354	0.77	15,560
3	529.89	525.20	25,110	3,052	0.58	12,310
4	525.34	549.89	25,600	2,415	0.43	9,050
1925	574.68	613.82	28,300	n.a.	n.a.	n.a.
6	667.84	551.78	26,600	n.a.	n.a.	n.a.
7	n.a.	n.a.	20,700	n.a.	n.a.	n.a.
8	n.a.	n.a.	17,200	n.a.	n.a.	n.a.
9	n.a.	n.a.	12,000	n.a.	n.a.	n.a.
1930	n.a.	n.a.	9,100	n.a.	n.a.	n.a.
1	n.a.	n.a.	8,500	n.a.	n.a.	n.a.
2	n.a.	n.a.	5,200	n.a.	n.a.	n.a.
3	n.a.	n.a.	4,500	n.a.	n.a.	n.a.
4	n.a.	n.a.	670	n.a.	n.a.	n.a.
1935	n.a.	n.a.	920	n.a.	n.a.	n.a.
6	n.a.	n.a.	670	n.a.	n.a.	n.a.
Total	(1913-1924)			26,870		122,604

Sources to Appendix Table 14:

Cracked gasoline output:

1913-1926—Standard Oil Company (Indiana), C. J. Barkdull, "Figures on Production of Gasoline by Burton Process...," February 10, 1928. Included in Indiana Standard output is that of custom plants, i.e., cracking units owned and operated by the Standard Oil Company (Indiana) and located in the refineries of other companies.

1927-1937—"Report on United States Operating Refineries," Oil and Gas Journal, Annual Refining Issues, Tulsa: The Petroleum Publishing Company. The figures on the various cracking processes were reported as the capacity per barrel of charge of operating equipment, and not as gasoline output. In order to change from charge capacity to product output, the author assumed that the Burton units were operated at full capacity throughout the year, and that the yield of gasoline was 25% of charge.

Royalties:

1914-1924—U. S. vs. Standard Oil Company (Indiana) et al., District Court of the United States, Northern District of Illinois, Eastern Division, In Equity No. 4131, Petitioners Book of Exhibits, vol. II, Exhibit No. 82, p. 1185.

Estimated operating profits from cracking in Indiana's refineries:

1913—Standard Oil Company (Indiana), Oil and Gas Evaluation Section, "Memorandum Showing Valuation of Burton Patent," February 21, 1922. (This represents a profit of 1.58 cents per gallon on the 131,838,000 gallons of gas oil charged during the year, and is equivalent to 4.08 cents per gallon on the 51,180,100 gallons of gasoline produced.)

1914-1924—There were not enough data to determine the profits from cracking directly from the records of the Standard Oil Company (Indiana), so they were estimated on the basis of the same average profit per gallon of gasoline as that achieved by the licensees of the Burton process. The royalty rate charged licensees was 25% of the net profits from operating the Burton process. Therefore Indiana's profit per gallon would be four times as much as its licensees' royalty rate.

Appendix Table 15

Estimate of Dubbs Process Royalties,
1922–1942

| Year | Capacity of Dubbs units in operation | | Royalty rate (¢/barrel) | Estimate of total royalties (000 $) |
	(000 barrels of charge per stream day)	(000 barrels of charge per calendar day)		
1922	0.25	0.18	15	6
3	8.0	5.6	15	305
4	33.4	23.4	15	1,277
1925	53.5	37.5	15	2,051
6	83.4	58.4	15	3,184
7	160	112	15	3,631
8	168	134	15	6,030
9	181	145	15	6,831
1930	229	183	15	10,000
1	198	158	15	8,650
2	216	173	15	9,460
3	217	173	15	9,460
4	218	174	10	6,350
1935	342	274	10	10,000
6	365	292	10	10,640
7	418	334	10	12,200
8	479	383	5	6,990
9	457	365	5	6,650
1940	469	374	5	6,820
1	495	396	5	7,220
2	517	413	5	7,540
Total				135,295

Sources to Appendix Table 15:

Capacity of Dubbs units in operation:

1922—see Chapter II.

1923-1926—The capacities in barrels per calendar day were
obtained by dividing the total yearly royalties (column 5)
by the number of days in the year, and subsequently dividing the quotient by the royalty rate of 15 cents per barrel of charge. In order to obtain the stream day figures,
a service rate of 70% was assumed.

1927-1942—Annual Refining Issues, Oil and Gas Journal.
No survey was made prior to 1927. After 1942, thermal
cracking capacity was not broken down by process. Capacities were reported on the basis of barrels per stream day.
In order to change to barrels per calendar day, the following utilization factors were assumed: 70% for 1927; 80%
for the period 1928-1935; and 90% for all subsequent years.

Royalty Rates:

See Chapter II. These are defined as cents per barrel of
fresh charge.

Total Royalties:

1922-1929—Universal Oil Products Company v. Winkler-Koch
Engineering Company and Root Refining Company, District
Court of the United States, District of Delaware, Nos. 716
and 895, vol. V, p. 48a, 49.

1930-1942—Calculated by multiplying the capacity (bpcd)
of the units by the royalty rate and the product of these
two by the number of days in the year. This assumes that
the units were always operated at full capacity.

Appendix Table 16

Estimate of Tube and Tank Process Royalties and Operating Profits,
1921-1942

Year	Cracked gasoline output from the Tube and Tank process (000 barrels of charge per year)	Capacity of Tube and Tank equipment (000 barrels of charge per day)	Royalties alone (000 dollars)	Royalties plus operating profits (000 dollars)
1921	24	.25	—	14
2	178	2	1	107
3	778	8	162	467
4	1,850	21	269	1,170
1925	3,830	42	n.a.	2,300
6	14,200	156	n.a.	8,520
7	19,700	211	n.a.	11,600
8	42,500	293	n.a.	16,000
9	48,000	431	n.a.	23,600
1930	n.a.	487	n.a.	26,700
1	n.a.	471	n.a.	25,800
2	n.a.	635	n.a.	34,800
3	n.a.	484	n.a.	26,500
4	n.a.	495	n.a.	18,100
1935	n.a.	503	n.a.	18,400
6	n.a.	467	n.a.	17,000
7	n.a.	449	n.a.	16,400
8	n.a.	466	n.a.	8,550
9	n.a.	414	n.a.	7,560
1940	n.a.	439	n.a.	8,010
1	n.a.	428	n.a.	7,810
2	n.a.	384	n.a.	7,010
Total				286,418

Sources to Appendix Table 16:

Cracked gasoline output from the
Tube and Tank process:

J. H. Westcott, Oil Gas Conservation and Waste, 4 ed., New
York: Beacon Press, 1930, p. 129.

Capacity of Tube and Tank equipment:

1921-1926—derived from cracked gasoline production, above.
In order to make the conversion from gasoline production to
equipment capacity it was assumed that gasoline yield was
25% on charge and that the equipment was operated at full
capacity.

1927-1942—Oil and Gas Journal, Annual Refining Issues,
capacity of operating units. The Annual Refinery Survey
was first made in 1927; after 1942 capacity of the different thermal cracking processes was not identified. For
1927-1929, the capacities calculated from Westcott's data
above are 216,000, 466,000, and 526,000 barrels per day respectively.

Royalties alone:

Standard Oil Company (Indiana) et al. v. United States of
America, 283 U. S. 163, Record of Hearings, vol. I, Peti-
tioner's Exhibit Number 87, p. 790.

Royalties plus operating profits:

These were estimated by multiplying the capacity of operating units by the royalty rate for the Dubbs process
(see Appendix Table 15); this assumes that the units were
operated at full capacity and that the profits accruing
to the owners of the process were equal to the royalty
rate charged to licensors.

Appendix Table 17

Estimate of Houdry Process Royalties,
1936-1944

| Year | Yearly installations of Houdry units | | Royalties (000 dollars) |
	Number	Capacity (000 barrels of charge per stream day)	
1936	1	2.	270
7	3	29.8	4,023
8	—	—	—
9	6	78.5	10,598
1940	4	50.	6,750
1	1	16.6	2,241
2	2	28.1	3,794
3	3	37.	4,995
4	4	47.5	6,412
Total	24	289.5	39,083

Sources to Appendix Table 17:

Yearly installations of Houdry units:

Houdry Process Corporation. Houdry units destined
for Russia and France are not included in the estimates although those installed by the Sun and
Socony-Mobil Oil companies are.

Royalties:

The royalty rate charged by Houdry was approximately
$150 per calendar day barrel of capacity. Assuming
a 90% service factor, this is equal to $135 per
stream day barrel of capacity. The capacities installed each year were multiplied by the latter
figure in order to give yearly royalties.

Appendix Table 18

Estimate of T. C. C. Process Royalties and Operating Profits,
1943-1957

Year	Capacity of T. C. C. units (000 barrels of charge per stream day)			Estimate of royalties and operating profits (000 dollars)	
	Total	Bucket elevator units	Air-lift units	Bucket elevator units	Air-lift units
1943	47	47	—	770	
4	75	75	—	1,230	
1945	195	195	—	3,200	
6	220	220	—	3,610	
7	241	241	—	3,960	
8	268	268	—	4,400	
9	293	293	—	4,810	
1950	311	296	15	4,860	246
1	355	312	43	5,120	706
2	385	328	57	5,350	936
3	510	344	166	3,390	1,630
4	580	360	220	3,550	2,160
1955	680	376	304	3,700	3,000
6	740	392	348	3,860	3,430
7	720	408	312	4,030	3,070
Total				55,840	15,178

Sources to Appendix Table 18:

Capacities:

Capacity of all T. C. C. units:

1943--see Chapter V.

1944-1957--Oil and Gas Journal, Annual Refining Issues. From 1943-1953, as of March 1; from 1954-1957 as of January 1.

Capacity of bucket elevator T. C. C. units:

1943-1949--see above.

1951-1956--Total capacity is assumed to increase in equal yearly increments of 16,000 bpsd from 295,000 bpsd in 1950 to a total, reported by Socony-Mobil Oil Company, of 408,000 bpsd in 1957.

Capacity of air-lift T. C. C. units:

1950--see Chapter V.

1951-1957--column 2 minus column 3

Royalties and operating profits:

The following assumptions are made: the units are on stream 90% of the time, the remaining time being consumed in maintenance (i.e., the service factor is 90%); when on stream, the units are operated at full capacity; the royalty rate is equal to five cents per barrel of charge from 1943 through 1952 and three cents per barrel of charge from 1953 through 1957; profit rate for equipment operated by the licensors is equal to the royalty rate licensees pay.

Appendix Table 19

Estimate of Houdriflow Royalties,
1950-1957

Year	Total capacity of Houdriflow units[a] (000 barrels of charge per stream day)	Estimated royalties (000 dollars)
1950	49,750	817
1	90,750	1,490
2	102,250	1,680
3	120,980	1,190
4	120,980	1,190
1955	171,980	1,690
6	186,000	1,830
7	180,000	1,770
Total		11,657

Note: a. As of December 31.

Sources to Appendix Table 19:

Capacities:
Oil and Gas Journal, Annual Refining Issues.

Royalties:
Units operated at full capacity with 90% service factor.
Royalty rate equal to five cents per barrel of charge from
1950 through 1952, and three cents per barrel of charge
thereafter.

Appendix Table 20

Estimate of Fluid Catalytic Cracking Process
Royalties and Operating Profits,
1942-1957

Year	Total capacity of Fluid units[a] (000 barrels of charge per stream day)	Estimate of royalties and operating profits (000 dollars)
1942	13	214
3	50	821
4	234	3,840
1945	409	6,720
6	419	6,890
7	559	9,190
8	717	11,800
9	834	13,700
1950	1,143	18,800
1	1,178	19,300
2	1,378	22,600
3	1,727	22,700
4	1,963	25,800
1955	2,341	30,600
6	2,609	34,300
7	2,927	38,400
Total		265,675

Note: a. As of December 31.

Sources to Appendix Table 20:

1942—see Chapter VI.

1943-1957—Oil and Gas Journal, Annual Refining Issues. The royalty rate was 5 cents per barrel of fresh feed from 1942 through
1952 and 4 cents thereafter. A 90% service factor was assumed in
changing from stream to calendar day rates.

Appendix Table 21a

Consumption of Inputs per Barrel of Cracking Charge,
1913–1955

Process	Date	Capacity of unit (barrels per stream day)	(barrels per calendar day)	Process labor (man-hours)	Capital (1939 dollars)	Cracking charge (barrels)	Representative gas oil (barrels)	Energy (millions of BTUs)
Burton	1914	197	88.5	0.172	0.387	1	1.67	0.534
	1922	479	221	0.046	0.307	1	1.33	0.782
Tube and Tank	1922	904	570	0.058	0.199	1	1.33	0.594
Holmes-Manley[a]	1938	7,500	6,750	0.035	0.150	1	1.67 (1.00 possible)	0.720
Houdry	1938	7,500	6,750	0.031	0.173	1	1.67	0.190
	1939–40	16,100	14,500	0.008	0.114	1	1.33	0.291
Fluid	1942	7,000	5,950	0.034	0.161	1	1.67	0.566
		15,000	12,750	0.016	0.145	1	1.67	0.578
		40,000	34,000	0.007	0.128	1	1.67	0.578
	1955	7,000	6,300	0.023	0.144	1	1.43 (1.00 possible)	0.272
		15,000	13,500	0.011	0.125	1	1.43 (1.00 possible)	0.273
		40,000	36,000	0.005	0.106	1	1.43 (1.00 possible)	0.273

Note: a. The Holmes-Manley was a continuous thermal cracking process.
By 1938 its design and that of the Tube and Tank process were
almost identical.

Appendix Table 21b

Consumption of Inputs per Gallon of Gasoline,
1913-1955

Process	Date	Capacity of unit		Process labor (man-hours)	Capital (1939 dollars)	Cracking charge (gallons)	Representative gas oil (gallons)	Energy (millions of BTUs)
		(barrels per stream day)	(barrels per calendar day)					
Burton	1914	197	88.5	0.0162	0.036	3.96	6.57	0.084
	1922	479	221	0.0026	0.018	2.42	4.04	0.045
Tube and Tank	1922	904	570	0.0036	0.012	2.56	3.42	0.036
Holmes-Manley[a]	1938	7,500	6,750	0.0013	0.005	1.52	2.53	0.026
Houdry	1938	7,500	6,750	0.0019	0.011	2.56	4.27	0.012
	1939-40	16,100	14,500	0.0005	0.007	2.70	3.60	0.019
Fluid	1942	7,000	5,950	0.0020	0.009	2.38	3.97	0.032
		15,000	12,750	0.0009	0.008	2.38	3.97	0.033
		40,000	34,000	0.0004	0.007	2.38	3.97	0.033
	1955	7,000	6,300	0.0009	0.006	1.70	2.43	0.011
		15,000	13,500	0.0004	0.005	1.70	2.43	0.011
		40,000	36,000	0.0002	0.004	1.70	2.43	0.011

Note: a. See Appendix Table 21a.

Appendix Table 21c

Consumption of Inputs per 100 Ton-Miles of Transportation, 1913–1955

Process	Date	Capacity of unit		Process labor (man-hours)	Capital (1939 dollars)	Cracking charge (gallons)	Representative gas oil (gallons)	Energy (millions of BTUs)
		(barrels per stream day)	(barrels per calendar day)					
Burton	1914	197	88.5	0.0560	0.126	13.63	22.8	0.290
	1922	479	221	0.0091	0.061	8.36	14.0	0.156
Tube and Tank	1922	904	570	0.0123	0.042	8.85	11.8	0.126
Holmes-Manley[a]	1938	7,500	6,750	0.0044	0.019	5.24	8.8	0.090
Houdry	1938	7,500	6,750	0.0047	0.02	6.49	10.8	0.030
	1939–40	16,100	14,500	0.0013	0.018	6.70	8.9	0.046
Fluid	1942	7,000	5,950	0.0040	0.018	4.78	8.0	0.065
		15,000	12,750	0.0018	0.016	4.78	8.0	0.066
		40,000	34,000	0.0008	0.014	4.78	8.0	0.066
	1955	7,000	6,300	0.0019	0.012	3.47	5.0	0.022
		15,000	13,500	0.0009	0.010	3.47	5.0	0.022
		40,000	36,000	0.0004	0.008	3.47	5.0	0.022

Note: a. See Appendix Table 21a.

Sources to Appendix Tables 21a, 21b, and 21c:

Appendix Tables 10, 22, 23; Appendix Chapter A, Figure 3.

Appendix Table 22

Calculation of Energy Consumption in Cracking
(per barrel of cracking charge)

Process	Date	Fuel (millions of BTUs)	Coke (#)	Coke (millions of BTUs)	Steam (net)[a] (#)	Steam (net)[a] (millions of BTUs)	Electricity (KWH)	Electricity (millions of BTUs)	Total (millions of BTUs)
Burton	1914	0.534	—	—	?	?	—	—	0.534
	1922	0.782	—	—	?	?	—	—	0.782
Tube and Tank	1922	0.594	—	—	?	?	—	—	0.594
Holmes–Manley	1938	0.620	—	—	?	0.083	?	0.017	0.720
Houdry	1938	0.159	11.9	0.160	?	(0.130)	?	0.001	0.190
	1939–40	0.158	9.8	0.141	(10.6)	(0.011)	0.149	0.003	0.291
Fluid (5,950 BPCD)	1942	0.320	12.6	0.179	75.3	0.075	0.143	0.003	0.566
(12,750 BPCD)	1942	0.320	12.6	0.179	76.8	0.077	0.151	0.003	0.578
(34,000 BPCD)	1942	0.318	12.6	0.179	78.0	0.078	0.148	0.003	0.578
Fluid (6,300 BPCD)	1955	0.025	12.5	0.178	63.0	0.063	0.360	0.006	0.272
(13,500 BPCD)	1955	0.025	12.5	0.178	63.1	0.063	0.360	0.006	0.273
(36,000 BPCD)	1955	0.025	12.5	0.178	63.2	0.063	0.360	0.006	0.273

Note: a. The figures in parentheses represent steam generated rather than consumed.

Source: Appendix Table 10.

Conversion Factors:
   Coke: One pound of coke on the catalyst will yield 0.0143 million BTUs
      when burned (R. V. Shankland, "Industrial Catalytic Cracking,"
      Advances in Catalysis, New York: Academic Press, Table V, p. 331).
   Steam: One pound of steam can be generated by 0.00100 million BTUs
      (W. L. Nelson, Petroleum Refinery Engineering, 3 ed., New York:
      McGraw-Hill Book Company, Inc., 1949, p. 698).
   Electricity: One kilowatt hour of electricity is assumed to require the
      following BTUs in its generation:

Year	# coal/KWH	Million BTU/KWH (assuming 13,100 BTU per # of coal)
1921	2.7	0.0367
1929	1.66	0.0224
1936	1.44	0.0195
1939	1.38	0.0187
1942	1.30	0.0176
1946	1.29	0.0175
(1955	assumed	0.0170)

   (William Staniar, ed., Plant Engineering Handbook, New York:
   McGraw-Hill Book Company, Inc., 1950, p. 20).

Appendix Table 23

Calculation of Capital Costs in Cracking,
1913–1955

Process	Date	Capital costs (1939 dollars per barrel [calendar] of charge)				
		Construction	Maintenance	Royalty	Catalyst	Total
Burton	1913	0.04014	0.02007	0.3263		0.3865
	1922	0.06758	0.03379	0.2059	—	0.3073
Tube and Tank	1922	0.05236	0.02618	0.1209	—	0.1994
Holmes-Manley	1938	0.07215	0.02786	0.05000	—	0.1500
Houdry	1938	0.08890	0.03024	0.04114	0.01270	0.1730
	1939–40	0.05850	0.02631	0.04073	0.00881	0.1344
Fluid						
Model I	1942	0.05228	0.02219	0.04585	0.04054	0.1609
		0.04060	0.01805	0.04585	0.04054	0.1450
		0.02904	0.01273	0.04585	0.04054	0.1282
Model IV	1955	0.06848	0.01524	0.0127	0.0477	0.1441
		0.05301	0.01188	0.0127	0.0477	0.1253
		0.03711	0.00849	0.0127	0.0477	0.1060

Source: Appendix Tables 6, 10, 13.

Appendix Table 24

Process and Non-process Labor Costs in Cracking,
1914-1955

Process	Date	Capacity of unit (barrels per calendar day)	Process labor cost (per barrel of cracking charge)	Ratio of non-process to process labor cost	Total of process and non-process labor costs (per barrel of cracking charge)
Burton	1914	88.5	$0.055	0.12	$0.061
	1922	221	0.0365	0.50	0.055
Tube and Tank	1922	570	0.0467	0.50	0.070
Holmes-Manley	1938	6,750	0.035	1.50	0.088
Houdry	1938	6,750	0.0308	1.50	0.077
	1939-40	14,500	0.008	1.50	0.025
Fluid					
Model I	1942	5,950	0.034	2.00	0.103
	1942	12,750	0.016	2.00	0.048
	1942	34,000	0.0069	2.00	0.021
Model IV	1955	6,300	0.058	2.50	0.203
	1955	13,500	0.027	2.50	0.095
	1955	36,000	0.0115	2.50	0.040

Source to Appendix Table 24:

Appendix Table 10. The ratio of non-process labor cost to process labor cost is customarily called "overhead."

BIBLIOGRAPHY

Ayres, C. E. *The Theory of Economic Progress.* Chapel Hill: University of North Carolina Press, 1944.

Bacon, R. F., and W. A. Hamor. *American Petroleum Industry.* New York: McGraw-Hill Book Co., 1916.

Bain, J. S. *The Economics of the Pacific Coast Petroleum Industry,* 3 vols. Berkeley: University of California Press, 1944–1947.

Beaton, Kendall. *Enterprise in Oil: A History of Shell in the United States.* New York: Appleton-Century-Crofts, Inc., 1957.

Bell, H. S. *American Petroleum Refining.* New York: D. Van Nostrand Co., Inc., 1923.

Clark, J. M. *Social Control of Business,* 2nd ed. New York: McGraw-Hill Book Co., 1939.

Cookenboo, Leslie, Jr. *Crude Oil Pipe Lines and Competition in the Oil Industry.* Cambridge: Harvard University Press, 1955.

De Chazeau, M. G., and A. E. Kahn. *Integration and Competition in the Petroleum Industry.* New Haven: Yale University Press, 1959.

Ellis, C., and J. V. Meigs. *Gasoline and Other Motor Fuels.* New York: D. Van Nostrand Co., Inc., 1921.

Forbes, R. J., and D. R. O'Beirne. *The Technical Development of the Royal Dutch Shell, 1890–1940.* Leiden: E. J. Brill, 1957.

Gibb, G. S., and E. H. Knowlton. *The Resurgent Years, 1911–1927: History of the Standard Oil Company (New Jersey).* New York: Harper & Brothers, 1956.

Giddens, P. H. *Standard Oil Company (Indiana): Oil Pioneer of the Middle West.* New York: Appleton-Century-Crofts, Inc., 1955.

Hidy, R., and M. Hidy. *Pioneering in Big Business, 1882–1911: History of the Standard Oil Company (New Jersey).* New York: Harper & Brothers, 1955.

Ickes, Harold L. *Fightin' Oil.* New York: Alfred A. Knopf, Inc., 1943.

Janeway, Eliot. *The Struggle for Survival: A Chronicle of Economic Mobilization in World War II.* New Haven: Yale University Press, 1951.

Larson, H. M., and K .W. Porter. *History of Humble Oil and Refining Company: A Study in Industrial Growth*. New York: Harper & Brothers, 1959.

Leontief, W., *et al. Studies in the Structure of the American Economy*. New York: Oxford University Press, Inc., 1953.

Lerner, A. P. *The Economics of Control*. New York: The Macmillan Co., 1946.

Maclaurin, W. R. *Invention and Innovation in the Radio Industry*. New York: The Macmillan Co., 1949.

McLean, J. G., and R. W. Haigh. *The Growth of Integrated Oil Companies*. Cambridge: Division of Research, Graduate School of Business Administration, Harvard University, 1954.

Manne, A. S. *Scheduling of Petroleum Refinery Operations*. Cambridge: Harvard University Press, 1956.

National Petroleum Council. *A National Oil Policy for the United States*. 1949.

Nelson, W. L. *Petroleum Refinery Engineering*, 3rd ed. New York: McGraw-Hill Book Co., 1949.

Passer, H. C. *The Electrical Manufacturers, 1875–1900*. Cambridge: Harvard University Press, 1953.

Petroleum Industry War Council, Technical Advisory Committee. *Wartime Petroleum Research*. May 8, 1945.

Popple, C. S. *Standard Oil Company (New Jersey) in World War II*. New York: Standard Oil Company (New Jersey), 1952.

Rostow, E. V. *A National Policy for the Oil Industry*. New Haven: Yale University Press, 1948.

Schumpeter, J. A. *Capitalism, Socialism and Democracy*, 3rd ed. New York: Harper & Brothers, 1950.

Standard Oil Company (Indiana) vs. Globe Oil and Refining Company, U.S. Circuit Court of Appeals, 7th Circuit, No. 5511.

U.S. Petroleum Administration for War. *History of the Petroleum Administration for War, 1941–1945*. Washington: Government Printing Office, 1946.

U.S. Senate, Temporary National Economic Committee. *Hearings*, Parts 14–17. Washington: Government Printing Office, 1940.

U.S. Senate, Temporary National Economic Committee. Monograph Number 39, *Control of the Petroleum Industry by Major Oil Companies*. Washington: Government Printing Office, 1941.

U.S. vs. Standard Oil Company (Indiana) *et al.*, District Court of the United States, Northern District of Illinois, Eastern Division, No. 4131.

U.S. vs. Standard Oil Company (Indiana) *et al.,* 173 Fed. Rep. 197–200.

U.S. vs. Standard Oil Company (Indiana) *et al.,* 283 U.S. 163.

Universal Oil Products Company vs. Winkler-Koch Engineering Company and Root Refining Company, District Court of the U.S., District of Delaware, Nos. 716 and 895.

Van Winkle, M. *Aviation Gasoline Manufacture.* New York: McGraw-Hill Book Co. 1944.

Wilson, R. E. "Pioneers in Oil Cracking." Address to the Newcomen Society, Chicago, October 29, 1946.

INDEX